MW01633296

NUCLEAR WEAPONS COUNTERPROLIFERATION

Nuclear Weapons Counterproliferation:

A New Grand Bargain

Jack I. Garvey

OXFORD UNIVERSITY PRESS

Oxford University Press is a department of the University of Oxford. It furthers the University's objective of excellence in research, scholarship, and education by publishing worldwide.

Oxford New York
Auckland Cape Town Dar es Salaam Hong Kong Karachi Kuala Lumpur Madrid
Melbourne Mexico City Nairobi New Delhi Shanghai Taipei Toronto

With offices in
Argentina Austria Brazil Chile Czech Republic France Greece Guatemala Hungary
Italy Japan Poland Portugal Singapore South Korea Switzerland Thailand
Turkey Ukraine Vietnam

Published in the United States of America by
Oxford University Press
198 Madison Avenue, New York, NY 10016

Library of Congress Cataloging-in-Publication Data

Garvey, Jack I.
Nuclear weapons counterproliferation : a new grand bargain / Jack I. Garvey.
p. cm.
Includes bibliographical references and index.
ISBN 978-0-19-984127-1 ((hardback) : alk. paper)
1. Nuclear nonproliferation. I. Title.
KZ5675.G38 2013
327.1'747—dc23

2012033752

9 8 7 6 5 4 3 2 1

Printed in the United States of America on acid-free paper

Note to Readers
This publication is designed to provide accurate and authoritative information in regard to the subject matter covered. It is based upon sources believed to be accurate and reliable and is intended to be current as of the time it was written. It is sold with the understanding that the publisher is not engaged in rendering legal, accounting, or other professional services. If legal advice or other expert assistance is required, the services of a competent professional person should be sought. Also, to confirm that the information has not been affected or changed by recent developments, traditional legal research techniques should be used, including checking primary sources where appropriate.

(Based on the Declaration of Principles jointly adopted by a Committee of the American Bar Association and a Committee of Publishers and Associations.)

For Monica

This book was inspired by the vision of a better world and instruction in the skills needed to achieve that world provided by my mentors, the late Professor Abram Chayes and Judge Hubert L. Will. In writing this book, my aspiration has been to contribute to that more secure world. That contribution was made possible also by the encouragement, support, and critical fortitude of Dean Jeffrey Brand and Professor Jesse Markham, Erin Garvey, and Rafael Aguirre-Sacasa. My thanks to the reference librarians of the University of San Francisco School of Law, especially Lee Ryan whose extraordinary talent and intellectual generosity were a consistent source of support. Thanks to my research assistants, Amol Mehra, Emily Corrigan, Alison Britton-Armes, Arash Yasrebi, and Brandon Clouse. Special thanks to my research assistant, Eric Sofge who, after serving as platoon leader and company executive officer in Iraq, served the cause of a safer world reflected in this book with similar dedication.

Contents

Between the potency
And the existence
Falls the shadow....
This is the way the world ends
This is the way the world ends
This is the way the world ends
Not with a bang but a whimper.
T.S. ELIOT, *The Hollow Men*

1

INTRODUCTION

A. The Need for a New Grand Bargain

The foundation for counterproliferation of nuclear weapons is failing. Fortunately, however, the whimper has come before the bang. We are well warned. T.S. Eliot had it not quite right in reference to nuclear weapons.[1] It is today widely understood and acknowledged that nuclear weapons risk is the greatest security risk facing the United States and the world.[2] President Obama called the nuclear threat the "threat that rises above all others in urgency" and warns that if we fail to fix the nonproliferation regime,

---

1 Though Eliot's poem, *The Hollow Men*, first appeared in 1925, Eliot himself later concluded that the H-bomb had come to be the allusion in common understanding. *See* "T.S. Eliot at Seventy," an interview with Eliot in SATURDAY REVIEW, Henry Hewes, Sept. 13, 1958, in Michael Grant, T.S. ELIOT: THE CRITICAL HERITAGE (Routledge & Kegan Paul 1982).

2 Today, the pre-eminent concern appears to be terrorist access. The Official Assessment of United States Security, the *National Security Strategy of the United States of America*, (National Security Strategy), declares that preventing the detonation of a nuclear weapon in the United States is the highest national security priority. George W. Bush, *National Security Strategy of the United States of America*, Sept. 2002, http://georgewbush-whitehouse.archives.gov/nsc/nss/2002/. At a Bush-Putin news conference two months after the 9/11 terrorist attacks, Bush declared: "Our highest priority is to keep terrorists from acquiring weapons of mass destruction." *See* The Acronym Institute, *US Wrestles with Huge WMD-Terrorism Agenda,* ISSUE NO. 65 DISARMAMENT DIPLOMACY (July-Aug. 2002), http://www.acronym.org.uk/dd/dd65/65nr09.htm. *See* Michael V. Hynes, John E. Peters, & Joel Kvitky, *Denying Armageddon: Preventing Terrorist Use of Nuclear Weapons*, THE ANNALS OF THE AMERICAN ACADEMY OF POLITICAL AND SOCIAL SCIENCE (2006), http://ann.sagepub.com/content/607/1/150.full.pdf. *See also* Pierre Goldschmidt, *The Increasing Risk of Nuclear Proliferation: Addressing the Challenge*, IAEA, Nov. 26, 2003, http://www.iaea.org/newscenter/statements/ddgs/2003/goldschmidt26112003.html. President Obama has agreed with this assessment, stating, "The single biggest threat to U.S. security, short-term, medium-term, and long-term, is the possibility of a terrorist organization obtaining a nuclear weapon.," *see* CNN Wire Staff, *Obama Hosts Leaders at Nuclear Summit,* CNN, Apr. 13, 2010, www.cnn.com/2010/POLITICS/04/12/nuclear.security.summit/index.html, as has former Secretary of Defense Robert Gates, "... if you ask every senior leader what keeps them aware at night, it's terrorists getting weapons of mass destruction, especially nuclear." *See* Jim Garamone, *Trip Was Gesture of Respect to Airmen,*

"we will invite nuclear arms races in every region and the prospect of wars and acts of terror on a scale that we can hardly imagine."[3]

There is consensus that current counterproliferation architecture is not up to the tremendous challenge presented by increasingly accessible nuclear weapons related material and technology. The same lament is heard in every arena of expert analysis, whether military, foreign policy, or nuclear science. The same anxiety pervades all academic discussion of proliferation, as well as nuclear strategic policy. The bang, they all say, may shortly be upon us, because the infrastructure upon which we have relied for non-proliferation is proving critically inadequate to constrain contemporary nuclear weapons risk.[4]

Nuclear weapons risk, today, is much more complex than ever before. Long gone is the simplicity and stability of cold war nuclear reality, compelled by the simple logic of mutually assured destruction (MAD). No longer is nuclear risk contained by the dark humor of MAD and Dr. Strangelove, which despite placing us all on the precipice, seems to have prevented what, we may no longer well enough recall, could have been our world ending by bang, then nuclear winter. Today, the spread and availability of fissile material and nuclear technology compounds nuclear risk on multiple fronts, generating a proliferation challenge of multiple dimensions. Nuclear terrorism, transcending any state-to-state confrontation, is the most significant new dimension, given the almost uncontrolled spread of nuclear material and technology. But ease of access has also resulted in new risk by way of the nuclear capability of some of the most dangerous governments on earth. Nuclear capability of the regimes in North Korea and Iran lays the basis for nuclear arms races in their own regions, and proliferation with regimes such as have ruled in Burma and Syria with their own apparent nuclear weapons ambitions. Even MAD is not gone. MAD can be found in the most volatile political confrontations on the planet, including the posturing of India and Pakistan; Israel hanging on to the "Sampson option" that equates survival with the threat of

---

Gates Says, American Forces Press Service, June 10, 2008, http://www.af.mil/news/story_print.asp?id=123102318 (Garamone, *Gesture of Respect*); *See also* former Senator Sam Nunn, "... preventing the spread and use of nuclear weapons should be the central organizing security principle of the 21st century." Sam Nunn, *Nuclear terrorism: Unite against the gravest threat*, CDI Russia Weekly, May 28, 2003, http://www.cdi.org/Russia/259-15.cfm.

3 President Barack Obama, Address at the United Nations (UN) General Assembly (Sept. 23, 2009) (*transcript available at* http://www.whitehouse.gov/the-press-office/remarks-president-united-nations-general-assembly).

4 In December 2004, a UN High Level panel mandated by the UN Secretary-General to assess major threats to the earth's peoples concluded that nuclear danger by way of the "erosion of the nonproliferation regime" was the prime threat. As to the spread of nuclear material technology, their conclusion was that "We are approaching a point at which the erosion of the nonproliferation regime could become irreversible and result in a cascade of proliferation." *See* UN Secretary-General, *Report of the High-level Panel on Threats, Challenges and Change: A More Secure World: Our Shared Responsibility*, (Dec. 2, 2004), http://www.un.org/secureworld/report2.pdf. "As we've said many times, the spread of nuclear weapons is the greatest threat facing our country." Vice-President Biden, Remarks at the National Defense University (Feb. 18, 2010) (*transcript available at* http://m.whitehouse.gov/the-press-office/remarks-vice-president-biden-national-defense-university).

apocalypse in the ever-volatile Middle East; and Syria, Egypt, and governments of other states in the Middle East claiming the right to nuclear capability to counter the nuclear options of Israel and Iran.

Non-proliferation of nuclear weapons is not the apparent future. The gamesmanship of North Korea and Iran, unrelenting in their work on nuclear weapons capacity, provides only the most evident failure of non-proliferation. The ostensible legal framework intended to ensure nonproliferation, the Treaty on the Non-Proliferation of Nuclear Weapons (NPT), adopted in 1970, is failing to contain the evolution and exponential growth of nuclear risk. The NPT remains the only comprehensive foundation for control. But despite the treaty and the multifaceted nonproliferation architecture it has engendered, the fissile material and the technology to make nuclear weapons are increasingly available for governments with aggressive ambitions and for malevolent non-state actors. These protagonists of nuclear risk, acting both overtly and in secret, motivated by regional power ambitions, money, or most dangerous of all, apocalyptic vision of reward in an afterlife, are moving outside effective control.

The result is a profound sense of inadequacy—truly much more than a whimper. That assassination of Iranian nuclear scientists[5] is the most innovative counterproliferation strategy of recent times, epitomizes the pervasive desperation of nuclear nonproliferation policy. The frustration is global, and pervades even the highest levels of counterproliferation infrastructure. The Secretary-General of the International Atomic Energy Agency (IAEA), Mohammad ElBaradei, upon his resignation, declared the architecture of nonproliferation to be "in tatters."[6] This depressive swan song simply reflects the general consensus that the legal and political infrastructure that has long appeared to contain nuclear weapons proliferation is failing as never before. President Obama, though endorsing the United States commitment to universal compliance with the NPT, nevertheless has identified out-of-control nuclear weapons risk as the principal security risk of our time. The President has characterized the non-proliferation regime by observing, "our efforts to contain these dangers are centered on a global non-proliferation regime, but as more people and nations break the rules, we could reach the point where the center cannot hold."[7] According to most experts, and as ElBaradei's capitulation indicates, we are already at that point.

---

5 Farnaz Fassihi & Jay Solomon, *Scientist Killing Stokes U.S.—Iran Tensions* WALL ST. J. 1 (Jan. 12, 2012), *available at* http://online.wsj.com/article/SB10001424052970204257504577153980963513686.html. L ST. J., Jan. 12, 2012, at 1, http://online.wsj.com/article/SB10001424052970204257504577153980963513686.html. Vincent Trivett, *Mossad Suspected In Murder Of Iranian Nuclear Scientists*, BUSINESS INSIDER, Aug. 05, 2011, http://articles.businessinsider.com/2011–08–05/news/29995816_1_nuclear-warheads-mossad-israeli-intelligence#ixzz1d3d4Fa5L. Farnaz Fassihi, *Bombs Target Iranian Nuclear Scientists*, WALL ST. J., Nov. 30, 2010, at A15. Farnaz Fassihi & Jay Solomon, *Scientist Killing Stokes U.S.—Iran Tensions*, WALL ST. J., Jan. 12, 2012, at 1, http://online.wsj.com/article/SB10001424052970204257504577153980963513686.html.

6 Joe Lauria, *ElBaradei Ends Term With Goals "In Tatters,"* WALL ST. J. (Nov. 5, 2009), *available at* http://online.wsj.com/article/SB125738716199429981.html.

7 President Barack Obama, Remarks in Prague, (Apr. 5, 2009) (*transcript available at* http://www.whitehouse.gov/the_press_office/Remarks-by-President-Barack-Obama-In-Prague-As-Delivered/).

The reasons are systemic and fundamental. Therefore, a systemic and fundamental response is required. Clearly now, this crisis cannot be allowed to continue—because it is a crisis of unequaled magnitude, magnitude that has always been inherent in nuclear risk, distinguishing it profoundly from any other danger the human species has invented for its own destruction. It is often recalled, that Robert Oppenheimer, seeing what he had orchestrated as the first atomic detonation, referenced the words of the Bhagavad-Gita; "... now I have become death, Shiva, the destroyer of worlds ...."[8] Shiva remains the relevant reference. The bottom line of nuclear risk today, according to all theoretical calculations of risk,[9] is a nuclear detonation in a major population center in five to ten years, and not more than twenty years going forward, absent radical improvement in our capacity to diminish that risk.

This book is about what we can make from the tatters of non-proliferation. It envisions not a phoenix rising to finally conquer nuclear weapons risk, but a new approach with significant promise for a much safer nuclear future. What is proposed here is a new regime for counterproliferation. It is a response to the need, not just for non-proliferation, but a regime of proactive counterproliferation.[10] It is about transmutation of what is still vital in the current infrastructure of counterproliferation to a comprehensive mandate of universal application that assures equity in nuclear security for all nations.

The task of creating a new legal and institutional framework requires, first, understanding why the current legal and institutional infrastructure is failing, and how contemporary nuclear risk defies containment. This in turn requires examination of nuclear risk in greater detail, to understand its components and its dynamics, at every principal stage, from source to detonation, to identify where in the process we can work a new regime to construct security. It requires, perhaps above all, understanding and engaging the political considerations that must be accommodated to achieve

---

8 Physicist Robert Oppenheimer, Supervising Scientist of the Manhattan Project on July 16, 1945, at 0529 HRS, in the Jomada del Muereto desert near the Trinity site in the White Sands Missile Range quoting from the Bhagavad-Gita upon witnessing the first atomic detonation by mankind. *See* James A. Hijiya, *The Gita of J. Robert Oppenheimer*, 144 PROCEEDINGS OF AMERICAN PHILOSOPHICAL SOCIETY 123 (2000), http://www.amphilsoc.org/sites/default/files/Hijiya.pdf.

9 *See generally* Graham Allison, NUCLEAR TERRORISM: THE ULTIMATE PREVENTABLE CATASTROPHE (Henry Holt & Company 2004); *See also* Commission on the Prevention of Weapons of Mass Destruction Proliferation and Terrorism, WORLD AT RISK (Vintage Books 2008).

10 There is no technically clear distinction between *non-proliferation* and *counterproliferation*. The terms are often conflated. See, e.g., Oxford Research Group, COUNTERPROLIFERATION IN A NON-PROLIFERATION WORLD, 4, (Apr. 2005), http://kms1.isn.ethz.ch/serviceengine/Files/ISN/90416/ipublicationdocument singledocument/a542a984-8c65-4986-93f5-322959c2a4b3/en/05-04+Counter-Proliferation.pdf. ("The PSI and other counter-proliferation initiatives should not be seen as a separate activity in a losing war against weapons proliferation, but as tools in the wider context of non-proliferation ..." It can be said that 'non-proliferation' puts the emphasis, consistent with its NPT origins, on the obligation not to proliferate, whereas 'counterproliferation' emphasizes proactive and preventative measures as seminally stated in the 1993 Defense Counterproliferation Initiative of the Clinton administration). Les Aspin, U.S. Dept. of Defense, The Defense Counterproliferation Initiative (Dec. 7, 1993).

the necessary legitimacy for any framework for counterproliferation to actually prove effective. That framework, if it is to work, must survive the test of historic experience and demonstrate viability in foreign relations.

Accordingly, this analysis, while focused on achieving a functional legal and institutional framework, draws from a variety of disciplines to achieve an integration of concerns. Such integration of understanding, characteristic of all truly functional architecture, is nothing less than what is required to meet the reality, the scope, and the depth of the critical challenge to our survival that nuclear weapons represent.

This book proposes a new foundation to transcend the limitations and failings of the Grand Bargain embodied in the NPT. The original Grand Bargain still remains the fundamental framework for non-proliferation of nuclear weapons. That bargain is simple in conception. It is composed of a trade of three commitments, sometimes called the "three-legged stool," or in a characterization that ignores its weakness, the "three pillars" of non-proliferation. The deal is, on the one side, the promise of the non-nuclear states not to acquire nuclear weapons; on the other, the promise of the nuclear states to provide assistance for the peaceful development of atomic energy, and to work to achieve nuclear disarmament and general disarmament.[11] The classification of nuclear and non-nuclear states is fixed, according to which governments "manufactured and exploded a nuclear weapon... prior to 1 January 1967."[12]

The Nuclear Non-proliferation Treaty is thus somewhat unusual among multilateral treaties, in that the party governments are drawn into two distinct classes as to their rights and obligations. The NPT, despite placing rights and obligations within the asymmetric reality of nuclear weapons possession as of a specified date, purports to achieve equity and legitimacy long term. It does so by tying non-proliferation obligation to the commitment to nuclear disarmament, and working towards a nuclear weapons free world, where the nuclear status of nations would finally become equal, i.e., zero nuclear weapons worldwide. The nexus between non-proliferation and disarmament

---

11 The Treaty on the Nonproliferation of Nuclear Weapons (Mar. 5, 1970) provides at Article II, "Each non-nuclear-weapon State Party to the Treaty undertakes not to receive the transfer from any transferor whatsoever of nuclear weapons or other nuclear explosive devices or of control over such weapons or explosive devices directly, or indirectly; not to manufacture or otherwise acquire nuclear weapons or other nuclear explosive devices; and not to seek or receive any assistance in the manufacture of nuclear weapons or other nuclear explosive devices." The NPT further provides at Article IV.2, "All the Parties to the Treaty undertake to facilitate, and have the right to participate in, the fullest possible exchange of equipment, materials and scientific and technological information for the peaceful uses of nuclear energy. Parties to the Treaty in a position to do so shall also co-operate in contributing alone or together with other States or international organizations to the further development of the applications of nuclear energy for peaceful purposes, especially in the territories of non-nuclear-weapon States Party to the Treaty, with due consideration for the needs of the developing areas of the world." Article VI provides the third pillar, the state parties committing to pursue "negotiations in good faith on effective measures relating to cessation of the nuclear arms race at an early date and to nuclear disarmament," and towards aTreaty on general and complete disarmament under strict and effective international control." Treaty on the Nonproliferation of Nuclear Weapons (Mar. 5, 1970), 21 U.S.T. 483, 729 U.N.T.S. 161.

12 *Id.*, art. IX.3.

thus became, both as international law, and politically, one of mutual dependency, promising ultimate equity in a nuclear weapons free world. The linkage of non-proliferation and disarmament, and the equity premise of that linkage, were pervasive in the negotiation of the NPT and framed and conditioned its resolution. That key dynamic of the NPT negotiations has been described as follows by scholars who have studied the negotiation history and travaux of the NPT:

> Because the non-nuclear states believed that permitting a few states to have nuclear weapons while barring most from doing so constituted a discriminatory feature of the Treaty, they were anxious to ensure during negotiations that the nuclear states would relinquish their nuclear weapons as soon as possible.[13]
>
> From the outset of the negotiations over the NPT, many non-nuclear states... were concerned with reducing and limiting what they regarded as the inherently discriminatory nature of the proposed treaty. At the 1965 session of the General Assembly, the eight non-aligned members of the ENDC—Brazil, Burma, Ethiopia, India, Mexico, Nigeria, Sweden and the United Arab Republic (Egypt)—proposed a resolution calling for a treaty on the non-proliferation of nuclear weapons. The proposed resolution, subsequently adopted by an overwhelming majority of the General Assembly as Resolution 2028 (XX), advanced five "main principles," the first three regarded as being the most important:
>
> (a) The treaty should be void of any loop-holes which might permit nuclear or non-nuclear Powers to proliferate, directly or indirectly, nuclear weapons in any form;
> (b) The treaty should embody an acceptable balance of mutual responsibilities and obligations of the nuclear and non-nuclear Powers;
> (c) The treaty should be a step towards the achievement of general and complete disarmament and, more particularly, nuclear disarmament.[14]

It is clear from the negotiating history that these principles, in manifesting the mutual dependency of the pillars of the NPT, and the ultimate claim to equity by way of the commitment to nuclear disarmament, "became the key demand of all non-nuclear countries,"[15] and the basis on which the essential bargain of the NPT was resolved.[16]

---

13 William Epstein & Paul C. Szasz, *Extension of the Nuclear Non-Proliferation Treaty: A Means of Strengthening the Treaty*, 33 VA. J. INT'L L. 735, 736 (1992–1993).

14 *Id.*, at 738–39.

15 *Id.*, at 740.

16 *Id.*, at 738–40. Ambassador Ecobesco from Romania, for example, proposed changes to the draft treaty in 1967 that demanded real disarmament measures on the part of the nuclear-weapon states that would show that nuclear and non-nuclear countries were being equally treated. United States Arms Control and Disarmament Agency, INTERNATIONAL NEGOTIATIONS ON THE TREATY ON THE NONPROLIFERATION OF NUCLEAR WEAPONS 87–88 (U.S. Government Printing Office 1969). Then, at Meeting 320 of the Conference of the Eighteen-Nation Committee on Disarmament, he specifically

The inherent imbalance in power between the nuclear-weapon states and the non-nuclear-weapon states remained a prevalent theme throughout the 10-year period during which the NPT was drafted, with the non-nuclear-weapon states repeatedly insisting that the final version require negotiation towards nuclear disarmament as the commitment of the nuclear-weapon-states to achieve ultimate equity, and the key trade-off for their own non-proliferation commitments as signatories to the NPT. This same dynamic has since dominated all discussion of respective rights and obligations. As the scholars who have studied this subsequent history have characterized the life of the NPT, "Throughout the history of the NPT, the non-nuclear states have striven for a universal and non-discriminatory regime . . . ."[17]

---

referred back to the principle articulated in paragraph 2(b) of Resolution 2028 (XX) stressing that it "implies, and in a very precise way, the character of equivalence of the responsibilities and obligations assumed by the parties to the treaty, the symmetry of the legal relations which this treaty would create... In order to conform to these requirements, which are of fundamental importance, the non-proliferation of nuclear weapons should be part of a whole series of measures whose final objective—which is both logical and necessary—would be nuclear disarmament... In our opinion, non-dissemination, if not accompanied by such measures, would only legalize the division of the world into nuclear and non-nuclear States. . . . " *Full verbatim record of the Conference of the Eighteen-Nation Committee on Disarmament [Meeting 320]*, Eighteen-Nation Committee on Disarmament (ENDC), http://quod.lib.umich.edu/e/endc/4918260.0320.001/10?rgn=full+text;view=image. Ambassador De Palma from the United States, during the Thirteenth Session of the ENDC, (the negotiations which produced the draft treaty of March 14, 1968), acknowledged the continuing pressure of the nuclear disarmament demand of the non-nuclear-weapon states, and its legal import which the NPT as finally agreed embodied, when he said that the U.S. did, of course, want to end the arms race but that the tendency of some non-nuclear-weapon countries to view nuclear disarmament as a *quid pro quo* overlooked the fact that the nonproliferation treaty would enhance the security of all parties, especially those which did not have nuclear weapons. United States Arms Control and Disarmament Agency, International Negotiations on the Treaty on the Nonproliferation of Nuclear Weapons 106 (U.S. Government Printing Office 1969). Attempting to resist the demand, he stated, "(t)hose who look for a *quid pro quo* seem to consider this treaty as if it were a commercial contract in which each party seeks to trade off concessions in order to gain equal financial or trade benefits." The Swiss stated the more general view that nevertheless there was mutual dependency of the promises of the NPT, declaring that "(t)he non-nuclear-weapon States certainly cannot take the responsibility of tying their hands indefinitely if the nuclear-weapon States fail to arrive at positive results in that direction. (nuclear disarmament) (parenthesis added). *Full verbatim record of the Conference of the Eighteen-Nation Committee on Disarmament [Meeting 362]*, Eighteen-Nation Committee on Disarmament, http://quod.lib.umich.edu/e/endc/4918260.0362.001/9?rgn=full+text;view=image. http://quod.lib.umich.edu/e/endc/4918260.0362.001/9?rgn=full+text;view=image. The Japanese representative, in statements echoed by the Pakistani delegation, commented in referring to the mutual commitments to nonproliferation and disarmament that the draft version did not yet provide an "acceptable balance of mutual responsibilities" for nuclear and non-nuclear states, as required under Resolution 2028. *Id.*, at 118. The Canadian ambassador expressed his country's similar concerns stating that, "if non-nuclear States are to be expected formally to renounce the right to acquire nuclear weapons, they can legitimately expect some *quid pro quo* in the form of progress towards halting the arms race in other sectors." *Full verbatim record of the Conference of the Eighteen-Nation Committee on Disarmament [Meeting 231]*, Eighteen-Nation Committee on Disarmament, http://quod.lib.umich.edu/e/endc/4918260.0231.001/33?rgn=full+text;view=image. These statements, and many others like them, are typical of the views expressed by the representatives of the non-nuclear-weapons states who attended the hundreds of meetings of the Eighteen-Nation Committee on Disarmament.

17 *Id.*, at 761.

Clearly it is not working as thus intended, or this book and many others would not be discussing the dramatic contemporary increase in nuclear weapons risk. However, most discussions concern how to improve the NPT, without considering the wisdom and viability of the original bargain as it plays out today. This book, instead, asks whether the NPT should be relied upon as the sole foundation for the future of counterproliferation, and whether, despite any accomplishment under the treaty, there should be a different framing of counterproliferation for a more secure future.

The proposal here is not to degrade or discard the considerable non-proliferation capital that has been built upon the NPT. However, the analysis begins with the necessity to understand why the Grand Bargain of the NPT is not succeeding as conceived, and why counterproliferation will continue to fall short in achieving nuclear security unless reinforced and eventually supplanted by a different legal and institutional framework. That framework, to be viable, must integrate different national interests of different states, and in that sense constitute a new Grand Bargain. It would build on the distinctive character of counterproliferation norms as universally applicable and would be implemented as a mandatory counterproliferation regime formulated by the United Nations Security Council through its authority under Chapter VII of the United Nations Charter (Charter), establishing uniform counterproliferation obligations for all states.

Though extending the parameters of Security Council legislation, the proposal here elaborated is not for an exercise in world government. Action by the Security Council cannot seriously advance counterproliferation without widespread support of governments. The viability of counterproliferation as an ongoing and improving endeavor will depend, as all matters of international law and organization depend, on securing legitimacy and compliance within the extant world of sovereign states. What is here proposed is to build on current capacities to develop a regime notwithstanding that it would be mandatory, is compatible with national sovereignty as we know it, that can capitalize on national interest to attain the legitimacy required for a much higher level of compliance.

This book is a plea to strike out on a new path to nuclear security. The entrance to this path, it will be explained, is already marked, though haltingly, deficiently, and, on the surface at least, without a plan for moving forward, by mandatory resolutions of the United Nations Security Council on the subjects of terrorism and weapons of mass destruction. The legal and institutional infrastructure here developed would similarly embody mutual perception of risk by the members of the Security Council; but it would represent a new conceptual framework, moving beyond the NPT with a new design and prospect for implementation, projecting a mandatory uniform set of standards to be consistently applied for all governments. The objective is to utilize the means available in this century, at this time, to achieve the security of fissile materials, better intelligence, control and monitoring of the nuclear fuel cycle, import-export control, interception of illicit transfer of nuclear materials, and attribution of responsibility through the remarkable new capacities of nuclear forensics, to achieve a containment and deterrence that meets the challenge of contemporary nuclear weapons risk. It is to organize anew the presently available components for effective counterproliferation.

How can this now be possible at a time when even the principal managers of nuclear risk, such as the former Secretary-General of the International Atomic Energy Agency, appear to have conceded defeat? Such progress is possible, because of the very fear they voice. We are all facing the same concern, whether voiced by nuclear weapons experts, academics, strategic policy planners, political leadership, or in communities far away from the actual work of nuclear weapons containment. There is the widespread realization that contemporary nuclear risk is out of control, if only brought to more general public consciousness by disasters in peaceful use of atomic energy such as Chernobyl or Fukushima. Thus the United Nations Secretary-General's High-level Panel on Threats, Challenges and Change reported as early as December 2004 that "we are approaching a point at which the erosion of the non-proliferation regime could become irreversible and result in a cascade of proliferation."[18] Subsequent developments, as in Iran and North Korea, have only confirmed this crescendo of risk.

Nuclear weapons risk has become identified as greatest in relation to international terrorism. 9/11 brought with it a change of consciousness concerning weapons of mass destruction and terrorism, and willingness to cope. 9/11 demonstrated that much will be done and money will flow for security, at least after the fact of a catastrophic event. As catastrophe, the scale of a contemporary nuclear detonation, in an urban setting, is barely imaginable. In the event of a nuclear detonation, it is likely the same sequence of disaster and response would occur as has occurred in much lesser crises, and that consequent to a detonation, the necessary political will to accomplish a mandatory regime along the lines of what is here proposed would appear. We already have demonstration enough in recent times, such as the Fukushima disaster, that corrective regulation mostly follows rather than precedes a nuclear event. But what comfort is that to the victims in Fukushima, or the human community that will suffer any future failure?

There is an alternative path. An aphorism attributed to Charles Darwin summarizes one of the great lessons of evolution to be that "it is not the strongest of the species that survives, nor the most intelligent, but the one most responsive to change." The attribution to Darwin is controversial, because it fails to acknowledge Darwin's discovery that just luck, by way of mutation, is key to survival of the fittest.[19] But because humankind is the most self-conscious of species, the luck of mutation does not describe the legal and institutional development of which human beings are capable. Our adaptive capability includes the capacity to prevent and pre-empt species catastrophe. Nuclear proliferation will not allow reliance on luck. This book is about our alternative, the capacity of our species, to create the legal and institutional framework for its own survival.

---

18 UN Secretary-General, *supra* note 4, at 39–40.

19 *Famous Darwin quotes wrong, says scholar*, COSMOS (Feb. 12, 2009), http://www.cosmosmagazine.com/news/2540/famous-darwin-quotes-are-wrong-says-scholar; John van Wyhe, *It Ain't Necessarily So . . .*, THE GUARDIAN, Feb. 8, 2008, http://www.guardian.co.uk/science/2008/feb/09/darwin.myths.

B. The Old Grand Bargain Breakdown

i. THE GOAL OF NUCLEAR DISARMAMENT

Of the three promises that constitute the core of the NPT, the disarmament promise has, in recent times, been given the most prominence. On January 4, 2007, by way of a joint declaration published in *The Wall Street Journal*, that commitment was newly made to resonate internationally. Former Secretaries of State George Shultz and Henry Kissinger, former Secretary of Defense William Perry, and former Senator Sam Nunn, called for the global abolition of nuclear weapons. In support of their call for "a nuclear free world," they referenced the Grand Bargain of the NPT and the commitment to nuclear disarmament embodied in Article VI of the treaty, thus reaffirming nuclear disarmament by the nuclear weapons states as the *quid pro quo* for non-proliferation. In another joint statement published in *The Wall Street Journal* one year later, the same senior statesmen made this connection even more emphatic and explicit, declaring that "without the vision of moving toward zero, we will not find the essential cooperation required to stop our downward spiral."[20] This follow-up declaration also noted the "general support" of many distinguished United States and international former officials for pursuit of abolition of nuclear weapons as reaffirmation of the Grand Bargain.[21]

The impact claimed was not overstatement. The four authors were soon internationally anointed "the four wise men."[22] And in his Prague speech, in April, 2009, placing nuclear risk at the top of the United States national security agenda, President Barack

---

20 George P. Shultz, William J. Perry, Henry A. Kissinger, & Sam Nunn, *Toward a Nuclear Free World*, WALL ST. J. A13 (Jan. 4, 2007) (Shultz et al., *Nuclear Free World*). Nunn also stated in Congressional testimony "we cannot get the cooperation of other nations without embracing the vision of a world free of nuclear weapons." *See* Senator Sam Nunn, Statement on Nuclear Weapons Policy to the House Committee on Foreign Affairs (May 10, 2007) (*transcript available at* http://foreignaffairs.house.gov/110/nun051007.htm).

21 Named supporters of U.S. government prominence included Madeleine Albright, Richard V. Allen, James A. Baker III, Samuel R. Berger, Zbigniew Brzezinski, Frank Carlucci, Warren Christopher, William Cohen, Lawrence Eagleburger, Melvin Laird, Anthony Lake, Robert McFarlane, Robert McNamara, and Colin Powell. Named international supporters included Mikhail Gorbachev and United Kingdom foreign secretary, Margaret Beckett. Shultz et al., *Nuclear Free World*, *supra* note 20.

22 *See*, e.g, David E. Hoffman, *Global Heroes: How the Cold War's wise men went anti-nuclear*, FOREIGN POLICY, Dec. 1, 2010, http://www.foreignpolicy.com/articles/2010/11/29/global_heroes; Ellen Tauscher, Under Secretary for Arms Control and International Security, Remarks at the Global Zero Summit in Paris, France (Feb. 3, 2010) (*transcript available at* http://www.state.gov/t/us/136425.htm). *See also* Conference Call with Charles D. Ferguson and Lieutenant General Brent Scowcroft, announcing the release of the Independent Task Force on U.S. Nuclear Weapons Policy report, Council on Foreign Relations, (May 1, 2009) (*transcript available at* http://www.cfr.org/proliferation/ferguson-scowcroft-conference-call/p19273); Franco Frattini, Introductory remarks at the Conference on Overcoming Nuclear Dangers in Rome, Italy, (Apr. 16, 2009) (*transcript available at* http://www.theworldpoliticalforum.net/wp-content/uploads/wpf2009/04_overcoming_nuclear_dangers_rome/doc/opening_speech_frattini.pdf).

Obama pledged "to seek the peace and security of a world without nuclear weapons." President Obama also reaffirmed the Grand Bargain of the NPT as the basis for this goal and its ultimate achievement.[23] In awarding President Obama the 2009 Noble Peace Prize, the Norwegian Nobel Committee stated that it "attached special importance to Obama's vision of and work for a world without nuclear weapons."[24]

President Obama was certainly not the first United States President to declare the goal of total elimination of nuclear weapons. A succession of presidents and foreign leaders endorsed that goal, most dramatically Ronald Reagan, along with Soviet Prime Minister Gorbachev, though fleetingly, at their summit meeting in Reykjavik, Iceland. No doubt each leader sincerely declaring the goal of abolition has been compelled by the terrible burden of responsibility nuclear weapons impose, and no doubt each could take no other moral position. But just as Reagan's vision quickly disappeared behind the United States' insistence on the development of an anti-ballistic missile program, each and every high-level declaration of the goal of abolition has been immediately contradicted in some form or other, by national security considerations. The four wise men, while calling for a world without nuclear weapons, also soon found themselves qualifying that vision. Before long, they stated in another *Wall Street Journal* op-ed pronouncement that "... as long as nuclear weapons exist, America must retain a safe, secure and reliable nuclear stockpile primarily to deter a nuclear attack and to reassure our allies through extended deterrence."[25] Henry Kissinger and George Shultz were soon criticized for hypocrisy for supporting upgrade of the U.S. nuclear weapons arsenal.[26]

That national security policies contradict the declared goal of abolition cannot simply be dismissed as hypocrisy. There is a trenchant critique of abolition as policy that warrants attention. It is a critique, that soon after the Shultz, Perry, Kissinger, Nunn declaration appeared, was voiced from prominent quarters of the national security community. In a response entitled "Nuclear Fantasy," former U.S. Secretary of Defense, Harold Brown, and John Deutch, director of the Central Intelligence Agency for the first Clinton administration, questioned the wisdom of the declaration of abolition

23 Obama, Remarks in Prague, *supra* note 7. "Today, the threat of global nuclear war has passed, but the danger of nuclear proliferation endures, making the basic bargain of the NPT more important than ever; nations with nuclear weapons will move toward disarmament, nations without nuclear weapons will forsake them, and all the nations have an "inalienable right" to peaceful nuclear energy." President Barack Obama, Remarks on the 40th Anniversary of the Nuclear Nonproliferation Treaty, (Mar. 5, 2010) (*transcript available at* http://www.whitehouse.gov/the-press-office/statement-president-obama-40th-anniversary-nuclear-nonproliferation-treaty).

24 Press Release, Norwegian Nobel Committee, *The Nobel Peace Prize 2009 Barack H. Obama*, Oct. 9, 2009, http://www.nobelprize.org/nobel_prizes/peace/laureates/2009/press.html.

25 George Shultz, William J. Perry, Henry Kissinger, & Sam Nunn, *Deterrence in the Age of Nuclear Proliferation*, WALL ST. J., Mar. 7, 2011, at A15.

26 *See* Philip Taubman, THE PARTNERSHIP: FIVE COLD WARRIORS AND THEIR QUEST TO BAN THE BOMB 1st ed., (Harper 2012). *See also*, Greg Webb, *Leading US Scientist Criticizes Warhead Effort*, GLOBAL SECURITY NEWSWIRE, Feb. 27, 2008, http://www.nti.org/gsn/article/leading-us-scientist-criticizes-warhead-effort/.

as policy. The sum and substance of their response was epitomized in the memorable phrase, "hope is not a policy."[27]

The Brown/Deutch distinction between hope and policy merits consideration. It highlights the fact that the abolition of nuclear weapons, though stated as legal obligation under the NPT, is essentially aspirational. Abolition has not been a factor in national security planning of governments as manifest throughout the history of the NPT. The distinction between hope and policy, indeed, gets us to the problem at the heart of the current framework for the non-proliferation of nuclear weapons. Abolition of nuclear weapons is, and will remain, for any foreseeable future of international security, aspirational. One of the "four wise men," Senator Sam Nunn, said as much in drawing a since often-repeated metaphor for achieving nuclear disarmament—that it is "like climbing a fog-shrouded mountain."[28] Getting to global nuclear disarmament is made a matter of faith, something like getting to heaven, akin to Lord Acton's reference to "the remote and ideal objective" that "captivates the imagination by its splendor and the reason by its simplicity."[29]

In going beyond simplicity, the discussion of getting to global nuclear disarmament, like getting to heaven, requires discussing the risk of the thermal alternative. But though the wise men and most other proponents of abolition always end up talking about counterproliferation, they insist on the firm connection between nuclear disarmament and counterproliferation embodied in the NPT. In their second declaration on a world without nuclear weapons, published in *The Wall Street Journal*, the four wise men declared "that continued reliance on nuclear weapons as the principal element for deterrence is encouraging, or at least excusing, the spread of these weapons, and will inevitably erode the essential cooperation necessary to avoid proliferation, protect nuclear materials and deal effectively with new threats."[30]

In the real world of strategic policy-making, we see no evidence of this alleged connection. What we do see is disjunction between the goal of global nuclear disarmament, and policies of counterproliferation. The disjunction can partly be explained in that counterproliferation strategy cannot wait for the political equivalent of heaven that is required for the abolition of nuclear weapons. Counterproliferation is about engaging present capacities to reduce nuclear risk, today, to confront and defeat its metastasis. Accordingly, real and present policy makers do not consider the abolition of nuclear weapons part of contemporary national security strategy.

But the respective timing for counterproliferation and abolition is only one aspect of the explanation for why total nuclear disarmament and counterproliferation are

---

27 Harold Brown & John Deutch, *The Nuclear Disarmament Fantasy*, WALL ST. J., Nov. 19, 2007, at A19.

28 Senator Sam Nunn's fog-shrouded mountain metaphor has become part of nuclear *lingua franca*, repeated both by his co-authors of the declaration published in THE WALL STREET JOURNAL and in nuclear disarmament discourse more generally. Sam Nunn, Co-Chairman and CEO, Nuclear Threat Initiative, Remarks to the InterAction Council 28th Annual Plenary Meeting in Hiroshima, Japan, (Apr. 18, 2010) (*transcript available at* http://www.nti.org/c_press/speech_Nunn_Hiroshima_InterAction_Council_041810.pdf).

29 Lord Acton, *Nationality*, HOME AND FOREIGN REVIEW (1862).

30 Shultz et al., *supra* note 20.

not connected in actual policy planning. That fuller explanation is not difficult to discover. There has been much study of why nations seek to develop nuclear weapons and why some nations have terminated their nuclear weapons programs. We know quite a bit about why the commitment to global nuclear disarmament does not command, or even influence, national policy, both at the theoretical and practical levels.

At the level of theory, those charged with national security policies simply do not see a viable stasis of nuclear weapons abolition. Advocates of abolition argue that other weapons have been banned—poison gas, for example, consequent to the horror of its widespread use in the First World War. But of course, legal ban does not prevent use. Poison gas has been used as a weapon, even in recent times; in the Iran–Iraq war; also by the Saddam Hussein regime against the Kurdish population of Iraq. Poison gas has also been used as a weapon of international terrorism, with the attack by Aum Shinrikyo in Japan. The global ban on such weapons has brought us to a stasis where use is the exception, not the norm. But the possible use of a nuclear weapon is of a dramatically different order. National security policies take account of the fact that nuclear weapons delineate, for any government, an existential dimension well beyond any weapon in human history. For strategic planning, the scale of the destructive power of nuclear weapons introduces unique considerations and dynamics. No other weapon comes even close to matching the strategic policy import of nuclear weapons—for intimidation, blackmail, deterrence, or destruction. One detonation, a single detonation in any major urban center anywhere in the world, would be truly a global catastrophe, not only in the extraordinary scale of immediate death and injury, but also in damage to the interdependent matrix of the global economy, damage to the environment, and damage to the human psyche of global security. The damage may be incalculable, but we can be sure it would be the supreme trauma of contemporary weapons use. So unlike the legal ban of any other weapon, the legal ban of nuclear weapons cannot possibly bring us to a condition of tolerable risk.

Much of the theoretical analysis of nuclear weapons risk also argues that a world without nuclear weapons would not be a world free of nuclear risk, and could be even more dangerous. Principal theorists of nuclear weapons policy, particularly strategic game theorists, maintain that reaching or even approaching zero nuclear weapons could actually result in greater danger of sudden and dramatic nuclear instability, and hence a greater likelihood of nuclear risk spiraling out of control.[31] They argue that nuclear disarmament would put a premium on speed and initiative for any miscreant government, and that it would afford greater advantage to smaller powers of relatively small conventional weapons strength. For adversaries, it would, consequently, also increase incentives toward the preemptive use of nuclear weapons, or

31 "If for a moment we imagine that Sagan's hoped-for world without nuclear weapons could be realized, what would anyone do if a major state revealed that it had secretly rebuilt a considerable nuclear arsenal? Would someone then attack the reborn nuclear state using the only weapons it would have, that is, conventional ones? I think not." Kenneth Waltz, *Waltz Responds: The Great Debate*, National Interest, Sept.-Oct. 2010, http://nationalinterest.org/greatdebate/waltz-responds-3953.

their conventional military power.[32] The game theorists generally conclude that zero would dramatically raise the risk of nuclear coercion that the cheating or "breakout" of a rogue or renegade government could achieve well beyond its capacity to do so in a nuclear armed world.

This is what security scholars sometimes call the "instability of offense dominance"—that even in a world of zero nuclear weapons, and perhaps most of all in a world of zero, there may be decisive advantage for the government initiating the reconstitution of a nuclear arsenal. Zero would contain a new dynamic. The breakout government, having developed even a nuclear weapons capacity small by today's standards, would be the proverbial one-eyed man in the kingdom of the blind. Zero would create new windows of opportunity for aggression, and new windows of vulnerability for former nuclear weapons states, leaving the latter more inclined to launch conventional pre-emptive strikes. Even those advocating abolition of nuclear weapons admit, there is no "technical fix" to the breakout problem.[33]

In light of such considerations, abolition is seen as unrealistic. Even in a world of zero nuclear weapons, the technology and material for manufacture would remain available. This allows the possibility, even likelihood, of breakout by any government or terrorist organization seeking to gain advantage in a variety of possible scenarios, such as positioning for nuclear blackmail, or simply acting out the irrationality of an apocalyptic ideology. Breakout could occur by way of concealment on the way to zero, or by the initiation of a clandestine nuclear weapons program on the way to zero. Breakout could occur after zero, given that the technology and the material for nuclear weapons manufacture would remain available. Actual abolishment of nuclear weapons would not abolish institutional memory, nuclear weapon expertise, experimental data, or designs, which could be quickly reconstituted. Even under the most optimistic nuclear disarmament scenarios, "surge capabilities" or "virtual arsenals"[34] would remain. Such risk would in turn make pre-emptive action by other states more likely. The argument is not merely theoretical. The George W. Bush Administration's justification of the invasion of Iraq, on the basis of Iraq's alleged programs to develop weapons of mass destruction (WMD), employed a related theory of pre-emptive self-defense.[35] It is also, of course, the reasoning behind threats to destroy Iran's nuclear facilities.

Thus policy makers perceive zero as creating its own world of nuclear weapons risk. Discovery, or even just fear that an adversary has hidden a militarily significant number of nuclear weapons, or has taken steps to reconstitute its nuclear weapons capacity in the midst of political crisis, could precipitate breakout in the most virulent form. The perennial confrontation between India and Pakistan, for example, could

32 *See* elaboration of this consideration in Thomas C. Schelling, *The Role of Deterrence in Total Disarmament*, VOL. 40, N.1.3 FOREIGN AFFAIRS at 396, (Apr. 1962).

33 *See*, e.g, Carl Kaysen, Robert McNamara, & George Rathgens, NUCLEAR WEAPONS AFTER THE COLD WAR, A NUCLEAR WEAPONS FREE WORLD at 33–51 (Westview Press 1993).

34 *See infra* pp. 41–42.

35 *See Agora: Future Implications of the Iraq Conflict*, 97 AM. J. INT'L L. 557 (2003).

easily devolve to such a post-zero scenario. Given the unendurable consequence of a nuclear strike, even a minor advantage in lead time would be seen as critical. It is therefore not surprising that Russia, China, France, Pakistan, and Israel all critique the security implications of zero.[36]

Without absolute assurance that all would comply with global nuclear disarmament, policy makers naturally conclude that universal compliance cannot be expected. And there is no such assurance for any government, so long as the political conditions that engendered its nuclear weapons capacity in the first place continue. We can have policy-driven reductions between states if fundamental political conditions do change, such as the importantly successful nuclear risk reductions between the former Union of Soviet Socialist Republics (Soviet Union) and the United States. But the risk of any weapon in the control of a state threatening another state, or a weapon that might be sold, stolen, or otherwise transferred from government to terrorist, is enough to convince the current nuclear weapons powers that nuclear risk might actually increase with progress towards global nuclear disarmament.

Current material and technological realities make it feasible for any national regime with a renegade or a revolutionary world vision, to play a nuclear weapons game wholly at odds with getting to zero. Policy makers do not have to see far ahead to be convinced of this strategic reality. It is evident in the stated ambition of Al Qaeda to achieve a nuclear armed caliphate commanding its own international order.[37] Terrorist risk will continue to strain nuclear deterrence theory with the problem of finding a return address. And between states nuclear weapons risk would still be inherent at zero, in the ambitions of the regimes in North Korea, Iran, and potentially other places, serving as sources for nuclear weapons related material and technology. That North Korea and Iran and Iraq and Libya were all able to turn their right to peaceful use of atomic energy to weapons related use, while remaining parties to the Nuclear Non-proliferation Treaty, has forever red-flagged the risk of moving towards zero.

Much of the risk that policy makers see as inherent in nuclear disarmament might be manageable if verification could provide at least a high probability of detecting a violation, sufficient to assure timely warning and response. All evidence is to the contrary. The failures of detection, extending over years, in the most threatening cases—Iraq, Iran, and North Korea—have left a legacy of extreme skepticism about monitoring and verification capability. Moreover, all the experts agree that inspection capacity and verification technology can be deceived and defeated. They also agree there is no technical prospect of assurance against clandestine nuclear weapons activity, such as smaller facilities or the below-ground enrichment plants that Iran is reported to have constructed. We can improve detection and monitoring, and make cheating more difficult. That is essential to effective counterproliferation. But in a zero nuclear weapons

36 George Perkovich & James M. Acton, *Abolishing Nuclear Weapons: A Debate*, Carnegie Endowment for International Peace (2009), http://carnegieendowment.org/files/abolishing_nuclear_weapons_debate.pdf.

37 *See*, e.g., Allison, *supra* note 9.

world, there would remain substantial risk of breakout that any known or contemplated means of verification could not negate.

Policymakers mapping nuclear risk must take account of these concerns. They circle the fact that nuclear weapons cannot be disinvented. They cannot ignore the availability, even after hypothetical zero, of expertise and material for the manufacture of nuclear weapons. They must account for the prospect that even in a "nuclear weapons free future" of abolishment, the burgeoning nuclear power industry worldwide will bring with it more and more significant "dual-use" technologies, that with the "turn of a screw" can transform peaceful use to weapons use.

It thus becomes understandable why nuclear disarmament does not even enter into current calculations of policymakers. Specific arguments cautioning against global nuclear disarmament may be debatable, even rebuttable, and there is much to be said for step-by-step long-term progress to the substantial reduction, or elimination of nuclear weapons.[38] The ineluctable point, however, is that global nuclear disarmament does not enter into the strategic prescriptions of policymakers for persuasive reasons. Strategic theory, particularly the arguments drawn from game theory, are naturally speculative. But speculative scenarios inevitably are the substance of present policy planning. So long as these speculations are persuasive, given the understandable bias against making fatal mistakes on a grandiose scale, abolition will not be on the policy-planning table.

If we look at the actual national security strategies in place, this is clearly the situation. For the United States, despite all the rhetoric, and the presidential declaration of a goal of getting to zero, the vision of nuclear zero is not even included in the official declaration of US nuclear weapons policy.[39] The same is true of Russian military doctrine.[40] Despite nuclear arms reductions achieved under START, all major nuclear weapons states have declared themselves, in some form or other, as definitively committed

---

38 For a comprehensive and thoughtful analysis, *see* Gareth Evans & Yoriko Kawaguchi, Co-Chairs, International Commission on Nuclear Non-proliferation and Disarmament, *Eliminating Nuclear Threats: a Practical agenda for Global Policymakers*, 59–100 (2009), http://icnnd.org./org/Reference/reports/ent/pdf/ICNND_Report-EliminatingNuclearThreats.pdf

39 *See* U.S. Department of Defense, *US Nuclear Posture Review Report*, at 19, (Apr. 2010), http://www.defense.gov/npr/docs/2010%20nuclear%20posture%20review%20report.pdf.

40 Russian Federation Military Doctrine, Decree No. 706, Apr. 21, 2000, provided by Nezavisimaya Gazeta, *Russian Federation Military Doctrine, Approved by Russian Federation Presidential Edict of April 21, 2000*, Apr. 22, 2000, at 5–6 [FBIS document CEP20000424000171]. The Russia Military Doctrine states "Under present-day conditions the Russian Federation proceeds on the basis of the need to have a nuclear potential capable of guaranteeing a set level of damage to any aggressor (state or coalition of states) under any circumstances." *Also see* "HK Paper Report PRC CMC Meeting on Nuclear Weapons Strategy," Hong Kong, *Tai Yan Pao*, Doc. ID: CPP20000717000021 (July 17, 2000). During the Central Military Commission conference, China outlined the "Five Musts" on nuclear weapons: "China must own strategic nuclear weapons of a definite quality and quantity in order to ensure national security. China must guarantee the safety of strategic nuclear bases and prevent against the loss of combat effectiveness from attacks and destruction by hostile countries. China must ensure that its strategic nuclear weapons are at a high degree of war preparedness. When an aggressor launches a nuclear attack against China, China must be able to launch nuclear counterattack and nuclear re-attack against the aggressor. China must pay attention to the global situation of strategic balance and stability and,

against their own nuclear disarmament. Leaders of governments speak praises of their nuclear arsenals that echo cold war rhetoric. As recently as 2006, French President Chirac declared, for example, that "nuclear deterrence remains the fundamental guarantee of our security."[41] More recently, President Nicolas Sarkozy of France called France's nuclear weapons "the nation's life insurance policy," and committed to modernization of France's nuclear arsenal as increasing France's insurance.[42] Given removal of the conventional weapons advantages of the Soviet Union, Russia is more reliant than ever before, in its strategic policies, on nuclear weapons, despite the reductions of START II.[43] China has shown no inclination to reduce its nuclear arsenal, and instead seems bent on its modernization and expansion. None of the five nuclear weapons states so classified under the NPT have promised not to develop new types of nuclear weapons, and neither have India, Pakistan, or Israel. Even in the context of obtaining U.S. Senate ratification for the new Start Treaty, indeed to secure that approval, President Obama promised $80 billion to modernize the U.S. nuclear arsenal.[44] More to the point, no present nuclear weapons state, certainly not one of the original five, has established any bureaucracy, or even any program, with the goal of total nuclear disarmament.[45] Sergio Duarte, UN High Representative for Disarmament Affairs, has seen the emperor without clothes, complaining that there is "still no sign of the infrastructure required

---

when there are changes in the situation, adjust its strategic nuclear weapon development strategy in a timely manner." *See also,* Peter Schwartz, *French President Chirac Threatens Nuclear Retaliation in the Event of Terrorist Attack*, WORLD SOCIALIST WEB SITE, Jan. 21, 2006, http://www.wsws.org/articles/2006/jan2006/chir-j21.shtml. "Leaders of states who use terrorist methods against us, as well as those who consider using in one way or another weapons of mass destruction, must understand that they would expose themselves to a firm and appropriate response on our part. This response could be a conventional one. It might be of a different kind." Gwynne Dyer, *France Knows the Nuclear Club is the Place To Be Demands by the haves on the have-nots are hypocritical and self-defeating*, SYDNEY MORNING HERALD, Feb. 12, 2006, http://www.commondreams.org/views06/0212-26.htm.

41 "Since 1964, France has had an autonomous nuclear deterrence. The lessons of history led General de Gaulle to make this crucial choice. During all these years, the French nuclear forces have ensured our country's defense and greatly helped to preserve peace. Today, they continue to keep watch, quietly, for us to be able to live in a land of freedom which is the master of its future and its destiny. They continue, and will continue tomorrow, to be the ultimate guarantor of our security. . . . " *See* Présidence de la République Française Jacques Chirac, Remarks to the Strategic Air and Maritime Forces at Landivisiau, (Jan. 19, 2006) (*transcript available at* http://www.acronym.org.uk/dd/dd82/82chirac.htm#en01)

42 President Nicola Sarkozy, Presentation of Le Terrible in Cherbourg, (Mar. 21, 2008) (*transcript available at* http://www.acronym.org.uk/docs/0803/doc09.htm).

43 For the proposition that Russia is reliant on nuclear weapons due to inadequacy of conventional weapons. *See* Lee Banville, *Tracking Nuclear Proliferation: Russia Nuclear Strategy*, PBS NEWSHOUR, May 2, 2005, http://www.pbs.org/newshour/indepth_coverage/military/proliferation/countries/russia.html.

44 *See* Rebecca Johnson, *NPT conference: half time glass half full*, OPEN DEMOCRACY, May 17, 2010, at 2, http://www.opendemocracy.net/5050/npt-conference-half-time-glass-half-full.

45 This state of affairs was summarized in a Carnegie Foundation report as follows: "Few, if any, top-tier issues attract as much simplistic analysis, as much rhetoric, and as little serious work by governments as does the feasibility of nuclear disarmament. As was pointed out in *Abolishing Nuclear Weapons*, none of the nuclear—weapons states 'has an employee, let alone an inter-agency group, tasked full time with figuring out what would be required to verifiably decommission all its nuclear weapons.'" Perkovich & Acton, *supra* note 36 (quoting Jessica T. Mathews President of the Carnegie Endowment for International Peace).

to achieve nuclear disarmament—no operational plans, deadlines, government disarmament agencies, budgets, and detailed domestic legislation."[46]

Is it that the governments have not caught up with the conditions of nuclear security? First to be noted is that we have not eliminated state-to-state risk and the logic of MAD, supposedly a relic of the Cold War. MAD remains very much present in regional confrontations of states, such as India/Pakistan, and potentially present between Israel and surrounding Arab states, and North Korea and the governments of East Asia that North Korea may seek to intimidate. Disarmament proponents point out that nuclear weapons, particularly as held within the arsenals of great powers, no longer have the strategic value they embodied in the cold war years of MAD. This *is* certainly true for the United States in light of its overwhelming conventional weapons capacity. In further support, disarmament proponents list the post-World War II conflicts such as the Korean and Vietnam wars and other conflicts in which nuclear weapons were available but not employed or even deployed.[47] But this does not take account of the utility and attractiveness of nuclear weapons for threat of use. And we have had plenty of that. The Bush administration, for example, sought to make clear to Saddam Hussein that any use of WMD would be met with total devastation, making the point that the nuclear option was on the table.[48] In the context of current nuclear confrontation, US Secretary of State Hillary Clinton has voiced a similar threat to Iran.[49] Such threats are not exclusive to great powers. Certainly, on the other side, the threats of North Korea to use its nuclear weapons have been treated with the utmost seriousness.[50] The utility of the threat, even during actual conflict, has been documented. It was reported that the threat of nuclear response was critical to Israel's survival in the 1973 Yom Kippur war, imposing constraint on Egypt's forward movement of its troops when Israeli lines were overwhelmed in the early hours of that war. Though Egyptian forces penetrated deep into the Sinai, to the very threshold of Israel's heartland, they

---

46 Sergio Duarte, *Disarmament: A Look Back, A Look Ahead*, DISARMAMENT TIMES, at 5, (Mar. 2008), http://disarm.igc.org/index.php?view=article%3B&catid=61%3Adt2008spring&id=63%3Adt2008springDuarte&format=pdf&option=com_content&Itemid=2.

47 *See*, e.g, Joseph Rotblat, Jack Steinberger, & Bhalchandra Udkaongar, A NUCLEAR-WEAPON-FREE WORLD: DESIRABLE? FEASIBLE? at 33–62 (Westview Press 1993).

48 "The United States is prepared to launch nuclear missiles against Iraq if President Saddam Hussein deploys chemical or biological weapons against American troops or allies, the White House said." Roland Watson, *Bush warns Saddam to expect a nuclear retaliation*, IRISH INDEPENDENT, Dec. 12, 2002, http://www.independent.ie/world-news/americas/bush-warns-saddam-to-expect-a-nuclear-retaliation-282234.html.

49 "In the next ten years, during which they [Iranians] might foolishly consider launching an attack on Israel, we would be able to totally obliterate them." Television interview by Chris Cuomo with Hilary Clinton, U.S. Secretary of State, (Apr. 23, 2008), *see* Jake Tapper, *Pennsylvania's Six Week Primary Ends Tonight*, ABC NEWS, Apr. 22, 2008, http://abcnews.go.com/WN/Vote2008/story?id=4698059&page=1#.Trt4wlYu6DI.

50 Pyongyang was ready to launch a "retaliatory sacred war" at any time, the state-run Korean Central News Agency (KCNA) said... North Korea says it will use its "nuclear deterrent" in response to joint US-South Korean military exercises this weekend. John Sudworth, *North Korea warns of nuclear "sacred war,"* BBC NEWS, Jul. 24, 2010, http://www.bbc.co.uk/news/world-asia-pacific-10748148.

stopped, apparently in deference to the prospect of an Israeli nuclear response, the so-called Samson Option.[51] It was and remains the essence of Israel's policy to retain a nuclear strike force, as the existential threat Israel makes to ensure its own survival.

Conversely, even a small number of nuclear weapons pose an existential threat to a small state such as Israel. This certainly was Israel's justification for destroying nuclear facilities in Iraq and Syria, and is the justification for the threat to do the same to Iran. Other governments, without solo ability to muster overwhelming conventional armament in their own defense, such as the United Kingdom (UK) and France, have adhered to a similar logic in retaining their nuclear weapons. Their nuclear weapons strategy may be thought to be flawed, even archaic, but it nevertheless persists, grounded in security concerns. Any enlightenment as to the disutility of nuclear weapons, if that is what is required, has only resulted in the reduction of nuclear armaments for reasons of cost and efficiency, not commitment to zero.

States of proliferation concern, such as Iran and North Korea, have seized upon perhaps the most persuasive rationale today for possession of nuclear weapons. Their strategic situation well illustrates the often stark contrast between hope and policy. Thus on the same editorial page of *The Wall Street Journal*, in which the disarmament manifesto of the four wise men was published, it has since been observed, "Respectable wise men, in and out of government, talk of the importance of arms control and a nuclear-free world, when the reality is that Iran, North Korea and other countries have made the acquisition of nuclear weapons their highest priority."[52]

It is a mistake to see such policy of the "states of proliferation concern" as simply reflecting rogue intention. The governments of North Korea and Iran have a variety of reasons for pursuing nuclear weapons-related programs. There are no doubt domestic political considerations involved. But these governments, most significantly, see nuclear weapons capacity as their best counter to the conventional weapons superiority of the United States and its allies, constraining the ability of the United States to project its power globally. The accessibility of nuclear weapons development has become the great equalizer. If there was any doubt about this before the invasion of Iraq, the Bush Administration's listing of an "axis of evil" made the invasion of Iraq on the rationale of preventing culmination of its alleged program to develop nuclear weapons, and the leverage it would thereby acquire, an indelible lesson for the regimes in Tehran, Pyongyang, and elsewhere. Even non-rogue governments drew the same lesson. Generals in charge of strategic planning for India and Pakistan declared the principal lesson of the invasion of Iraq to be that possession of nuclear weapons is the best means to counter US conventional force dominance.[53] And they are probably

51 Mark Helprin, *Why Israel Needs the Bomb*, WALL ST. J., Oct. 18, 2010, at A19.

52 Stephen Peter Rosen, *The Emperor's Nuclear Clothes,* WALL ST. J., Nov. 29, 2010, *available at* http://online.wsj.com/article/SB10001424052748704693104575638671591044484.html.

53 Interview by Hugh Gusterson with Gen. Atta M Iqhman, *see* Hugh Gusterson, *U.S. nuclear double standards*, BULL. OF THE ATOMIC SCIENTISTS, Feb. 20, 2008, concurring in this view as "famously stated" by India's General Sundarji, "the lesson of the 1991 war between the United States and Iraq was not to get into a conflict with the United States unless you already had nuclear weapons."

correct, as the common quotation of their observation confirms. Some commentators even see this equalizer effect as indicating a greater likelihood of conventional wars, absent the nuclear weapon threat.[54]

This rationale, sometimes called *denial of access*, operates despite a government's understanding that its use of nuclear weapons would be met with its own annihilation. The risk of nuclear annihilation is unlikely to dissuade a regime from developing nuclear weapons, given its choice to be between conventional or nuclear annihilation, if the threat posed by its demonstration of the actual possession of its own nuclear weapon may spare it from either alternative. One can suppose, that during the first US/NATO cruise missile strike against Libya in 2011, someone in Muammar Qaddafi's inner circle must have wondered along these lines about the wisdom of having dismantled the Libyan nuclear weapons program. If the Libyan regime was in position to respond with a nuclear weapon, would NATO have agreed to a military campaign against Libya?

For the "states of proliferation concern," nuclear weapons are additionally attractive as means to extract economic and political concessions that would not otherwise be obtainable. Thus we have the gamesmanship of North Korea, promising non-proliferation compliance, then refusing, then obtaining concessions for rejoining talks, then withdrawing again; a sequence which has impressed the Iranian regime as similarly advantageous.[55] For North Korea especially, the nuclear threat has become its most significant means for achieving international advantage, given its otherwise desperate domestic situation, and general alienation from the benefits of global integration. The threat of what amounts to nuclear suicide is employed as the means to secure the mundane but substantial benefits of money, goods and services otherwise unobtainable.

Beyond strategic theory and strategic policy, states seek other benefits from their nuclear weapons programs. These include intangible benefits described colloquially as prestige or political status, including nuclear weapons as a symbol of modernity, regional power, and defiance. That weapons systems create this kind of political value is surely not a new observation about the reasons that nations seek weapons, and

---

54 This has led some strategic analysts to even argue in the extreme that more nukes is better. *See* Steve Chapman, *Learning to Love the Bomb: Is nuclear proliferation inherently dangerous?*, REASON, Feb. 2003, http://reason.com/archives/2003/02/01/learning-to-love-the-bomb. Columbia University political scientist Kenneth Waltz argued that "the gradual spread of nuclear weapons is more to be welcomed than feared." Scott D. Sagan & Kenneth N. Waltz, THE SPREAD OF NUCLEAR WEAPONS: A DEBATE RENEWED at 45 (W. W. Norton & Company 2003).

55 *See* Kim Murphy, *North Korea Nuclear Deal May Be Inspiration for Iran; Analysts See Tehran is in Mood to Negotiate, But Hard Liners Sense the U.S. Is Weakened*, L.A. TIMES A4 (Feb. 15, 2007) (quoting Professor Sadegh Zibakalam, a professor of politics at Tehran University), "The hard-liners, perhaps impressed by North Korea's achievement, are now inclined to be more resilient and uncompromising. They say if North Korea could do it, why shouldn't we? Why should we let the United States dictate to us, rather than negotiate with us? .... This scenario has been at the back of the minds of some Iranian leaders; that if we reach a stage that we would be respected as an equal partner, then we could do real negotiations and reach a deal over our nuclear program."

submerge other interests to obtain them. Thucydides long ago identified honor as one of the reasons for war, and human history bears all too much testimony to the truth of his observation. France is certainly not alone in claiming a standard of *honneur* as emblematic of its history. Today a similar standard is raised highest by the states of proliferation concern, such as Pakistan, India, Iran, and North Korea; although in the case of North Korea, one might more accurately conclude its greatest motivation is not *honneur*, but not to be ignored.

Moreover, there is significant domestic political appeal to be obtained in pursuing nuclear weapons programs. This is dramatically evident in the pro-nuclear street demonstrations in Tehran and Pyongyang, and the fact that A.Q. Khan, the man identified as running the most significant nuclear black market ever discovered, is to this day treated as a national hero in Pakistan for his role in Pakistan's nuclear weapons development. As Pakistan's Foreign Minister has described the broader implication of the popular sentiment, "nuclear weapons are the currency of power and many countries would like to use it."[56] The proposition, often heard from proponents of nuclear disarmament, that nuclear disarmament can demonstrate to non-nuclear weapons states that they do not need nuclear weapons,[57] therefore misses the point. Non-nuclear weapons states may know they do not need nuclear weapons, but still want them.

Perhaps all the reasons preventing global nuclear disarmament, theoretical and real, can eventually be overcome by developing trust between nations, such as has been achieved, for example within the European Community (EC), where we see what looks like permanent peace among historic enemies. But under any reasonable analysis, a comparable global state of international affairs is a long way off, certainly as distant as the fog-shrouded mountain top of global nuclear disarmament envisioned by the four wise men, and far beyond the current realities of nuclear risk with which counterproliferation must contend. Perhaps the prospect of sufficient psychological and political transformation is not beyond possibility in the long term of an increasingly interdependent world. But the risk presented by nuclear proliferation is here and now. There is one conclusion about getting to zero on which everyone who has seriously looked at the matter can agree—we won't get there any time soon.[58] The most ambitious and optimistic estimates typically postulate at least a 50-year time frame. For most of us, that leaves nuclear risk as a clear and present danger for the remainder of our adult lives, and for our children.

---

56 Jo Johnson & Farhan Bokhari, *Pakistan Warns on India-US Deal*, FINANCIAL TIMES, Mar. 16, 2006, http://www.ft.com/intl/cms/s/0/674bb44c-b51f-11da-aa90-0000779e2340.html#axzz1dHv38ppH.

57 *See*, e.g, Christopher C. Joyner & Alexander Ian Parkhouse, *Nuclear Terrorism in a Globalized World: Assessing the Threat and the Emerging Management Regime*, 45 STANFORD J. INT'L L. 203 (2009) (repeating the comment of Graham Allison, *supra* note 9, at 240).

58 Consistent with this, President Obama reiterates whenever speaking of getting to zero, that he does not think it will occur in his lifetime. Obama, Remarks in Prague, *supra* note 7. *See also* Evans & Kawaguchi, *supra* note 38, at 67. "For the time that will be needed to overcome the political, strategic, psychological and other obstacles to abolition, the retention of nuclear weapons in sufficient numbers and configuration to deter others from threatening or using them is something that policymakers on all sides of the argument are going to have to accept."

ii. THE FLAWED CONNECTION OF NUCLEAR DISARMAMENT AND COUNTERPROLIFERATION

Even if nuclear disarmament is a viable goal, not just a hope, it is therefore counterproductive for its achievement to be made the condition for substantial progress on counterproliferation. Nuclear disarmament may be the long-term objective, but counterproliferation is the immediate requirement for reduction of nuclear risk. The unrealized goal of disarmament should not be allowed to undermine progress on counterproliferation by serving as the excuse for resistance. But that is what will continue to occur so long as counterproliferation remains wholly referable for its sole foundation to the NPT, in which disarmament and counterproliferation are bound together. Nuclear risk, to the contrary, is not somewhere high on that same fog-shrouded mountain of a world without nuclear weapons. It is down here on the plains of real risk, where counterproliferation must be made effective within the limits of current political and strategic reality.

Down in the real world of nuclear risk, the nexus of non-proliferation and global disarmament embodied in the NPT is the cross that counterproliferation bears in every venue of nuclear weapons discourse. There is consistently the insistence from many governments, most emphatically from the non-nuclear weapons states (NNWS), that progress in non-proliferation as promised in Article I of the NPT depends upon progress in achieving nuclear disarmament seen as a *quid pro quo* as stated in Article VI of the Treaty. At the NPT review conference that occurs every five years, this central tenet is always repeated, however much frustration and dispute it engenders. The most recent review conference that took place in 2010 once again called for the "full, effective and urgent implementation" of nuclear disarmament, and proclaimed, as a cardinal principal, the "unequivocal undertaking" by nuclear weapons states to eliminate their nuclear arsenals as the basis for moving forward.[59]

This insistence on a conditional dependency between nuclear disarmament and counterproliferation for any counterproliferation progress dominates all discussion. It is the view put forward by the four wise men when they speak on either topic, though their version is primarily about atmospherics and securing cooperation. They declare, for example, "We believe that without the bold vision of a nuclear weapons-free world as called for in the Non-proliferation Treaty, the actions (counterproliferation and other threat reduction such as weapons and other fissile material security and reduction) will not be perceived as fair or urgent."[60] They also say, "We cannot take these steps without the cooperation of other nations. We cannot get the cooperation

---

59 United Nations, *Final Document, 2010 Review Conference of the Parties to the Treaty on the Nonproliferation of Nuclear Weapons*, NPT/CONF.2010/50 Vol. 1 2010, http://cns.miis.edu/treaty_npt/pdfs/2010_FD_Part_I.pdf

60 Former Senator Sam Nunn, Nuclear Threat Initiative, Speech at American Nuclear Society Annual Meeting (June 15, 2009), http://www.nti.org/c_press/speech_Nunn_American_Nuclear_Society061509.pdf.

of other nations without the vision and hope of a world that will someday end these weapons as a threat to mankind."[61]

The assertion of a necessary nexus between counterproliferation and nuclear disarmament appears pre-eminent in many forms and fora. Throughout the literature of disarmament and non-proliferation the same proposition is restated, and is claimed to represent the consensus view among principal non-nuclear states. The Carnegie Report on "Abolishing Nuclear Weapons" declares, "Key non-nuclear weapons states say that motivation is undermined by the failure of the nuclear-armed few to work in good faith towards fulfilling the disarmament bargain. Seriously pursuing disarmament is therefore necessary to prevent proliferation and make the probably inevitable expansion of nuclear energy safe."[62] The Carnegie Report also makes clear that lack of progress on nuclear disarmament becomes the basis for real resistance to counterproliferation measures, observing that "... non-nuclear weapons states oppose any tightening that would affect non-nuclear weapons states without corresponding concessions by the nuclear weapons states in the area of disarmament ...."[63] Some commentators declare a direct dependency between non-proliferation and nuclear disarmament in even more categorical terms, concluding "it will be impossible to curtail nuclear weapons proliferation without serious progress toward nuclear disarmament."[64]

That reliance on nuclear weapons by the nuclear weapons states is used to justify resistance to counterproliferation is undeniably true. That it is the real reason, all evidence indicates, is not true. There is no evidence, other than rhetorical, of a functional nexus between disarmament and counterproliferation. Reducing nuclear risk just does not work this way. Counterproliferation is a much more differentiated, diverse, and nuanced matter.

This is evident, for example, in the irony that one state's nuclear arsenal may actually secure non-proliferation of other states. Thus it has long been a primary element of United States strategic policy to extend a nuclear umbrella over allies, both in Europe and East Asia, not only for deterrence, but for its value in preventing those allies from developing their own nuclear arsenals. The nuclear umbrella extended to allies is also intended to serve counterproliferation by preventing the increase in risks of security of weapons and fissile material, accident, miscalculation, or dangerous turn of leadership; risks that acquisition of nuclear weapons always brings with it. Many governments have been able to foreswear nuclear weapons just because they are under

---

61 Former Senator Sam Nunn, Nuclear Threat Initiative, "The Race Between Cooperation and Catastrophe" (June 12, 2008), http://www.nti.org/c_press/speech_Nunn_Germany61208.pdf; *See also*, Sidney Drell & James Goodby, *The Reality: A Goal of a World Without Nuclear Weapons Is Essential*, THE WASHINGTON QUARTERLY, Summer 2008 at 30, http://www.twq.com/08summer/docs/08summer_drell-goodby.pdf; George Perkovich et al., *Universal Compliance: A Strategy for Nuclear Security*, CARNEGIE ENDOWMENT FOR INTERNATIONAL PEACE June 2007 at 150, http://carnegieendowment.org/files/univ_comp_rpt07_final1.pdf

62 Perkovich & Acton, ABOLISHING NUCLEAR WEAPONS, supra note 36, at 130-31.

63 Perkovich, et al. *supra* note *id*, at 214.

64 Perkovich & Acton, *supra* note 36, at 13.

the nuclear umbrella of the United States. South Korea, Japan, Taiwan, and various European states with capability to produce nuclear weapons have not acquired nuclear weapons at least in part because of the U.S. nuclear umbrella. This has become increasingly so for East Asia in relation to North Korea's development of nuclear weapons, and the North Korean regime's expressed willingness to proliferate. For Europe, though now well beyond the dynamics of the Cold War and MAD, this rationale also remains relevant, particularly in the current face-off with Iran's nuclear threat.[65] Relatedly, the United States nuclear arsenal as nuclear guarantee may also leverage states such as Iran and North Korea to avoid a regional nuclear arms race.

Some states enjoying a nuclear umbrella today are capable of rapid development of nuclear weapons. It is likely some would develop their own nuclear weapons if the nuclear umbrella were removed. This appears true even of Japan, despite the traumatic legacy of the Hiroshima and Nagasaki detonations, and the recent trauma of Fukushima. Japan is probably the state most easily identified as a "virtual nuclear weapons state," known to be fully nuclear capable, having the material and technology to develop its own nuclear weapons within a matter of months. Prominent Japanese politicians have indeed floated the proposition that Japan would proceed with development of its own nuclear weapons if it should determine it to be necessary to counter the nuclear risk presented by North Korea.[66]

In the Nuclear Posture Review Report released in April 2010, then U.S. Secretary of Defense Robert Gates made clear the nuclear umbrella strategy remains critical in United States strategic planning. He reiterated in diplomatic, but nevertheless certain terms, that the United States requires a reliable nuclear inventory because "more than two dozen allies and partners rely on our nuclear umbrella."[67] In other words, one state's nuclear arsenal, in the official view, does serve non-proliferation by others. What this also illustrates is that the core *quid pro quo* of the NPT does not accurately describe the relationship between nuclear weapons programs and non-proliferation as it actually occurs in the practice of states; that, indeed, in some respects, the relationship is the opposite of what the NPT Grand Bargain anticipates, and is counterintuitive, with one state's arsenal actually deterring the creation of nuclear weapons arsenals by others.

---

65 Judy Dempsey, *US says antimissile shield in Europe will be ready by* 2011, N.Y. TIMES, Mar. 15, 2007, http://www.nytimes.com/2007/03/15/world/europe/15iht-shield.4919630.html. *See also* Mail Foreign Service, *U.S. vows to "100 per cent" cover Europe with an anti-ballistic missile shield by 2018*, THE DAILY MAIL ONLINE, Apr. 16, 2010, http://www.dailymail.co.uk/news/article-1266492/U-S-vows-100-cent-cover-Europe-anti-ballistic-missile-shield-2018.html.

66 Kyodo News, *Nakagawa floats sobering option: going nuclear*, JAPAN TIMES, Apr. 20, 2009, http://www.japantimes.co.jp/text/nn20090420a3.html; *See also* David McNiell, *Japan: The Land of the Rising Nationalism*, THE INDEPENDENT, Nov. 5, 2010; *See also* David McNiell, *Japan Must Develop Nuclear Weapons, Warns Tokyo Governor*, THE INDEPENDENT, Mar. 8, 2011, http://www.independent.co.uk/news/world/asia/japan-must-develop-nuclear-weapons-warns-tokyo-governor-2235186.html.

67 Secretary Robert Gates, Department of Defense, Briefing on the Announcement of the New START Treaty (Mar. 26, 2010), http://www.state.gov/secretary/rm/2010/03/139147.htm.

More generally, even putting aside the contradictory premise at the heart of the NPT, there appears to be no significant relationship in the actual practice of states between counterproliferation and nuclear disarmament. The historical record, without exception, bears this out. The reductions and eliminations of nuclear weapons programs that have occurred, have not reduced resistance to counterproliferation measures, nor prevented proliferation. In fact, the greatest proliferation occurred when the states holding 90 percent of the world's nuclear weapons, the Soviet Union and the United States, were cutting their nuclear armaments from the 1970s through the 1990s. Proliferation and expansion of the nuclear arsenals of former non-nuclear weapons states during the same period included Israel, India, Pakistan, Iran, Iraq, Libya, and North Korea. More recently, United States and Russian reductions achieved through the SALT and START negotiations have not resonated with non-nuclear state governments, who understand that the nuclear weapons reductions by the U.S. and Russia are designed for their own immediate security objectives, which do not include getting to zero. Reduction to 1550 warheads in Start II is also seen as permission for 1550, leaving Russia and the United States still with the capability for mutual destruction, or the destruction of any state, many times over.

Nevertheless, the NPT continues to be relied upon as the foundation for claims of legitimacy in relation to nuclear weapons. In announcing the signing of the START II Treaty for nuclear weapons reductions on April 8, 2010, President Obama declared, "We are keeping our commitments under the NPT."[68] But given the lack of any response to other nuclear arms reductions, there is no reason to suppose that this claim of NPT compliance will have any traction whatsoever with the non-nuclear weapons states for furthering counterproliferation. If past experience is at all indicative, any arms reductions that are accomplished by the major powers short of total nuclear disarmament, will not end the disarmament complaint of the NNWS.

There is also no discernible relationship between counterproliferation and the national motivations of lesser powers that have abandoned nuclear armament. The motivations for nuclear disarmament have been various, but wholly devoid of any motivation to secure other states non-proliferation. All the situations of major reductions or elimination of nuclear weapons, if examined, confirm this. The demise of the Soviet Union naturally brought with it a fundamentally altered strategic relationship between the United States and the states of the former Soviet Union. That made possible new historic agreements to reduce weapons, and terminate the nuclear weapons status of the Ukraine, Belarus, and Kazakhstan. It also made possible cooperation for the highly successful Nunn-Lugar Cooperative Threat Reduction Program securing nuclear weapons and fissile material scattered throughout the former Soviet Union. The former Soviet republics reasonably concluded they were better off without nuclear weapons and the associated risks, such as accident and associated health and

---

68 President Barack Obama, Comments made upon the signing of the START II Treaty (Apr. 8, 2010), http://www.whitehouse.gov/blog/2010/04/08/new-start-treaty-and-protocol.

environmental risk, in light of the Chernobyl disaster. This was particularly true for Belarus, the Chernobyl disaster having contaminated 20 percent of Belaran territory. The incentives for the former Soviet republics also importantly included economic benefit. For example, the Ukraine was able to negotiate compensation from both Russia and US. This included Russian multi-billion dollar debt forgiveness for oil and gas and the US commitment of $900 million in American assistance and investment, at a time when the new Ukrainian government needed aid. The mix of incentives culminated in the 1994 Trilateral Agreement of the United States, Russia, and the Ukraine, which provided financial and technical incentives to compensate Ukraine for its highly enriched uranium. Other reasons for the abandonment of nuclear weapons programs, for Argentina, Brazil, Kazakhstan, Libya, and South Africa have included avoidance of the costs involved, economic incentives, security assurances, and political change. South Africa's termination of its nuclear weapons program was surely the result of the revolution in its politics ending apartheid. Libya is a more controversial case, with the George W. Bush Administration claiming Libya gave up its nuclear weapons program as a consequence of the threat implicit in the invasion of Iraq, and the interdiction of Libyan nuclear supplies. Other analyses dispute this, crediting the abandonment of Libya's program to such factors as the negotiations over the Lockerbie bombing and the Libyan regime's recognition that its economic interests would be best served by integration with the global economy. Whatever the truth of Libyan motivation, no historical analysis maintains that Libya's abandonment of its nuclear program, or any other termination or reduction by any other nation, was brought about as payment for counterproliferation. In view of the now fully revealed nature of the Gaddafi regime, such suggestion would be ludicrous.

Conversely, counterproliferation measures that have been accomplished have not depended for their success on corresponding reductions in nuclear weapons arsenals. There is not the least evidence establishing that nuclear arsenal reductions or eliminations have improved the atmospherics for securing counterproliferation cooperation. There is simply no basis for concluding that numerous states agreeing to such important counterproliferation measures as the Additional Protocol enlarging inspection rights of the IAEA, implementation of export-import controls, provision of data for nuclear forensics capability, or arrangements for sharing counterproliferation intelligence, have depended on steps towards nuclear disarmament. There is not the slightest indication that any such progress on counterproliferation has been retarded, enhanced, or affected in any way by developments in nuclear arms reductions.

It is, however, surely the historical experience that when states resist counterproliferation measures, they justify their resistance as based on the NPT nexus between counterproliferation and disarmament. Thus a recent survey addressing the question, "Why Do States that Oppose Nuclear Proliferation Resist New Non-proliferation Obligations?" summarized its findings as demonstrating, "(t)here is something approaching consensus among scholars and policy-makers that many states resist proposals to strengthen the non-proliferation end of the NPT bargain largely because

America and other nuclear-weapon states haven't made satisfactory progress towards nuclear disarmament."[69] The finding is certainly superficial as stated. In light of the actual evidence of state practice, the more accurate interpretation of the consensus would have to be that nuclear disarmament is "*the favorite excuse*" governments employ to resist counterproliferation.[70] For not only is there no evidence whatsoever that disarmament induces acceptance of measures for counterproliferation, but without exception, the evidence is that proliferation motivation has nothing to do with nuclear disarmament progress by the nuclear weapons states. The so-called rogue states, the ones that most matter for counterproliferation, are not influenced by US-Russian reductions that are an echo of the bipolar world gone by. Such reductions have little if any relevance to the interests at stake in nuclear relations with governments such as that of North Korea and Iran. The Iranian, Iraqi, Libyan, and North Korean proliferations are all traceable to factors such as regional strategic policies, leverage to intimidate other regional powers, insurance against foreign conventional superiority, and internal and external political prestige. For much of proliferation, there is also the importance of the considerable profits involved in the nuclear weapons-related trade. Sale of missiles capable of carrying nuclear warheads, for example, has been an important source of income for a financially desperate North Korea. But in none of the specific cases of proliferation, does general or specific failure of the nuclear weapons states to make progress on nuclear disarmament even appear as relevant.

Any reduction of nuclear armament capability no doubt reduces nuclear risk, if only through reduction of the risks of accident, theft, or sabotage. But the proposition that nuclear weapons reduction among the nuclear weapons states is necessary for counterproliferation steps to be implemented by governments, has no grounding beyond overoptimistic speculations about the atmospherics of negotiation. There is a priority global interest in reducing or eliminating nuclear armaments, and a priority global interest in counterproliferation. Both objectives serve nuclear security. But neither history nor logic establishes that success in achievement of one goal depends upon the other. The actual successes of counterproliferation and elimination or reduction of nuclear arsenals, as historical fact, consistently demonstrate the contrary.

Though the historical experience exposes the nexus at the heart of the NPT to be entirely unrealized and unsupportable, that nexus has been important in negatively impacting counterproliferation. Probably the most significant example is the opposition to universalization of the Additional Protocol of the IAEA. The Additional

---

69 Andrew Grotto, *Why Do States that Oppose Nuclear Proliferation Resist New Nonproliferation Obligation?: Three Logics of Nonproliferation Decision-Making*, VOL. 18, NO. 1 CARDOZO J. INT'L & COMP. L. 1, 1–2 (2010) (discussing how the failure of nuclear states to disarm has prompted many non-nuclear states to strengthen the nonproliferation end of the NPT).

70 The point is thus apparent in Graham Allison's observation that "... demonstration of the haves living up to NPT obligations would erase the have-nots' favorite excuse for resisting essential actions." *See* Graham Allison, NUCLEAR DISARMAMENT AND NONPROLIFERATON 14–15, (Trilateral Commission 2011). "But without the NPT obligation to disarm being realized, we accordingly expect the favorite excuse for resisting essential actions to remain."

Protocol was developed in response to the inability of the IAEA to detect Iraq's nuclear weapons programs before it operated for almost seven years. The Additional Protocol is specifically designed to achieve much greater effectiveness in detection, by extending inspection authority beyond declared nuclear facilities to include undeclared facilities. Yet at the NPT review conference in 2010, non-nuclear weapons states within the non-aligned movement opposed universalization of the Additional Protocol as an international norm of counterproliferation. The only justification offered for this position was the claimed linkage to nuclear disarmament. This was despite a draft report that declared the Additional Protocol to "represent the verification standard that best fulfills the objectives of Article III of the Treaty."[71] That so important an advance in counterproliferation capability, though legitimated through its acceptance by numerous states, could be denied universalization on the basis of failure of global nuclear disarmament, demonstrates just how damaging the nexus that is the core of the NPT can be.

Examination of the major arenas of counterproliferation, as we will explore them in this book, makes clear that real resistance to counterproliferation results not from failure of disarmament, but from concerns of sovereign interest distinct to each arena of counterproliferation. For export-import control, there is the concern that the controls are being used to preserve nuclear supplier monopolies, and that they may operate as a barrier to economic development. Constraining counterproliferation intelligence-sharing are concerns of disclosure of sources and methods, and free-riding by states with relatively limited intelligence capabilities. Preventing the adoption of proposals for multi-nationalization of the nuclear fuel cycle are concerns of energy independence and other concerns of national sovereignty. The great potential for enhanced deterrence through the revolutionary new technologies of nuclear forensics is stifled by concerns about disclosure of proprietary and national security related data. But nowhere, in the real world of securing counterproliferation measures, is the impediment related in any respect to failures of nuclear disarmament.[72]

Though the claimed nexus between counterproliferation and nuclear weapons disarmament demonstrates no cause and effect relationship in either direction, it does have a retrograde impact on the status of the NPT as its source and inspiration. Former Secretary of State George Shultz, for example, asserts that the NPT is "unraveling because there hasn't been significant commitment on the part of countries that have nuclear weapons to get rid of them."[73] What is not acknowledged is that any such unraveling is in fact in significant measure a result of the fictitious nexus and dysfunction at the core of the NPT. The critical lesson we can usefully draw from the unraveling of the NPT, is not the "full, effective and urgent implementation" of global nuclear

---

71 William Potter, Patricia Lewis, Gaukhar Mukhatzhanova, & Miles Pomper, *The 2010 NPT review Conference: Deconstructing Consensus*, CNS Special Report June 17, 2010, http://cns.miis.edu/stories/pdfs/100617_npt_2010_summary.pdf.

72 Grotto, *supra* note 69, at 1–2.

73 Remarks by Secretary Shultz quoted in the Christian Science Monitor. *See* Robert Marquand, *Nuclear weapons: Is full Disarmament Possible?*, Christian Science Monitor, Apr. 6, 2010, http://www.csmonitor.com/World/Global-Issues/2010/0406/Nuclear-weapons-Is-full-disarmament possible, at 5.

disarmament called for at the 2010 NPT Review Conference.[74] The critical lesson is that we cannot continue to rely exclusively on a legal formulation that is not working. It is not working, not because of lack of weapons reductions, but because it depends upon and projects a fictitious relationship between nuclear disarmament and counterproliferation as the sole basis for any counterproliferation progress.

We have failed to achieve total nuclear disarmament for about 40 years since that objective was declared and frozen as concurrently conditional with counterproliferation, and there is no such prospect for the foreseeable future. It is therefore counterproductive to continue to rely exclusively on the NPT as the foundation for counterproliferation infrastructure. The immediate need for effective counterproliferation is not well served by a framework that includes, as a principal element, an excuse for proliferation. This is why it is essential to explore a new formulation, and build a new foundation, to move forward to actually reduce nuclear risk.

This does not, and should not, in any respect, diminish the nuclear security advantage to be gained from measures of nuclear disarmament, such as strategic arms reduction treaties and other arms agreements, improvements in security of weapons and fissile materials, and reduction of alert levels and trigger times of nuclear forces among the nuclear weapons states. Moreover none of these nuclear arms control measures require the radical transformation on which disarmament to zero is premised. These are the step-by-step advances that thoughtful nuclear disarmament proponents, including the four wise men, endorse and have worked to promote with some degree of success.[75] These are risk reductions which have proved doable, as exemplified by the nuclear arms agreements and nuclear security arrangements achieved between the United States and the states of the former Soviet Union. These are achievements that demonstrate, unequivocally, that important progress in weapons reduction is possible. Collectively they indicate, however, that with a more propitious foundation for nuclear risk reduction, much more significant progress could be achieved.

C. Legitimacy; The Challenge of Asymmetric Possession of Nuclear Weapons

The rhetorical nexus between nuclear disarmament and non-proliferation has framed the views of scholars and policymakers to a remarkable degree, considering the extensive literature indicating proliferation has no connection, logical or empirical, with disarmament.[76] Those interested in nuclear trade, or the development of clandestine

---

74 United Nations, *supra* note 59, at 19.

75 Shultz et al., *Nuclear Free World*, *supra* note 20. *See also* Nuclear Threat Initiative, *About NTI: Fact Sheet*, (Nov. 9, 2011), http://www.nti.org/b_aboutnti/b4_programs.html.

76 John Warden, *Are Disarmament and Nonproliferation Two Sides of the Same Coin?*, Center for Strategic and International Studies (Nov. 11, 2011), http://csis.org/blog/are-disarmament-and-nonproliferation-two-sides-same-coin. *See also* Jacques E. G. Hymans, The Psychology of Nuclear

nuclear weapons related capacity, may find advantage in perpetuating the presumed connection, as the excuse for their resistance to counterproliferation.[77] But why is the presumed connection taken so seriously, and made central by so many scholars and statesmen of global security policy? Characterizing this phenomenon as "The Emperor's Nuclear Clothes," an editorial in *The Wall Street Journal* recently observed, "Enough is enough. Every day, the events of the real world reveal that the American foreign policy establishment is wearing nothing but the emperor's new clothes—policies that make proper people murmur 'how Nobel worthy' while looking around to see if anyone else notices something odd."[78] What is the explanation for why nuclear weapons abolition, as a precondition for counterproliferation, however odd, so dominates the discussion?[79]

The rhetorical perpetuation of the connection of disarmament and counterproliferation *is* revealing. It tells us something important about what is required to move forward with counterproliferation in a world of nuclear weapons haves and have nots. The explanation is the need to legitimate counterproliferation despite asymmetry in the possession of nuclear weapons. That reason is in the origin of the NPT bargain. In freezing the distinction of nuclear and non-nuclear states as of 1967, the NPT became the embodiment of the political and strategic nuclear weapons asymmetry of its time. But that asymmetry in itself would have denied the NPT legitimacy. The solution was to establish the nexus between a goal of nuclear disarmament and non-proliferation. The promise of negotiation towards nuclear weapons disarmament in Article VI (along with sharing in peaceful use of atomic energy in Articles IV and V) could justify non-proliferation, despite the actual asymmetry of possession of nuclear weapons, because its idealized dialectic promised that all states eventually would become non-nuclear weapons states. The Grand Bargain of the NPT offered at least an ultimately equitable resolution of the matter of legitimacy.[80] Though the reasons states

---

PROLIFERATION (Cambridge University Press 2006). *See also* Robert Rauchhaus, Matthew Kroenig, & Erik Gartzke, CAUSES AND CONSEQUENCES OF NUCLEAR PROLIFERATION, 1st ed., (Routledge Global Security Studies 2011).

77 For a discussion of how this is played on by Iran *see* Nazila Fathi & David E. Sanger, *Iran Won't Give Up Right to Use Atomic Technology, Leader Says*, N.Y. TIMES, June 28, 2006, http://www.nytimes.com/2006/06/28/world/middleeast/28iran.html.

78 Rosen, *supra* note 52.

79 Thus Egypt, which held the NAM chair during the 2010 NPT Review Conference declared in the 2005 Conference, presumably speaking for the non-nuclear weapons states, that progress on disarmament should be "the determining factor with regard to acceptance by the states-parties of any further obligations under the NPT." Ahmed Gathalla, Egyptian Foreign Ministry, Statement Before the General Debate of the 2005 Review Conference of the NPT 1 (May 3, 2005). *See also* position of South Africa, similarly prominent in the two most recent NPT review conferences, highlighting nuclear disarmament as the controlling dynamic for nonproliferation progress under the NPT. *See* Christopher F. Chyba, *Time for a Systematic Analysis: U.S. Nuclear Weapons and Nuclear Proliferation*, Vol. 38 ARMS CONTROL TODAY (Dec. 2008) (discussing how South Africa should be considered a nuclear power because of the 300 kilograms of weapons-grade uranium it possesses), http://www.armscontrol.org/act/2008_12/Chyba.

80 *See* pages 5–7 and notes 13–17, *supra*.

have since reduced or eliminated their nuclear arsenals, or adopted measures of counterproliferation, bear no real relationship to that scheme, adherence to the presumed nexus and the outcome it promised remains an article of faith. That nexus continues because it provides the only claim to fairness and legitimacy for non-proliferation, despite the continuing asymmetry of the nuclear/non-nuclear classification of states. Moreover, there is understandably a sustaining disinclination to any critique that could undermine the NPT, because the NPT is all we have as the foundation for counterproliferation.

So what is done, in attempting to move forward, is to repeat the catechism of a connection between non-proliferation and disarmament, without acknowledging its irrelevance. For counterproliferation, the result is a paradoxical and negative nuclear security dynamic. The commitment to negotiate towards global nuclear disarmament, awaiting a different world and time, becomes increasingly with time, the excuse for undermining the infrastructure of counterproliferation. But how can nuclear risk be diminished, when we have a foundational deal which, over time, increasingly casts doubt on its own legitimacy? There was no intention for it to work that way of course. The authors of the NPT had a different view of the future than the future has become; but it does work that way.

The NPT does not, however, erect an insurmountable legal barrier to moving forward on counterproliferation without disarmament, and moving forward does not require abandonment of the NPT. There is enough play in the disarmament language of Article VI of the NPT to accommodate the new architecture here proposed. Article VI is not quite what it is represented to be by proponents of disarmament and proliferating governments. It does not commit the nuclear weapons states to a substantive requirement of immediate steps to global disarmament. The stated commitment is that "Each of the Parties to the Treaty undertakes to pursue negotiations in good faith on effective measures relating to cessation of the nuclear arms race at an early date and to nuclear disarmament . . . ." The commitment is to negotiate in good faith. This is not just a matter of literal reading. A legal duty to negotiate in good faith is importantly distinct from a substantive commitment, and has been so employed in both United States domestic law, and in public international law.[81]

What the negotiators of the NPT must have intended by stipulating a duty to negotiate in good faith in Article VI, was to walk a fine, but important line. To obtain

81 A prominent example of its use in domestic law is the duty of employers and employees to negotiate in good faith as the central obligation of both under the National Labor Relations Act. *See* 29 U.S.C.A. § 158(d). *See also* Jack Garvey, *Trade Law and Quality of Life—Dispute Resolution Under the NAFTA Side Accords on Labor and the Environment*, VOL. 89, NO. 2 AM. J. INT'L. L. 439 (Apr. 1995) (describing the NAFTA dispute resolution process). The duty to negotiate in good faith has been employed in international law, for example, by way of the "good faith accord" that United Nations Secretary General Dag Hammarskjöld negotiated between Israel as the legal framework for termination of hostilities after the invasion of Egypt by Israel, France and Britain in 1956. *See* Jack Garvey, *United Nations Peacekeeping and Host State Consent*, VOL 64, NO. 2 AMER. JOURNAL OF INT'L LAW 241 (Apr. 1970).

endorsement for the treaty, most importantly the commitment of the non-nuclear weapons states to non-proliferation, they had to address the asymmetry that would remain. The nuclear weapons reality they faced at the time was MAD—possession of nuclear weapons as the irreducible deterrent dynamic of the cold war. The legal invention, to bridge the gap between the nuclear states and non-nuclear states, and provide a promise of eventual equity, was to articulate a commitment to negotiate in good faith towards the stated goal of zero.[82]

Proponents of nuclear disarmament have understandably sought to ignore the distinction between a substantive commitment to nuclear disarmament and the promise to negotiate in good faith. They have been quite successful at it, to the point where the review conferences for the NPT repeatedly proclaim, without any qualification, that the NPT embodies a legal commitment to global nuclear disarmament. The point here, though, is simply that we need to move beyond the NPT and its flawed foundation, and that the legal analysis for doing so, whatever the political rhetoric, includes the proposition that there is no legal barrier to developing a new foundation for counterproliferation.

That there is no near-term prospect of global nuclear disarmament is widely acknowledged even by its most dedicated proponents. Former Senator Sam Nunn's metaphor of the fog-shrouded mountain top was well chosen. The nuclear landscape today indubitably demonstrates that nuclear disarmament, which the NPT under Article VI establishes as the *quid pro quo* for non-proliferation, is nowhere in sight. The Thirteen Steps to nuclear security articulated in the Final Document of the 2000 NPT Review Conference accordingly remain idealized and unrealized. The effort to draft a consensus document at the 2005 review conference ended in utter failure, and the Final Document issued by the 2010 Review Conference acknowledged there was still "the urgent need for the nuclear-weapons states to implement the steps leading to nuclear disarmament agreed to in the Final Document of the 2000 Review Conference."[83]

Even if one or another of the likely flash points of contemporary nuclear risk should disappear; indeed, even if the goal of global nuclear disarmament were achieved, nuclear risk is here to stay. Nuclear weapons risk will always be with us because its material and technology will be with us. Even the most optimistic view of political evolution does not alter this reality. There is no such thing as political stasis. Fissile material and fissile humanity will remain a volatile mix. New bad actors replace the old, although occasionally we may not see any. Colin Powell, when he was Chairman of the Joint Chiefs of Staff, on one occasion discussing global security said, "I'm running out of demons, I'm running out of villains. I'm down to Castro, Kim Song II."[84] But it did not take long to discover new demons, with potentially suicidal and catastrophic policies, to bedevil non-proliferation—President Mahmoud Ahmadinejad of Iran, leaders of Burma, that son of a demon, Kim Jong-il, himself fathered by the demon

---

82 *See* pages 5–8 and 13–17, *supra*.

83 United Nations, *supra* note 59.

84 Jim Wolffe, *Powell: "I'm Running Out of Demons,"* ARMY TIMES 4 Apr. 15, 1991.

Kim II-Sung, now followed by Kim Jong-Un—probably to be followed by some other yet-to-be born dangerous child. We can be sure we will not run out of nuclear villains. We need a new way forward, because though a world without nuclear weapons may be the ideal and the goal, nuclear risk will remain.

Indeed, nuclear risk is spreading well beyond what can be attributed to malign governments. The Chernobyl, Three-Mile Island, and the Fukushima disasters generated hesitation, and even apparent termination of peaceful use programs, such as that of the government of Germany. However, initiatives for nuclear development continue to appear. Concerning official reports that the Obama Administration and Saudis were planning for nuclear cooperation to box in Iran, the chairwoman of the US House of Representatives Foreign Affairs Committee declared, "I am astonished that the Administration is even considering a nuclear agreement with Saudi Arabia. Saudi Arabia is an unstable country in an unstable region, with senior officials openly proclaiming that the country may pursue a nuclear-weapons capability."[85] She should not be astonished. Saudi Arabia has been reported to be pursuing nuclear–cooperation agreements also with South Korea, Japan, France, and Russia.[86] And Saudi Arabia is only one current example of how open for business—big business—is the dual-use nuclear market. A US deal with Saudi Arabia would be intended to replicate the deal signed with the United Arab Emirates in 2010, not only to pressure Iran, but as means to address proliferation by gaining some control on the flow of nuclear material and technology, particularly by way of a commitment by Saudi Arabia not to produce its own nuclear fuel.[87] And there is no sufficient international control presently in place to prevent any of the contemplated deals, certainly not the NPT, with its Article IV guarantee of nuclear development for peaceful use. Moreover, with suppliers from numerous states competing for great profits, there is less and less leverage for US-imposed restrictions.

Meeting all these challenges of the apparent future of proliferation requires a new architecture for counterproliferation. The failures of counterproliferation are not all attributable to the flaws of the NPT. But clearly the NPT has proved inadequate to the challenge, with even its most vociferous supporters calling for improvement and amendment.[88] And as the work of counterproliferation struggles to go on without realization of the promise of nuclear weapons abolition, it engenders, over time, increasing cynicism, and the sense of unraveling of the NPT. The NPT is simply not a prescription for progress, and its delegitimization is likely to continue. What is needed, therefore, is a means for progress on counterproliferation that is viable, notwithstanding the continuing asymmetry of the possession of nuclear weapons by states and the failures of progress towards global nuclear disarmament.

---

85 Jay Solomon, *U.S. Saudis To Discuss Nuclear Agreement*, Wall St. J. A7 (July 30, 2011).

86 *Id.*

87 *Id.*

88 *See* Jozef Goldblat, *Amending the nonproliferation regime*, United Nations Institute for Disarmament Research (2009), http://www.unidir.org/pdf/articles/pdf-art2862.pdf.

2

FUTILITY OF NUCLEAR WEAPONS RISK MANAGEMENT IN A CONSENSUAL REGIME

THE UNITED NATIONS (UN) Security Council has imposed sanctions in the few limited cases of most egregious and dangerous proliferation, namely North Korea and Iran and Saddam's Iraq. However, the mandatory proscriptions that have resulted from Security Council action under Chapter VII of the United Nations Charter (Charter) do not address counterproliferation directly or exclusively. Moreover, sovereign consent is the dominant principle of counterproliferation, as it now exists. The present capabilities and limitations of counterproliferation are best described by the voluntary adherence of governments to the different agreements and structures that are its components. These include, most prominently, the safeguards and inspection regime of the International Atomic Energy Agency (IAEA) and a collection of international agreements, both formal and informal.

Building a better counterproliferation regime requires understanding, first, why this consent-based architecture is not working well enough for the management and containment of contemporary nuclear weapons risk. If the system is unraveling and "in tatters," as those most knowledgeable claim, why? We need to understand the nature of the vulnerability of what we now have, before reaching for a better design. This in turn requires identifying the distinctive nature of contemporary nuclear weapons risk, and the challenges it presents.

A. Nuclear Terrorism

In the view of recent presidents of the United States, statesmen throughout the world, and principal commentators, nuclear terrorism is at the top of the list of what we should worry about.[89] Nuclear terrorism is so distinctively new a threat, and so threatening, as to confound former approaches to nuclear risk containment, which

89 Obama, Remarks in Prague, *supra* note 7.

depend wholly on influencing states, not controlling non-state actors. The collapse of the Nuclear Non-proliferation Treaty (NPT) regime is most apparent in that it was not designed to address what is today probably this most serious counterproliferation concern. In the old world of nuclear weapons risk the NPT was designed to fit, only states possessed nuclear weapons, and it was not within the realm of likelihood that non-state actors could become nuclear weapons capable. Indeed terrorism did not exist as the international phenomenon it is today. International terrorism and its likely linkage to nuclear weapons capability was simply not present at the conception of the NPT in 1967. Nor was much consideration given to the related nuclear weapons risk that dual-use now implicates. Even today, the threat generated by non-state actors is at best addressed only indirectly, to the extent transparency is achieved by accounting, monitoring and inspection of state facilities by the IAEA.

The diverse collection of ad hoc efforts to address the nuclear terrorism threat, such as securing the weapons of the former Union of Soviet Socialist Republics (Soviet Union), export controls, the Proliferation Security Initiative (PSI), and national anti-terrorism legislation, bespeak the necessary invention of a contemporary response to this distinctively contemporary threat. The reality, however, has been little if any strategic coherence. This is so though the scenarios of nuclear terrorism are well identified.[90] This is so though a nuclear detonation in an urban setting as predicted, in any one of these scenarios, given the incomparable magnitude of consequence, may well be the holy grail of terrorist weapons of mass destruction (WMD) ambition.

That the international terrorist threat is connected to nuclear weapons risk is well established. The ambition of al-Qaeda to commit nuclear terrorism, for example, is documented. It has been reported that shortly before the 9/11 attacks, two Pakistani nuclear experts met with Osama bin Laden in Afghanistan to discuss al Qaeda building a nuclear device.[91] There is also evidence that as early as 1993, agents of al Qaeda acted to acquire nuclear materials or warheads from former Soviet republics.[92] In a December

90 The IAEA has described four principal categories wherein the means and the methods for nuclear terrorism are apparent and available: (1) detonation of a stolen or purchased nuclear weapon; (2) detonation of an improvised nuclear explosive device made from stolen or purchased nuclear material; (3) sabotage of, or attacks on, installations, locations, or transport containing nuclear material which could result in severe and widespread dispersal of radiation; and (4) detonation of a radiological dispersal device; in popular jargon, the "dirty bomb" scenario. IAEA Doc GOV/2002/50 (48)/6 Nuclear Security—Measures to Protect Against Nuclear Terrorism 4 (Aug. 11, 2004), http://www.iaea.org/About/Policy/GC48/GC48Documents/English/gc48-6_en.pdf

91 It was discovered that Bin Laden met with scientists from the Pakistani nuclear program, from which the CIA's Weapons Intelligence, Nonproliferation and Arms Control Unit determined that Al-Qaeda "probably had access to nuclear expertise and facilities and that there was a real possibility of the group developing a crude nuclear device." Rudimentary diagrams of the essential components of nuclear weapons were found inside a suspected Al Qaeda safe-house in Kabul. David Albright, *Al-Qaeda's quixotic quest to go nuclear*, Asia Times, Nov. 22, 2002, http://www.atimes.com/atimes/Middle_East/DK22Ak01.html; National Commission on Terrorist Attacks upon the United States, *The 9/11 Commission Report* (2004), http://www.911commission.gov/report/911Report.pdf. *See also* Joyner & Parkhouse, *supra* note 57, at 207, 210–11.

92 Bill Gertz, *Russian Renegades Pose Nuke Danger*, Wash. Times, A1 (Oct. 22, 1996).

1998 interview, Bin Laden called the acquisition of weapons of mass destruction a "religious duty," and declared al Qaeda's objective "to kill four million Americans."[93]

9/11 demonstrated al Qaeda's capacity to plan and carry out a terrorist attack that was probably more complicated than seizing, transporting, and detonating an unsecured nuclear weapon. Any other terrorist organization might also achieve that capability. There are in fact reports of other terrorists groups seeking fissile material and nuclear weapons. These include repeated efforts by Chechen separatists.[94] And the terrorist fixation on nuclear is not limited to extremist Islamic groups. Seized documents of the terrorist organization responsible for the sarin nerve gas attack in the Tokyo subway, Aum Shinrikyo, indicates it sought development of nuclear weapons.[95] In 2008, the Colombian government reported that Fuerzas Armadas Revolucionarias de Colombia (FARC) rebels had been attempting to obtain highly enriched uranium.[96]

These are only some of the known situations of terrorist groups attempting to obtain nuclear weapons, but reveal such motivation to be widespread, and we can presume similar activity is yet unknown. 9/11 was evidence enough of the attraction to terrorist groups, to the point of suicide, of the opportunity to reduce the towers of 21st century civilization to rubble. The likely operational calculus for a terrorist organization is that the greater the terror and destruction, the greater the risks they will undertake; and accordingly, the less the deterrent effect of possible failure, exposure, and punishment. Nuclear, by this calculus, is their most appealing option. Experts differ markedly as to the likelihood of a terrorist nuclear attack, and such projections are naturally highly speculative. However, the most informed projections are more than enough cause for apprehension. A 2005 U.S. Senate survey of experts is illustrative, resulting in a projection of the average likelihood of a terrorist nuclear event at about 30 percent by 2015.[97]

Nuclear terrorism threat reduction is beyond the capacity of any state or even collective regional action. To address this threat, it is necessary to secure fissile material worldwide, combat nuclear trafficking worldwide, and constrain the spread and availability of nuclear material and technology worldwide. Each of these arenas of concern present distinct requirements for implementation. Nuclear security requires securing

---

93 Rahimullah Yusufzai, *World's Most Wanted Terrorist: An Interview with Osama Bin Laden*, ABC News Online, Jan. 2, 1999, http://cryptome.org/jya/bin-laden-abc.htm. *See also* Joyner & Parkhouse, *supra* note 57, at 207, 210–11 (describing Al Qaeda's efforts to obtain a nuclear device). *See also* George Tenet, Central Intelligence Agency, Written Statement for the Record of the Director of Central Intelligence before the Joint Inquiry Committee (Oct. 17, 2002), https://www.cia.gov/news-information/speeches-testimony/2002/dci_testimony_10172002.html.

94 *See*, e.g., Allison, *supra* note 9, at 31–34.

95 *Id.*, at 40–42.

96 Tom Gjelten, *Colombia Reflects Rising Threat of Nuclear Terrorism*, NPR, Apr. 21, 2008, http://www.npr.org/templates/story/story.php?storyId=89803657.

97 In a U.S. Senate 2005 survey of experts on terrorist threats, opinions differed markedly as to the risk of a terrorist nuclear attack, but on average the experts surveyed indicated the risk at about 30 percent by 2015. Richard J. Lugar, *The Lugar Survey on Proliferation Threats and Responses*, Senate Foreign Relations Committee, June 2005 at 13–14, http://lugar.senate.gov/nunnlugar/pdf/NPSurvey.pdf.

all nuclear weapons, including the thousands of nuclear weapons in existing stocks that may be present in politically unstable circumstances such as the breakup of the Soviet Union,[98] or prospectively in Pakistan.[99] It requires securing the material that could be used to make a nuclear weapon in the form of a dirty bomb; any device that employs a conventional explosion to spread nuclear contamination. The scenarios of terrorist plans to obtain any such material that must be anticipated include seizure from nuclear weapons or fissile material inventory (the IAEA has documented many such thefts[100]), attack on a nuclear facility or the transport of nuclear material, or purchase on the blackmarket from already stolen or illicitly marketed materials. The history of proliferation indicates such black marketing of nuclear material is of perhaps greatest concern, given the fact that the "nuclear Wal-Mart" of Dr. A.Q. Khan of Pakistan went on for many years without detection, involving numerous governments and considerable cross-border trafficking. Operating in some 20 countries for decades, its discovery dramatically exposed the inadequacy of contemporary nonproliferation infrastructure, and there is considerable evidence of other black marketing in nuclear materials and technologies.[101] Moreover, the increase in dual-use technology and capabilities being transferred through regular commercial channels considerably compounds the challenge.

Although the infrastructure and associated costs for building nuclear weapons may be beyond the capacity of most terrorist organizations, some analyses conclude a terrorist organization, despite the difficulty, could build a crude nuclear weapon; if it can obtain the fissile material. And a dirty bomb, using conventional explosive such as dynamite or C-4 to disperse radioactive material, presents virtually no barrier other than obtaining the nuclear material. It could be made using about a dozen radioisotopes that are widely available as radioactive sources for medicine, industry, and agriculture.

---

98 This particular risk of "loose nukes" was addressed to a significant extent by the Lugar-Nunn program, though with many of these weapons and with weapons grade material having gone unaccounted. David E. Hoffman, *Victories Come Slowly in Cleanup of Soviet Bloc Nuclear Materials*, THE WASHINGTON POST, Aug. 30, 2007.

99 As to Pakistan, there is already planning within the U.S. government for the scenario of terrorists stealing the material that could be used to construct a nuclear weapon, or obtaining it through conspiracy with individuals with authority in the government. *See* Greg Miller, *Emergency Rule in Pakistan; Pakistan's Nuclear Arsenal a U.S. Worry*, THE L.A. TIMES, Nov. 8, 2007, at A10. *See also* Allison, *supra* note 9, at 20–24.

100 As of December 31, 2011, the IAEA had confirmed 2,164 incidents of illicit trafficking of nuclear material, 500 of which showed evidence of theft or loss. IAEA ILLICIT TRAFFICKING DATABASE 2 (2011), http://www-ns.iaea.org/downloads/security/itdb-fact-sheet.pdf. Between July 2009 and June 2010 another 222 incidents were reported, 61 of which were classified as thefts or losses. *Illicit Trafficking Database*, IAEA (Apr. 5, 2011), http://www-ns.iaea.org/security/itdb.asp.

101 According to the IAEA's Illicit Trafficking Database (ITDB), a majority of the reported incidents between 1993 and 2004 involved some form of criminal activity "such as theft, illegal possession, illegal transfer or transaction." The IAEA concluded that the data indicated a demand for nuclear and radioactive materials on a black market and that the primary motive for the incidents was profit seeking. IAEA, *Illicit Trafficking Database* (Nov. 12, 2011), http://www.iaea.org/newscenter/features/radsources/pdf/itdb_31122004.pdf.

Though the detonation of such a device would not be of the incomparable magnitude of a nuclear detonation, it could cause massive casualties and civil disruption.

Nuclear terrorism is especially problematical for managing nuclear weapons risk because of the deterrence and prevention conundrums it presents. Because the protagonists of nuclear terrorism would be non-state actors motivated primarily by ideology, the avenues for addressing nuclear risk that exist in other contexts are largely, if not entirely, foreclosed. Negotiation is not an option. The extreme nature of a terrorist agenda characteristically leaves nothing to discuss. Fear of punishment is overcome by promises of carnal bliss and martyrdom. The terrorist also enjoys the advantage perhaps most disabling of traditional deterrence—the ability to attack and fade back into the general population of any state, even one entirely unrelated to the attack. Deterrence is most frustrated, by what has become a cliché of national security jargon, the "lack of a return address." All previous deterrence theory has been premised on ability to identify the state perpetrator of attack, and deter attack with the threat of retaliation. 9/11 brought home a befuddlement of deterrence and retaliation in relation to non-state actors. The confusion became manifest as two wars in two countries, Iraq and Afghanistan, attacks in others for now more than ten years, costs of hundreds of billions of dollars, gross failures of cultural understanding, alienation of occupied populations, altogether generating more terrorism and more terrorists.

A terrorist organization may have connections to an established government, but we learned how speculative, problematic, and lacking in credibility claims for such connections may be. The invasion of Iraq, on the basis of never substantiated claims of connections to international terrorism and WMD is, of course, the principal case in point. Such failures to find any real connections defy the resources of even the best endowed national intelligence agencies, particularly when suffering from political manipulation, as for that misbegotten conflict. The requirement of governmental consent as the precondition for effective monitoring, which is a premise of counterproliferation as it currently operates, dramatically increases the challenges. It is especially difficult to monitor small clandestine nuclear weapons programs, which can be hidden in dual-purpose facilities using dual-purpose equipment. Nuclear weapons development today does not require extremely large infrastructure, and therefore is easier to conceal from visual detection, particularly imagery satellites. Indeed, verifiability is so dependent on physical and documentary access, that without commensurate consent, there cannot be adequate verifiability. Moreover, no government that collaborates with a terrorist organization is going to enter any agreement for monitoring or inspection of its nuclear facilities, or any other arrangement, that could compromise or disclose such connection.

Current counterproliferation capacity, as consensual, is almost wholly dependent on what governments will volunteer, and depends on cooperation of national intelligence agencies on an ad hoc case-by-case basis. There has been some degree of informal and formalized cooperation between national intelligence agencies. Some international agencies involved in counterproliferation have a limited intelligence capacity defined by their function, such as the Nuclear Suppliers Group effectuating export-import controls, or the IAEA in its operations.[102] Countering nuclear terrorism, however, is naturally a more broadly international enterprise. Terrorist activity as it relates to securing weapons of mass destruction, operates through cross-border networks at all levels; in obtaining and unleashing its operatives, for its financing and money laundering, and for obtaining and transporting material. It is constantly moving across borders to secure its objectives, and for its own security. Accordingly, the intelligence needed is broadly international. Connecting the dots means connecting dots that appear across many borders, and move across borders. But the international character of intelligence capability is dominated by discretion of national intelligence agencies. Intelligence tends to be fragmentary, coming from different governments in different forms and format. Each national resource is inhibited by its own national and bureaucratic sensibilities and claims of national security. National intelligence agencies, operating independently, give priority to jealously guarding their sources and methods. The result is that the dots are mostly seen only separately, within separate borders.

There is thus great need for monitoring, collating, and corroborating capability that works across borders. In other words, the maximization of intelligence, so critical to addressing nuclear terrorism, requires transcending traditional claims of sovereignty and national security. A consent-based regime is naturally antithetical to this need. By positioning claims of sovereignty and national security as controlling, both for the targeted state, and the targeting community, no matter how unreasonable or excessive such claims may be, the current intelligence regime precludes the maximization of existing intelligence resources to detect and prevent nuclear terrorism. Counterproliferation intelligence is simply out of sync with the subject matter it is supposed to reveal. With intelligence coordination limited to government-to-government agreement in specific cases, there has developed little global coordination, certainly nothing approaching a comprehensive global capability equal to the threat.

In light of the frustration of deterrence and limits on intelligence inherent in the existing architecture of counterproliferation, attempts to manage the risks of nuclear terrorism have turned mainly to securing the materials that would be the source of nuclear empowerment for a terrorist organization. Given the lack of means to deter potential nuclear terrorists directly, and the ease of transport of a nuclear weapon or fissile material without detection, the primary strategy is to prevent terrorists from obtaining the materials in the first place—at source. There is a consensus, therefore, that securing fissile material wherever and to whatever extent feasible, is probably the best means we have to prevent nuclear terrorism, not only by making the material hard to obtain, but by increasing the risks and costs of trying to obtain it. However, because nuclear materials are today so multifarious and omnipresent, the challenge is overwhelming all present counterproliferation capacity. It is estimated that there are approximately two million kilograms of highly enriched uranium (HEU) in stockpiles

---

102 *See infra,* pages 141–142.

all over the world.[103] It requires just 15–24 kilograms of HEU to produce a nuclear weapon.[104] Securing all this fissile material requires more than merely lockdown. Fissile material exists in a wide variety of forms and facilities, not only in standing nuclear weapons, but in fuel fabrication facilities, and in reprocessing, research and storage facilities. Plutonium and highly enriched uranium (HEU) are used not only in weapons, but in research reactors around the world in about 40 countries, as well as in power reactors and industrial applications that can be converted to weapons usable material by standard known chemical processes. Given the variety of nuclear materials and their placement, there is similar variety of vulnerability. The need, accordingly, is for nothing less than a globally comprehensive strategy for containment.

B. State-to-State Nuclear Weapons Risk

The landscape of nuclear risk with which the enterprise of counterproliferation must contend also includes state-to-state risk. Nuclear terrorism has warranted special attention because of the extraordinary challenge it represents for the established architecture of counterproliferation, and traditional deterrence theory. Nuclear weapons security is, however, an enterprise necessarily of much broader dimension.

Inadequate lockdown and accounting for nuclear weapons and fissile materials affects international nuclear security in a variety of ways. When any state goes nuclear, a variety of risks are raised in that development. These risks include accident, miscalculation, false alarms that might precipitate a nuclear launch, failures of command and control of nuclear forces involving rogue officers, or a mentally unhinged officer in the launch chain of command. Regime collapse of a nuclear armed state, such as the Soviet Union, or as now feared for Pakistan, is new. But even the Dr. Strangelove scenario of nuclear weapons confrontation is still with us. Indeed, MAD is alive and well in state-to-state relations. All the same risks that were there in the Cold War are still present, if only reduced to regional scale, such as between India and Pakistan. But state-to-state risk is not absent on a more global scale. It runs in chains of threat and response, beyond Pakistan and India, to India threatened by China's nuclear weapons, threatened by Russia's nuclear weapons threatened by the nuclear weapons of the United States. These more global threats may be at profoundly lower levels than they once were, but the risks of nuclear security and control they include are not. Many of the remaining nuclear weapons of the United States and Russia are apparently still pointed at one another. This may be a strategic anachronism. But the retention of thousands of nuclear weapons generates similar risks as during the cold war, such as false alarms that could trigger catastrophic response.

---

103 Nuclear Age Peace Foundation, *Ten Facts about Nuclear Weapons* (Sept. 2009), http://www.wagingpeace.org/articles/2009/09/facts_myths.pdf.

104 As of 2009, it is estimated there were 28 countries with a least one bomb's worth of HEU and 12 countries with at least 20 bombs' worth. *Id.*

Nuclear security, especially as it now may involve regime collapse of a state with nuclear weapons, demands the highest feasible standard for securing nuclear weapons arsenals and preventing and controlling access to their launch or other misappropriation. The stunning reality remains that, at the low end, nuclear security may be only a locked warehouse or a watchman, as has been repeatedly documented in reference to nuclear inventories in the former Soviet Union. We need to achieve, as has been proposed, a gold standard for the security of nuclear materials.[105] But how to do this, despite unwilling governments, is a conundrum that has stymied counterproliferation progress. Moreover, many of the risks of security and control that come with a state's possession and strategic deployment of nuclear weapons have actually increased in the world of computerized command and control, in which decisions, associated miscalculations, mistakes, and malevolence, are communicated at cyber-speed. Proliferation entails similar nuclear weapons risk as it did yesterday, but in some respects, significant new risks and even greater danger.

With proliferation on the rise, particularly by way of dual-use technologies, risk appears also on the rise in the form of so-called "virtual nuclear states." So far as generally known, there are currently nine countries in possession of nuclear weapons: the United States, Russia, the United Kingdom, France, China, Israel, India, Pakistan, and North Korea. Iran and Syria are at least two more states that recently have presented immediate nuclear proliferation concerns. The only real barrier, the experts tell us, just as for nuclear terrorism, is access to the fissile material, since the technology and engineering to build a bomb are widely available. Any state that has the ability to produce highly enriched uranium or plutonium is a virtual nuclear weapons state, and can become a real nuclear weapons state simply by choice. The prospects for conversion from virtual nuclear weapons state to actual nuclear weapons state are greatest in the regional hot spots, the Middle East and East Asia, mainly in relation to the nuclear weapons threat posed by Iran and North Korea. Japan, as noted, has indicated it may develop nuclear weapons to respond to North Korea.[106] Saudi Arabia has indicated it will not accept a strategic situation in which Iran, its Shiite rival, has nuclear weapons.[107] Other governments in the Middle East have expressed a similar reaction to Iran's nuclear program.[108] However, if any state with a fully developed fuel-cycle

105 Allison, *supra* note 9, at 143.

106 Chester Dawson, *In Japan, Provocative Case for Staying Nuclear*, WALL ST. J., Oct. 28, 2011, at A14.

107 Graham Allison, *Nuclear Disorder: Surveying Atomic Threats*, 89 FOREIGN AFFAIRS 74, 77 (Jan./Feb. 2010). *See also* former U.S. National Security Adviser Brent Scowcroft in testimony before the Senate Foreign Relations Committee, (Mar. 2009) "We're on the cusp of an explosion of proliferation, and Iran is now the poster-child. If Iran is allowed to go forward, in self-defense or for a variety of reasons, we could have half a dozen countries in the region and 20 or 30 more around the world doing the same thing just in case." Reuters, *"Iran Could Trigger Nuclear Arms Race in Middle East,"* HAARETZ, Mar. 6, 2009, http://www.haaretz.com/news/iran-could-trigger-nuclear-arms-race-in-middle-east-1.271591.

108 *See* Hassan Fattah, *Arab Nations Plan to Start Joint Nuclear Energy Program*, N.Y. TIMES, Dec. 11, 2006, at A10; William J. Broad & David E. Sanger, *With Eye on Iran, Rivals Also Want Nuclear Power*, N.Y. TIMES 1 (Apr. 15, 2007).

capability should decide to produce a nuclear weapon, experts agree it could do so in a matter of months. Moreover, informed estimates, as early as 2007, were that about 40 states already possessed enough fissile material to produce a bomb.[109]

The number of states seeking capacity to enrich uranium and separate plutonium amounting to dual-use capacity is rising. Numerous countries without any current dual-use nuclear capability, including several in the Middle East, have indicated an interest in developing nuclear power. Many have indicated their intention to enrich or reprocess nuclear fuel. Such latent nuclear capability may be, for some of these countries, what the Director-General of the IAEA likened to an "insurance policy" or "hedge" strategy, whereby a government finds it advantageous to deny weaponization while achieving the capacity for rapidly developing nuclear weapons. The record of Iranian brinksmanship on its nuclear weapons program gives reason to think Iran may be pursuing just such a strategy, if not, as now seems more likely, outright pursuit of nuclear weapons.

Studies of why states seek nuclear weapons identify various motivations,[110] including what seems a compulsion in the very psyche of sovereignty. Charles de Gaulle's declaration that "a great state" that does not have nuclear weapons when others do, "does not command its own destiny,"[111] is a sentiment that still resonates with political leaders; even the peacefully inclined. Former President Lula of Brazil declared during his first successful election campaign that military strength, including nuclear weapons, is one way a state gains respect.[112] That nuclear weapons remain a currency of foreign relations for many states, notwithstanding the stated goal of nuclear disarmament, reflects also how well possession of nuclear capacity can play in the streets, despite the suicidal implications, as evidenced by pro-nuclear weapons demonstrations not only in Tehran and Pyongyang, but also in Mumbai and Islamabad.

C. Risk Reduction by Consent

An exclusively consent-based nuclear weapons containment regime is wholly beholden to claims of sovereignty, whether from governments or their publics. Consent, as it appears in the current legal structure of counterproliferation, does not simply describe the basis for the general commitments articulated in the NPT. The concession to sovereignty of consent-based obligation runs throughout the current infrastructure of

109 Matthew Bunn, *Securing the Bomb*, NUCLEAR THREAT INITIATIVE (2010), http://www.nti.org/e_research/securingthebomb.pdf.

110 Scott D. Sagan, *Why do States Build Nuclear Weapons?: Three Models in Search of a Bomb*, 21 INT'L SECURITY 54, (1996). *See also* Hymans, *supra* note 76. *See also* Rauchhaus, et al., *supra* note 76.

111 Thomas Graham Jr., COMMON SENSE ON WEAPONS OF MASS DESTRUCTION, at 66 (University of Washington Press 2004).

112 Anthony Faiola, *As His Country Stumbles, the Practical "Lula" Soars; Candidate Taps Into Brazilians' Desire for Respect*, WASH. POST A16 (Sept. 22, 2002).

counterproliferation. Each and every government retains a veto over each and every form of regulation, whether export-import controls, inspection and monitoring, or intelligence or data sharing. The result is that we have no comprehensively international rules on nuclear security.

Under the nonproliferation regime of the NPT, where the need for agreement to security standards is most serious, it is most likely to be blocked by denial and rejection. Governments with enterprises benefiting from sales of nuclear-related materials and technology will avoid any agreement that could impair that financial return, quite besides any strategic motivation. This is true especially of the states of proliferation concern and their customers. Governments with relationships with extremists groups will limit their consent to prevent discovery of any such connections. Governments with clandestine nuclear weapons programs will limit the scope and depth of inspections.

The criterion of consent also prevents discovery of state involvement in the black marketing of nuclear material and technology. The A.Q. Khan network transferred weapons related technology to Iran between 1989 and 1991, to North Korea and Libya between 1991 and 1997, and technology to North Korea until 2000. The limits imposed on IAEA authority to monitor or investigate, resulted in none of this being identified until intelligence disclosures by Western intelligence agencies in 2003. Iran managed to keep the scope of its nuclear program a secret from the IAEA for 20 years, and now openly presses ahead, while denying nuclear weapons development and blocking inspection and verification.

In sum, a consensual regime for policing proliferation is, operationally, a non-sequitor. It is the governments that most require policing that set limits other governments generally accept and abide. For states, as for individuals, self-policing is not generally the best prescription for assuring good behavior, especially when there is enticement such as profits to be had. Yet non-proliferation is fixed in a framework that allows those attracted to proliferate to reject regulation that most states accept.

The requirement of sovereign consent has major negative impact on counterproliferation. Its most extreme manifestation is the NPT allowing a state to acquire nuclear technology and material while a member, then withdraw, using that same technology and material for a weapons program. North Korea acquired plutonium, ostensibly for its civil energy program, and was able to do so, with legal justification, while a member of the NPT. When pressed with charges of weapons development and demands for inspections, North Korea withdrew from the NPT in 2003 by asserting its freedom to withdraw under Article X of the Treaty. It then continued to pursue its nuclear weapons program, openly taking advantage of nuclear development gains it had obtained while under the NPT. There is no basis in the law of counterproliferation for demanding that safeguards continue after such withdrawal, nor is there any clarity as to whether termination constitutes a threat to international peace and security such as to invite action by the UN Security Council under Chapter VII of the UN Charter, that might deter termination. Iran has asserted NPT Article IV peaceful use rights to continue its enrichment program, while rejecting IAEA and even Security Council admonitions of violation. Iraq, under Saddam, employed a similar pattern in attempting to develop its nuclear weapons program.

The requirement of consent operates as an absolute limitation at every level of counterproliferation management. Even though parties to the NPT are obligated to secure their materials once having signed on, the terms of any nation's security, reporting, and inspection arrangements are negotiated as bilateral agreements between the IAEA and each party government. These agreements begin with general models, model safeguards agreements, and model inspection protocols, but will vary depending on the demands of a particular government. These may include outright refusal to sign on to one of the standard agreements. Most significantly, this includes for many states the refusal to adopt the Additional Protocol, designed to expand inspection authority of the IAEA, primarily in relation to undeclared nuclear activity sites.

This inspires the perpetuation and enlargement of nuclear weapons risk. The NPT with its consensual limitation in effect instructs would-be proliferators that if they withdraw from the NPT or impose severe limits on IAEA inspection, then make threats and demonstrate nuclear weapons capability by means such as weapons testing and the firing of missiles capable of carrying nuclear warheads, they may be paid substantial rewards for temporarily backing off. The Grand Bargain has become a formula for nuclear blackmail. North Korea and Iran have demanded economic assistance and the release of sanctions as the condition for returning to the path of non-proliferation and weapons denuclearization, basing such demand on the aid that was promised under Articles III and IV of the NPT. The 2007 agreement with North Korea, providing it with such assistance, as critics even from within the George W. Bush Administration immediately pointed out, sent precisely the wrong message to both North Korea and Iran.[113]

President George W. Bush's proclamation of an "axis of evil" sent an even more compelling message to North Korea and Iran—that actual possession of nuclear weapons was the best defense to avoid the fate of Saddam Hussein. The Iranian and North Korean governments could conclude not only that nuclear blackmail is profitable, but that it can checkmate any outside attempt at regime change. Nuclear blackmail becomes a survival imperative, a lesson that was not lost on Iranian or North Korean leadership.[114]

---

113 John R. Bolton, former U.S. Ambassador to the United Nations, criticized the pact as "too weak... it 'contradicts fundamental premises' of the administration's approach to North Korea during the past six years." Helene Cooper & Jim Yardley, *Pact With North Korea Draws Fire From a Wide Range of Critics in U.S.*, N.Y. TIMES A10 (Feb. 14, 2007).

114 The North Korean regime's understanding was declared by its "Committee for Solidarity with the World Peoples": "The Iraq war taught the lesson that 'nuclear suspicion,' 'suspected development of WMD' and suspected 'sponsorship of terrorism' touted by the U.S. were all aimed to find a pretext for war and one would fall victim to a war when one meekly responds to the IAEA's inspection for disarmament. Neither strong international public opinion nor (other members of the Security Council's) opposition to war nor the UN Charter could prevent the US from launching the Iraqi war. It is a serious lesson the world has drawn from the Iraqi war that a war can be averted and the sovereignty of the country and the security of the nation can be protected only when a country has a physical deterrent force, a strong military deterrent force capable of decisively repelling any attack to be made by any types of sophisticated weapons." *U.S. to Blame for Derailing Process of Denuclearization on Korean Peninsula*, KOREAN CENT NEWS AGENCY, May 13, 2003, http://www.kcna.co.jp/item/2003/200305/news05/13.htm.

The current legal regime for counterproliferation of nuclear weapons is certainly not devoid of accomplishment. Multiple programs involving many dedicated individuals both in and out of government have worked for many years with some success to secure nuclear weapons and related materials in military, energy and research facilities in the former Soviet Union and elsewhere. There have been some extraordinary accomplishments such as the Nunn-Lugar Cooperative Threat Reduction Program to help countries of the former Soviet Union dismantle many nuclear weapons and their means of delivery, and to upgrade nuclear security measures. The NPT and the uneven safeguards adopted under the NPT by the member states have been supplemented by a variety of counterproliferation initiatives, largely at the behest of the United States. Principle among these are the Proliferation Security Initiative,[115] the Global Initiative to Combat Acts of Nuclear Terrorism, the Code of Conduct on the Safety and Security of Radioactive Sources, the Convention for the Suppression of Acts of Nuclear Terrorism, and the Convention on the Physical Protection of Nuclear Material and the Global Threat Reduction Initiative for removing highly enriched uranium from sites around the world and improving security for research reactors and radiological sources.

To the extent governmental cooperation can be achieved, each such initiative promises counterproliferation enhancement and improvement. But all ultimately depend on the discretion of the governments involved. With varying parties and various degrees of commitment, each initiative remains subject to great variation and fragility. There is no leverage for compliance beyond the political embarrassment entailed in failing to achieve jointly declared goals. There is no obligatory implementation of uniform standards of safety, security, or safeguards.

Addressing the failings of the NPT regime by amendment of the NPT might seem to offer the means to secure improvement. But amendment is generally regarded as a non-starter. The former deputy director general of the IAEA, and head of the Department of Safeguards, has written, "In the present geopolitical environment and considering in particular the frustration of most NNWS regarding the lack of progress in nuclear disarmament by the five nuclear weapons states, any attempt to amend the NPT, Comprehensive Safeguards Agreement, or the Model Protocol Additional would be doomed to failure and possibly counter-productive."[116] Moreover, commentators see a general collapse of the consensual architecture, notwithstanding all such efforts to reinforce it through other treaties, agreements, and legal interpretations. The dismal prospect for the NPT regime of counterproliferation has been well summarized:

> In fact, the growing perception that the treaty is in deep trouble has resulted in two opposing responses, neither of which has helped salvage it. One was to propose a series of scaffoldings designed to artificially support it, either by adding

---

115 *See infra*, pp. 193–213.

116 Pierre Goldschmidt, *Priority Steps to Strengthen the Nonproliferation Regime*, Carnegie Endowment Policy Outlook (Feb. 2007), http://carnegieendowment.org/files/goldschmidt_priority_steps_final.pdf.

a series of reinforcing treaties (such as the Comprehensive Test Ban Treaty and the Fissile Material Cutoff Treaty), by reinterpreting some of its provisions.... The opposite direction has been to conclude side deals that bypass the treaty (the U.S.-India nuclear deal, for example) or hold support for the treaty hostage to some other concessions.... the treaty-based regime seems increasingly headed toward unraveling ....[117]

The United States-India deal *is* particularly pertinent. That deal established a new and important stage in the unraveling of the NPT and counterproliferation. India was the first state to openly develop nuclear weapons while refusing to sign on to the NPT. It did so, despite widespread international condemnation, including official condemnation by the United States. Now India reaps reward through a bilateral agreement with the United States, and the NPT is seriously delegitimized by India's deal with its former critic. Many informed commentators view the deal as fatal for the NPT, despite explicit affirmation of the deal by the Nuclear Suppliers Group and the IAEA, at the prompting of the United States. The precedent is now established for a nonsignatory to the NPT to develop nuclear weapons in defiance of the NPT, then make a bilateral deal for dual-use nuclear material and technology with a state within the NPT nuclear weapons club; in effect joining that club, with all attendant privilege. The fact that the IAEA and Nuclear Suppliers Group supported the U.S.-India deal, on the grounds that it is a means to bring India into the club of "responsible" nuclear powers, simply confirms the incompatibility of the NPT with the contemporary politics of nuclear risk.

There is no likelihood the Grand Bargain of the NPT will be redeemed, and dual-use masquerading as peaceful use continues to be a matter of increasing concern. The nuclear weapons states show no greater real commitment to nuclear disarmament than they ever did. Indeed, there has been major movement in the contrary direction as evidenced by the United States nuclear posture review and National Security Strategy of the United States calling for modernized nuclear policy,[118] including the testing of "mini-nukes,"[119] the Reliable Replacement Warheads program,[120] and experiments for development of space-based weapons.[121] Moreover, the NPT enshrinement of a sovereign right for development of peaceful use, in light of dual-use, renders the Grand Bargain not simply more and more irrelevant to nuclear risk, but ever more dangerous. The distinction between nuclear technology for weapons purposes and

117 Ariel E. Levite, *Rethinking Nuclear Abolition*, NUCLEAR DISARMAMENT AND NONPROLIFERATION, A REPORT TO THE TRILATERAL COMMISSION at 80 (2010).

118 *See* Ralph Vartabedian, *U.S. to Develop New Hydrogen Bomb; Lawrence Livermore May Take the Lead in an Effort by Three National Labs. Aging Warheads Would be Replaced*, L.A. TIMES A21 (Mar. 2, 2007).

119 *See* William J. Broad, *Ideas & Trends: Chain Reaction; Facing A Second Nuclear Age*, N.Y. TIMES § 4, at 1 (Aug. 3, 2003).

120 *Id.*

121 *See* William J. Broad, *Administration Conducting Research Into Laser Weapon*, N. Y. TIMES, A22 (May 3, 2006); *See also*, William J. Broad, *Look Up! It's No Meteor, It's an Arms Race*, N.Y. TIMES § 4, at 3 (Jan. 21, 2007).

peaceful uses has always been problematic. But the distinction has become increasingly blurred as nuclear weapons technology evolves, increasing the risk of crossover from peaceful use to weapons use. As nuclear technology has become cheaper and more accessible, it becomes more troubling that the NPT promises non-nuclear weapons states acquisition of nuclear related materials and technology that can bring them well along the path to nuclear weapons production. The NPT has facilitated, not prevented, an increase in this risk through the commitment to spread peaceful use. Thus Iraq maintained its status under the NPT while importing weapons grade nuclear fuel and related equipment ostensibly for peaceful use, which in fact was used by the regime of Saddam Hussein for a nuclear weapons program.

There is no assurance that any regime that acquires nuclear technology for peaceful purposes will not cheat or be replaced by a hostile regime committed to weapons production. But intrusive IAEA inspections, which are necessary to ferret out important nondisclosure and clandestine activity, are inevitably constrained by the consensual nature of the NPT counterproliferation regime. Until the adoption of the Additional Protocol to the NPT in 1997, the IAEA did not even have the authority to inspect undeclared facilities. It should not be surprising, therefore, that the IAEA failed, for so many years, to detect noncompliance in Iraq, Iran, and Libya. And although the Additional Protocol now expands the authority of the IAEA to inspect undeclared facilities, many states still have not ratified the Additional Protocol.[122]

The NPT regime, as essentially a consensual regime, is also necessarily dependent for effectiveness on the degree to which state parties will give the IAEA an accurate and complete inventory of all their nuclear material and activities. The governments without nuclear weapons ambitions provide information as requested. The governments interested in developing nuclear weapons do not. If a government with a clandestine program deems it advantageous, that government, like North Korea, can assert its own determination under Article X of the NPT that "extraordinary events... have jeopardized the supreme interests of its country," and thereby legally withdraw from the NPT according to its terms.[123]

In sum, the NPT is not preventing radical increase in nuclear weapons risk. That is the true story of the contemporary enterprise of nuclear weapons counterproliferation. Surely, therefore, it is time to move on and to seek a different foundation for the future management of nuclear weapons risk. The purely consensual model has been well tested. Too often and too importantly, it fails the test of counterproliferation effectiveness.

---

122 136 signatories of the NPT have also signed the Additional Protocols, but only 112 of these states have put the Additional Protocol into force. IAEA, *Conclusion of Additional Protocols: Status as of Oct 31, 2011* (Oct. 31, 2011), http://www.iaea.org/OurWork/SV/Safeguards/documents/AP_status_list.pdf.

123 Article X provides, "Each Party shall in exercising its national sovereignty have the right to withdraw from the Treaty if it decides that extraordinary events, related to the subject matter of this Treaty, have jeopardized the supreme interests of its country." Treaty on the Non-Proliferation of Nuclear Weapons, *supra* note 11, art. X, 1.

3

SECURITY COUNCIL MANDATE OF UNIVERSAL STANDARDS

A. Global Legislation by the United Nations Security Council

i. THE SECURITY COUNCIL AS LEGISLATOR

The United Nations (UN) Security Council broke new ground with the passage of Resolution 1373 on the subject of international terrorism, and then most importantly for counterproliferation, Resolution 1540, on the subject of weapons of mass destruction (WMD). These resolutions are now seen as marking a profound shift of the Security Council as global legislator. What is new is the mandate of obligation for all states to counter both terrorism and proliferation of WMD, as global threat to international peace and security, under the authority of Chapter VII, unconfined to any specific event or state(s).[124]

Though inspired by the specific event of 9/11, Security Council Resolution 1373 articulated a list of general categories of measures for all states to undertake to combat terrorism, focusing terrorism as a global phenomenon. Resolution 1540 on WMD, prompted especially by the discovery of the proliferation network orchestrated by Dr. A.Q. Khan of Pakistan, was designed to address proliferation involving non-state actors. Prior to Resolution 1540, a number of Security Council resolutions had designated WMD as constituting a "threat to peace and security," the triggering language of Chapter VII of the United Nations Charter (Charter).[125] Resolution 1540 moved forward to provide a similarly legislative mandate for WMD as Resolution 1373 did for terrorism, imposing general obligations on all states for the purpose of preventing non-state actors from obtaining WMD and their means of delivery, but not directed to

124 UNSC Res. 1373 (28 September 20010 UN Doc. S/RES/1373; UNSC Res. 1540 (April 28, 2004) UN Doc. S/RES/1540. *See* as noting this significance, Stefan Talmon, *The Security Council as World Legislature*, 99 AM. J. INT'L L. 175, 176–77 (2005); Eric Rosand, *The Security Council as "Global Legislator": Ultra Vires or Ultra Innovative?* 28 FORDHAM INT'L L.J. 547, 542 (2004).

125 In 1991, SC Resolution 687 defined weapons of mass destruction as constituting a threat to international peace and security, as did 1172 in 1998.

any specific event or states. Before Resolutions1373 and 1540, the Security Council had never acted so comprehensively under its Chapter VII authority as to a given subject, be it terrorism, weapons of mass destruction, or any other matter, to impose mandatory obligations without any temporal or situational limitation.

Resolution 1373 was passed unanimously only 17 days after 9/11. No doubt its quick passage was propelled by the global shock of that day's events. It was passed, however, without any vocal acknowledgement that it marked a transition of broader significance for the role of the Security Council. By the time Resolution 1540 came around, though it was also adopted unanimously, the significant enlargement of the role of the Security Council was questioned, with some governments objecting that the Charter did not grant the Security Council legislative authority.[126] That Resolution 1540 represented new "global legislation" by the Security Council, and was seen as the precursor of more to come, was expressly stated during its formulation.[127] Soon thereafter, Resolution 1566, coming in response to a terrorist attack in Beslan, Russia, by Chechen separatists, evidenced the more to come.[128]

Notwithstanding the stated reservations, there is attraction in the Security Council wielding a so-called legislative power. Its exercise is expeditious, in contrast to the laborious, sometimes to the point of impossible, process of obtaining the agreement of large numbers of states to a treaty or convention on the same or similar subjects. It is universal; binding all. It enables focus, without the dispersion and descent to the least common denominator, that consensual process so often demands for achieving agreement.

However, any further Security Council legislative action on counterproliferation would engage a larger debate. Notwithstanding such action as has occurred, there is legal controversy over whether the Security Council has any legal authority to legislate.[129] That legal debate has roiled through a variety of contexts as the Security Council designation of "a threat to the peace" under Chapter VII has enlarged from the early view as applying

---

126 *See* U.N. SCOR, 59th Sess., 4950 mtg. at 23, U.N. Doc. S/PV.4950 (Apr. 22, 2004) (India); *Id.* at 30 (Cuba); *Id.* (resumption 1) at 4–5 (Mexico); *Id.* (Resumption 1) at 13–14 (Nepal); and *Id.* (Resumption1) at 16–17 (Namibia), at 31 (Indonesia), at 32 (Iran), at 5 (Algeria); UNDoc. Discussing the critique of SC "legislative resolutions" and summarizing the misgivings of member states, *see* Ian Johnstone, *Legislation and Adjudication in the UN Security Council: Bringing Down the Deliberative Deficit*, 102 Am. J. Int'l. L. 275 (2008).

127 The President of the Security Council, in referring to the planned adoption of Resolution 1540, characterized it as "the first major step towards having the Security Council legislate for the rest of the United Nations' membership" and that the "Council would be needed more and more to do that kind of legislative work." Press Conference by Security Council President (Apr. 2, 2004), http://www.un.org/News/briefings/docs/2004/pleugerpc.DOC.htm.

128 S.C. Res. 1566, U.N. Doc. S/RES/1566 (Oct. 8, 2004).

129 A definition of *legislative* that has been often employed in the debate was first propounded by Edward Yemin as follows: "Legislative acts have three essential characteristics: they are unilateral in form, they create or modify some elements of a legal norm, and the legal norm is general in nature, that is, directed to indeterminate addresses and capable of repeated applications in time." Edward Yemin, Legislative Powers in the United Nations and Specialized Agencies 6 (A.W. Sijthoff) eds., 1st ed. 1969. Some commentators, on the basis of this particular definition, have argued that the Security Council has always had legislative authority. *See* e.g., F.I. Kirgis Jr, *The Security Council's First Fifty Years*, 89 Am. J. Int'l. L. 506, 520–28 (1995).

to actual conflict between states, to internal national conflicts,[130] to potential conflicts of either sort, and now, by way of Resolutions 1373 and 1540, the global threats to international peace and security of international terrorism and its potential connections to WMD. The Security Council's determination of "a threat to the peace," the trigger for mandatory prescription under Chapter VII of the Charter, has been the principal device for this expansion, which has provoked not only debate among legal scholars, but statements of concern from a significant number of member states of the United Nations.[131]

Before the passage of Resolutions 1373 and 1540, the Security Council's prescription of normative standards that have been characterized as asserting in some respect legislative, or relatedly quasi-judicial action, included determining the boundary between Kuwait and Iraq,[132] establishing an intrusive arms regime for Iraq,[133] a claims commission,[134] and international criminal tribunals for the former Yugoslavia and Rwanda.[135] Some commentators also have seen such action by the Security Council inherent in Resolutions 1422 and 1487 concerning the International Criminal Court (ICC), where the Security Council imposed obligations of a general character on all member states, not even specifying a threat to the peace.[136]

---

130 In recent years, this has included action with respect to Albania, Angola, Burundi, the Central African Republic, the Democratic Republic of the Congo, East Timor, Liberia, Rwanda, Sierra Leone, Somalia, and Sudan.

131 With respect to the adoption of Resolution 1373, a number of states declared concern on such grounds. *See* e.g, Statement by H.E. Ambassador Christian Wenaweser, Permanent Representative of the Principality of Liechtenstein, to the United Nations, Question of the Equitable Representation on and Increase in the Membership of the Security Council and Related Matter. (Oct. 11, 2004), http://www.regierung.li/uploads/media/pdf-fl-aussenstelle-newyork-dokumente-uno-10-10–2004-statement-sc-reform_01.pdf (stating that with the adoption of Resolution 1373, the Security Council has expanded its activities into the field of law-making, a sphere that is reserved to the General Assembly under the Charter, adding that this "raises fundamental questions which affect the institutional balance of the organization"); The consideration and adoption of Resolution 1540, further removed in time from the impetus generated by 9/11, occasioned even broader objection. *See* UNSC, S/PV. 4950, at 23 (India), at 30 (Cuba), at 5 (Mexico, at 14 (Nepal) and at 17 (Namibia), at 3 (Egypt), at 31 (Indonesia), at 32 (Iran); at 5 and 20 (Algeria), (2004), http://www.un.org/ga/search/view_doc.asp?symbol=S/PV.4950.

132 S.C. Res. 687, UN SCOR, 46th Sess., Res. & Dec., at 11, UN Doc. S/INF/47 (1991).

133 *Id.*, pt. C.

134 S.C. Res. 692, UN SCOR, 45th Sess., 2987th mtg., U.N. Doc S/RES/692 (1991). *See*, Erika de Wet, "The Security Council as a Law Maker: The Adoption of (Quasi)-Judicial Decisions," in Rudiger Wolfrum and Volker Roben, DEVELOPMENTS OF INTERNATIONAL LAW IN TREATY MAKING 217 (Springer) eds., 2005, asserting this action was *ultra vires* and illegal ("In essence, therefore, the illegality of the Compensation Commission is to be found in the Security Council's excessive control over the exercise of the Compensation Commission's adjudicative function. The lack of independence that the Compensation Commission enjoys in this regard, combined with Iran's lack of standing before it are in violation of the principles of justice as outlined in article 1(1) of the Charter.")

135 S.C. Res. 827, UN SCOR, 48th Sess., Res. & Dec., at 29, UN Doc. S/INF/49 (1993) (International Criminal Tribunal for the Former Yugoslavia); S.C. Res. 995, UN SCOR, 49th Sess., Res. & Dec., at 15, UN Doc. S/INF/50 (1994) (International Criminal Tribunal for Rwanda).

136 S.C. Res. 1422, U.N. Doc. S/RES/1422 (July 12, 2002), 41 I.LM. 1276 (2002); SC Res. 1487, U.N. Doc. S/RES/1487 (June 12 2003), 42 I.L.M. 1025 (2003); See, Stefan Talmon, *The Security Council as World Legislature, supra* note 124, at 177–178.

However, it is Resolutions 1373,[137] addressing terrorism, and 1540, identifying its potential connections to WMD, that have come to represent the extreme of legislative action by the Security Council under Chapter VII of the Charter. These resolutions are distinguished by their enunciation of global norms as binding obligations on all states. Prior to their passage, even positivist commentators supporting a broad view of Security Council authority, such as Hans Kelsen, had not gone beyond the capacity of the Security Council to create new law for a specific case.[138] The mandates of Resolutions 1373 and 1540, that all states take measures to deny safe haven to terrorists, criminalize terrorist financing, and prevent the proliferation of WMD and their means of delivery clearly staked new ground for Security Council action under Chapter VII. The measures listed in these resolutions go well beyond the sanctions measures listed in Article 41, and are no doubt normative. They are mandated to be taken by all 193 member states of the United Nations, and are therefore no doubt global in their imposition.

Following on the trauma of 9/11, Resolutions 1373 and 1540 were expressly adopted by the Security Council pursuant to its responsibility for the maintenance of international peace and security enshrined as a primary purpose of the United Nations in Article 1 of the United Nations Charter. International terrorism and its potential linkages with WMD were seen as urgent threats made real by 9/11, requiring avoidance of the difficulty and time necessary to achieve a consensual response to the immediate risk of non-state actors acquiring WMD. In adopting Resolution 1373, the Security Council went well beyond what consensual process had been able to achieve, drawing on standards that had not been widely adopted. When the Security Council adopted the resolution 17 days after 9/11, only two states were party to all 12 of the existing international conventions and protocols on terrorism developed by the General Assembly and in other consensual fora, none with any mechanism for implementation.[139]

There is no authority in sight that suggests a power of review, or likely reversal, of Security Council legislation. There is no clear standard for judicial review of

137 A number of commentators have identified Resolution 1373 as marking the first time the Security Council fully assumed the role of legislator. See, e.g., Michael C. Wood, "The Security Council as Lawmaker," in DEVELOPMENTS OF INTERNATIONAL LAW IN TREATY MAKING 217, at 234 (Springer) eds., 2005 ("a defining moment"); George Nolte at p. 238 in same text; Paul Szasz, *The Security Council Starts Legislating*, 96 AM. J. INT'L. L. 901 (2002); Judge Gilbert Guillaume, *Grotius Lecture on Terrorism and International Law*, 53 INT'L. AND COMP. L. QUARTERLY 3, 537, 543 (2004).

138 Hans Kelsen, THE LAW OF THE UNITED NATIONS 259 (Praeger) 1950; See also comments on Kelsen's position; Michael Wood, *The Security Council as Lawmaker*, *supra* note 137 and Georg Nolte, *The Limits of the Security Council's Powers and its Functions in the International Legal System: Some Reflections*, *supra* note 137.

139 All 12 conventions are available at United Nations, *Text and Status of the United Nations Conventions on Terrorism*, UNTC (last visited Sep. 3, 2012), http://treaties.un.org/Pages/DB.aspx?path=DB/studies/page2_en.xml&menu=MTDSG

Security Council action under Chapter VII.[140] The International Court of Justice (ICJ) has declined any authority to challenge a determination by the Security Council under Chapter VII.[141] And in the limited contexts in which judicial consideration has occurred, such as the establishment of the International Criminal Tribunal for the former Yugoslavia (ICTY), Security Council action though challenged as legislative and beyond its powers was confirmed as a proper exercise of its authority.[142] So there are no international institutional limits, outside the Security Council itself that presently can act to constrain Security Council legislative action.

Some international law scholars have argued that the absence of provision for judicial review does not mean there are no limits *of law* to action by the Security Council.[143] So the acquiescence in Security Council action of a legislative character has not eliminated the legal controversy. And to the extent there are legal questions as to the Security Council's authority to mandate normative standards, such questions may affect the willingness of states to cooperate in the implementation of any Security Council mandate. Hence, such questions may also influence how much further the Security Council may be willing to go as "legislator."

Concerning achievement of more proactive and effective counterproliferation, therefore, it is important to consider the legal debate, and what it indicates as to state acceptance, particularly in comparing the other arenas in which the Security Council has taken, or is proposed to take, so-called legislative action. This requires assessment of the claims of legal limits on the Chapter VII authority of the Security Council in relation to the political practice of the Security Council. What we find, propitious for a safer world, is that a counterproliferation resolution promises greater legal merit and political viability than virtually any other legislative initiative by the Security Council of the United Nations, past or prospective.

---

140 See, W. Michael Reisman, *The Constitutional Crisis in the United Nations*, 87 AM. J. INT'L. L. 83, 93–94 (1993).

141 The ICJ declared in its judgment in the Namibia case, "undoubtedly, the court does not possess powers of judicial review or appeal in respect of the decisions taken by the United Nations organs concerned." Legal Consequences for States of the Continued Presence of South Africa in Namibia (South West Africa) Notwithstanding Security Council Resolution 276 (1970), Advisory Opinion, 1971 ICJ, 16, 45 § 89; *Id.* at 51–52, §§ 109–110; *Id.* at 53, § 115. See also, *Prosecutor v. Tadic*, Case No.: IT-94-1-AR72, Decision on the Defense Motion for Interlocutory Appeal on Jurisdiction, October 2, 1995, §§ 26–40; Ian Brownlie, PRINCIPLES OF PUBLIC INTERNATIONAL LAW 666 (Oxford University Press), 6th ed. 2003.

142 In the *Tadic* decision, the Appeals Chamber of the ICTY validated the establishment of an international criminal tribunal as an instrument for the exercise of its own principal responsibility for the maintenance of international peace and security. *Prosecutor v. Tadic, supra* note 141.

143 See Antonios Tzanakopoulos, DISOBEYING THE SECURITY COUNCIL 54–84 (Oxford), 1st ed. 2011; Stefan Talmon, *The Security Council as World Legislature,* 99 AM. J. INT'L. L. 175, 178 (2005); Susan Lamb, "Legal Limits to United Nations Security Council Powers," in Guy S. Goodwin-Gill & Stefan Talmon (eds.), THE REALITY OF INTERNATIONAL LAW 361–88 (Oxford) 1999; Stefan Talmon, *The Security Council as World Legislature,supra* note 124, at 178, 182–186; Gaetano Arangio-Ruiz, *On the Security Council's "Law-Making,"* 83 Rivista di Diritto Internazionale 610, 622–725 (2000).

ii. THE LEGAL DEBATE

The legal debate over Security Council authority to mandate general standards binding all states focuses the Charter of the United Nations as a constitutional document defining the powers of the respective organs of the United Nations. Indeed, the legal debate is somewhat akin to the perennial constitutional debates over relative powers in United States constitutional litigation. On one side are those who assert colorings of original intent as constraint on the exercise of power. They argue essentially that the Security Council is constitutionally authorized only to act as international policeman enforcing rules, not as rule maker, and is therefore not empowered to legislate standards addressing global and ongoing threats under Chapter VII.[144] This is complemented by a separation of powers conception emphasizing that the Security Council is not representative of the greater membership of the United Nations. It refers to original intent manifest in the drafting of the UN Charter to restrict Chapter VII action to a particular situation of international conflict, consistent with the original vision of the Security Council as international policeman, and argues that it is the General Assembly that is charged with recommending prescriptions for the general conduct of states. Any normative mandate by the Security Council not grounded in a particular situational conflict is seen as invasive of the role of the General Assembly as the fully representative body exclusively charged to develop and recommend any measures and standards applicable to states at large. Norms, it maintains, must be developed within the constraints of the consensual context of treaties, conventions and other expressions of consensus. From this perspective, the distinct powers and roles of the organs of the United Nations are regarded as limiting rather than enlarging the potential for the Security Council to undertake functions traditionally viewed as adjudicative or legislative. The proponents of this view generally insist on the impliedly restrictive provisions of the Charter, such as the domestic jurisdiction provision Article 2(7), and the Article 1(1) requirement that the United Nations act "in conformity with the principles of justice and international law."[145]

It is also argued by commentators objecting to Security Council legislation that, as in international security and conflict law more generally, the Security Council is limited by the proportionality principle. *Proportionality*, as claimed to apply to Chapter VII

---

144 Some commentators see the legislative assertion of Security Council authority as unduly expansive and some see it as *ultra vires*. *See* Matthew Happold, *Security Council Resolution 1373 and the Constitution of the United Nations, supra* note 136, LEIDEN J. INT'L. L. 593, 593–610 (September 2003); Jose Alvarez, *Hegemonic International Law Revisited*, 97 AM. J. INT'L. L. 874 (2003); Roberto Lavalle, *A Novel, If Awkward, Exercise In International Law-Making: Security Council Resolution 1540*, 51 NETH. INT'L L. REV. 411 (2004); Gaetano Arangio-Ruiz, *On the Security Council's "Law-Making," supra* note 143, RIVISTA DI DIRITTO INTERNAZIONALE 610, 622–725 (2000). Erika de Wet, THE CHAPTER VII POWERS OF THE UNITED NATIONS SECURITY COUNCIL (Hart Publishing) 2004.

145 See, e.g., Erika de Wet, "The Security Council as a Law Maker: The Adoption of (Quasi)-Judicial Decisions," in Rudiger Wolfrum and Volker Roben, DEVELOPMENTS OF INTERNATIONAL LAW IN TREATY MAKING 187–88 (Springer) eds., 2005); Gaetano Arangio-Ruiz, *On the Security Council's "Law-Making," supra* note 143 (2000).

action by the Security Council, is variously defined, but as a limitation on the authority of the Security Council is generally understood to confine Security Council action to the exigencies of particular cases for the maintenance of international peace and security, not to be extended disproportionally to other interests.[146] As to measures under Chapter VII taken for the maintenance of international peace, application of the principle of proportionality is taken to mean that the action undertaken must be proportional to counter or remove a particular threat.[147] Some commentators carry a proportionality constraint so far as to contradict Security Council assertion of any legislative role, arguing that Security Council authority under Chapter VII is limited by the proportionality principle to peace-enforcing measures addressing a particular situation and that any legislative or quasi-judicial action the Security Council purports to assert as authorized under Chapter VII is *ultra vires* as beyond its authority when extended to rules of general conduct with no temporal limitation.[148]

Scholarship that takes the more expansive evolutionary view of the powers of the Security Council focuses particularly on the Security Council's responsibility for maintenance of international peace and security ordained in Article I of the United Nations Charter, and the principle broadly stated by the ICJ in the *Certain Expenses* case, that "when the Organization takes action which warrants the assertion that it was appropriate for the fulfillment of one of the stated purposes of the United Nations, the presumption is that such action is not *ultra vires* the Organization."[149] This construction of the Charter grounds action by the Security Council on Article 24 of the Charter which empowers the Security Council with primary responsibility for the maintenance of international peace and security through "prompt and effective action," which is seen to require, particularly in response to the new challenges presented by contemporary global threats, action without a requirement of temporal or situational limitation.

Here the complementary jurisprudential perspective is not emphasis of the distinction of the relative roles of the Security Council and General Assembly under the Charter, but that interpretation of the Charter is properly evolutionary—that its

---

146 See Arrangio-Ruiz, *supra* note 144, at 628–30; Nicolas Angelet, INTERNATIONAL LAW LIMITS TO THE SECURITY COUNCIL, IN UNITED NATIONS SANCTIONS AND INTERNATIONAL LAW 72 (Vera Gowland-Debbas et al.) eds., 2001; J.A. Frowein & N. Kirsch, "Introduction," in THE CHARTER OF THE UNITED NATIONS, A COMMENTARY 701, 711–12 (Bruno Simma et al.) eds., 2d ed. 2002; Georg Nolte, *The Limits of the Security Council's Powers and its Functions in the International Legal System: Some Reflections, supra* note 138. See commentary on Article 2(7) of the Charter regarding the proportional use of Security Council power in THE CHARTER OF THE UNITED NATIONS, A COMMENTARY 148, 171 (Bruno Simma et al.) eds., 2d ed. 2002.

147 Stefan Talmon, *The Security Council as World Legislature, supra* note 143, at 184 Antonios Tzanakopoulos, DISOBEYING THE SECURITY COUNCIL, *supra* note 143, at 54–84.

148 See e.g., Gaetano Arangio-Ruiz, *On the Security Council's "Law Making", supra* note 143, at 723-724. Matthew Happold, *Security Council Resolution 1373 and the Constitution of the United Nations, supra* note 143, at 608. Daniel H. Joyner, *The Security Council as a Legal Hegemon* 43 GEORGETOWN J. INT'L. L., 225 (2012).

149 *Certain Expenses Case*, ICJ Reports (1962) at 168.

creature, the United Nations, if it is to be relevant, vital, and useful, must act as fundamental purpose instructs through time.[150] This must include both the express powers of the Security Council and such implied or residual powers as may be required to account for the changing nature of threats to international peace and security.[151] Most notably for contemporary times, of course, this includes adaptation to the distinctively new challenge posed by the non-state actor and WMD threat that Resolutions 1373 and 1540 were designed to address.

The argument proceeds that the UN members have agreed that in carrying out its Article 24 responsibility, the Security Council acts on behalf of the members, who under Article 25 are committed to carry out the decisions of the Security Council, and under Article 48, paragraph 1, more particularly, have agreed to carry out the determinations of the Security Council that are directed to the maintenance of international peace and security.[152] Members are bound also because there was universal consent to

---

150 See Paul C. Szasz, *General Law-Making Processes*, in 1 United Nations Legal Order 35, 61–68 (Oscar Schachter & Christopher C. Joyner, eds.), 1995; Eric Rosand, *The Security Council as "Global Legislator": Ultra Vites or Ultra Innovative?, supra* note 124, at 542. Some commentators, while even acknowledging an original separation of powers conception, take the position that as Security Council legislative and quasi-judicial initiative is endorsed by states more generally, the original Charter conception can legitimately be regarded as having changed. See, e.g. Bruno Simma, THE CHARTER OF THE UNITED NATIONS, Volume I, supra note 146 at 709. See Paul C. Szasz, *General Law-Making Processes, supra* note 137. Anne-Marie Slaughter, AN AMERICAN VISION OF INTERNATIONAL LAW, 97 AM. SOC'Y INT'L L. PROC. 125, 128 (2003): Keith Harper, *Does the United Nations Security Council have the Competence to Act as a Court and Legislature?*, 27 N.Y.U. J. INT'L L. & POL. 103, 149 (1994); Frederick L. Kirgis, Jr., *The Security Council's First Fifty Years, supra* note 129.

151 The International Court of Justice in the Namibia advisory opinion, endorsed the theory of residual powers of the Security Council as follows:

> The reference in paragraph 2 of (Article 24 of the Charter) to specific powers of the Security Council under certain chapters of the Charter does not exclude the existence of general powers to discharge the responsibilities referred to in paragraph 1. Reference may be made in this respect to the Secretary-General's Statement, presented to the Security Council on 10 January 1947, to the effect that 'the powers of the Council under Article 24 are not restricted to the specific grants of authority contained in Chapters VI, VII, VIII and IX... The members of the United Nations have conferred upon the Security Council powers commensurate with its responsibility for the maintenance of peace and security. The only limitations are the fundamental principles and purposes found in Chapter I of the Charter.' ICJ Reports (1971) at 52, para. 110. *See also*, Frederick L. Kirgis, Jr., *The Security Council's First Fifty Years, United Nations at Fifty, supra* note 129, at 521, 524 (citing Reparation for Injuries Suffered in the Service of the United Nations, 1949 ICJ Rep. 174, 179, 182) (Advisory Opinion of Apr. 11); *Certain Expenses Case*, ICJ Reports (1962) at 168.

On implied UN powers as required by the functional requirements of maintenance of international peace and security, *see Reparation for injuries suffered in the service of the United Nations*, 1949 ICJ Reports 174,179, 182 (Advisory Opinion of Apr. 11); *See also Certain Expenses Case*, ICJ Reports (1962) at 167.

152 Frederick L. Kirgis, *The Security Council's First Fifty Years, supra* note 129, at 526–527 (1995) *See also, Legal Consequences for States of the continued presence of South Africa in Namibia (South West Africa) notwithstanding Security Council Resolution 276 (1970)*, Advisory Opinion, ICJ Reports 1971, p. 16, 562–63, in which the International Court of Justice held that Security Council Resolution 276 calling on all states to refrain from dealings with South Africa was binding on all states under Article 25.

the powers of the Security Council among the member states of the United Nations broadly implicit in ratification of the Charter.[153] Even non-members are bound under Article 2(6) which requires the United Nations to "ensure that states which are not Members act in accordance with these Principles so far as may be necessary for the maintenance of international peace and security." Also, noted in direct support of this more expansive view of the powers of the Security Council, is that its Chapter VII authority is the one exception expressly appended to the Article 2(7) domestic jurisdiction reservation. A more controversial point, but also part of the argument, is that the Chapter VII power of the Security Council to adopt normative prescription is not limited by the Article 1(1) requirement that the United Nations act "in conformity with the principles of justice and international law."[154] Additionally, so the argument goes, the primacy of prescription by the Security Council over other sources of international standards is assured by the primacy given the UN Charter relative to the consensual process of treaties, embodied in the provision of Article 103 of the Charter that "(i)n the event of a conflict between the obligations of the Members of the United Nations under the present Charter and their obligations under any other international agreement, their obligations under the Charter shall prevail."[155]

As to a principle of proportionality, there is commentary as well as case law that denies the Security Council is bound by any strict principle of proportionality.[156] Sometimes the proponents of an evolutionary legislative role for the Security Council assert that Chapter VII of the Charter allows the Security Council broad leeway that renders its legislative forays, such as they have been, generally consistent with a principle of proportionality.[157] They note that Chapter VII does not mention any limit and

---

153 Eric Rosand, *The Security Council as "World Legislator": Ultra Vires or Ultra Innovative, supra* note 124, at 542.

154 There is considerable authority, supported by the language of the Charter, that Article 1 (1) requires compliance with international law only for peaceful settlement of disputes under Chapter VI, not collective measures under Chapter VII, buttressed by the exception for enforcement measures made explicit in the domestic jurisdiction reservation of Article 2(7). See, e.g. Frowein/Krisch, "Action with respect to Threats to the Peace, Breaches of the Peace, and Acts of Aggression" in Bruno Simma (ed.), THE CHARTER OF THE UNITED NATIONS: A COMMENTARY, Volume I, 710–11 (Oxford University Press) 2002. See contra, Erika de Wet, *"The Security Council as a Law Maker, supra* note 145, at 187–188, arguing on the basis of unclear preparatory travaux that Chapter VII action by the Security Council is limited by the inclusion of "justice and international law" in the first sentence of article 1(1) of the Charter.

155 *See* Thomas Franck, RECOURSE TO FORCE: STATE ACTION AGAINST THREATS AND ARMED ATTACKS 5 (Cambridge) 2002.

156 Kirgis, *The Security Council's First Fifty Years, supra* note 129, at 517; Frowein/Krisch in Bruno Simma, THE CHARTER OF THE UNITED NATIONS, Volume I, 710–12 (Oxford University Press) 2002; Eric Rosand, *The Security Council as "Global Legislator", supra* note 153, at 542. See *Case Concerning the Air Service Agreement of March 27, 1946 (U.S. v. Fr.)*, 18 R.I.A.A. 417, 54 I.L.R. 304, 338 (1978).

157 See Ian Brownlie, PRINCIPLES OF PUBLIC INTERNATIONAL LAW, *supra* note 141, at 666–667. (Oxford University Press) 6th ed. 2003; Jochen Abr. Frowein & Nico Krisch, "Introduction to Chapter VII," in Bruce Simma (ed.) THE CHARTER OF THE UNITED NATIONS: A COMMENTARY VOL. I. 701, 712, para. 30 (Oxford University Press) 2d ed. 2002. Even commentators asserting significant limits on the authority of the Security Council to act under Chapter VII may concede that the Security Council is not limited

gives broad discretion to the Security Council, referring in Article 40 to those measures the Security Council "deems necessary or desirable." Additionally, they note the flexibility inherent in the Article 42 provision for military action if the Security Council "considers" that measures under Article 42 would be inadequate.[158]

iii. THE LEGAL DEBATE ENLIGHTENED BY POLITICAL REALISM

The legal debate, insofar as it would negate Security Council legislative authority, has been trumped by real world exigency. The record of legislative or quasi-judicial action demonstrates the Security Council is willing to do what the permanent members, in perception of mutual interest, deem doable for the maintenance of international peace and security, and that the international community has acquiesced. The Security Council, acting with such authority, has become the post Cold War resurrection of the political realism present at the origination of the United Nations, originally manifest in designing the Security Council to reflect existing realities of power and interest to avoid another catastrophic war. Its most emphatic expression became Chapter VII of the United Nations Charter, under which the Security Council has crafted its newly legislative role.

The most extreme recent expression of legislative action by the Security Council, the post 9/11 passage of Resolution 1373 on terrorism, flagged what has been called the "defining moment" of Chapter VII authority.[159] As a result, even commentators considering the legal objections have concluded that "the sustained general acceptance of Resolution 1373 trumps all traditional legal arguments which challenge its legality."[160] Reinforcing this conclusion is that the Security Council action in determining a threat

---

by the principle of proportionality, defining the principle as implying that the means should not be disproportionate to the end, which they see as unduly restrictive of the Security Council efficiency for the maintenance of peace, including use of force. *See* Erika de Wet, THE CHAPTER VII POWERS OF THE UNITED NATIONS SECURITY COUNCIL, 184–85 (Hart Publishing) 2004 and authorities cited therein.

158 *See*, Frowein/Krisch, *supra* note 156, at 712. Similarly as to the related question whether the "measures" taken under Chapter VII can include the mandate of general obligations for all states, Article 41 of the Charter is understood to be only a representative listing of measures available because of the use of the phrase "may include." This interpretation received judicial confirmation in the Tadic case where the court stated, "Article 39 (which provides that the Security Council shall decide what measures shall be taken in accordance with Article 41 to maintain or restore international peace and security) leaves the choice of means and their evaluation to the Security Council, which enjoys wide discretionary powers in this regard; and it could not have been otherwise, as such a choice involves political evaluation of highly complex and dynamic situations." *Prosecutor v. Tadic, supra* note 141, paras. 35, 39.

159 *See supra*, note 137.

160 Georg Nolte, "Lawmaking through the UN Security Council," in DEVELOPMENTS OF INTERNATIONAL LAW IN TREATY MAKING 217 (Springer) eds., 2005. See also, Georg Ress, "Interpretation MN 5," in Bruce Simma (ed.) THE CHARTER OF THE UNITED NATIONS: A COMMENTARY VOL. I. (Oxford University Press) 2d ed. 2002. Comment by Michael C. Wood, "*The Security Council as Lawmaker, supra* note 137, at 217. ("Assertions based on abstract interpretation lead to claims of illegality which simply do not square with reality. Indeed, they are potentially damaging to the international order and to the standing of international lawyers.")

to the peace as the basis for action involving the setting of standards has been treated as essentially unreviewable.[161] The Security Council also has been able to legislate without significant political opposition, though with varying degree of success in implementation, using virtually whatever mechanisms or tools it determines to employ, both those specifically listed in Chapter VII, such as sanctions and use of force, and innovative strategies beyond the specific listing of measures, such as adjudicative process. The ICTY Appeals Chamber in the *Tadic* case recognized this in confirming its own legitimacy as a creature of the Security Council, declaring, "'the threat to the peace' is more of a political concept," which gives the Security Council broad discretion under Chapter VII.[162]

So the evolution of Security Council action indeed appears to have a certain inevitability about it as the international community has been compelled to confront new global threats and now, most profoundly, the mutually magnifying threats of WMD and international terrorism, that are seen as large, and looming ever larger, on the horizon of nuclear risk. The legal accommodation to this reality is seen by many to require a generally prescriptive and global response to meet the nature of the threat and satisfy the Security Council's primary responsibility for the maintenance of international peace and security.[163] This interpretation is seen as especially compelling as well as proportional because there is no alternative in sight today other than unilateral action by states including use of force, as Israel and the United States are now threatening against Iran.[164] Even the most vociferous critics charging that "legislative" initiative by the Security Council is *ultra vires* and illegal acknowledge that there is no reason to think the Security Council will not continue to exercise such initiative if the sense of urgency and common interest in the maintenance of international peace and security are sufficient. Thus one of the critics writing most extensively on the legislative phenomenon, in a representative statement of disdain for such concession to the political realities that have generated legislative action under Chapter VII, complains, "For the time being, the international community remains confronted with a Security Council that will only engage in law-making activity if and to the extent that it serves the interests of a few powerful states and, where necessary, at the expense of the very norms on which the United Nations is based."[165]

But such reaction to the Security Council addressing the new global challenges to international peace and security is misguided and misguiding, especially as it would play in relation to counterproliferation of nuclear weapons. This should be recognized in a number of important respects. First, the Security Council has gauged, and can be expected to gauge, its willingness to legislate according to the degree of general

161 *See* W. Michael Reisman, *The Constitutional Crisis in the United Nations, supra* note 140, at 83.

162 *Prosecutor v. Tadic, supra* note 141, paras. 29, 31.

163 *See, e.g,* Stefan Talmon, *The Security Council as World Legislature, supra* note 136.

164 David Feith, *What Obama Isn't Saying About Iran*, WALL ST. J., Aug. 17, 2012, p. A11.

165 Erika de Wet, *The Security Council as Lawmaker, supra* note 145 at 225.

support among the membership of the United Nations. Thus the outstanding and still distinct examples of legislation obligating states generally without temporal or situational limitation, remain subject matters such as the global threats to the peace of terrorism and weapons of mass destruction, threats which have been seen as "threats to the peace" by virtually all states except the few miscreants. Second, counterproliferation as a subject matter is the pre-eminent candidate for further action under Chapter VII because the Security Council, in its most legislative action, namely the passage of Resolutions 1373 and 1540, is already seized of nuclear risk as a subject matter requiring its legislative attention. Third, action already taken by the Security Council indicates that though there is serious division of scholarly opinion on the question of Security Council authority to legislate, as to counterproliferation, that question has been answered unequivocally by the Security Council. If there is clear linkage between nuclear threat, and the responsibility of the Security Council for the maintenance of international peace and security enshrined as the priority objective in Article I of the United Nations Charter, the record demonstrates that the Security Council is increasingly inclined to act by way of mandatory prescription under Chapter VII.

That any legislative expression of the collective will of the members of the Security Council will be limited and conditioned by the need for support and cooperation from the membership at large does mean, though, dependency on legal justification. There is a correlative relationship between any legal basis for Security Council action under Chapter VII and global support. This is especially so as to a subject matter such as counterproliferation, which relies so significantly on global implementation. Some commentators, while asserting an original separation of powers conception as to the respective roles of the Security Council and General Assembly, even take the position that as Security Council legislative and quasi-judicial initiative is endorsed by states more generally, the original Charter conception can legitimately be regarded as having changed. Altogether, then, it is instructive in regard to the relationship of legality and legitimacy, which the so-called legislative activity of the Security Council implicates, to contrast the proposed counterproliferation mandate by way of a new Security Council resolution with the principal contexts in which the Security Council can be said to have mandated or is proposed to mandate international standards.

a. Inconsistency with Treaty Rights and Obligations and Customary International Law

The critique of Security Council legislation includes, as a principal contention that in acting under Chapter VII, and relying on Article 103's provision that Chapter VII action takes precedence over any international agreement, the Security Council has abused and ignored rights and obligations properly relegated to the consensual process of treaty law. One example employed in this critique is that Resolution 687 prohibited Iraq from possessing chemical and biological weapons, though the 1925 Geneva Protocol, the only consensual instrument obligating Iraq, only banned their use.[166] Another is that the Security Council included in 1373 certain provisions from the International Convention for the Suppression of the Financing of Terrorism, but omitted others such as rights of extradited persons, the convention's provisions on international humanitarian law, and the provisions on judicial dispute settlement, and did not limit itself to measures provided in the convention.[167]

This critique, that Security Council legislative action under Chapter VII, has been in excessive denigration of consensual process, is most heightened with respect to Security Council action in direct contravention of treaty rights and obligations. In Resolution 731 (1992) and Resolution 748 (1992)[168] the Security Council asked Libya to surrender for trial two Libyan officials who had been indicted in the United States and Scotland for implication in the destruction of an American civilian airliner over Lockerbie, Scotland. Libya insisted on its rights under the Montreal Convention for the Suppression of Unlawful Acts Against the Safety of Civil Aviation and its customary right under international law to try the officials itself. The Montreal Convention did appear to accord Libya the right to itself conduct any related prosecution.[169] Nevertheless, the ICJ determined that when the Security Council makes a decision under Chapter VII of the Charter that is inconsistent with a treaty-based right, the Security Council decision prevails.[170]

The court reasoned, in line with the liberal evolutionary view of Security Council authority under Chapter VII that the Security Council's decisions bind the member states under Article 25, and under Article 103, its decisions are deemed to prevail over any international agreement. The ICJ affirmed the Security Council's legislative authority, when exercised in discharging its primary responsibility for the maintenance of international peace and security, though at odds with international customary law and/or treaty-based rights. The legal arguments that the Libya resolutions went beyond the authority of the Security Council were overridden or ignored. And the acquiescence in this result indicates that there was general recognition among the state members of the United Nations that this was a useful and proper exercise of authority by the Security Council, notwithstanding the claims and arguments that it

---

166 Protocol for the Prohibition of the Use of Asphyxiating, Poisonous or Other Gases, and of Bacteriological Warfare, (1925) 44 LNTS 65.

167 Compare, *International Convention for the Suppression of the Financing of Terrorism*, Dec. 9, 1999, arts. 9, 15, 17, 21, 39 I.L.M. 270 (2000), and S.C. Res. 1373, U.N. Doc. S/RES/1373 (Sep. 28, 2001), 40 I.L.M. 1278 (2001).

168 S.C. Res. 731, U.N. Doc. S/RES/731 (Jan. 21, 1992), *reprinted in* 31 I.L.M. 732 (1992). S.C. Res. 748, U.N. Doc. S/RES/748 (Mar. 31, 1992), *reprinted in* 31 I.L.M. 750 (1992).

169 Under the Montreal Convention for the Suppression of Unlawful Acts Against the Safety of Civil Aviation, Libya had the option to prosecute *or* extradite. See MONTREAL CONVENTION FOR THE SUPPRESSION OF UNLAWFUL ACTS AGAINST THE SAFETY OF CIVIL AVIATION, Sep. 23, 1971, art. 7, 24 U.S.T. 564, 974 U.N.T.S. 177.

170 *Questions of Interpretation and Application of the 1971 Montreal Convention arising from the Aerial Incident at Lockerbie (Libya v. UK; Libya v. U.S.), Provisional Measures,* ICJ REPORTS 3, 144 (Orders of Apr. 14, 1992).

was *ultra vires* as beyond the constitutional limitations of the United Nations Charter, as well as basic principles of due process.[171]

Primacy accorded the Security Council determination over treaty or custom-based rights does not necessarily remove the political tension such inconsistency may reflect. That tension may still serve to undermine Security Council action under Chapter VII. However, concerning counterproliferation, serious tension between any treaty right and a counterproliferation mandate is not likely to arise. A counterproliferation mandate might well provoke the complaint that bedevils progress under the Nuclear Non-Proliferation Treaty (NPT), the perennial and overworked complaint that the nuclear weapons states are not living up to their NPT disarmament commitment. But a Security Council counterproliferation resolution would not be inconsistent with any promise of the NPT, and would constitute a dramatic reinforcement of counterproliferation. It would also effectively transcend the NPT controversy concerning disarmament. That is, it would give counterproliferation a new basis of justification under Chapter VII and the Security Council's primary responsibility to maintain international peace and security. Any tension between counterproliferation and treaty based rights would be minimized, if appearing at all.

There also would be no question of consistency with customary law. Custom has come to support counterproliferation by way of the broad range of counterproliferation measures already accepted in some degree by a significant majority of states. There *would be* the profound difference between counterproliferation commitments currently discretionary for each state, becoming enforceable as mandatory obligations under Chapter VII of the Charter, which is the central theme of this book. But unlike the situation in the Lockerbie litigation, for example, there is no apparent substantive conflict between counterproliferation measures, and other international rights or obligations, whether customary or treaty-based.

b. "Threat to the Peace"

On the political front that is the real world test for any legislative action of the Security Council, it is instructive to compare a proposal repeatedly made by a leading UN scholar and the former Director of the General Legal Division of the United Nations, Paul Szasz, for achieving the equivalent by Security Council resolution of the long stymied Comprehensive Test Ban Treaty. The proposal is that "... (t)he Council could reasonably determine that, since any nuclear explosion would constitute a threat to

171 For the articulation of such claims and arguments, see Arrangio-Ruiz, *On the Security Council's Lawmaking*, *supra* note 144, at 702–712; Susan Lamb, "*Legal Limits to United Nations Security Council Powers*," *supra* note 143, at 376–378. in Guy S. Goodwin-Gill and Stefan Talmon (eds.), THE REALITY OF INTERNATIONAL LAW 376–378 (Oxford) 1999; Erika de Wet, "The Security Council as a Law Maker: The Adoption of (Quasi)-Judicial Decisions," in Rudiger Wolfrum and Volker Roben, DEVELOPMENTS OF INTERNATIONAL LAW IN TREATY MAKING 202–205 (Springer) eds., 2005; Erika de Wet, *The Chapter VII Powers of the United Nations Security Council*, *supra* note 145 (Hart Publishing) 2004; Paul C. Szasz, SELECTED ESSAYS ON UNDERSTANDING INTERNATIONAL INSTITUTIONS AND THE LEGISLATIVE PROCESS 60 (Transnational Publishers) 1st ed. 2001.

the peace within the meaning of Article 39, all such explosions would be henceforth be prohibited and the control system of the Comprehensive Test Ban Treaty would be an appropriate means of ensuring compliance with that edict."[172]

In arguing for his proposal, Szasz references Lockerbie as precedent, stating that "if the Security Council can hold that the non-extradition of two persons accused of having bombed a civilian airliner some years ago is a threat to the peace—a determination the World Court declined even to question—then the proposed determination with respect to nuclear testing is evidently well within the Council's wide discretionary power under the Charter."[173] Citing the UN Secretary-General's declaration in January 1992, that the proliferation of nuclear, and indeed "all weapons of mass destruction, constituted a threat to international peace and security,"[174] Szasz argues that nuclear testing should be subject to ban by the Security Council in that "nuclear testing actually or potentially furthers . . . proliferation."[175]

"Threat to the peace," the triggering term for action by the Security Council under Article 39 of Chapter VII, has never been defined other than as given content by the Security Council. It is generally viewed as a determination to be made at the Security Council's discretion notwithstanding the controversy over whether there are any legal limits.[176] Though given the opportunity, the ICJ has not asserted authority to second-guess the Security Council's determination of "a threat to the peace." As much legal scholarship acknowledges, this is surely both in recognition of the political nature of the determination, and that there would be an absence of judicially manageable standards for any court to apply.[177] It is generally acknowledged that Article 39 was adopted with the declared purpose of allowing the Security Council discretion in designating a threat to peace, including rejection of any specification other than the obligation "to act in accordance with the Purposes and Principles of the Organization and the provisions of the Charter."[178] And it is widely recognized that maintenance of international peace and security may require acting pre-emptively or preventively without waiting for a threat to the peace to become a breach of peace, though there is considerable argument over how this proposition played in the Bush pre-emption doctrine as it was employed to justify the invasion of Iraq.[179]

Even in its most extreme expression, however, determination of a "threat to the peace" is not arbitrary. It is subject to the limiting framework of the deliberative and

---

172 Paul C. Szasz, *The Security Council Starts Legislating*, 96 AM. J. INT'L L. 901, 904 (2002).

173 Paul C. Szasz, *A New Approach to Achieving a CBT*, DISARMAMENT TIMES, Nov. 24, 1992, at 3.

174 U.N. Doc. S/23500 (Jan. 31, 1992), at 4, http://www.un.org/Docs/journal/asp/ws.asp?m=s/23500.

175 Paul C. Szasz, DISARMAMENT TIMES, *supra* note 173, at 3.

176 *See* Hans Kelsen, THE LAW OF THE UNITED NATIONS 727 (Praeger) 1950; Stephan Talmon, *The Security Council as World Legislature, supra* note 124, at 179–82; Eric Rosand, *The Security Council as "Global Legislator," supra* note 124, at 554–55.

177 *See* W. Michael Reisman, *The Constitutional Crisis in the United Nations, supra* note 140 at 93–94.

178 UNCIO XII 334 *seq*. 379–81, 505.

179 *See Agora: Future Implications of the Iraq Conflict, Iraq and International Law, supra* note 35; Jose E. Alvarez, *Hegemonic International Law Revisited, supra* note 144, at 882.

voting process of the Security Council. Designation of "threat to the peace" is confined within the procedural requirement of a concurring vote of all five permanent members, which naturally engages their concerns as to creating precedent and need for achieving legitimacy and support among nations outside the Security Council. The process, while principally political, allows a complex of considerations, both political and legal, to be brought to bear. It is undeniable that the phrase "threat to the peace" "has proved to be quite elastic in the hands of the Council," affording broad discretion as to that determination and the measures to be employed under Chapter VII.[180] But the institutional means for control is the precondition for action under Chapter VII of shared perception among the members of the Security Council of the intertwined limitations of politics, effectiveness, and legitimacy.

What the Security Council has done, in actual fact, indicates ample precedent to support an Article 39 determination by the Security Council for establishment of a broad counterproliferation mandate. As Szasz noted as the basis for his proposal of a ban on nuclear testing, the Security Council has already made the determination that nuclear proliferation is a "threat to the peace," both through official declaration of the President of the Security Council, and as reiterated in a number of Security Council resolutions.[181] Insofar as some scholarship has argued that the term "threat to the peace" does have substantive content, such as that the situation addressed "has to have the potential of provoking armed conflict between states,"[182] what subject could be more connected to the potential for armed conflict on a grand scale than proliferation of the capacity to create nuclear weapons? Certainly that was the thinking behind the public relations campaign of the Bush administration in claiming the presence of WMD programs, particularly nuclear, as justification for the invasion of Iraq. In present policy, clearly proliferation is the "threat to the peace" the United States and Israel have declared as justifying the "on table option" of use of force for dealing with the Iranian nuclear weapons threat if diplomacy and sanctions should fail.[183]

c. Proportionality

If the proportionality principle is a limit or condition for action by the Security Council under Chapter VII, as previously noted a matter much in controversy in legal scholarship,[184] the principle nevertheless applies in favor of a counterproliferation mandate.

---

180 W. Michael Reisman, *The Constitutional Crisis in the United Nations*, *supra* note 140, at 93; Rosand, *The Security Council as Global Legislator*, *supra* note 124, at 555; *Prosecutor v. Tadic*, *supra* note 141, 144.

181 See statement by president of the Security Council declaring that "(t)he proliferation of all weapons of mass destruction constitutes a threat to international peace and security." U.N. Doc. S/23500 (Jan. 31, 1992), at 4, http://www.un.org/Docs/journal/asp/ws.asp?m=s/23500.

182 See Erika de Wet, THE CHAPTER VII POWERS OF THE UNITED NATIONS SECURITY COUNCIL *supra* note 144, and authorities cited therein.

183 David Feith, *What Obama Isn't Saying About Iran*, *supra* note 164.

184 See *supra* page 53 and notes 146–148, and pages 56–57 and notes 156–158.

Given the global and dispersed nature of the threat of proliferation, which cannot be overcome by restriction to particular situational conflict or only immediate measures as listed in Article 41 of Chapter VII, a broad mandate is no doubt a proportionate response. Also in reference to proportionality, it must be recognized that the Security Council is the *only* institutional resource we have available to establish broad-based institutional tools for addressing proliferation risk. Some legal commentators denounce this as "hegemonic," a term that has become a cliché of scholarship decrying the Security Council's assumption of any legislative role.[185] However, the great significance of the lack of acceptable alternatives can be appreciated best in light of the current threats emanating from Israel and the United States to employ use of force as a last resort in meeting the nuclear weapons challenge of Iran. So desperate is the situation that some commentary has posited such use of force by individual states as a permanent alternative, arguing it is the "20 percent solution"[186] for nuclear proliferation. This solution would be a permanent prescription of use of force by ad hoc alliances of states against any proliferation miscreant; clearly a course fraught with greater danger for the maintenance of international peace and security than any legislative initiative by the Security Council. A Security Council Counterproliferation Resolution, by contrast, not only promises the procedural restraint of institutionalization of international use of force, but could make clear that any use of force would require an additional Security Council resolution, such as the Security Council assured the UN membership at large in adopting Resolution 1540.[187]

Surely, in light of the limitations of real world choice for how to deal with any nuclear weapons threat, legislative action by the Security Council, and the requirement of its imprimatur before the use of force, would be well within the bounds, and affirmation, of proportionality. The linkage of "threat to the peace" and the critical counterproliferation measures here to be discussed is certainly at least as clear and definite than in relation to a proposed ban of nuclear testing. That "threat to the peace" encompasses proliferation is no longer at issue, having not only been declared by the Security Council as a general proposition, but in multiple resolutions and

185 See, e.g., Jose Alvarez, *Hegemonic International Law Revisited, supra* note 144, at 873-888.; Daniel H. Joyner, *The Security Council as Legal Hegemon supra* note 148.

186 Matthew Lund, *The Eighty Percent and Twenty Percent Solutions to Nuclear Proliferation*, 2009 BRIGHAM YOUNG UNIV. L. REV. 741 (2009), proposing application of the Pareto 80/20 economics rule to nuclear proliferation, to address the 20 percent nuclear weapons proliferating governments with use of force.

187 Resolution 1540 does not refer to taking action against noncompliant states, and implies the need for a resolution for enforcement action by noting that it "*Expresses* its intention to monitor closely the implementation of this resolution and at the appropriate level, to take further decisions which may be required to this end." See S.C. Res. 1540 *supra* note 124, 11. See also statement by Adam Thomson, Deputy Permanent Representative of the United Kingdom to the United Nations, U.N. SCOR, 59th Sess., 4950th mtg. at 11, U.N. Doc. S/PV. 4950 (2004) (stating that any enforcement action would require a new Council action); Statement by James Cunningham, Deputy Permanent Representative of the United States to the United Nations, U.N. SCOR, 59th Sess., 4950th mtg. at 17, U.N. Doc. S/PV.4950 (2004) (stating that "the draft resolution is not about enforcement.").

their implementation.[188] So the legal case for adoption of global counterproliferation measures by the Security Council is at least as strong and proportional as the Szasz proposal concerning a universal nuclear test ban, and indeed has already achieved a principled status dimensionally beyond that proposal. Of even greater significance in relation to what is politically practicable, is that the Comprehensive Test Ban Treaty, after years of pressures for approval, still languishes. This is because of the opposition or resistance of key governments, most importantly the permanent members of the Security Council, the United States and China, and firm and continuing opposition of not-to-be-ignored governments, such as India, Israel, Egypt, North Korea, and Pakistan, who all refuse to sign, though for different reasons.[189] The Szasz proposal for a nuclear test ban by means of a Security Council resolution under Chapter VII is a non-starter so long as such opposition continues. By contrast, the measures that would be mandated through a Security Council counterproliferation resolution would not invite significant political opposition, except from the governments of miscreant status, such as Iran and North Korea. To the negative, there is no permanent member of the Security Council generally opposed to improved counterproliferation. To the positive, the actions to date by the Security Council to promote counterproliferation, the ongoing operations of the IAEA, and the cooperation of most governments when called upon for implementation of the major aspects of counterproliferation certainly distinguishes counterproliferation as highly proportional, and propitious for obtaining political support.

d. Invasion of Domestic Jurisdiction

Objection to the Security Council acting as legislator has been most pronounced in reference to Security Council action not only to dictate, but to trump domestic criminal law. This may be explained in that criminal law jurisdiction is among the most politically and sovereignty sensitive areas of traditional domestic jurisdiction. The principle Security Council initiatives that have provoked such objection are the establishment of international tribunals for Yugoslavia and Rwanda, and Resolution 1373's global mandate to criminalize terrorism. The objection, articulated as legal argument, is generally based on the Article 2(4) reservation of domestic jurisdiction and the Article I requirement for the United Nations to act "in conformity with principles of international law." This includes the customary distinction of domestic and international criminal jurisdiction, though the assertion of a requirement of conformity to international law

188 See statement by president of the Security Council declaring that "(t)he proliferation of all weapons of mass destruction constitutes a threat to international peace and security." U.N. Doc. S/23500, *supra* note 181.

189 *See*, William S.W. Chang, *China and the Comprehensive Test Ban Treaty Negotiations*, 1 STANFORD J. OF EAST ASIAN AFFAIRS 34 (2001); Kaegan McGrath, Stephanie Bobiak and Jean du Preez, *The Future of the Nuclear Test Ban Treaty: The Good, the Bad, and the Ugly*, JAMES MARTIN CENTER FOR NONPROLIFERATION STUDIES (Mar. 7, 2008); Sean Dunlop, *The United States and the CTBT: Renewed Hope or Politics as Usual*, MONTEREY INSTITUTE OF INTERNATIONAL STUDIES (Feb. 1, 2009).

is controversial as applied to Chapter VII, with some commentators interpreting the Charter and its negotiating history as establishing that the requirement of conformity to international law does not apply to Chapter VII.[190]

In establishing the ad hoc criminal tribunal for the former Yugoslavia, the Security Council adopted new rules that purported to modify or contravene legal process in member states. It asserted that states must stay or defer domestic criminal proceedings for cases falling within the ICTY's jurisdiction when requested by the ICTY to do so, and that no person could be tried for violations of international humanitarian law if already tried by the ICTY.[191] Some of the rules prescribed clearly went beyond what domestic legal process of the states affected by the mandate would have allowed, such as requiring host or transit states to enforce orders of the ICTY for the surrender of indicted individuals.[192] The Appeals Chamber of the ICTY nevertheless determined the Security Council did have the authority to establish the ICTY with such effect.[193]

Security Council Resolutions 1373 and 1540, especially, are said to have illegally invaded domestic criminal law jurisdiction, not only in mandating that states criminalize certain activity, but by then leaving considerable uncertainty as to any assurance of due process rights for targeted individuals. Resolution 1373, most directly concerning criminal prosecution, did not provide any assurance of the protection of international human rights or humanitarian law, and did not indicate any due process limitation as to sanctions, though the clash of targeted sanctions and human rights concerns was naturally to be anticipated as inherent in the Resolution 1373 counterterrorism mandate.[194]

The *Kadi* case, brought before the European Court of Justice (ECJ), addressed the tension between the Security Council counterterrorism mandate and due process concerns. Kadi challenged the implementation of UN Security Council resolutions requiring enforcement by UN member states of financial sanctions against persons the Security Council's Sanctions Committee targeted as being involved in terrorism. The ECJ struck down the applicable European Union (EU) Council regulation, finding

---

190 *See* e.g., Frowein/Krisch, THE CHARTER OF THE UNITED NATIONS, *supra* note 146, at 710; Rosand, *The Security Council as "Global Legislator," supra* note 124, at 556; Gaetano Arrangio-Ruiz, *On the Security Council's Law Making*, supra note 144, at 644–645. Georg Nolte, *The Limits of the Security Council's Powers and its Functions in the International Legal System, Some Reflections supra* note 138.

191 Statute of the Yugloslavia Tribunal, S.C. Res. 827, UN SCOR, UN Doc. S/25704, annex (1993), arts. 9(2), 10(1), reprinted in 32 I.L.M. 1192(1993); Statute of the Rwanda Tribunal, arts. 8(2), 9(1), SC Res. 955, annex (Nov. 8, 1994), reprinted in 33 I.L.M. 1602 (1994).

192 Kirgis, *supra* note 129, at 523. See Statute of International Tribunal for the Prosecution of Persons Responsible for Serious Violations of International Humanitarian Law Committed in the Territory of the Former Yugoslavia since 1991, art. 29, annexed to Report of the Secretary-General Pursuant to Paragraph 2 of Security Council Resolution 808, U.N. Doc. S/25704/Annexes (1993).

193 *See Prosecutor v. Tadic, supra* note 141, para. 38.

194 For an extensive discussion of these lapses and apparent contravention of international standards, See Jose D. Alvarez, *Hegemonic International Law Revisited, supra* note 144.

that the regulation violated certain fundamental due process rights guaranteed to EU nationals under EU law. There has been other litigation indirectly challenging implementation of Security Council resolutions, in reference to national implementation measures.[195]

There is no such significant tension or clash likely between counterproliferation and regional or national law. A Security Council resolution that would mandate counterproliferation would prescribe the implementation of standards that are already being implemented cooperatively to some degree by most states. This is true of all the principal areas of counterproliferation concern. As will be explained for each arena of counterproliferation, achieving a much more robust architecture does not require invasion of domestic jurisdiction that cannot be reasonably accommodated. Neither enhanced nuclear forensics capability, intelligence sharing, multi-internationalization of the nuclear fuel cycle, interdiction of nuclear weapons related transport, nor export controls need seriously undermine what is traditionally designated domestic jurisdiction. As to export controls, the area most likely to involve any criminal aspect, national law would remain the basis, as it is today, for any criminal penalties. Criminalization of violation of export controls and illicit transfer of nuclear weapons related material, along the lines already developed and implemented by the Nuclear Suppliers Group and other control regimes, *would* have to be extended globally. But there is no obvious and direct conflict with domestic substantive or procedural criminal law, certainly not anything in the nature of the extreme due process and other concerns relating to protection of individual human rights that counterterrorism, in its many manifestations, has inevitably provoked.

There is also a complementary aspect to prescription of standards by the Security Council that should not be ignored, that works as to standards of counterproliferation in a more robust and less objectionable way, than as to other legal prescriptions by the Security Council. Whenever the Security Council affirms norms consistent with state practice, those norms are reinforced as candidates for constituting customary international law. Indeed, it is recognized that Security Council action can help produce new international law, where state practice reflects the same standards.[196] The Security Council's adoption of the statutes of the international tribunals for Yugoslavia and Rwanda thus surely was an affirmation of individual criminal responsibility under international law, despite the invasion of domestic criminal jurisdiction, and the criticism it occasioned. The standards of counterproliferation, if prescribed under Chapter VII, being already the subject of widespread implementation and cooperation among states, would certainly benefit from even significantly greater support, given all the challenges by contrast that international criminal adjudication typically confronts, as

---

195 See, Nada v. Switzerland, App. No. 10593/08 (Eur. Ct. H. R. Sept. 12, 2012), *available at* http://hudoc.echr.coe.int/sites/fra-press/pages/search.aspx?i=001-11318; A. Tzanakopoulos, *Domestic Court Reactions to UN Security Council Sanctions* in A. Reinisch (ed), CHALLENGING ACTS OF INTERNATIONAL ORGANIZATIONS BEFORE NATIONAL COURTS (Oxford) 2010.

196 Georg Nolte, *The Limits of the Security Council's Powers and its Functions in the International Legal System: Some Reflections, supra* note 138.

the adjudications for Yugoslavia and Rwanda and the due process concerns raised by Resolutions 1373 and 1540 attest.

iv. COUNTERPROLIFERATION AS THE BEST PROSPECT FOR SECURITY COUNCIL LEGISLATION

Insofar, then, as the Security Council may undertake further legislative action under Chapter VII, a broad counterproliferation mandate under Chapter VII would minimize both the legal and political objections that have plagued other legislative initiatives. Counterproliferation is at the epitome of legal, logical, and empirical justification, in its direct tie to the primary Charter objective of the maintenance of international peace and security ordained in Article 1, the objective which all sides of the legal debate agree is the touchstone for legitimacy of Chapter VII action by the Security Council. Contrasted with other actual or seriously proposed Security Council legislation, counterproliferation norms are more easily reconciled to existing consensus, whether reflected in international agreement or customary international law. Indeed, the increasing consensus supporting the established measures of counterproliferation has been identified as on its way to achieving, at least as to some elements, the status of customary international law. This evolution of the body of counterproliferation standards and its interconnectedness was explicitly noted at the 2011 meeting of the American Society of International Law, where it was stated,

> As this web grows stronger, certain components may evolve to the point of becoming customary international law, which would make them binding on all states. Indeed, the nuclear commodity controls lists of the 46-member NSG may arguably be on their way to achieving this status—they have been widely adopted by non-NSG states in implementing their export control rules under UNSCR 1540 and have been made mandatory for all states by UNSCR 1929 for controlling nuclear commodity transfers to Iran.[197]

As such development proceeds, even the critics relying on Article 1 of the UN Charter as imposing a legal limit of international law on Security Council legislation would have to concede that any such limit would be surmounted. Even more importantly, such development indicates the firming up of a broadly based political consensus to support the articulation of a global counterproliferation mandate. Indeed, the interconnectedness of counterproliferation standards, being a web, makes counterproliferation the quintessential candidate for application through comprehensive mandate.

The counterproliferation norms that would be legislated would not be at odds with other norms of either national or international law, whether legislative, customary, or treaty based. They would be, as the above comment indicates, the standards currently

197 Leonard S. Spector, *Responding to Nuclear Security Challenges in a Fragmented World*, Proceedings of the 105th Annual Meeting, 105 AM. SOC. OF INT'L L. 133, 137 (Mar. 23–26, 2011).

administered by the IAEA, the Nuclear Suppliers Group, and other institutional mechanisms that currently define counterproliferation. Adoption could be determined by the degree of consensus any particular norm or set of norms has already demonstrated. For example, the Additional Protocol is currently adopted and operates in about 134 states, and there is no good reason, given such widespread adoption, that it could not be mandated as an international standard, under a new regime disallowing exceptional status for any state.

A counterproliferation mandate, as among Security Council legislative initiatives, would be of the highest compatibility with established standards and practice, and accordingly most promising of success. The standards developed by the IAEA through its long in-depth operational experience implementing measures of nuclear security are already available. The very fact of their implementation on a broad basis, and the educational resources widely provided by the IAEA to the many governments with which it has agreements, have already generated significant positive dynamics for further acceptance and success. Indeed, the rich articulation of standards and their widespread implementation, though often not formalized, characterizes all of the areas of principal counterproliferation concern, with acceptance enhanced by the cooperative nature of the collective enterprise. This has been the nature of progressive acceptance and enhancement of counterproliferation capacity, whether the subject is nuclear forensics, export controls, intelligence gathering, multi-internationalization of the fuel cycle, or interdiction of nuclear weapons related transport. Moreover, given the nature of counterproliferation, as highly dependent on technology and expertise, it is simply and naturally more inclined to participatory and consultative process than other subjects of Security Council legislation such as counterterrorism and international criminal adjudication. During the consideration of Resolution 1540, the Security Council engaged in consultations not only internally, but with regional groups and held a public meeting to hear comments from the wider UN membership on the draft text.[198] Similar consultation, enlisting a similar source of consensual process, would be even more appropriate and feasible for consideration of a comprehensive counterproliferation mandate, and there is no reason, any more than there was for the adoption of Resolution 1540, to avoid such broader participation.

Just as was done for the Counter Terrorism Committee established under Resolution 1373, the specific requirements for effective implementation of a broad counterproliferation resolution would be borrowed from existing best practices, codes, and standards. This is the methodology the Security Council mandated in 1373, and accordingly the Counter Terrorism Committee created pursuant to that resolution utilizes standards developed by international institutions such as the International Civil Aviation Organization and the World Customs Organization. Resolution 1373, by its own

198 See U.N. SCOR, 59th Sess., 4956th Mtg. at 14, U.N. Doc. S/PV.4950 (2004) (This public meeting included statement of the views of all 15 Council members and more than 30 states not members of the Security Council.

terms, drew upon prior standards developed through consensual process; particularly in drafting the provisions of operative paragraph 1 to cut off terrorist financing. These provisions were based on the International Convention for the Suppression of the Financing of Terrorism, adopted by the General Assembly on December 9, 1999,[199] though at the time of the adoption of Security Council resolution 1373 only four states had ratified the Convention and 46 others had signed it.

The normative content of what would be a counterproliferation resolution can be importantly distinguished, though, from Resolutions 1373 and 1540. Resolutions 1373 and 1540 can be analogized to directives in EC law in that they bind member states only to objectives, but leave to those states the substantive means for achieving the stated objectives. This requires large staffs of persons to monitor compliance of such bottom-up implementation. Similarly, bottom-up implementation has become a considerable burden for the implementing committees for the mandates of Resolutions 1373 and 1540, which is especially problematical given the challenge of contending with the devils of diverse national legal systems. By contrast, counterproliferation standards are standards designed to be universally applied as common standards, without substantial variation in implementation in different states, reducing by considerable dimension the tasks and numbers of personnel required for monitoring and supervision.

There is no reason to think the Security Council cannot or will not continue to legislate if there is mutual perception among the members of global threat, urgency, and a commonality of interest that compels action. Terrorism, WMD, and the possible connections between them demonstrate this to be the likely future. The ongoing assumption among the political players, if not all legal scholarship, is as the president of the Security Council stated upon the passage of resolution 1373; that the "Council would be needed more and more to do that kind of legislative work."[200]

There has been relative inactivity of the Security Council as legislator since its adoption of Resolutions 1373, in 2002, and 1540, in 2004. What this indicates is that the Security Council is not inclined to aggressively or frequently assume the role of legislator, and that such role is reserved for matters of great urgency and consequence. There is evident concern among the members of the Security Council not to tred beyond measures that can find support in a broad if not universal consensus of the member states of the United Nations. In other words, there is an effort to maximize legitimacy through consensual process notwithstanding dependency on the mandatory character of Security Council action under Chapter VII. This is indicated not only

---

199 GA Res. 54/109, annex (Dec. 9, 1999), 39 ILM 270 (2000). *See also*, the 1994 Declaration on Measures to Eliminate International Terrorism and the 1996 Declaration to Supplement the 1994 Declaration on Measures to Eliminate International Terrorism, adopted by General Assembly Resolutions 49/60 of December 9, 1994, and 51/210 of December 17, 1996, to which they are annexed. The General Assembly reaffirmed these resolutions in GA Res. 55/158, para. 9 (Dec. 12, 2000).

200 "Press Briefing," United Nations, *Press Conference by Security Council President*, Apr. 2, 2004, at http://www.un.org/News/briefings/docs/2004/pleugerpc.DOC.htm.

by the bottom-up approach undertaken for Resolutions 1373 and 1540, leaving the specific legal implementation of general objectives to the governments of states, but in the selection of measures. It is notable, for example, that the Security Council did not include in Resolution 1373 certain provisions of the Convention for the Suppression of the Financing of Terrorism, such as those relating to prosecution or extradition of offenders. There are other examples of such restraint by the Security Council resisting proposed legislative action in deference to consensual process. For example, the Security Council resisted proposed action to counter attacks on UN personnel and left that work to the General Assembly's Legal Committee,[201] which work became the UN Convention on the Safety of UN and Associated Personnel.[202] What we see is that the Security Council as legislator choses carefully to enlist only those provisions for which it can anticipate general cooperation in implementation, and generally shared perception of pre-eminent importance and urgency. This practice is designed to secure legitimacy even in the context of movement from consensual to mandatory measures. Counterproliferation of nuclear weapons is already and undeniably identified as a subject of pre-eminent importance for which there is a relatively highly developed level of international cooperation. Counterproliferation consequently affords the greatest potential for a legislative Security Council resolution to truly serve the maintenance of international peace and security.

B. Counterproliferation Beyond Current Legislation

In addressing the critical real world concern—whether Security Council action by way of a counterproliferation mandate can actually improve international security—it is important to see that it is an overstatement to characterize as legislation the functional transition the Security Council realized in Resolutions 1373 and 1540. Though Resolutions 1373 and 1540 are legislative in articulating general mandates for all states, the resolutions are not legislative of any specific laws or guidelines.[203] The mandate is

201 *See* Rosand, *The Security Council as "Global Legislator,"* supra note 124, at 580–581, concerning the Council's deference to the General Assembly's Legal Committee to develop the UN Convention on the Safety of UN and Associated Personnel when pressed to define attacks on UN personnel as crimes, and require all states to prosecute or extradite the perpetrators of such attacks. Similarly, Rosand notes that in drafting Resolution 1373, the Security Council avoided addressing issues on which there was little or no international consensus, such as the definition of terrorism, thus allowing each state to employ its own definition. *Id.*

202 UN General Assembly, *U.N. Convention on the Safety of U.N. and Associated Personnel*, Dec. 9, 1994, http://www.un.org/law/cod/safety.htm.

203 The level of generality is apparent in operative paragraph 2(a) of Resolution 1373, which provides "all States shall: Refrain from providing any form of support, active or passive, to entities or persons involved in terrorist acts, including by suppressing recruitment of members of terrorist groups and eliminating the supply of weapons to terrorists." S.C. Res. 1373, *supra* note 124, at 2(a) U.N. Doc. S/RES/1373 (Sept. 28, 2001); Resolution 1540 similarly provides in its operative paragraph 1 that "all states shall refrain from providing any form of support to non-State actors that attempt to develop, acquire, manufacture, possess, transport, transfer or use nuclear, chemical or biological weapons and their means of delivery." S.C. Res. 1540, *supra* note 124 1.

for all states to "adopt and enforce appropriate effective laws." Resolution 1373 requires all states to criminalize terrorist funding, and any other form of support or safe haven for terrorists or their supporters. Resolution 1540, in operative paragraph 3, provides a short generalized list of areas of concern identifying the modalities for "appropriate effective" laws to be realized. These include measures to account for and secure WMD materials, border controls, export and transshipment controls, and end user and financial controls.[204] But neither resolution indicates what the rules should be, nor even any guidelines for specific legislation. There is no top-down provision of rules, nor any top-down process for their articulation. A host of specific guidelines and available regulations for achieving counterproliferation have in fact already been articulated at the international level, principally through the work of the IAEA. But there is no mandate to implement any one of these. Most notably, there is no mandate for all states to adopt or implement such legal instruments as the IAEA's Additional Protocol expanding inspection of nuclear activity sites, despite its adoption by many states, both nuclear and non-nuclear. Resolutions 1373 and 1540 quite clearly bow before national discretion, following in the tradition of the NPT, thus marking only a partial evolution beyond the purely consensual nature of the NPT regime.[205]

Resolution 1540 also falls short in addressing nuclear risk. It speaks to the relationship between terrorism and weapons of mass destruction, but is devoid of any distinction between nuclear, chemical, and biological threats, whether in relation to terrorism, or in any other respect. This is despite the profoundly greater magnitude of nuclear weapons risk. More to the point of achieving effective nuclear counterproliferation, it evidences no recognition that nuclear WMD threat presents a very different set of challenges than other WMD, in virtually every respect.[206] It does not distinguish the scale and growth of the nuclear threat, how it is created, its transit from creation to target, and the means for counterproliferation, dictated by the nature of nuclear technology, nor does it address the nuclear fuel cycle, and means of preventing or interdicting transit to target. Casting nuclear together with chemical and biological threats, as Resolution 1540 does, only muddles the picture and is accordingly counterproductive for actual implementation.

As to international standards and enforcement, there is next to nothing stated. Resolution 1540 only reiterates the Security Council's prerogative to take action on a

---

204 S.C. Res. 1540, *supra* note 124 at 3.

205 Resolutions 1373 and 1540 do indicate a common legal format for the relationship between the United Nations Security Council and national legislation. First, the Security Council "calls upon" states to take particular actions "in accordance with their national legal authorities and legislation and consistent with international law." *Id.* 3(c). Second is the declaration that the Security Council will "monitor closely the implementation" of the resolution. *Id.* 11. Third, the Security Council declares its decision to "remain seized of the matter," opening the door to escalation of its action under Chapter VII. *Id.* 12. Fourth, each resolution provides for the creation of a subsidiary committee to monitor and help implement the resolution's mandate by serving as liaison between states that require assistance in carrying out the mandate, and those willing to provide it. *Id.* 7. *See also* S.C. Res. 1373, *supra* note 124, 6.

206 See discussion of the confusion engendered by the use of the term WMD to cover a variety of threats in, Christopher F. Chyba, *Toward Biological Security*, 81 FOREIGN AFFAIRS, 123–127 (May/June 2002).

matter of proliferation concern. Insofar as Resolution 1540 addresses states as proliferators, it goes no further than imposing the obligation on states to take action under their national laws to prevent trafficking in nuclear, chemical, or biological weapons, their means of delivery, and related materials.[207]

The reliance of Resolutions 1373 and 1540 on national legislation, such as financial controls and export controls, is a matter of preaching to the converted. The states cooperating in counterproliferation will most rigorously legislate, and those resisting will most rigorously refuse. Without the international mandate, perhaps some governments would ignore counterproliferation that can be accomplished through national legislation. However, with the only standards mandated being as formulated and implemented under national law, it can be anticipated, as now, that counterproliferation action will occur least where it is needed most.

Furthermore, Resolution 1540 did not target states as proliferators. It addressed state proliferation, only indirectly, prohibiting the aiding or abetting of non-state actors. Surely the passage of the resolution was facilitated by designing it this way. The Security Council was able more easily to assume a legislative role by confining the mandated obligations to terrorism and weapons of mass destruction, and avoiding the NPT's nexus of counterproliferation and disarmament, that targeting states more directly as proliferators would have provoked. It avoided the threat the Chinese government and others already perceived in the targeting of states implicit in the U.S. initiated Proliferation Security Initiative.[208] The Security Council did so simply by shifting the focus to non-state actors.

Similarly, when it came to monitoring and compliance, Resolutions 1373 and 1540 avoided targeting states. The Security Council established a 1373 Committee and 1540 Committee to accept compliance reports from member states, and assist implementation. As the 1540 Committee mechanism now operates, it provides a number of functions to that end.[209] However, it depends wholly on national discretion. Resolution 1540 instructs bottom-up reporting from each government, which includes reports made directly to the 1540 Committee and, additionally, information made available by governments, such as by way of official websites or in international fora. It is essentially, however, a process of self-reporting. The language of Resolution 1540, in regard to

---

207 S.C. Res. 1540, *supra* note 124, 1–3.

208 *See infra*, pages 199, 202.

209 The 1540 Committee assists member states in generating the reports the resolution requires by holding workshops, sponsoring outreach events, serving as a clearing house to pair up states needing assistance with more sophisticated states or other organizations such as the IAEA and Organization for the Prohibition of Chemical Weapons (OPCW), and also by offering technical assistance in drafting reports and in submitting requests for assistance. It collects reports submitted by member states and collates the data from those reports into a spreadsheet known as a 1540 Matrix that reflects a state's efforts and progress in complying with the resolution's requirements. The data from those spreadsheets is then used to generate a report for the Security Council summing up global state-level efforts to prevent the proliferation of nuclear, chemical, and biological weapons and material. It also maintains a database of state-level legislation enacted in accordance with the resolution based on the reports it has received.

reporting, is not mandatory. The Security Council simply "calls upon" states to comply.[210] The same nonmandatory "calls upon" preface appears even more importantly in operative paragraph 10 of 1540, which addresses states taking action to prevent WMD trafficking. The essential dependency on the consensual regime is thus again reiterated.[211]

The problems with Resolution 1540 monitoring were quickly evident, beginning with the fact that only one-third of all states submitted reports by the stipulated deadline: some were only a few pages while others were long. It also became apparent, as the reports began to accumulate, that they lacked coherence. The 1540 Committee quickly sought to address the problem by developing a matrix of relevant information that is now in place for each state. However, extreme variation in reporting and implementation remains characteristic of the system. The explanation given by some governments for the relative shortfall of their response was their lack of any nuclear weapons technology or materials. The United States criticized the latter view for ignoring the reality that proliferation occurs through front companies and false end-use destinations listed in export transactions, and because shipments are routed through countries with weak trade regulations, none of which can be tracked without the fullest cooperation of states ostensibly unconnected to nuclear facilities.[212]

It was no doubt to be expected that reporting and implementation would vary, given the variance among national legal systems, and the variance of national nuclear activity and trade. But the more fundamental problem is that there are no specific standards mandated for universal implementation. All that is internationally designated are the general areas for implementation referenced in operative paragraph 3 of Resolution 1540. Because there are no mandated controls, there is no meaningful measure of the effectiveness of national legislation supposed to carry out the Resolution 1540 mandate. Since the reporting system is consensual, there is also no means of enforcement, even the enforcement of monitoring. The committee's role is, in fact, truncated and not fit within any power or process for ensuring compliance. The committee itself has made clear that it, "does not investigate or prosecute alleged violations of non-proliferation obligations."[213]

Under this arrangement, there is no reason for confidence that states will accurately report their activities. As with all aspects of the current consensual regime, this is especially so of the states of proliferation concern, where nuclear activities, transfers, and transactions are most likely to be inconsistent with the mandate of Resolution 1540. There is a corresponding absence of any method of verification of the accuracy or

---

210 S.C. Res. 1540, *supra*, note 124, 4, 6.

211 Resolution 1540 simply declares that the members of the Security Council note "the importance for all States parties to these treaties to implement them fully in order to promote international stability." *Id.* preamble.

212 *See* Wade Boese, *U.S. Disappointed With Worldwide Response to WMD Resolution*, Vol. 34 ARMS CONTROL TODAY (Dec. 2004), http://www.armscontrol.org/act/2004_12/WMDResolution.

213 *Frequently Asked Questions on UNSC Resolution 1540*, 1540 COMMITTEE: SECURITY COUNCIL COMMITTEE ESTABLISHED PURSUANT TO RESOLUTION 1540 (2004) (last visited Nov. 27, 2011), http:/www.un.org/sc/1540/faq.shtml#7 (1540 FAQ).

completeness of the data reported, other than what can be deduced by the experts now employed to support the committee's work.

Presumably the information gathered by the 1540 Committee could be collated with other sources of information such as the IAEA or national intelligence agencies, but there is no mandate to do so. No external audit is provided, nor any other analysis to be conducted at the behest of an international agency. The quality, depth, and comprehensiveness of reports vary widely from state to state. Not surprisingly, of states with nuclear production facilities, the states that are of the least proliferation concern in relation to the illicit transfer of nuclear weapons-related material or technology tend to provide the most comprehensive reports. The states of greatest concern submit the least comprehensive reports, if any.

Despite best efforts, the 1540 Committee has presided over reporting that is uneven and suffers from incoherence no doubt attributable, not only to varying inclinations of governments to cooperate, but also to the lack of a mandate for international standards. For reporting and monitoring, it is especially significant that Resolution 1540 does not identify or impose any specific measures, or an international mechanism for articulating uniform measures for all states. The statement of general areas for standards in operative paragraph 3 of Resolution 1540 is not sufficient to generate coherence of standards, other than what might be accomplished through guidance by the 1540 Committee, subject to each state's voluntary adoption. At the extremes of the variable adoptions, what is illegal in one state may be legal in another, notwithstanding that WMD proliferation is a first priority security concern for all responsible governments, presenting similar challenges for containment wherever it may occur.

This is not to deny that utility for counterproliferation can result from consensual pursuit of the objectives recited in Resolutions 1373 and 1540, and the empowerment of expert resources, which are now provided. But in the final analysis, notwithstanding Security Council resolutions in the nature of "global legislation" under Chapter VII, there is no reliable engine for global compliance with uniform standards. Indeed, during the debates concerning Resolutions 1373 and 1540, some states voiced the fear that the passage of those resolutions, being under Chapter VII, would be seen as available for controversial claims of enforcement authorization, as had been the experience with "no-fly" zones in Iraq to protect the Kurdish population and the George W. Bush Administration's claimed legal authorization for the invasion of Iraq.[214] Several

214 The debate over the adoption of Resolution 1540 included expressions of concern by several states that the resolution would be used as a means to institute sanctions against states, being forced to implement certain measures. Resolution 1343 had stated that the Security Council was determined to "take the necessary measures" to accomplish its implementation, raising the specter of interpretation that might be the basis for similarly proactive interpretation. Resolution 1540, in contrast, made explicit that any enforcement action would require a separate Security Council resolution, and a number of prominent delegations, including that of the United States, assured the membership that the resolution did not carry with it enforcement. *See*, e.g., Statement by James Cunningham, Deputy Permanent Representative of the United States, to the United Nations, U.N. SCOR, 59th Sess., 4950th mtg. at 17, U.N. Doc. S/PV.4950 (2004) (declaring that "the draft resolution is not about enforcement.").

states expressed concern that Resolution 1540 would be used as a means to institute sanctions against states, to force them to implement certain measures. The response to this concern, and pragmatically to the variation of national systems supposed to implement counterproliferation, was to declare that implementation was entirely a matter of national discretion. The British delegate, for example, stated that "the draft [of Resolution 1540] was not about coercion or enforcement .... [T]he draft did not authorize enforcement action against State or non-state actors in the territory of another country. Any enforcement action would likely require new Security Council measures."[215] Accordingly, the resolution instructs but does not compel states to implement nuclear security. Presumably an egregious violation of Resolution 1540's general mandate would enhance the legal basis for the initiation of action by way of sanctions or the application of force by the Security Council. However, implementation and its monitoring, so far as the express terms of the resolution go, are limited to national law.[216] Thus despite its universal mandate of state responsibility, Resolution 1540 failed to achieve universality as to what matters most—universal implementation of uniform standards that can secure high quality counterproliferation.

Nevertheless, despite all the real differences from legislation, Resolutions 1373 and 1540 did open the door to internationally mandated protection of nuclear material. Physical protection of nuclear material within any state before Resolution 1540 was always addressed under international agreement, subject therefore to the complete discretion of national government. Thus even though the 1980 Convention on Physical Protection of Nuclear Material (CPPNM) and its 2005 amendment require international standards for the transport of nuclear material from one country to another, standards under the convention concerning physical protection of nuclear material once located within a state, are left essentially a matter of national choice. There is a certain irony about the discretion allowed. Thus, the 2005 amendment to the convention states that physical protection required "should be based on the state's current evaluation of the threat."[217] This may be sound in reference to design basis threat assessment, which can adjust to the particularity of different particular facilities. However, more generally the state for which mandated requirements are most needed, surely, is the state with an inadequate national perception of the threat, which explains why there is inadequate protection of its nuclear material in the first place.

Notwithstanding that Resolution 1540 does not address states as perpetrators of proliferation, and does not require the implementation of international standards, it is unique and evolutionary as an international mandate. It indicates progress towards international implementation of uniform standards. Consistent with this new

215 Press Release, Security Council, Speakers in Security Council Debate on Weapons of Mass Destruction; Express Doubts Over Content of Proposed Nonproliferation Text, U.N. Doc. SC/8070 (Apr. 22, 2004).

216 S.C. Res. 1540, *supra* note 124, §4.

217 IAEA, *Nuclear Security—Measures to Protect Against Nuclear Terrorism Amendment to the Convention on the Physical Protection of Nuclear Material*, IAEA Doc. Gov/INF/2005/10-G(49)/INF/6 (Sept. 6, 2005) (http://www.iaea.org/About/Policy/GC/GC49/Documents/gc49inf-6.pdf).

direction, the 1540 Committee has asked the IAEA to advise on physical protection measures, in reference to aiding states to improve physical protections. More generally of note is that the Security Council is charged with enforcement of Resolution 1540's requirements on noncompliant states, including the requirement of "appropriate effective" physical protection of nuclear material. The IAEA is naturally positioned to articulate what that means as the content of an international counterproliferation mandate. Without baseline definition of "appropriate effective" requirements, and the requisite inspection capacity to check their implementation, the mandate is likely still to be rendered least effective where it matters most. But it is some movement in the right direction. Though Resolution 1540 as a counterproliferation mandate suffers the limitation of being targeted directly at non-state actors, not states, it does achieve an important advance by placing legal obligation concerning weapons of mass destruction squarely within the action authority of Chapter VII of the United Nations Charter. Presumably, after Resolution 1540, just as before it, any state providing support or sanctuary to non-state actors in their pursuit of weapons of mass destruction, could be sanctioned if the IAEA brings to the attention of the Security Council suspected violation of safeguards agreements. But since enactment, implementation, and the reporting of "appropriate effective" counterproliferation measures under Resolution 1540 are exclusively a matter for national legislation and national law enforcement, that ultimately brings the entire structure back to a legal regime, very much akin to what we have now under the NPT, whereby any measures depend wholly on negotiation with the different state signatories. In sum and at best, then, though Resolution 1540 opens the door to a mandatory system, it leaves counterproliferation a hybrid and compromised endeavor.

C. Universal Standards

1. NUCLEAR SECURITY AS AN INDEPENDENT INTERNATIONAL INTEREST

To assess the potential of legislative Security Council action for empowering counterproliferation, it is necessary to see how its legal, practical, and political components could best be developed. For its legal component, a counterproliferation resolution going forward would necessarily begin with the premise that proliferation of nuclear weapons is a threat to international peace and security. This would be to place it firmly within the mandatory framework of Chapter VII of the United Nations Charter. The linkage between Chapter VII and counterproliferation is already well established. It was declared as early as 1992, on behalf of the Security Council, that "(t)he proliferation of all weapons of mass destruction constitutes a threat to international peace and security." and that the members "commit themselves to working to prevent the spread of technology related to the research for or production of such weapons and to take appropriate action to that end."[218] Since 1992, the Security Council has further

218 Note by President of the Security Council, UN Doc. S/23500, at 4 (Jan. 31,1992), http://daccess-dds-ny.un.org/doc/UNDOC/GEN/N92/043/34/PDF/N92/043/34/PDF/N9204334.pdf?OpenElement

additionally classified a variety of situations relating to weapons of mass destruction and their means of delivery as constituting a "threat to the peace."[219] But there is today still no clear and comprehensive affirmation of Chapter VII as the means for nuclear counterproliferation management, notwithstanding the beginning constituted by Resolutions 1373 and 1540.

A Security Council Resolution under Chapter VII, to address counterproliferation management, would have to more directly target states than did Resolutions 1373 and 1540. More resistance, accordingly, can be expected. However, the targeting of states, along with non-state actors, within a mandatory counterproliferation regime, would be well supported by established international law. A particularly relevant principle from international law would be, for example, the so-called Trail Smelter Principle, originated in the international arbitration of the same name.[220] That principle declares that states are legally responsible for harm caused to other states.[221] Further, it is understood to establish a duty of prevention, whereby states are obligated to prevent extraterritorial harm they might generate. The Trail Smelter Principle, including this duty of prevention, has become a principle of more general application than its origin and principal development in environmental law, given its reiteration without significant opposition in numerous international conventions and fora.[222] Most significantly for

---

219 *See* "Statement by the President of the Security Council," United Nations Security Council, *S/PRST/1996/17*, para. 4, Apr. 12, 1996, http://www.un.org/ga/search/view_doc.asp?symbol=S/PRST/ 1996/17. *See also* "Statement by the President of the Security Council," United Nations Security Council, *S/PRST/1998/12*, para. 4, May 14, 1998, http://daccessods.un.org/access.nsf/Get?Open&DS=S/PRST/1998/12&Lang=E&Area=UNDOC. *And also* S.C. Res. 1172, U.N. Doc. S/RES/1172 (June 6, 1998), http://www.undemocracy.com/S-RES-1172(1998).pdf.

220 Trail Smelter Arbitration (*U.S. v. Can*), 3 R.I.A.A. 1905 (1938).

221 For an analysis of the Trail Smelter Principle's influence on the International Law Commission's 2001 adoption of *Draft Articles on the Responsibility of States for Internationally Wrongful Acts, see* Mark A. Drumbl, *Trail Smelter and the International Law Commission's Work on State Responsibility for Internationally Wrongful Acts and State Liability*, WASHINGTON & LEE LAW RESEARCH PAPER NO. 03-06 (May 2003).

222 The Trail Smelter proposition is today consistently affirmed in international law, as not only establishing compensation liability for harm done, but also the duty to prevent harm. The principle arose and was first developed in the arena of environmental law. The 1972 UN Conference on the Human Environment, also known as the Stockholm Conference, formally adopted the no-harm principle of Trail Smelter. *See* United Nations, Report on the United Nations Conference on the Human Environment, A/CONF.48/14/REV.1, DECLARATION OF THE UNITED NATIONS CONFERENCE ON THE HUMAN ENVIRONMENT (June 16, 1972), http://www.un-documents.net/unchedec.htm. The Trail Smelter ruling was also followed in the 1992 UN Conference on Environment and Development under Principle 2 of the Rio Declaration. *See* United Nations, Report of the United Nations Conference on Environment and Development, A/CONF.151/5/REV.1, REPORT OF THE UNITED NATIONS CONFERENCE ON ENVIRONMENT AND DEVELOPMENT (June 14, 1992), http://www.un.org/documents/ga/conf151/aconf15126-4.htm. The no-harm rule can be found in Article 194(2) of the 1982 UN Law of the Sea Convention and in the Preamble of the 1992 UN Framework Convention on Climate Change. *See* S. Treaty Doc No. 102–38, 1771 U.N.T.S. 107, UNITED NATIONS FRAMEWORK CONVENTION ON CLIMATE CHANGE, (May 9, 1992), http://www.unfccc.int/resource/docs/convkp/conveng.pdf. The International Court of Justice has confirmed the Trail Smelter principle. *Gabcikovo Nagymaros Project (Hung. v. Slovk.)*, 1997 I.C.J. 7, (Sept. 25), para 53.

counterproliferation, the International Court of Justice, in its 1996 Advisory Opinion on the Legality of the Threat or use of Nuclear Weapons, acknowledges the principle in relation to possession of nuclear weapons technology and material.[223] Further, in 2006, the International Law Commission (ILC), in adopting the Draft Principles on the Allocation of Loss in the Case of Transboundary Harm Arising out of Hazardous Activities, characterized nuclear technology as "ultra hazardous" and therefore the "subject of special regulation."[224] The varied attention to the Trail Smelter Principle in connection with nuclear security, supports the proposition that every state has the legal responsibility to secure its nuclear material and technology, and to prevent its territory from being used for activity that would cause harm to other states. A counterproliferation resolution under Chapter VII of the United Nations Charter would capitalize on this development, by mandating the basis for its implementation.

Besides compatibility with international principle, it is important that a counterproliferation resolution not conflict with, or alter the rights and obligations of the parties to the NPT, the status of related conventions and agreements, or diminish the responsibilities of the IAEA. It can be anticipated resistance will be based on questions of such compatibility, and it can be expected there will be the usual charge that any progress on counterproliferation must depend upon progress on nuclear disarmament. But notwithstanding reiteration of the false nexus drawn from the NPT, a broad counterproliferation resolution can be justified on its own terms and need not be put forward as a rejection of the NPT or any related counterproliferation infrastructure. That transition to a mandatory regime can be accomplished without clash with the NPT promise of nuclear disarmament was already confirmed in the negotiation of Resolution 1540 that resulted in its referencing affirmatively the core deal of the NPT. The Security Council declared, in the preamble to Resolution 1540, "the need for all Member States to fulfill their obligations in relation to arms control and disarmament and to prevent proliferation in all its aspects of all weapons of mass destruction."[225] A nuclear counterproliferation resolution could repeat the same injunction. Over time, infrastructure reconstructed on the new foundation would supplant the established consent-based architecture with safeguards and inspection protocols more congruent with the new mandatory regime. But this should not require any sacrifice of counterproliferation progress that has already been achieved.

---

223 The International Court of Justice, in its advisory opinion on the legality of the threat or use of nuclear weapons, acknowledged that "the existence of the general obligation of states to ensure that activities within their jurisdiction or control respect the environment of other states is now part of the corpus of international law relating to the environment." *Advisory Opinion on the Legality of the Threat or Use of Nuclear Weapons, I.C.J. 1996*, at para. 29, http://www.icj-cij.org/docket/files/95/7495.pdf.

224 This was despite the ILC declining to list activities likely to produce transboundary harm. See International Law Commission, DRAFT PRINCIPLES ON THE ALLOCATION OF LOSS IN THE CASE OF TRANSBOUNDARY HARM ARISING OUT OF HAZARDOUS ACTIVITIES 9 (2006). http://untreaty.un.org/ilc/texts/instruments/english/draft%20articles/9_10_2006.pdf

225 S.C. Res. 1540, *supra* note 124.

What a counterproliferation resolution would make much more likely is a better integration of counterproliferation architecture. Counterproliferation is commonly characterized as being "multilayered," that is, composed of a variety of international and national regulatory mechanisms and capabilities. These include aspects such as safeguards, inspection protocols, export-import controls, monitoring, and policing for interdiction, nuclear forensics, and intelligence resources. But there is a synergistic character to the counterproliferation enterprise. Effective interdiction requires meaningful substantive definition of what transfers are illegal, and that is the task for export-import control. Both interdiction and export-import regulation are dependent on the quality of intelligence, and the coordination and cooperation of national intelligence agencies. Intelligence resources depend on technical capacities, such as satellite surveillance, and the work of nuclear forensics scientists. Bringing this all together, and more, as one coherent legal mandate under Chapter VII of the Charter is, accordingly, the logical and practical formulation for a more robust nuclear counterproliferation capability.

A counterproliferation resolution that constitutes a reinvigoration of counterproliferation must be designed, most importantly, as making mandatory, international standards of counterproliferation. In this respect, it would be a major advance over the limitation of Resolutions 1373 and 1540 to prescription by way of diverse national laws. Standards for effective counterproliferation are presently a toolkit for counterproliferation that could and should be employed globally on a uniform basis. They are the known standards to which most states already subscribe.[226] This would substantially reduce or eliminate the need to negotiate specific monitoring and regulatory capacity on a state-by-state basis. It would avoid the erratic and uneven reporting, quantitative and qualitative, that occurs under the current mechanisms of Resolutions 1373 and 1540, which simply require states to report what they are doing under their own national legislation to fulfill the resolutions' mandates.[227] It would serve uniformity and thereby facilitate both the reporting and measuring of actual compliance. The implementation of counterproliferation through national laws that was envisioned in Resolutions 1373 and 1540 is inevitably multifarious given the many and different legal systems and legislatures involved. But for the most important aspects of counterproliferation, there is a well-established resource of rules that can be globally applied.

The IAEA currently attempts to achieve uniformity and universal application through the issuance of general guidelines, model safeguards agreements, and inspection protocols; and the negotiation of their adoption and implementation with any government with nuclear activities. The guidelines, safeguards agreements, and protocols

---

226 *See infra*, pages 105–109.

227 *See*, e.g., Boese, *supra* note 212 (detailing the U.S. disappointment over the failure of 120 countries to comply with Resolution 1540's reporting requirements). For example, as to the initial requests for information under Resolution 1540, only about one-third of UN members replied with the request to detail their efforts to prevent non-state actors from acquiring or developing WMD, with the substance of the submissions varying widely.

allow the IAEA the means to verify that a state is fulfilling its NPT non-proliferation obligation.[228] According to the former IAEA Director-General Mohamed ElBaradei, the safeguards system has three main functions: it operates as a "confidence-building measure, an early warning mechanism, and the trigger that sets in motion other responses by the international community if and when the need arises."[229] The NPT does look to the application of international standards in requiring the party governments each to implement comprehensive safeguard agreements. Article III of the NPT provides that all non-nuclear-weapon states must "accept safeguards, as set forth in an agreement to be negotiated and concluded with the IAEA, for the exclusive purpose of verification of the fulfillment of its obligations assumed under [the NPT]. . . . "[230] And the IAEA's stated purpose is universal—to "accelerate and enlarge atomic energy's contribution to world peace, health, and prosperity throughout the world," and ensure that atomic energy is not used for military purposes.[231] According to former Director-General ElBaradei, adherence by as many states as possible to the strengthened safeguards system is a crucial component of this endeavor.[232] Also, the United Nations General Assembly, the NPT Review Conference, and the IAEA General Conference have made repeated calls for universal application.[233] Global non-proliferation initiatives have also identified universal compliance with the comprehensive safeguard agreement and the model additional protocols as essential.[234]

However, with adoption remaining at the discretion of governments under the NPT regime, any government seeking to avoid transparency and engage in proliferation currently can reject or qualify any safeguard or any other international guideline. Of the 185 non-nuclear-weapon states parties to the NPT, 15 have yet to bring into force a comprehensive safeguards agreement.[235] There is still significant non-adoption of the Additional Protocol and comprehensive safeguards agreements. Without having the Additional Protocol in force for any state, the IAEA is disabled from detecting illicit activity for that state.[236] As of the IAEA Safeguards Statement for 2010, only 99 States had both comprehensive safeguards agreements and the Additional Protocol in force.[237] This is of particular concern, as 28 of the non-complying states are engaged in

---

228 *See* IAEA, *IAEA Safeguards Overview: Comprehensive Safeguard Agreements and Additional Protocols*, (last accessed Dec. 30, 2011), http://www.iaea.org/Publications/Factsheets/English/sg_overview.html.

229 *See* IAEA, *Nonproliferation of Nuclear Weapons & Nuclear Security: IAEA Safeguards Agreements and Additional Protocols*, IAEA.ORG (May 2005), http://www.iaea.org/Publications/Booklets/nuke.pdf.

230 Treaty on the Nonproliferation of Nuclear Weapons art. III, *supra* note 11.

231 Statute of the IAEA art. II, Oct. 23, 1956, 8 U.S.T. 1039, 276 U.N.T.S. 3.

232 *See* IAEA, *Non-Proliferation of Nuclear Weapons & Nuclear Security: IAEA Safeguards Agreements and Additional Protocols*, *supra* note 229.

233 *Id.*

234 *See* IAEA, *NPT Comprehensive Safeguards Agreement: Overview of Status*, IAEA.ORG (last accessed Dec. 30, 2011), http://www.iaea.org/Publications/Factsheets/English/nptstatus_overview.html.

235 *Id.*

236 *Id.*

237 *See* IAEA, *Safeguards Statement for 2010 and Background to the Safeguards Statement*, IAEA (last accessed Sept. 20, 2011), http://www.iaea.org/OurWork/SV/Safeguards/es/es2010.html.

significant nuclear activities, and their number includes such significant nuclear players as Argentina, Brazil, Egypt, North Korea, Syria, and Iran.

Under the current system, the IAEA is limited to different degree depending on state-by-state consent. At the extreme, are the outliers to the NPT, Israel, India, and Pakistan, not bound by the NPT but only through other agreements. The signatories to the NPT and the IAEA have called upon the three to accede to the treaty "without any conditions, and to bring into force the required comprehensive safeguards agreements and additional protocols consistent with the model additional protocol."[238] This call, we know, has not been answered. Then there are the states that are signatories to the NPT, but refuse to sign comprehensive safeguards agreements or agree to inspection protocols, and instead agree only to specific-item safeguards or inspection. The specific-item agreements are more restrictive, essentially preventing the IAEA from assuring adherence to comprehensive non-proliferation standards. Finally, it is a truism that the IAEA has no direct information where states simply refuse inspections or safeguards, as North Korea and Iran have done.

A counterproliferation resolution that included the mandate for all states to employ the measures adopted by the board of the IAEA as appropriate for uniform international adoption would cast all these refusals and qualifications in a different light. The board would designate as mandatory those measures that are currently the subject of guidelines and model protocols precisely because they are significant for nuclear security and not subject to reasonable objection. For example, the Additional Protocol, which has been implemented in many states and extends IAEA inspection authority to undeclared nuclear activities, and safeguards model agreements, would be precisely the sort of statements of requirements that would be appropriately mandated as uniform and universal. With a comprehensive counterproliferation resolution in place under Chapter VII, the refusal to comply would no longer be only a matter of withdrawing consent to the NPT. It would place a rejecting government in breach of the resolution and its subsidiary process and standards.

A Security Council Resolution under Chapter VII, sufficiently comprehensive to empower counterproliferation, in contrast to Resolutions 1373 and 1540, would also have to target states directly as subject to enforcement of such obligation. It would put all governments on notice that failure to take the steps universally mandated would trigger the risk of sanctions, and increasingly serious costs as noncompliance continues. It would operate as a warning to governments, not just as to their responsibility to prevent and punish proliferation activities of non-state actors within their jurisdiction, but as to their state responsibility *qua* state, to prevent proliferation or suffer consequences. Would-be proliferators, whether states, companies, or other entities or organizations would be forewarned that discovery of significant and willful proliferation could trigger a collective response, and that if sanctions or domestic criminal law enforcement should be deemed inadequate by the Security Council, force might be

238 *Id. See* United Nations, *supra* note 59.

employed. The actual imposition of sanctions might occur no more than at present, but the threat would be made clear by way of the universally applicable mandate, reducing much of the uncertainty that today surrounds response to continuing violations of counterproliferation commitments. A counterproliferation resolution declaring standards for all states, and referencing Chapter VII for enforcement, would much more certainly establish risk for proliferators, by moving counterproliferation from the realm of the ad hoc and purely political, to the status of a priori legal obligation.

As previously noted, a Security Council resolution declaring proliferation a threat to the peace that triggers Chapter VII would be no more intrusive or offensive to national sovereignty than the mandates the Security Council set forth in Resolutions 1373 and 1540. Indeed, it would be significantly less intrusive. Under Resolutions 1373 and 1540, the Security Council purported to instruct governments to doctor their national laws, including the laws within their national criminal jurisdiction, thus intruding on the most sovereignty sensitive arena of national law. The proposed Security Council mandate would only concern, by contrast, international obligation of states, based on the now unimpeachable proposition that failure of nuclear security is a threat to the security of all states.

That the Security Council has authority to specify what measures are needed under Chapter VII is well established.[239] Thus a "gold standard" of nuclear security, such as has been proposed as the best antidote to nuclear terrorism,[240] could be set as the universal standard, no longer subject to the vagaries and trade-offs of international politics and the hit-or-miss negotiation with each government. Standards uniform and based in international legitimacy also are more likely to be actually meaningfully implemented and monitored than the national law mandates of Resolutions 1373 and 1540. This would avoid the surely perplexing task of monitoring the national laws of the world's great variety of national legal systems, a task with no common standard to measure effectiveness.

Mandatory counterproliferation under a Chapter VII authorization could also serve to strengthen the inspection and verification effectiveness of the IAEA. It would enable uniform mandatory reporting of categories of informational detail and improve rights of inspection. A key problem under the current legal regime has been the lack of completeness of nuclear material declarations by states. Informational access is currently limited to whatever a particular state may have stipulated under its safeguards agreement, or by way of its particularized adoption of the inspection protocols of the IAEA. With all states bound by the same standards, no such limitations would be justified.

---

239 "Article 39 (which provides that the Security Council shall decide what measures shall be taken in accordance with Article 41 to maintain or restore international peace and security) leaves the choice of means and their evaluation to the Security Council, which enjoys wide discretionary powers in this regard; and it could not have been otherwise, as such a choice involves political evaluation of highly complex and dynamic situations." *Prosecutor v. Tadic supra*, note 141, 143.

240 Allison, *supra* note 9.

Moreover, a mandatory regime would allow a single, unified "integrated safeguards" State Evaluation Report (SER) for each state as a whole (as distinct from separate facility reports). This would allow the IAEA to articulate basic standards of completeness designed to achieve the most politically viable balance of disclosure objectives and national security concerns. Any limitation would be only as determined through the multilateral legitimizing consensus of the board of the IAEA, or the Security Council. Within a regime of uniform standards equally applied, there would still be discretion as to verification intensity for different states and the relative risks each presents. Upon persuasive evidence of violation under the standards to be articulated, the state-specific situation would be referred to the Security Council, as is presently the process. However, the denouement would be fundamentally different in that the assessment would be on the basis of uniform standards, not dependent on what may have been negotiated with the targeted state.

Such implementation of peremptory norms on a uniform basis is simply not feasible under the consensual modality of the NPT. Mohamed ElBaradei, former IAEA Director-General, did argue during his tenure that non-proliferation "should be regarded as a 'peremptory norm' of international law—not vulnerable to any nation subsequently withdrawing, based on the whim of a new government or a vote of the latest parliament."[241] But such vulnerability is precisely what the NPT does guarantee under the Article X withdrawal provision. Moreover, there seems to be consensus that the NPT cannot be amended to remove this undermining provision. The International Commission on Weapons of Mass Destruction, while recognizing the retrograde nature of the Article X withdrawal provision, expressed "doubt that it would be either possible or desirable to seek to eliminate the right of withdrawal from the NPT or other WMD treaties."[242] Apparently, any such effort to improve the NPT as a counterproliferation regime will be seen as further discrimination against the non-nuclear weapons states. And the same justification for refusing to amend the NPT is always available to proliferating governments—that permanent members of the Security Council have failed in their principal obligations under the Nuclear Non-proliferation Treaty—the promised transfer of nuclear technology under Articles III and V, and nuclear disarmament under Article VI. The North Korean and Iranian governments have in fact responded to condemnation of their proliferation by claiming precisely this justification.[243] For enforcement within a Chapter VII mandatory regime, by contrast, it would be legally, if not politically irrelevant whether the permanent members have complied with the Grand Bargain of the NPT.

Further, proliferation as a violation triggering Chapter VII would eliminate any basis for the targeted state to demand a *quid pro quo* for turning to the path of

---

241 Mohamed ElBaradei, *Towards a Safer World*, ECONOMIST 66 (Oct. 18, 2003).

242 Weapons of Mass Destruction Commission, final report, *Weapons of Terror: Freeing the World of Nuclear, Biological, and Chemical Arms*, Stockholm, Sweden, June 1, 2006, http://www.blixassociates.com/wp-content/uploads/2011/02/Weapons_of_Terror.pdf.

243 *See* Nazila Fathi & David Sanger, *Bracing for Penalties, Iran Threatens to Withdraw From Nuclear Treaty*, N.Y. TIMES § 1, at 16 (Feb. 12, 2006).

non-proliferation. This is another major dimension of difference between the current treaty regime and the regime here proposed. Both North Korea and Iran have openly admitted that their noncompliance with the NPT was to obtain concessions on other issues.[244] The proposed mandatory regime and its authorizing resolution would make it clear, that in the event of a finding of proliferation, the only subject to be discussed is compliance, not payment for compliance.

For a mandatory regime, just as under the NPT regime, enforcement would remain within the discretion of the Security Council. That is the design of Chapter VII as intended by the framers of the United Nations Charter to reflect the reality of international power upon creation of the Security Council as an institution. The exercise of Security Council discretion, accordingly, always involves a mix of objective fact and legal and political considerations, ultimately realized, if realized at all, through expression of the mutual interests of the members of the Security Council. The stipulation of a priori benchmarks and standards thus cannot dictate particular enforcement. However, stipulation of benchmarks and standards would establish and focus the prohibition for would-be proliferators and inform and focus the Security Council's deliberative process. The Security Council would focus on established criteria,[245] as first applied by the IAEA, and then the Security Council, for determining whether to designate a situation one of nuclear proliferation, and therefore a threat to the peace triggering Chapter VII. That the established criteria cannot dictate the result does not mean that counterproliferation must be relegated to the ad hoc process that has in the past characterized Security Council sanctions.

Accomplishing actual retrenchment in nuclear weapons development will likely require negotiation with the targeted state, as it does today. The Security Council would and should have at its disposal the full range of diplomatic alternatives for countering proliferation. But under the proposed regime, any negotiation would take place unburdened by the claims of legitimacy and justification that, under the current consent-based regime, crucially undermine efforts to quell nuclear weapons development.

Security Council mandated counterproliferation under Chapter VII of the United Nations Charter, in contrast to the NPT, would frame counterproliferation as focused singularly on the global interest in reducing proliferation risk. This was the thrust of Resolutions 1373 and 1540 as "global legislation." These resolutions reflected the change of consciousness, brought about by the interconnected risks of terrorism and weapons of mass destruction, with which counterproliferation now contends. They indicate new opportunity for a much more robust counterproliferation capability worldwide, by centering counterproliferation as an independent objective, worthy in itself,

---

244 Murphy, *supra* note 55.

245 For specific possible benchmarks, though some probably too specific, see the compliance assessments and categories of violation detailed in Michael Moodie & Amy Sands, *New Approaches to Compliance with Arms Control and Nonproliferation Agreements*, 8 THE NONPROLIFERATION REVIEW 1, 1–9 (Spring, 2001), http://cns.miis.edu/npr/pdfs/intro81.pdf (describing possible benchmarks).

notwithstanding the NPT or the division between nuclear weapons and non-nuclear weapons states. These resolutions shifted the focus from inequality in the possession of nuclear weapons to the shared interest of the international community in countering proliferation. That interest can now be capitalized.

Under a broad Security Council counterproliferation mandate, the actual work of counterproliferation would be, as it is now, adapted to different state nuclear facilities, and anticipation of risk through design basis threat analysis for each particular facility. But it would be operating, particularly as to "states of proliferation concern" on the same basis as for all other states, applying common standards and best practices. This would include physical security and accounting and measurement of materials, personnel screening, and reporting and monitoring of facilities through inspection protocols. There would be international authority equally intrusive as to all states, and uniform standards of safety, security, and safeguards. No longer would the agenda of the IAEA be fractionated according to what each particular government might be willing to negotiate.

A mandatory regime of uniform standards uniformly applied would also help diminish the negative impact on global counterproliferation, of asymmetry in the possession of nuclear weapons. To the extent that the nuclear facilities of all states, both nuclear weapons states and non-nuclear weapons states, are subject to the same international regulation under the same requirements and management, the legitimacy gap is reduced. And it cannot and should not be ignored that much of the proliferation that has occurred involves nuclear weapons states. Some of the most significant proliferation has involved principal members of the nuclear weapons club. The governments of Russia, China, Israel, Pakistan, and even Canada, have all been named as witting or unwitting proliferators on the supply side of proliferation. The extensive spread of nuclear material and technology that occurred under early "peaceful use" programs, such as the Atoms for Peace Program of the United States, also in light of dual-use, can now be seen as having supported proliferation. The nuclear weapons states must be bound to the same standards as the non-nuclear weapons states, so long as within reasonable "national security" limitations as now do exist as to weapons related facilities.[246] To the extent of such national security limitations, asymmetry remains a problem. But a great measure of the nuclear activity that presents proliferation risk, such as enrichment and reprocessing facilities, could be subject to the same international regulation, notwithstanding the national security limitations imposed by nuclear weapons states.

---

246 *See* Eva C. Uribe, M. Analisa Sandoval, Marisa N. Sandoval, Brian D. Boyer, & Rosalyn M. Leitch, *A Comparison of the Additional Protocols of the Five Nuclear Weapon States and the Ensuing Safeguards Benefits to International Nonproliferation Efforts*, INMM 50th Annual Meeting (July 12–16, 2009), http://permalink.lanl.gov/object/tr?what=info:lanl-repo/lareport/LA-UR-09-04012. *See also, infra* note 297.

II. NO CLASSIFICATION OF STATES

Legitimacy surely would require acceptance beyond the permanent membership of the Security Council. Any further global legislation by the Security Council to build counterproliferation capability must, if it is to be effective, receive at least the tacit endorsement of the greater international community. Legitimacy is what propels compliance. For legitimacy, it is necessary that the principles of equality and non-discrimination be furthered to the greatest extent feasible. That would be one dynamic and measure, among the most important, of counterproliferation effectiveness.

There is, however, a strong dynamic contrary to furthering the equality of application that generates legitimacy. Discrimination among states in the spread of nuclear weapons related technology and materials has become a hallmark of counterproliferation policy, particularly for the United States. This occurs through various classifications of states as good or bad for proliferation; most notoriously through the George W. Bush Administration's "axis of evil" designation. The states in the "axis of evil", North Korea, Sadam's Iraq and Iran are of course deemed to be the bad. A democracy such as India, is deemed to be the good.

a. Proliferation to 'Democratic' States

The U.S. agreement with India, especially, belied the Grand Bargain of the NPT. The agreement was done apparently without any consultation with any relevant international organization, or even any other states. After the fact, the United States did obtain, through pressure, the approval of the membership of the Nuclear Suppliers Group, which only accentuated the exceptionalism of the deal.[247]

The authorizing legislation approved by the United States Congress for the US-India deal, the Henry J. Hyde United States-India Peaceful Atomic Energy Cooperation Act of 2006,[248] equips India with the ability to boost its nuclear sector by allowing U.S. companies to sell it equipment, nuclear fuel, and reactors. The perceived benefits are considerable profits for both sides, and the transfer of energy consumption by India from highly polluting forms, such as coal, to nuclear power. Another motivation commentators have suggested is that in making the deal, the United States was countering China's ascendancy in the region.[249]

The U.S. Secretary of State, at the time, Condoleezza Rice, also represented the agreement as benefiting counterproliferation.[250] But contrary to her characterization, the

---

247 *See* reports of resistance within the NSG, *Fighting the Nuclear Fight: When Nuclear Sheriffs Quarrel*, ECONOMIST 68–69 (Oct. 30, 2008), http://www.economist.com/node/12516611; FT Reporters, *Objectors Bar Path to Indian Nuclear Accord*, FIN. TIMES, Sept. 4, 2008, at 3, http://www.ft.com/cms/s/0/a25e9816-7a1a-11dd-bb93-000077b07658.html#axzz1j11PMFdF.

248 22 U.S.C. §§ 8001–8008

249 Somini Sengupta, *Interests Drive U.S. To back a Nuclear India*, N.Y. TIMES, Dec. 10, 2006, at 10, http://www.nytimes.com/2006/12/10/world/asia/10iht-web.1210nuke.3843419.html?pagewanted=all. *See also* Ashley J. Tellis, *India as a New Global Power*, CARNEGIE ENDOWMENT FOR INTERNATIONAL PEACE (July 2005), http://carnegieendowment.org/files/CEIP_India_strategy_2006.FINAL.pdf.

250 Secretary Rice stated in Congressional Hearings, "[I]magine the alternative: Without this initiative, 81 percent of India's current power reactors—and its future power and breeder reactors—would

deal included exemptions from safeguards for nuclear reactors that expand India's nuclear weapons potential. Fast breeder test reactors and prototype fast breeder reactors under construction are not under safeguards under the agreement, and only 14 of 22 power reactors in India are safeguarded, leaving eight not safeguarded.[251] Most significant, the agreement impacted the established regime at its core, constituting the first time a state that had developed a nuclear weapons capacity while refusing to sign the Nuclear Non-proliferation Treaty, was granted rights for the import and export of nuclear materials and technology that can be used for nuclear weapons. Supporters as well as critics saw the U.S.-India deal as not only out of keeping with the non-proliferation legal regime based on the Nuclear Non-proliferation Treaty, but as fundamentally undercutting the NPT and the architecture of non-proliferation. As precedent, it allows a nonsignatory to the NPT to take the benefits of peaceful uses reserved by the NPT to states that have committed to non-proliferation.

In promoting the nuclear agreement with India, the Bush administration did not deny its departure from past non-proliferation policy.[252] However, the public relations campaign for approval of the United States-India Agreement portrayed it as doing little damage to the established non-proliferation legal regime, because it was between the world's largest democracies. Political classification was the overarching justification. The Bush administration also indicated that the U.S.-India deal, while exceptional, was open to other nations, depending on their political personality. When signing the US-India Nuclear Agreement, President George W. Bush emphasized that message, stating that "nations that follow the path to democracy and responsible behavior will find a friend in the United States of America."[253]

It is clear this is an approach to non-proliferation that did not simply fade away after the demise of the Bush Administration. Such classification has become common in official pronouncements by the United States on non-proliferation policy, not only in regard to the U.S.-India deal, but with respect to the prospects for other nuclear cooperation agreements.[254] Recognizing that the U.S.-India deal might lead

---

continue to remain outside of IAEA safeguards. The Indian nuclear power program would remain opaque, a nuclear black box." Secretary of State Condoleezza Rice, Remarks at the Senate Foreign Relations Committee on the U.S.-India Atomic Energy Cooperation, (Apr. 5, 2006) (*transcript available at* http://www.carnegieendowment.org/static/npp/reports/rice_4-5-06.pdf).

251 *See* Paul K. Kerr, U.S. Nuclear Cooperation With India: Issues for Congress 8–9 (Dec. 15, 2011), http://www.fas.org/sgp/crs/nuke/RL33016.pdf.

252 The prior administration of President Clinton had, by contrast, "an undifferentiated concern about proliferation." Defense Science Board Chairman William Schneider quoted by Edward Alden & Edward Luce, *A New Friend in Asia*, Fin. Times, Aug. 21, 2001.

253 *Bush Signs US-India Nuclear Bill*, BBC News, Oct. 8, 2008, http://news.bbc.co.uk/2/hi/7660310.stm.

254 *See*, e.g, Presidential Determination No. 2009-7, Proposed Agreement for Cooperation Between the Government of the United States of America and the Government of the United Arab Emirates Concerning Peaceful Uses of Nuclear Energy, 73 FR 70583 ("... the performance of the Agreement will promote, and will not constitute an unreasonable risk to the common defense and security."); and United States-United Arab Emirates Joint Statement, Office of the Spokesman, Nov. 17, 2008, *http://merln.ndu.edu/archivepdf/NEA/State/111954.pdf* ("The U.A.E. has played a positive role in advancing democratic reforms in the region... The United States welcomes U.A.E.'s decision to pursue the development of peaceful nuclear energy.").

other nuclear powers outside the NPT to demand equal treatment, the U.S. Congress included in the authorizing legislation a test of political classification, along with other non-proliferation criteria.[255] Declaring that it can be in the interest of the United States to enter into an agreement for nuclear cooperation with a country that has never been a state party to the NPT, Congress outlined the terms for doing so.[256] Among them is that "the country must have a functioning and uninterrupted democratic system of government" and "have a foreign policy consistent with that of the United States."[257] The clear import of the legislation, therefore, is that the US-India deal is the archetypical model for future nuclear cooperation agreements being based on the political character of a state.

The United States-India agreement, turning the trade in nuclear weapons related material and technology on distinguishing good proliferation from bad, is a reversal of U.S. policy. Previously, the United States opposed the spread of nuclear weapons related materials and technology not conditional on ideological or political affinity with the receiving state. For most of the nuclear weapons era, the United States declared its opposition, though to varying degree, to the acquisition of nuclear weapons related technology and material by states of such diverse political, strategic, and economic character as Argentina, Brazil, South Africa, Taiwan, South Korea, and Pakistan and India. Though never estranged from the United States to the degree Iran and North Korea are today, the governments of these states did present a wide range of relationships with the United States, and included some of highly dubious democracy.

Given the implication of the U.S.-India deal, that transfer of nuclear weapons related material and technology should turn on political classification, the question for counterproliferation policy is the extent to which such political characterization is reliable. More importantly, the question is how such classification, correct or incorrect in any particular case, relates to nuclear risk. The answer is that the exceptionalism of the U.S.-India deal is grounded in fallacy. It is fallacy of both fact and logic that is fated to confound any counter proliferation context in which it is employed.

Any objective view of the history of India over the last quarter century demonstrates the fallaciousness of the assertion that India is a best case for politically based non-proliferation exceptionalism. The facts are that India, in its modern history, has shown substantial political instability, wholesale lack of transparency on matters of national security, and repeated confrontation with Pakistan that is heavily laden with nuclear risk. Indeed, the confrontation with Pakistan, given the status of both states as nuclear weapons powers, may be the most dangerous nuclear confrontation extant on the planet today and, accordingly, a most dangerous field for enhancing nuclear weapons capacity.

The India-Pakistan confrontation has been the justification for both states to stay outside the legal regime of the Nuclear Non-proliferation Treaty. Pakistan, in its

---

255 *Congress Authorizes the President to Waive Restrictions on Nuclear Exports to India*, 120 HARV. L. REV. 2020, 2022 (2007).

256 22 U.S.C. §8001(6) (2006).

257 *Id.* § 8001(6)(B).

decision not to sign the NPT, stated that so long as India failed to sign the agreement, Pakistan would not sign.[258] The tension between India and Pakistan, focused primarily on the disputed territory of Kashmir, has continued in varying degree, but has consistently factored in both states' development of nuclear weapons and trade in nuclear technology and material. Moreover, when engaged in conventional conflict, Pakistan and India have repeatedly threatened each other, in official statements, with nuclear retaliation.[259] This is evident, for example, in the nuclear rhetoric of the Indian response to a terrorist attack India identifies as originating in Pakistan.[260]

Thus even if it were the case that India could be depended upon not to increase the nuclear risk it might generate unilaterally, the nuclear risk presented by proliferation to India is revealed in an entirely distinct and dangerous dimension when considered in relation to nuclear-armed Pakistan. Pakistan understandably perceives the U.S.-India deal as severely increasing nuclear risk for Pakistan. The increased access to nuclear material and technology that India achieves under the U.S.-India Agreement thus surely enhances the level of nuclear risk inherent in any confrontation between India and Pakistan.

If there were to be a radical Islamic takeover in Pakistan, a scenario of risk now real enough to be accounted for in United States strategic planning, the Pakistan-India confrontation could become as or more dangerous than any scenario involving Iran or North Korea in their respective regions of the world. This is quite besides the danger such a takeover would present for global security, a prospect real enough for the United States already to have engaged in planning for the seizure of Pakistan's nuclear sites.[261]

Indeed, the folly of basing proliferation policy on political affinity is most evident in the proliferation history of democratic Pakistan. It is well established that Pakistan has a complete infrastructure for nuclear weapons, a history of severe political instability, and serves as a sanctuary for terrorists, including terrorist ties within the Pakistani intelligence and nuclear engineering communities. Proliferation from Pakistan has

---

258 Mubashar Nizam, *Pakistan Refuses to Sign NPT*, PAKISTAN TIMES, Aug. 27, 2007, http://www.pak-times.com/2007/08/27/pakistan-refuses-to-sign-npt/.

259 *See*, e.g., Chadinand Rajghatta, *Pak's Retaliation Threat to US Sucks in India*, THE TIMES OF INDIA, Nov. 13, 2007, http://articles.timesofindia.indiatimes.com/2007-11-13/us/27967983_1_nuclear-doctrine-nuclear-posture-nuclear-weapons (A 2002 elaboration of Pakistan's nuclear doctrine said its nuclear weapons are aimed only at India and identified four triggers that would cause Islamabad to use the weapons. The triggers included: (1) India attacks and conquers a large part of its territory, (2) India destroys a large part of either its land or air forces, (3) India proceeds to the economic strangulation of Pakistan, and (4) India destabilizes Pakistan through domestic subversion.).

260 For example, commentators noted in reference to the terrorist attacks in Mumbai that the "familiar specter of Indo-Pakistani war quickly reared its head, recalling the nuclear standoff of 2001–2002, a crisis triggered by the December 13, 2001 assault on the Indian parliament by Pakistan-based militants." Daniel Markey, *Mumbai: A Battle in the War for Pakistan*, COUNCIL ON FOREIGN RELATIONS, Dec. 12, 2008.

261 Adrien Levy & Cathy Scott-Clark, *Bush Handed Blueprint to Seize Pakistan's Nuclear Arsenal*, THE GUARDIAN, Nov. 30, 2007, http://www.guardian.co.uk/world/2007/dec/01/pakistan.iraq.

been, so far as we know, without equal. Over decades, even though Pakistan was considered a staunch ally of the United States, claiming to be a democracy when not under military rule, it was engaged in the most extensive and unprecedented, and clandestine, proliferation, though not necessarily in the trade of nuclear weapons as such. During the period that includes the dramatic rise of the international terrorist threat, Pakistan was thought to have a responsible record of non-proliferation. Yet only as late as 2005, it was discovered that it was Pakistan, not a listed state sponsor of terror, not a failed state, that generated the greatest international proliferation risk.[262] It was Pakistan, long secure on the list of U.S. allies, relatively ignored as to proliferation risk, that enabled the so-called "nuclear Wal-Mart" of Dr. A.Q. Khan, whereby nuclear material and technical information was transferred to Iran, North Korea, and Libya. Though the United States government attributed responsibility to Khan as a nongovernmental entity, so that no presidential waiver was needed in order to provide military aid to Pakistan, it was Khan's official position, as the head of Pakistan's nuclear program, that allowed him to gain the access that led to the creation of the greatest nuclear proliferation operation yet known.

So as to Pakistan as well as India, the true nature of what is at issue, namely nuclear risk, is only camouflaged and confused by evanescent categorizations such as democracy. Pakistan and India have both had their periods of more or less democracy. But both have enlarged proliferation risk, with Pakistan making a major business of it. And the presumptive political category of "stable democracy" not only fails in reference to India and Pakistan, but also as to other relationships involving consistently steadfast alliances of the United States. Though Israel has long been a known nuclear weapons state, it continues to be the largest recipient of U.S. military aid; and some of that aid relates to nuclear weapons delivery systems, if not the actual nuclear components. Moreover, there is substantial evidence that, despite its long-standing special security relationship with the United States, Israel collaborated with the South African white regime in its nuclear weapons development.[263]

Implicit in the claim of exceptionalism upon which the U.S.-India deal and similar initiatives have been promoted are assumptions of classification as uncertain and unstable as the political world they purport to reflect. The consequence is incoherence in counterproliferation policy. Being classifications, they assume a fictional stasis. Being absolute, they fail to accommodate the multiple and evolving requirements of managing effective counterproliferation on a global basis. But most importantly, such classifications are dangerous, because they enhance rather than diminish nuclear weapons risk.

The interests generating the U.S.-India deal, while accentuated by the size of both economies, are certainly not unique to the U.S.-India bilateral relations, nor are the

---

262 *See*, e.g., Luke Baker, *"Failed State" Pakistan raises Nuclear Threat*, NATIONAL POST, Dec. 28, 2007; *and* United States National Intelligence Council and Central Intelligence Agency, *Global Futures Assessment Report* (2005).

263 *See*, e.g., Chris McGreal, *Brothers in Arms—Israel's Secret Pact with Pretoria*, THE GUARDIAN, Feb. 7, 2006, http://www.guardian.co.uk/world/2006/feb/07/southafrica.israel.

stipulated political qualifications.[264] There is already significant pressure to replicate the deal with other governments. Any such exceptionalism in international counterproliferation policy sets in motion a most-favored-nation clamor and dynamic. The U.S.-India deal set a dangerous precedent, upon which other governments quickly seized. Pakistan immediately laid claim to the same rights, affecting its nuclear dealings with China.[265] Commentators in Egypt and elsewhere were soon arguing that similar benefits should follow as a matter of equity from their own important political relationships with the United States.[266] Soon after the U.S.-India Agreement, as might have been expected, Pakistan asked the U.S. for a similar deal. The U.S.-India bilateral agreement consequently thrust a major irritant into the critical strategic relationship with Pakistan and U.S. efforts to get Pakistan to move against Islamic extremists. As should have been expected, Pakistan now demands nuclear parity with the India as a price for its strategic support.[267]

It is not only on the demand side of proliferation that the political categories have proven mistaken and counterproductive. Political categorization as the basis for counterproliferation policy ignores the general impact on nuclear supplier states, in relation to concerns of competitive advantage. Thus the U.S.-India nuclear deal has already been cited by China, a nuclear exporter, and an alleged source of Pakistan's nuclear weapons-related technology, as precedent for a similar exceptionalism. China has taken the position that "if America can bend the rules for India, then China can break them for Pakistan."[268] A similar rationalization has been stated by Brazil in refusing to

---

264 *See*, e.g., 22 U.S.C. § 8001(6)(B) stating the qualification that "the country has a functioning and uninterrupted democratic system of government, has a foreign policy that is congruent to that of the United States, and is working with the United States on key foreign policy initiatives related to nonproliferation."

265 *See* Johnson & Bokhari, *supra* note 56; *Pakistan, India and the Anti-Nuclear Rules: Clouds of Hypocrisy*, ECONOMIST (June 24, 2010), http://www.economist.com/node/16425914; "China, unhappy at America's coddling of India, is exploring more nuclear co-operation with Pakistan—which in turn threatens to match India, should it step up weapons production or test again." *The America-India Nuclear Deal: Worse Will Come*, ECONOMIST (Aug. 25, 2007), http://www.economist.com/node/9687395.

266 Egyptian commentators ask, "Why should the U.S. assist India in its nuclear program and not Egypt?" Michael Slackman & Mona El-Naggar, *Mubarak's Son Proposes Nuclear Program*, N.Y. TIMES A14 (Sept. 20, 2006) *available at* http://www.nytimes.com/2006/09/20/world/africa/20egypt.html. "Certainly Egypt's role in the service of critical United States strategic objectives in the Middle East is at least equally critical as the role of India in its strategic zone. With what justification can the United States publicly continue to ignore the Egyptian complaint, notwithstanding United States interest in maintaining the nuclear security of Israel? More broadly, given the economic and ecological interest infusing the U.S.-India deal, why should other technologically advanced NPT signatories, such as Brazil, Egypt, Saudi Arabia, and Japan continue to restrain themselves from similar perceived advantage? Moreover, what is to stop other nuclear weapons nations, including China and Russia, from negotiating their own side agreements with states anxious to benefit from the nuclear materials and technology marketplace, through agreements similar to the U.S.-India deal, outside of the structure of the NPT?" Jimmy Carter, *India Deal Puts World at Risk*, INTERNATIONAL HERALD TRIBUNE, Sept. 11, 2008.

267 Tom Wright, *Pakistan Looks For U.S. Deal*, WALL ST. J. A8 (Oct. 16, 2010).

268 *Nuclear Proliferation in South Asia: The Power of Nightmares*, ECONOMIST 61, 61 (June 26, 2010) http://www.economist.com/node/16426072 (discussing the Brazilian refusal to accept controls in light of

accept controls in light of the U.S.-India deal.[269] Supplier states are now staking their own claims of national interest as similarly justified, with severe consequences, including in the most important geographical arenas for counterproliferation. And each deal, by whatever supplier state, inspires others, notwithstanding the mutual interest in nuclear weapons non-proliferation. Thus Russia's interest in an enormous trade with Iran, including weapons-related trade, has motivated its opposition to sanctions on Iran, and Russia opposed sanctions on India because the sale of a $2.6 billion nuclear reactor would have been jeopardized.[270] The Europeans have similarly compromised non-proliferation policy in relations with Iran.[271]

The incentives are already apparent and in place for multitudinous global development along the same dangerous lines, as political classification opens the gates. Counterproliferation depends upon common international purpose. Bilateral transfer based on political rationalization, to the contrary, is inherently antithetical to the goal of strengthening the constraints that can apply to all governments. The government of Russia or China, North Korea, or of any state, to be sure, can formulate its own political justifications to match the claim of democracy under which the United States has sought to justify transfer. China could argue for democratic communism as justifying nuclear trade with Venezuela or Cuba. And what of the U.S. designation of democracy as marking states appropriate for nuclear trade if radical fundamentalists take over in Syria or Egypt as the result of free and fair elections?

Political grounding of nuclear non-proliferation policy in state classification, as the U.S.-India deal demonstrates, is too unstable, too fraught with delusion and fallacious characterization, to serve as the basis for a secure nuclear future. The political classification of states is simply at odds with the necessary evolution of international nuclear security. It generates a dynamic that undercuts the universalism necessary to strengthening appropriate institutional mechanisms, the standards they employ, and the capacity for monitoring, verification and enforcement. This negative dynamic is very strong and potentially

the U.S.-India deal). *See also* George Perkovich, *Faulty Promises; the U.S.-India Nuclear Deal*, No. 21 CARNEGIE ENDOWMENT FOR INTERNATIONAL PEACE POLICY OUTLOOK (Sept. 2005), http://carnegieendowment.org/2005/09/07/faulty-promises-u.s.-india-nuclear-deal/bxg.

269 "An immediate casualty was the effort to get all members of the Nuclear Nonproliferation Treaty (NPT), who have already promised not to seek the bomb, to sign up to an additional protocol on toughened safeguards. Many have, but on hearing of the America-India deal Brazil's president is reputed to have flatly ruled that out. And where Brazil has put its foot down, others have also hesitated." Economist, *supra* note 268.

270 *See* Howard Diamond, *Russia, India Move Forward with Deals on Arms, Nuclear Power*, ARMS CONTROL TODAY 25 (June-July 1998), http://www.armscontrol.org/print/373.

271 *Europe and the Mullahs, How the EU Subsidizes Trade With Iran*, WALL ST. J. (Feb. 20, 2007). And also the United States, even before the deal with India, did not always align proliferation policy with proliferation risk, after taking into account economic and other strategic interests. For example, the United States lifted sanctions on India and Pakistan so that American farmers could bid on wheat sales to Pakistan. Eric Schmitt, *Senators Back Sale of Wheat to Pakistanis*, N.Y. TIMES A1, A1 (July 10, 1998), *available at* http://www.nytimes.com/1998/07/10/world/senators-back-sale-of-wheat-to-pakistanis.html.

overwhelming, because it draws upon the economic competition among nuclear supplier states, and compounds its strength with the equity claims of governments arguing they are disadvantaged, generating a process of breakdown of the technical and material barriers between nuclear weapons states and non-nuclear weapons states. Not surprisingly, a government of proliferation concern, such as that of Iran, points to the inconsistency of U.S. policy in attempting to prevent the transfer of enrichment technology to a non-nuclear weapons state party to the Nuclear Non-proliferation Treaty (Iran), while undertaking nuclear trade with a nonsignatory to the Nuclear Non-proliferation Treaty (India) that has a long-standing and extensive nuclear weapons program.[272] Iran's principal negotiator on nuclear matters and Secretary of Iran's National Security Council has fastened on the contradiction, declaring "India does not accept the NPT and has nuclear weapons. But America has no problem with this and is also concluding a long-term nuclear energy agreement with India."[273] The official response of the United States has been only to further emphasize political classification, arguing that "Comparing India to the North Korean or the Iranian regime is not credible. India is a democracy, transparent and accountable to its people, which works within the international system to promote peace and stability and has a responsible nuclear non-proliferation record."[274] It is thus evident that the important lesson has not been learned.

Given the nuclear materials sales interests of other nuclear weapons states besides the United States, such as China and Russia, the U.S.-India Agreement opens a door for proliferation not just for India, but globally, as a precedent that destroys any remaining credibility of the NPT Grand Bargain. Indeed, it cannot be assured even that India, the principle beneficiary of state classification under current United States proliferation policy, will restrict transfers of nuclear technology and materials according to the political preference of the United States government. India has already indicated as much by its refusal to join in the Proliferation Security Initiative designed to interdict WMD-related transport, declaiming it as a threat to its sovereignty, and by its refusal to join in nuclear-related sanctions on Iran, actually increasing its imports from Iran.[275]

b. Proliferation to 'Non-Democratic' States

In taking the path of political distinction, United States non-proliferation policy dictates not just that a government can receive nuclear materials and technology

---

272 Simon Tisdall, *Tehran Accuses US of Nuclear Double Standard*, THE GUARDIAN, July 28, 2005, at 14, http://www.guardian.co.uk/world/2005/jul/28/iran.usa.

273 *See* N. Ram, Siddharth Varadarajan & John Cherian, *For the U.S., the Nuclear Issue of Iran is Just an Excuse*, THE HINDU, Aug. 7, 2006, http://www.hindu.com/2006/08/07/stories/2006080703931100.htm.

274 Andrew K. Semmel, Deputy Asst. Secretary, Nuclear Nonproliferation Policy and Negotiations, Remarks on the U.S.-India Civil Nuclear Cooperation Initiative (May 6, 2006) (*transcript available at* http://www.nti.org/media/pdfs/69_1.pdf?_=1316568793).

275 *See* Mark J. Valencia, THE PROLIFERATION SECURITY INITIATIVE; MAKING WAVES IN ASIA at 376 (International Institute for Strategic Studies 2005); Jim Yardley, *India Defends its Oil Purchases from Iran*, WALL ST. J., Feb. 12, 2012, at 11.

because of its status as a democracy, but that states such as Iran and North Korea must be prohibited because of their estrangement from the United States, and their aggressive ideologies. The most prominent and extreme manifestation of this was of course President George W. Bush's categorization of Iraq under Saddam Hussein, and North Korea and Iran as constituting, in his now famously infamous phrase, an "axis of evil".[276]

What is evident in the public responses of governments so designated, is that their listing as nuclear pariah states results in severely negative, not positive, consequences for proliferation of nuclear weapons. As previously noted, the invasion of Iraq sent the message to others on the "axis of evil" list, that they could expect a similar fate as Saddam Hussein, unless they obtained the necessary strategic and political leverage to restrain the United States. The obvious strategy in response was to obtain a nuclear weapons capacity before the United States could strike. The North Korean regime flat out stated this was how it perceived its "axis of evil" classification.[277] The Iranians, more discreetly, stated as much.[278] And there was another major lesson these governments took from their inclusion in the classification of states as bad proliferators—that the aggressive pursuit of a nuclear weapons capacity not only is the best strategy to restrain the United States, but also the best strategy to gain economic and other benefits from the United States, its allies, and the international community in general.[279]

The Bush Administration claimed the utility of the negative listings was demonstrated by the dramatic announcement by Libya on December 19, 2003, that it had decided to eliminate all WMD materials, components, and programs. The Bush Administration thus sought to tie the Libyan reversal exclusively to the invasion of Iraq.[280] It was indeed reported to have timed the WMD deal with Libya to fill the legitimacy void that the failure to find WMD in Iraq created.[281] The facts are that the Libyan turn-around on

---

276 President George W. Bush, State of the Union Address (Jan. 29, 2002), *available at* http://www.whitehouse.gov/news/releases/2002/01/20020129-ll.html.

277 *U.S. to Blame for Derailing Process of Denuclearization on Korean Peninsula*, *supra* note 114.

278 *See* Murphy *supra* note 55. (quoting Professor Sadegh Zibakalam, a professor of politics at Tehran University.)

279 *See id.*, "The hard-liners, perhaps impressed by North Korea's achievement, are now inclined to be more resilient and more uncompromising." "They say if North Korea could do it, why shouldn't we? Why should we let the United States dictate to us, rather than negotiate with us?"; *and* L. Feinstein and A.M. Slaughter, *A Duty to Prevent*, FOREIGN AFFAIRS 146 (Jan./Feb. 2004), "[w]here a state trades in sensitive technologies in exchange for hard currency, economic incentives- including assistance from international financial institutions, direct bilateral aid, and trade incentives—may be more appropriate." The authors are referring to "where a state seeks WMD for their perceived deterrent value."

280 *See* Eben Kaplan, *How Libya Got off the List*, COUNCIL ON FOREIGN RELATIONS BACKGROUNDER (updated Oct. 16, 2007), http://www.cfr.org/libya/libya-got-off-list/p10855.

281 *See* Marin Indyk, *The Iraq War Did Not Force Gadaffi's Hand*, FIN. TIMES, Mar. 9, 2004; and Flynt Leverett, *Why Libya Gave Up on the Bomb*, N.Y. TIMES, Jan. 23, 2004, http://www.nytimes.com/2004/01/23/opinion/why-libya-gave-up-on-the-bomb.html?pagewanted=all&src=pm; Robert Suskind, *The Tyrant Who Came in from the Cold*, WASHINGTON MONTHLY 38 (Oct. 2006), http://www.washingtonmonthly.com/features/2006/0610.suskind.html.

the issues of proliferation occurred only after a long course of negotiations involving international criminal responsibility and compensation by Libya for the families of the victims of the 1988 bombing of Pan American Flight 103 over Lockerbie, Scotland. Moreover, there is substantial evidence from the reports of the officials involved, that Libya was interested in working a deal for the removal of its WMD programs and material in exchange for lifting of sanctions, well before the invasion of Iraq. But whatever the truth as to motivations within the Bush Administration or the Libyan government, it is evident that in the Libyan case, deferral of any non-proliferation deal was probably inevitable given the outrage over the 1988 Lockerbie bombing and the necessary negotiation of a compensation scheme for the families of the victims.[282]

There will always be such other considerations and trade-offs in negotiating non-proliferation with a pariah government, as there has been in the carrot and stick packaging with North Korea, by way of energy supplies and the removal of sanctions. There may be prospects for similar trading with Iran. But these trade-offs concern objective factors that have no necessary connection with democracy or dictatorship or theocracy, and can be better addressed without the burden of political classifications. The denouement with Libya only confirms this. In the series of agreements that constituted the Libyan package, neoconservative critics saw a betrayal of President Bush's freedom agenda, because the Qaddafi regime could not credibly be classified as democratic, given its abysmal human rights record.[283] Fortunately for non-proliferation, the focus became one of monitoring, verification, and compliance to eliminate the Libyan nuclear weapons program, and a substantial nuclear weapons risk was removed, not because of but in spite of the political classification of Libya.

North Korean proliferation history is similarly revealing. In October 2008, the Bush Administration claimed, as its foreign policy swan song, a step in the elimination of North Korea's capacity to construct nuclear weapons. It traded the delisting of North Korea as a state sponsor of terrorism, along with energy assistance, for the North Korean resumption of the disablement of its nuclear facilities, access by nuclear experts to its nuclear facilities, and an agreement to the limited verification of nuclear technology transfers.[284] The listing of North Korea as a state sponsor of terrorism had

---

282 This was the U.S. position communicated to Libya according to Flynt Leverett (former senior director of the National Security Council and State Department Policy Planning Office member), Leverett, *supra* note 281. *See also*, Suskind, *supra* note 281. The eventual rapprochement with Qaddafi, also involved his regime's renunciation of terrorism, and assistance against terrorist organizations. *See* Jonathan B. Schwartz, *Dealing with a "Rogue State": The Libya Precedent*, 101 AM. J. INT'L L. 553 (2007), for a comprehensive recounting of the negotiations.

283 *See*, e.g., Guy Dinmore, *Neo-cons Question Bush's Democratization Strategy*, FIN. TIMES, May 29, 2006, http://www.ft.com/cms/s/0/1f808bd2-ef54–11da-b435–0000779e2340.html#axzz1j6laY5hE; Vance Serchuk & Thomas Donnelly, *Beware the "Libyan Model,"* AMERICAN ENTERPRISE INSTITUTE FOR PUBLIC POLICY RESEARCH 6 (Mar. 1, 2004), http://www.aei.org/article/foreign-and-defense-policy/regional/middle-east-and-north-africa/beware-the-libyan-model/.

284 Press Release, U.S. Department of State, *U.S.-DPRK Agreement on Denuclearization Verification Measures*, Oct. 11, 2008.

been a response to the bombing of a Korean Airlines flight in 1987,[285] not proliferation of nuclear weapons, and there was never any demonstration of linkage to nuclear, just as there was never any demonstration of linkage for Iraq with terrorists. However, by asserting a tie between the terrorism listing and counterproliferation,[286] the United States created the *quid pro quo* that North Korea was later able to demand as the price for not backtracking on a course of denuclearization. And North Korea was able to accomplish this without providing information on two critical matters, a covert program of uranium enrichment, and prior transfers of nuclear materials and technology to other countries.[287]

The folly of negative state classification is thus also well demonstrated by the North Korea negotiations, in which the political categorization appropriate to the designation of state-sponsored terrorism was conjoined with counterproliferation, to the detriment of each of these objectives. The Bush administration allowed removal from the list of state sponsors of terrorism to become a bargaining chip, paying North Korea to abide by its international commitment to dismantle weapons related nuclear production facilities, undoing the original terrorism listing and its rationale.

There were other more negative consequences. It was during the "axis of evil" listing of North Korea that its nuclear weapons were constructed and it conducted nuclear bomb tests. North Korea's "axis of evil" classification relieved it of any pressure for negotiation, helping to make this nuclear weapons development more politically feasible. Moreover, during this same period, North Korea was able to sell ballistic missile technology to Syria, Iran, Pakistan and others, and was suspected of helping Syria to build a nuclear facility, presenting sufficient nuclear weapons risk for Israel to undertake the political risk of bombing that facility in late 2008.

In sum, criteria focused primarily on the political character of a state do not serve the reduction of nuclear risk, and can undermine counterproliferation. The states with respect to which there is the greatest need to achieve agreement on nuclear safeguards, are not characteristically the friends of the nations most committed to counterproliferation. The challenge is to get all governments, and especially the known miscreants, to commit to adequate monitoring, verification, and enforcement of non-proliferation safeguards. It is no accident that the Bush Administration sought to claim a nuclear deal with North Korea as an important success. That deal, if actually

---

285 In fact, the terrorism risk presented by North Korea pales in comparison with the nuclear risk. According to the State Department's Country Reports on Terrorism for 2007, North Korea has not actively sponsored terror attacks since 1987, in spite of giving sanctuary to members of the Japanese Red Army. United States Department of State Publication Office of the Coordinator for Counterterrorism, COUNTRY REPORTS ON TERRORISM 2007 at 173 (Apr. 2008).

286 *See*, e.g., Bush, *supra* note 276, stating "Our second goal is to prevent regimes that sponsor terror from threatening America or our friends and allies with weapons of mass destruction. Some of these regimes have been pretty quiet since September the 11th. But we know their true nature. North Korea is a regime arming with missiles and weapons of mass destruction, while starving its citizens."

287 *A Nuclear Deal Worth Keeping*, BOS. GLOBE A10 (Sept. 1, 2008).

implemented, would have constituted a counterproliferation achievement of the first order. Counterproliferation agreement with governments inclined to nuclear weapons development is the best we can achieve, short of use of force. In other words, the more alien the political context for achieving counterproliferation, the more important it is to achieve nuclear cooperation agreements, and the more counterproductive the political classification. It is precisely because Iran and North Korea are the extreme cases, not conforming to the criteria of democracy and "a foreign policy consistent with the United States," as the U.S. legislation states its criteria,[288] that it is most urgent to achieve nuclear cooperation agreements with these states.

Avoiding the political classification of states is also necessary because the politics that occasion political classification are always changing. The relationship of governments, both "good" and "bad," to proliferation, is always in flux according to changes in domestically defined demands and strategic policy. Moreover, the proliferation consequences of one government's policies at any point of a nation's history are not easily understood, particularly by outsiders, and therefore cannot be a reliable basis for counterproliferation.

The judgments underlying political classification also too easily tend to the culturally obtuse. The classification of Iran, for example, as part of the "axis of evil," played directly into Iranian paranoia and the cultural narrative of the long troubled relationship between Iran and the West. From the perspective of Iran's hard-line regime, there was no honest broker with whom to negotiate. Its listing on the "axis of evil" gave the Iranian regime greater credibility domestically for coloring counterproliferation as a conspiracy of its enemies, making its defiance of the West on its nuclear program a centerpiece for its survival. The situation was quite different when, in May 2010, the governments of Turkey, Brazil, and Iran announced that they had reached an agreement on restricting Iranian uranium enrichment and gaining some transparency as to the Iranian nuclear program through that process, subject to the approval of the Vienna Group (The United States, Russia, France, and the IAEA).[289] The initiative of Brazil and Turkey on the critical matter of controlling Iranian uranium enrichment failed, but Iran at least gave the appearance of being receptive to an initiative that was not stamped, "made in the West." The role of the West in the overthrow of Mossadeq in 1952, and subsequent support of the Shah, as well as Shia resistance and political identity,[290] remains the revolutionary narrative on which the ruling elite depends. Political

---

288 *See supra* p. 89.

289 *Nuclear Fuel Declaration by Iran, Turkey and Brazil*, BBC NEWS, May 17, 2010, http://news.bbc.co.uk/2/hi/middle_east/8686728.stm. *See also* Gregory Ciscusi, *Sarkozy Calls Iran Nuclear Offer a "Positive," Seeks More Steps*, BLOOMBERG BUSINESS WEEK, May 18, 2010, http://www.bloomberg.com/news/2010-05-18/sarkozy-calls-iran-nuclear-offer-positive-now-seeks-stop-to-enrichment.html; *See also* Margaret Besheer, *Clinton: Iran Fuel Swap Has "Deficiencies,"* VOICE OF AMERICA, May 25, 2010, http://www.voanews.com/content/clinton-iran-fuel-swap-deal-has-deficiencies --94832089/118282.html.

290 *See* Ira M. Lapidus & Edmund Burke III, ISLAM POLITICAL AND SOCIAL MOVEMENTS at 283, (University of California Press 1988).

classification, instead of serving counterproliferation, simply strikes a most sensitive nerve in that narrative, making agreement even less likely. The negative impact is compounded because other significant nuclear states will not conform their policy to the U.S. classification, and regard such unilateral designation by the United States as an affront to their own sovereign rights to trade in nuclear materials and technology. Thus governments as diverse as those of Spain, China, and Russia have all declared policies contrary to the United States concerning the provision of nuclear materials and technology to Iran.[291]

Internationalizing counterproliferation under a Security Council Chapter VII mandate could instead provide a productive path to influence domestic political considerations constructively for both sides in the confrontation with Iran over its nuclear development. What is required is to transform the discourse as much as possible from one between Iran and the established nuclear weapons states, to one between Iran and the international community focused on counterproliferation. An international mandate under Chapter VII of the United Nations Charter can be the means to accomplish this.

The same value of formalized multilateralism applies for North Korea. It is notable that Secretary of State Rice defended the deal with North Korea during her time in office by declaring that "this... agreement has the advantage, first and foremost, of being, multilateral."[292] In other words, the six power talks involving China, North Korea's principal patron, buttressed by the establishment and implementation of sanctions under United Nations Security Council resolutions, was understood to provide the best chance of achieving sufficient leverage to put North Korea on the path of eliminating its nuclear weapons program, and keeping North Korea on that path.[293] There is a larger lesson though—that non-proliferation can best be achieved by avoiding the burden of political classification, and instead maximizing the advantages of multilateralism through application of uniform and nondiscriminatory international requirements. Indeed, China, whose cooperation on North Korea is the most critical, has been emphatic about this basic principle, declaring the priority of a "non-discriminatory non-proliferation regime."[294]

---

291 *See*, e.g., Neil King, Jr., *China-Iran Trade Surge Vexes U.S.*, WALL ST. J. (July 27, 2007) (referencing a range of specialty metals and other dual-use items going from China to Iran that could aid Tehran's missile and nuclear program); *Russia, Iran "agree nuclear deal,"* BBC NEWS, Dec. 13, 2007 (referencing Russian support for building a nuclear plant in Iran).

292 Condoleezza Rice, Secretary of State, Interview on The NewsHour with Jim Lehrer (Feb. 13, 2007) (*transcript available at* http://www.pbs.org/newshour/bb/asia/jan-june07/koreadeal_02-13.html).

293 Critics from President Bush's own administration castigated the deal, including Elliot Abrams, a deputy national security advisor, and former Ambassador to the United Nations John Bolton. In responding to the criticism, the President in effect indicated his concurrence with the Iranians, that they could draw lessons from the North Korean example, stating, "I have told the American people, like the Iranian issue, I wanted to solve the Korean issue—North Korean issue—peacefully.... " *See* Murphy, *supra* note 55.

294 Information Office of the State Council of the People's Republic of China, CHINA'S NON-PROLIFERATION POLICY AND MEASURES (Dec. 2003), http://www.china.org.cn/e-white/20031202/1.htm.

Political classification unnecessarily complicates and burdens the global counterproliferation objective given the multilateral interests necessarily involved. The North Korean situation is illustrative. The six powers meeting to secure the dismantling of North Korea's nuclear weapons program all share that objective, but vary widely in their political perceptions and assessments of national interest in relation to North Korea. China strongly supports North Korea in challenging U.S. efforts to sanction North Korea, and has indicated it rejects international intervention in North Korea. It clearly has rejected U.S. policy of isolating North Korea.[295] South Korea looks forward to possible unification with the North, and has been inclined to provide what North Korea demands, in the name of South Korea's "sunshine" policy towards North Korea and in order to prevent war. Japan and Russia have their own complex sets of interests, as illustrated by the abduction of Japanese citizens by North Korea introducing a wholly distinct dynamic in the North Korea-Japan relationship. So any political categorization by the United States, such as North Korea's inclusion on an "axis of evil" listing, in the context of multilateral counterproliferation negotiation, necessarily draws in a multitude of countervailing political and economic interests. These other interests only diffuse the focus, creating additional obstacles to achieving counterproliferation.

If counterproliferation is sought, instead, exclusively on the basis of the multilateral interest inherent in the multilateral institutions and procedures of counterproliferation, counterproliferation is easier to achieve. This is because other states can be enlisted more easily to put pressure on the proliferator, without severe risk of sacrificing their other interests. Multilateralism also renders it more tolerable for the subject government to move against proliferation in reference to its own national and regional constituencies. The story of Libya's transition from "bad" to "good" is particularly instructive on this. When press reports noted that the U.S. ships taking away Libya's nuclear materials had publicly displayed those materials on deck, a senior Libyan official is reported to have protested, "Libya was quite unhappy with this dog-and-pony show because it hurts (Libya) domestically (and) in the Arab world. It makes (it) look like unilateral US disarmament of Libya, and Libya wants it recognized as disarmament under the Nuclear Non-proliferation Treaty and IAEA auspices."[296]

III. INTERNATIONAL ADMINISTRATION OF UNIFORM STANDARDS

The greatest counterproliferation challenge is to bring along the governments inclined to resist and cheat. Universal compliance is the raison d'etre for a mandatory regime. Presently, monitoring, verification, and accounting are critically impaired on the basis of claims of secrecy relating to national security or other excuse, including of course the complaint that the nuclear weapons states are not complying with their NPT promise to disarm. Enforcement for violation of mandatory uniform standards could achieve

---

295 George Bunn & John B. Rhinelander, *NPT Withdrawal: Time for the Security Council to Step In*, ARMS CONTROL TODAY (May 2005), http://www.armscontrol.org/act/2005_05/Bunn_Rhinelander.asp.

296 *Libya Insulted by U.S. Display of Recovered Nuclear Materials, Official Says*, REUTERS, Mar. 17, 2004.

the legitimacy and political leverage to overcome these claims. This would avoid the perception of illegitimacy inherent in the present system in which only non-nuclear weapons states signatory to the NPT are obligated to negotiate a safeguards agreement for all declared facilities. Any one state could not justify resistance to standards legitimated by application to all states.[297] A mandatory regime would generalize the logic of equal application of law to the whole of counterproliferation, opening a much greater potential for moving the goal of a "gold standard"[298] for nuclear security from aspiration towards accomplishment.

Administration and management of a comprehensive Security Council counterproliferation mandate would have to be detailed contextually through implementation. There are distinct needs for effective counterproliferation for each of the arenas in which counterproliferation can be improved. There is the work of the IAEA to improve nuclear safety, security, and safeguards. There is the need to achieve an effective system of international export-import controls and the very different task of assembling the wherewithal for a robust nuclear forensics capability. The maximization of counterproliferation intelligence requires creation of mechanisms and standards for international intelligence sharing. Interdiction is an arena for professional security services and detection specialties. All of these arenas present distinct requirements of substance and process.

The need, however, is not to reinvent counterproliferation. Though the counterproliferation enterprise is large and multifaceted, there is already considerable capital assembled, principally under the aegis of the IAEA. Indeed, the expertise, experience, and present capacity of the IAEA positions it as the natural choice for the broadest management role for refinement of counterproliferation under the authority of Chapter VII. Some aspects must be left to other organizational forms and institutions, such as interdiction arrangements between national security agencies and military organizations. However, the whole of the counterproliferation enterprise is greater than the sum of its parts. Reduction of nuclear weapons risk must be a comprehensive project to secure synergies that are available, and to overcome the debilitating fractionalization that currently characterizes the entire enterprise.

The IAEA's mission is stated comprehensively, to "assist States in their efforts to prevent the further spread of nuclear weapons and to prevent, detect and respond to illicit uses of nuclear material."[299] Its current operations are devoted to detection of diversion of material or undeclared activities or nuclear material, providing assistance

297 A similar logic is behind the entry of the United States and other nuclear weapons states into IAEA safeguards agreements, though excluding facilities with direct national security identity. This is to demonstrate there is no reason why we cannot have uniform standards that includes all governments. The exemption for dedicated weapons facilities does not negate the value of a baseline of standards for all facilities identified as exclusive to peaceful use.

298 Allison, *supra* note 9, at 143.

299 *Verifying Compliance with Nuclear Nonproliferation Undertakings*, IAEA SAFEGUARDS AGREEMENTS AND ADDITIONAL PROTOCOLS 2, 2 (Apr. 2008), http://www.iaea.org/Publications/Booklets/Safeguards3/safeguards0408.pdf.

to countries to protect nuclear material and facilities, detecting and responding to illicit trafficking in materials, and responding to nuclear and radiological emergencies. It publishes guidelines and recommendations for securing and transporting nuclear material. It provides nuclear security training courses for individual country representatives on topics such as nuclear security awareness, combating illicit trafficking and nuclear forensics. The scale of these operations of the IAEA would have to be significantly enlarged to implement a comprehensively effective counterproliferation mandate. But functionally, the IAEA is presently addressing much of the variegated character of nuclear risk.[300]

The IAEA would be the natural locus not only for management of a Security Council counterproliferation mandate, but also for accommodating the politics of counterproliferation. The IAEA's record of integrity and expertise in working with individual governments suits it for the political challenges, notwithstanding charges of political bias coming from the noncompliant governments such as Iran and North Korea. The IAEA is best positioned to smooth the transition to a comprehensive mandatory regime. Particularly significant is its experience in pragmatic adjustment to national security limitations, limitations imposed by commercial proprietary interests and the related complex of concerns such as protection of intellectual property rights.

Presently, though, the IAEA's counterproliferation potential suffers from the same false nexus between counterproliferation and disarmament that infects other aspects of counterproliferation. A report prepared by an independent commission at the request of the Director-General of the IAEA on its role to 2020 and beyond declares that "progress towards disarmament, or the lack of it, deeply affects the IAEA's non-proliferation mission."[301] No evidence is offered for the proposition, because there

---

300 In its current incarnation, the IAEA is functionally the implementing body under Article 3 of the NPT that requires each nonnuclear weapons state party to the treaty to accept safeguards. It is important to understand that IAEA safeguards, despite the appellation, are not for safety or guarding, but designed to detect any diversion of nuclear material to military purpose. They are not designed to prevent theft or accident. The IAEA does employ nuclear security specialists and safeguard inspectors to visit and report on safety, security, and safeguards implementation at nuclear facilities. However, apart from bilateral inspection agreements or implementation of UN sanctions, inspectors are not normally charged with reporting any security weaknesses they observe. The safeguards agreements require that the agency use information obtained only for safeguards purposes and keep it confidential.

Currently, the IAEA also provides assistance for governments in establishing security practices, and detecting and responding to nuclear security events. It collects, distributes, and coordinates security-related information including best practices, interceptions of illicit transfers of nuclear material, and has developed its own code of conduct for the safety and security of nuclear materials. The IAEA helps states through training, development of regulation, and coordination of national, and international nuclear security programs. It operates an advisory and peer review service, available to member states on request, and maintains an Illicit Trafficking Database Program whereby governments notify it of illicit trafficking incidents, which helps for the analysis of threats, vulnerabilities, and response. The IAEA also works to improve nuclear detection methodology and equipment, and to develop sabotage resistant designs for nuclear reactors and research facilities.

301 IAEA, *Reinforcing the Global Nuclear Order for Peace and Prosperity, The Role of the IAEA to 2020 and Beyond* (May 2008), http://www.iaea.org/newscenter/news/pdf/2020report0508.pdf (prepared by an independent Commission at the request of the Director-General of the IAEA).

is none, other than rhetorical. It is simply the same cliché that burdens all current counterproliferation, affording the usual excuse for those governments resisting.

The IAEA is thus foiled in its mission by the same foundational deficiency that pervades all current counterproliferation. Any achievement is dependent on what each state member will concede in its own Comprehensive Safeguards Agreement. The IAEA does not have independent authority to critique or take action as to the measures a state chooses to apply for physical protection, and can only act in its advisory capacity.[302] It has no authority to require a state to establish a certain nuclear security system, nor does it have the authority to verify physical protections without the agreement or request of the subject state.[303] All safety reviews are subject to national acceptance. The result is that in-depth reviews have been conducted by the IAEA for only a fraction of the world's nuclear reactors, and there is no requirement for a government to report the results of any IAEA safety review. The IAEA also has a similarly limited role in relation to any peer review process, national or international.

The result is that a government can easily block information at the threshold of discovery. The IAEA may have sufficient evidence to find a government not in compliance with its Comprehensive Safeguards Agreement, and even then be stymied. This was the case for Iraq, Iran, and North Korea. The IAEA must depend upon voluntary compliance by the subject government, and as could be expected, the IAEA is denied access when it matters most.[304] Even a Comprehensive Safeguards Agreement and the Additional Protocol can carry it only so far, and no further. The IAEA does not have any legal follow-up authority that might help leverage compliance; at least not without action by the Security Council. Thus notwithstanding Iraq, Iran, and North Korea having entered into safeguards agreements, the government of each of these states was able to use its safeguard agreement as political cover for nuclear weapons related work.

Comprehensive Safeguards Agreements and the Additional Protocol no doubt reduce nuclear risk insofar as governments cooperate to achieve security for their nuclear materials. But this does not serve to reveal the machinations of a government

---

302 Ed Lyman, *Role of Nuclear Material Accounting and Control in the NPT* (Apr. 9, 2002), http://www.ieer.org/latest/npt02el.html (prepared for the IEER Conference: Nuclear Dangers and the State of Security Treaties).

303 Mark S. Soo Hoo, *IAEA-Activities for the Physical Protection: Role and Importance of IPPAS Missions*, http://www.eurosafe-forum.org/files/euro2_5_7_iaea_phys_pro.pdf.

304 For example, in September 2005, the Board of Governors of the IAEA passed a resolution calling upon Iran "to implement transparency measures... which extend beyond the formal requirements of the Safeguards Agreements and Additional Protocol." IAEA, *Implementation of the NPT Safeguards Agreement in the Islamic Republic of Iran* at 3 (Sept. 24, 2005), http://www.iaea.org/Publications/Documents/Board/2005/gov2005-77.pdf. The Director-General's report of April 28, 2006 to the IAEA Board of Governors stated that "the Agency is unable to make progress in its efforts to provide assurance about the absence of undeclared nuclear material and activities in Iran," nor can it evaluate "the role of the military in Iran's nuclear program." IAEA, *Implementation of the NPT Safeguards Agreement in the Islamic Republic of Iran, Report by the Director General* at 7 (Apr. 28, 2006), http://www.iaea.org/Publications/Documents/Board/2006/gov2006–27.pdf.

that will do everything it can to hide its dereliction. For Iraq, Iran, and North Korea, it took years, not months, to confirm illicit transfer of nuclear weapons and technology, or the production of enriched uranium or plutonium. And in each case, the revelation was not the result of voluntary reporting of information, but information provided by national intelligence agencies such as the CIA.

Whenever the IAEA has been especially proactive, as in flagging nuclear weapons development in North Korea and Iran, it has been accused of exceeding its legal authority. When in November 2011, the Director-General delivered a formal report on Iran's nuclear program indicating Iranian development of nuclear weapons, the IAEA was criticized even by some U.S. commentators as exceeding its authority under the NPT and any safeguards agreement. It was charged that IAEA discussion of Iran's development of non-fissile material activities to develop a nuclear warhead was beyond IAEA authorization for only monitoring safeguards and diversion of fissile material to weapons use.[305] When North Korea withdrew from the NPT, its purported justification was that the IAEA was acting with bias in using intelligence gathered by third-party governments, thereby going beyond the NPT or any other agreement or authorization, and that the IAEA was thus supporting espionage. Such literalist readings of the authority of the IAEA as so limited are not without merit as legal arguments, and therefore simply demonstrate the dramatic incongruity of the current legal framework and the fundamental goals of counterproliferation.

The failures *have* provoked steps forward in the development of counterproliferation. Thus the Additional Protocol, which is designed to help determine whether there are undeclared nuclear materials and activities in a NNWS, was primarily a reaction to the discovery that Saddam Hussein had been secretly developing nuclear weapons at undeclared sites. But the Additional Protocol, whatever its merits when seriously adopted and implemented, is still not in force in a couple score NNWS states having nuclear enrichment activities. Among them, Argentina, Brazil, and Iran all have dual-use centrifuge uranium enrichment facilities adaptable without significant barrier to production of weapons grade fissile material.

IAEA administration of safeguards agreements, as presently structured in relation to national sovereignty, is simply inadequate to the challenge of contemporary nuclear risk. Its goal is to assure implementation of best practices at all the world's reactors and nuclear installations, including research reactors and fuel-cycle facilities. Responding to risk at source *is* critical, particularly with respect to the threat of nuclear terrorism. Production of weapons grade material requires substantial capital infrastructure. So lockdown at the source is the best prevention. By increasing the costs of concealment and risks of exposure of illicit transport, it is also the best deterrent to the diversion or theft of fissile material for weapons use. However, the scale of the challenge is to lock down the over 2,000 tons of plutonium and highly enriched uranium that are spread

---

305 *See*, e.g., Daniel Joyner, *Iran's Nuclear Program and the Legal Mandate of the IAEA*, JURIST, Nov. 9, 2011, http://jurist.org/forum/2011/11/dan-joyner-iaea-report.php.

through dozens of countries. Because the IAEA can only act pursuant to the request or agreement of a government, it is impossible to establish uniform baseline standards, which is the only way to achieve comprehensive containment of risk of this scale.

The uncertainty generated by absolute dependence on what governments will do voluntarily reflects itself also in the consistently uncertain and problematical budgeting for nuclear security activity by the IAEA. Dependency on what each government will accept makes it difficult to anticipate financial needs and helps explain the crippling gap between the time funds are pledged and when they are available.[306] Relying on voluntary pledges from governments also results in conditions being imposed on how donated funds may be used, which obstructs the ability of the agency to allocate funds as needed to maximize its counterproliferation activities.[307]

Despite current limitations, the IAEA *is* positioned for a natural transition to a mandatory system. The IAEA has developed numerous significant capacities and standards addressing a wide range of nuclear security matters. If mandated under Chapter VII of the United Nations Charter, this broad capacity could metamorphose counterproliferation from a system that is unraveling to one of considerably greater dimension and effectiveness. The IAEA has already developed much of the substance of what is required. The safeguards agreements give the IAEA authority to collect reports and implement verification to confirm their accuracy.[308] All safeguards agreements require the state to maintain a system of accounting for and controlling nuclear material. Although terms vary according to the nuclear materials and facilities present in a particular state, if the Additional Protocol is in place, it allows access for verification by IAEA inspectors that includes going beyond declared facilities.

The IAEA is already working to assist states in implementing their mandatory obligations under Security Council Resolution 1540. It works in conjunction with the 1540 Committee in considering the adequacy of reports submitted by states on their adherence to Resolution 1540 imposed obligations. There is no reason to doubt the ability of the IAEA to further develop such capabilities and standards, but of mandatory and

---

306 U.S. Government Accountability Office, GAO-06-93, *Report to Congressional Requesters, Nuclear Nonproliferation: IAEA Has Strengthened Its Safeguards and Nuclear Security Programs, but Weaknesses Need to be Addressed* at 49–53 (Oct. 2005), http://www.gao.gov/new.items/d0693.pdf.

307 *Id.* at 49–53. Efforts to harmonize pledges and needs have been largely frustrated by donor stipulations, *See* IAEA, GC(49)/17 *Nuclear Security Measures to Protect Against Nuclear Terrorism: Progress Report and Nuclear Security Plan for 2006–2009,, Report by the Director General* at 3 (Sept. 23, 2005), http://www.iaea.org/About/Policy/GC/GC49/GC49Documents/English/gc49-17_en.pdf.

308 There are three elements of a robust and comprehensive safeguards system: physical protection, control, and accounting. The system first developed in the United States about 40 years ago was the original scheme for the IAEA safeguards system. Its modus operandi is to verify non-diversion of declared nuclear material by focusing on the correctness of a state's declaration. The system's principal deficiency was that it did not address undeclared sites and materials. That is the reason for the drafting and adoption of the Additional Protocol after the Gulf war, which is designed to provide verification authority to assure absence of undeclared nuclear materials, by focusing on the question of completeness of a government's declaration. Nuclear materials in military programs are not included in its purview, thus acknowledging the essential asymmetry of the distinction between nuclear weapons states and non-nuclear weapons states.

uniform character, depending on authority and resources.[309] Other such important standards and procedures include threat-based risk assessment enabling member states to put in place effective nuclear security programs. The IAEA's Nuclear Security Guidelines, updated numerous times, are adopted by most states with significant nuclear activities. No doubt the expertise is available to develop similar standards for a uniform and universal baseline for universal mandatory compliance.

Applicable standards that would constitute the substance of a mandatory counter-proliferation regime are also articulated to different degrees in a variety of organizational contexts, international conventions and other international instruments that the IAEA or other institutional mechanism could utilize. These include the International Convention for the Suppression of Acts of Nuclear Terrorism, the Convention on the Physical Protection of Nuclear Material,[310] and The G-8 Global Partnership Against the Spread of Weapons and Materials of Mass Destruction.[311] There are also national resources and a wealth of experience available for standards development such as the U.S. Global Threat Reduction Initiative, established by the U.S. National Nuclear Security Administration (NNSA) to act "as quickly as possible, identify, secure, remove and/or facilitate the disposition of high risk vulnerable nuclear and radiological materials around the world."[312] There are significant nongovernmental initiatives and projects such as the World Institute for Nuclear Security (WINS), established in 2008, which brings together nuclear security experts, industry personnel, governmental agencies, and international organizations in a forum in which they may focus on the rapid and sustainable improvement of security of nuclear and radiological materials worldwide,

---

309 "There is no doubt that the IAEA could do more to strengthen and solidify the international nuclear security regime into a defined set of principles and practices that could ensure the best possible protection against malicious nuclear acts. However, the agency lacks the authority and resources to rapidly expand and improve upon its core functions and to develop new tools and functions to fill the gaps in the nuclear security regime." Jack Boureston & Andrew K. Semmel, *The IAEA and Nuclear Security: Trends and Prospects*, THE STANLEY FOUNDATION (Dec. 2010), http://www.stanleyfoundation.org/policyanalysis.cfm?id=436.

310 The Convention on the Physical Protection of Nuclear Material (CPPNM) entered into force on Feb. 1987, and establishes measures related to the protection of nuclear material, and the prevention, detection, and punishment of offenses related to nuclear material, and is almost fully international (142 parties as of March 2010). Convention on the Physical Protection of Nuclear Material, *opened for signature* Mar. 3, 1980, T.I.A.S. No. 11080, 1456 U.N.T.S. 101; International Convention for the Suppression of Acts of Nuclear Terrorism, G.A. Res. 59/290, U.N. Doc. A/RES/59/290 (Apr. 13, 2005).

311 Since its initiation in 2002, the partnership has made progress on nuclear safety through cooperative projects such as the dismantlement of decommissioned nuclear submarines, the security and disposition of fissile materials, and rechanneling employment of former weapons scientists. *The G-8 Global Partnership*, U.S. DEPT. OF STATE (last visited Dec. 3, 2012), http://www.state.gov/t/isn/gp2012/rls/docs/184759.htm

312 The initiative specifically focuses on the securing of nuclear and radiological materials located at civilian sites worldwide by employing three primary strategies: Convert, Remove, and Protect. The NNSA has requested $2.5 billion for the office for FY 2012 and $14.2 billion over the next five years. *Fact Sheet GTRI: Reducing Nuclear Threats*, NATIONAL NUCLEAR SECURITY ADMINISTRATION (Feb. 1, 2011), http://nnsa.energy.gov/mediaroom/factsheets/reducingthreats.

and develop and promulgate best practices.[313] These institutionalizations, both governmental and nongovernmental, constitute a substantial and significant resource—effectively a library of the practicable. They are realizable enough to have involved expenditures not just in millions, but also billions of dollars; such as the Nunn-Lugar Cooperative Threat Reduction Program, established in 1991 to secure and dismantle the nuclear arsenal spread out among the former Soviet states, providing funding and technical expertise.[314]

Operating under an express counterproliferation mandate of the Security Council, the IAEA presumably would continue in its role of setting nuclear security standards, and their implementation, monitoring and verification. The IAEA could continue to administer the large corpus of the relevant standards already articulated and available to be drawn from the long-standing operations of the IAEA and national and regional nuclear regulatory experience. The IAEA also could and should continue in its role of guidance and assistance to governments in implementing nuclear security, safeguards, and safety standards, counterproliferation measures, and interdiction of illicit shipment of nuclear weapons related material and technology.

The most obvious and important mandate for immediate implementation would be universal application of the Additional Protocol, which expands inspection authority to non-declared sites and is already widely applied. The Security Council has repeatedly "called upon" all states to adopt the Additional Protocol.[315] Adoption of the Additional Protocol could be made a condition of supply of nuclear material and technology, as has been suggested within the present counterproliferation regime for operation of the Nuclear Suppliers Group.

More generally, the inspection mandate should move in the direction of unfettered inspection rights for the IAEA. Presently, the IAEA can only inspect as far as the agreement with any government allows, even if the Additional Protocol is in place. Though the purpose is to discover undeclared sites, additional information and access requests

---

313 WINS, *WINS-Introducing WINS*, (last visited Dec. 3, 2012), http://www.wins.org/front/about_introducing_wins.php *Who Wins, Nukes* ECONOMIST (Oct. 2, 2008), http://www.economist.com/node/12339535.

314 The Nunn-Lugar Cooperative Threat Reduction Program expends about $500 million annually towards nuclear disarmament. Kennette Benedict, *Nunn-Lugar: 20 Years of Cooperative Threat Reduction*, BULL. OF THE ATOMIC SCIENTISTS (Dec. 19, 2011), *available at* http://www.thebulletin.org/web-edition/columnists/kennette-benedict/nunn-lugar-20-years-of-cooperative-threat-reduction.

315 The Additional Protocol was developed because under the original IAEA safeguards, the IAEA could only verify the correctness of the reports for a country's declared facilities, such as power and research reactors. To address the important suspicions of weapons programs or diversion that have been at issue, particularly after the 1991 Gulf War, a Model Additional Protocol on verification was negotiated and adopted by the IAEA, providing authority for off-site inspections and other means to verify the "completeness" of a country's declaration, as for instance sampling river water to disclose upstream nuclear activity. *Verifying Compliance with Nuclear Non-Proliferation Undertakings*, *supra* note 299, at 2–7. IAEA, *Model Protocol Additional to the Agreement(s) Between State(s) and the International Atomic Energy Agency for the Application of* Safeguards, IAEA Doc. INFCIRC/540 (1997), http://www.iaea.org/Publications/Documents/Infcircs/1997/infcirc540c.pdf.

are subject to timed notice provision, as well as visa requirements and travel notifications.[316] The IAEA needs, on a comprehensive basis for all states, the sort of ongoing authority that the Security Council, acting under Chapter VII, did provide for IAEA inspections in Iraq.[317] This would include the right to designate for inspection any site anywhere in the state suspected of noncompliance without satisfying any evidentiary threshold; the right to demand inspection of undeclared sites on short notice; and no right of the subject state to refuse or limit inspectors' access to such sites.[318] Other elements for expanded authority could be full access to information on imports and exports of nuclear material, and the right to enhance safeguards by employing environmental monitoring and other technological tools. The IAEA should have the authority to request additional information as it sees fit, which allows taking into account differences between the need to monitor different states, and different threat levels that different governments represent.

A robust accounting and detection capability is the essence of IAEA authority even as presently limited, and must be part of an effective non-proliferation regime.[319] Diversion of fissile material is detected by comparing reported information against information obtained from inspections and intelligence to expose discrepancies. To detect undeclared nuclear facilities, a counterproliferation regime requires a source of clues to trigger its attention. Thus the secretariat of the IAEA has called for better and more extensive information to be provided as to exports of nuclear materials, procurement inquiries, and export denials.[320] This is another area, however, in which a mandatory regime can achieve counterproliferation beyond present capability. The more reporting is established in a format that is mandatory and comprehensive, the more likely illicit transfer will be detected. A Chapter VII mandate could also make feasible an international registry of nuclear material, modeled on present commitments of states such as the United States and several European countries, to make annual declarations of plutonium holdings and weapons-grade enriched uranium, which could be expanded worldwide to include plutonium holdings for a global accounting of weapons usable material.[321] As the result, detection capability, to the extent known to be more robust, would enhance deterrence by way of the message it sends to those governments with nuclear weapons ambitions. The greater the capability, the more potential proliferators would risk being found out, and not at a time of their own choosing.

---

316 *See* U.S. Government Accountability Office, *supra* note 306, at 21.

317 *See* David Sloss, *It's Not Broken, So Don't Fix It: The International Atomic Energy Agency Safeguards System and the Nuclear Nonproliferation Treaty*, [35] VA. J. INT'L L. 841, 884–887 (1995).

318 S.C. Res. 707, U.N. Doc. S/RES/707 (Aug. 15, 1991); U.N. SCOR, 46th Sess., 3004 mtg. at 3.

319 IAEA, *Nuclear Material Accounting Handbook* at 1 (May 2008), http://www-pub.iaea.org/MTCD/publications/PDF/svs_015_web.pdf.

320 The secretariat's recommendation "requests all States to provide to the Agency relevant information on exports of specified equipment and non-nuclear material, procurement enquiries, export denials, and relevant information from commercial suppliers in order to improve the Agency's ability to detect possible undeclared nuclear activities." Goldschmidt, *supra* note 116, at 10 n.3.

321 Perkovich et al., *supra* note 61, at 108–109.

For the ultimate objective—compliance—the IAEA, under a Security Council mandate, could still work within the current process. Article II B.4 of the IAEA statute stipulates that the agency shall submit reports "when appropriate to the Security Council if in connection with the activities of the Agency there should arise questions that are within the competence of the Security Council . . . ."[322] Thus the board does not and should not have to establish weaponization to trigger reference to the Security Council. If that were the requirement, the government in non-compliance could simply refuse access that would allow proof of weaponization, as North Korea did prior to its first nuclear detonation. Though it may be without definitive proof as to the target state, the board of the IAEA already has authority to make compliance judgments, and to refer suspected noncompliance to the Security Council. The shortcoming has been enforcement, and credibility of the threat of enforcement by the Security Council. With a comprehensive counterproliferation resolution under Chapter VII in place, the improvement would be that reference to the Security Council would be based on suspected violation of clarified, uniform, established rules binding all states, not just ad hoc reference for political targeting. That in itself would add credibility to the threat of enforcement. It would put all governments on notice of international expectations and the likely cost and risk for proliferation. It would set the direction, in specific pre-established terms for any delinquent, and serve to focus and project political pressure and political risk on proliferators.

There are other tools for compliance that a mandatory regime could provide, more in the nature of intermediate steps. It is neither realistic nor necessary to rely on actual imposition of sanctions by the Security Council for an effective counterproliferation regime. Besides the value of the threat of Chapter VII sanctions to persuade general compliance, there are a variety of other means that can be employed to considerable effect as carrots and sticks for compliance. These include, for example, substantive requirements such as making adoption of the Additional Protocol by seller and purchaser's government an absolute condition of supply of dual-use technology and material, and for technical assistance. Intermediate means could also include procedural requirements, for example along the lines of a 2007 U.S. State Department proposal, that if the IAEA reports a state to be in substantial noncompliance, the IAEA be given additional necessary verification authority until it can conclude that there is no undeclared nuclear activity.[323] The Security Council mandate could prescribe that preliminary to economic, financial, or military sanctions under Chapter VII, if there is a finding of noncompliance, there will be access to documents, persons, and locations without restriction; prohibition on any transfer of nuclear material or technology to the subject state; and the suspension of all sensitive nuclear fuel cycle activities. Such measures as part of a counterproliferation mandate under Chapter VII would

---

322 Statute of the IAEA, *supra* note 231.

323 *See* International Security Board, *Report on Discouraging a Cascade of Nuclear Weapons States* at A-1 (2007), http://belfercenter.ksg.harvard.edu/publication/17705/report_on_discouraging_a_cascade_of_nuclear_weapons_states.html.

overcome the present calculus, whereby a noncomplying government can gamble on a lack of movement towards compliance. The discretion of the Security Council to employ economic sanctions or use of force would of course remain. That discretion is enshrined in the design of the United Nations Charter. However, this does not require abandoning other counterproliferation leverage that is available, notwithstanding the lack of the exceptional circumstances needed to generate Security Council sanctions under Chapter VII.

4

ELEMENTS OF AN EFFECTIVE COUNTERPROLIFERATION ARCHITECTURE

A. Expanding Deterrence; An International Nuclear Forensics Data Bank

1. CONTEMPORARY NUCLEAR FORENSICS CAPABILITY

In Resolution 1887, adopted in 2009, the United Nations (UN) Security Council stated it "(e)mphasizes that a situation of non-compliance with non-proliferation obligations shall be brought to the attention of the Security Council, which will determine if that situation constitutes a threat to international peace and security."[324] Despite the reference back to the Non-proliferation Treaty "non-proliferation obligations," the resolution indicates the potential within Chapter VII. The critical counterproliferation step forward, however, is yet to be taken—authorization of the imposition of the specific international standards and requirements of nuclear security for all states.

That this is what is most needed is perhaps best illustrated by the unrealized value of the science of nuclear forensics. Nuclear forensics can provide a new dimension of deterrence, reaching even the most dangerous nuclear risk that confounds traditional deterrence theory; the risk presented by non-state actors, including international terrorism. As to these new dimensions of nuclear risk, especially, the challenge is to reconstruct nuclear deterrence beyond its Cold War meaning. Nuclear forensics can provide that resource if enabled for internationalization under a United Nations Security Council resolution establishing a truly international nuclear forensics resource.

To appreciate the significance of such authorization, it is necessary to understand the nature, current limitations, and potential of the science of nuclear forensics. Nuclear forensics provides a means to identify who, what entity, what government, contributed to any specific nuclear weapons-related event, whether that event is the interdiction of fissile material or interdiction of a weapon, or the world-altering event of a nuclear detonation. During the Cold War, attribution was not a critical concern;

324 S.C. Res. 1887, U.N. Doc. S/RES/1887 (Sept. 24, 2009).

it was not even significant. Given the small size of the nuclear weapons club, and the well-defined alignment of adversary states, governmental responsibility was likely to be obvious. Strategic planning allocated little if any resource to establish a capacity to attribute responsibility for a nuclear event. When President Kennedy, in his Cuban Missile Crisis speech, declared that any nuclear missile launched from Cuba would be treated as an attack by the Soviet Union on the United States,[325] that attribution was unquestioned, and was most certainly confirmed by events. Resolution of the crisis was reached between the United States and the Soviet Union, though the nuclear-tipped missiles were located in Cuba, and despite Fidel Castro's claim of absolute authority to determine their disposition. Contrast this to the original claim to support the invasion of Iraq to destroy weapons of mass destruction (WMD)—that Saddam Hussein was developing WMD, including nuclear, that he might be transferring to a terrorist network. Those murky claims, based in fictions such as Saddam's purchase of yellowcake in Africa and meetings with al Qaeda, were trumpeted to the world.[326] That attribution was not based in any science, but it *was* used to determine events, and the world learned—too late—that targeting Iraq to pre-empt a terrorist nuclear event was not only mistaken, but the result of deliberate selection and distortion of intelligence to justify the decision to invade.[327]

As all too well demonstrated by the invasion of Iraq, correct determination of the pathway of nuclear risk today is critical. Attribution can negate false justification for application of military force. But there is much more to it. Attribution capacity can be critical to achieving a new dimension of deterrence. Attribution capability is in fact perhaps the best means—meaning the most practical and achievable means—to reduce nuclear risk by deterrence. Indeed, it may be the saving grace of the evolution of nuclear technology that, along with amplification of risk, a new capacity for identifying the pathway of nuclear material has also evolved. That new capacity is the modern science of nuclear forensics.

Nuclear forensics is a science born during the Cold War as a means for analyzing weapons development and determining the nature of the weapons possessed by the Cold War adversaries. Its processes were devoted to examining the debris and fallout from nuclear weapons tests. Nuclear forensics technology today, by contrast, is a science of a very different objective and capability. Its technology has been developed to the point where credible attribution can be made, not only if a weapon or weapons-related material is seized through interdiction, but also, if it should come to the worst of scenarios, post-detonation. So though the spread of nuclear technology and material has undermined cold war deterrence theory, there is available a new

325 President John F. Kennedy, Cuban Missile Crisis Address to the Nation (Oct. 22, 1962), http://www.americanrhetoric.com/speeches/jfkcubanmissilecrisis.html.

326 *See* Derrick Z. Jackson, *Still No Mass Weapons, No Ties to 9/11, No Truth*, BOS. GLOBE, Dec. 17, 2003, at A23.

327 *See* David E. Sanger, *On Iran, Bush Confronts Haunting Echoes of Iraq*, N.Y. TIMES 1 (Jan. 28, 2007).

capacity for identification, and a new deterrence, that is pertinent to 21st century strategic planning.

International cooperation in nuclear forensics research, and international cooperative examination of interdicted material does occur currently. But internationalization has remained just that—cooperation—limited by an antiquated legal and political infrastructure, confined to the form and limits of ad hoc consent among governments, with governments imposing many and varied barriers to the maximization of forensics capability. The barriers are erected under the rubric of national security and private claims of proprietary commercial interest, such as intellectual property concerns arising from the nuclear power industry. There is no consensus as to what barriers are legitimate or illegitimate, nor any institutional format for designing standards. Most importantly, there is no means, legal or institutional, to assure the appropriate collection and handling of the data involved. There are some agreements for cooperation in nuclear forensics, but these are mostly informal, and the existing agreements certainly do not comprise anything approaching the global scale of the challenge. In sum, there is a critical gap between the scientific capability, and international legal and institutional capability that must be overcome if we are to achieve the significant diminishment of nuclear risk that is within reach.

What is needed is dictated by the science. Nuclear forensics today includes physical, isotopic, and chemical analysis of interdicted material or post-detonation material to determine its composition and history of transformation, from origination to culmination. The processes of nuclear forensics rely on sampling materials and computer modeling. Both sampling and computer modeling depend upon the quality and comprehensiveness of information made available. Hence, the critical importance of data.

There has been a fundamental evolution in the collection and analysis of the data that is the subject matter of nuclear forensics. In the early years of the nuclear stand-off between the United States and Soviet Union, when nuclear forensics was first initiated as a national security science, it was in relation to the intelligence dynamic of that standoff. The earliest technologies were principally for the analysis of weapons development—one's own and that of potential adversaries. Nuclear forensics concerned primarily analysis of atmospheric fallout from the Soviets' development of the hydrogen bomb, to determine characteristics, such as yield, materials used, and weapons design.[328]

The techniques of nuclear forensics have cumulated and evolved to a different risk environment and a different purpose. Given their Cold War origins, the early techniques of nuclear forensics were designed to examine samples for which the origin was known and the goal was to gain intelligence on the design process within an adversary's nuclear weapons program. With nuclear material in the control of the few nuclear weapons powers, the origin or pathway of the material was not a significant

328 Richard Rhodes, Dark Sun: The Making of the Hydrogen Bomb at 525 (Simon and Schuster 1995).

subject for questions before the dissolution of the Soviet Union. Determining the origin of the material, (generally meaning where it was last processed), and the chain of custody including the source, (generally meaning the last legal guardian), became increasingly complex with the increase in nuclear weapons, increase in the number of nuclear weapons states, and the spread of nuclear weapons-related materials, ostensibly for peaceful use. But *peaceful use* has proved an elusive and ever more troubling designation, as the dual-use phenomenon has made it increasingly difficult to distinguish peaceful use from nuclear weapons-related use. With the spread of nuclear facilities of dual-use potential into more and more states, the focus of nuclear forensics has accordingly switched from a risk environment in which the source was known, to a risk environment in which identification of source is both the most significant and most problematical aspect of the nuclear security challenge.

Identification of the chain of custody is generally referred to as *attribution*, and attribution is now the driving heart of nuclear forensics. Attribution is a dynamic process that combines forensics science with other intelligence resources. Nuclear forensics science, unlike other forensics science, is distinguished, however, by dependence on a pre-defined set of scientific measurements and analyses, reflecting the dynamic nature of its subject matter, which changes form from origination to application. The contemporary science of nuclear forensics is used to determine from what origination, by what means, and through what transfers, interdicted nuclear material or post-detonation nuclear material was generated. It identifies different points in the history of nuclear material, but is about material in process and in transit. It leads from point to point, through iterative examination and discovery, with data revealed, revealing the next questions, next answers, and so on.

Taking a nuclear forensics case from beginning to end involves initially the collection of data, and then its subjection to numerous scientific tests and calibrations. Collection is from nuclear or radiological material that is interdicted in illicit shipment, or obtained post-detonation, from the debris at, around, and in the air above an explosion. The analysis phase involves extracting the data that can be used to compare the collected material to archived samples and/or computer modeling of known nuclear processes.

Source identification, which is the central focus of the science, is also the bridge between the science, and the assignment of legal and political responsibility. Though nuclear forensics is a science of technical attribution, it becomes of profound strategic consequence in relation to nuclear security, whether by indicating where there was a breach of security, or by indicating who orchestrated an attempted or consummated attack. The information obtained through nuclear forensics may even supply, or at least indicate, "the return address" made so elusive by the advent of non-state actors and rogue state nuclear risk. But the capacities of nuclear forensics relate importantly to nuclear security in other ways; for example, by informing as to whether there is more such material at risk, the likely transit route, and where and how control may have been lost. Whether for targeting the guilty or instructing where to rectify breached security, it is a rich source of important intelligence. Consequently, the more robust and accurate the techniques of nuclear forensics, the more they are likely to influence the decision-making process of nuclear security, in all its phases—lockdown, planning, physical protection, and response.

The capabilities of modern nuclear forensics even pertain directly to determination of the involvement of non-state actors in a nuclear weapons-related event, whether as to interdicted materials, or post-detonation. Because nuclear forensics can reveal characteristics of a nuclear weapon and the sophistication of its design, the science can indicate whether a weapon was or is being designed by terrorists on their own, or was obtained from a particular nation's nuclear weapons stockpile. Upon interdiction of a terrorist weapon, forensic analysis can be critical to understanding not only the weapon's design, but also its mobility and how to disable it.[329] Post-detonation, such information could be critical to determining appropriate response through indicating whether the targeted state is dealing with another state's failure of nuclear security, and/or a link with terrorists.

Much of the science of nuclear forensics was and continues to be highly classified. The work is known to be ongoing at various laboratories, both in the United States and in other nations, to further refine the processes involved.[330] Though many of its methods have stayed similar, as has the type of information used to draw forensics conclusions, refinement has meant significant progress in improving portability, efficiency, and timeliness in reaching those conclusions.[331] This is not limited to refinement of the analysis. New techniques have been developed as well for collecting samples, even from ground-zero after detonation, sufficient to measure such data as isotopic ratios, the age of the nuclear material, and the efficiency of the fuel burn in the detonation. This is all information that can be compared to prerecorded nuclear data to determine the origin and history of the material. The U.S. Department of Defense and nuclear scientists more generally state that we possess the technical capability to collect and identify nuclear materials in even the worst of circumstances.[332]

Any conclusive evaluation of reliability is difficult, if not impossible, to come by. Until the last few years, there was very little public information about nuclear forensics attribution. There were a few articles by those working within government, but few

329 Jonathan Medalia, *Nuclear Terrorism: A Brief Review of Threats and Responses* (Feb. 10, 2005), http://www.fas.org/sgp/crs/terror/RL32595.pdf.

330 John M. Doyle, *U.S. Faces Shortage Of Nuclear Investigators*, Aerospace Daily & Defense Report 3, (June 9, 2009) (It is reported, for example, that the Lawrence Livermore National Laboratory in California is developing technology to accelerate chemical analysis of samples from a nuclear event, and that Pacific Northwest National Laboratory in Washington is working on faster analytical instruments, such as for accelerating and expanding the capacity for chemical analysis).

331 Though there is serious shortfall in producing the scientists necessary for a significant ongoing forensics capability to utilize these technological developments. *See*, e.g, U.S. Government Accountability Office, GAO-09-527R, *Nuclear Forensics: Comprehensive Interagency Plan Needed to Address Human Capital Issues* (Apr. 30, 2009), http://www.gao.gov/new.items/d09527r.pdf.

332 *See* U.S. Department of Homeland Security, *Budget-in-Brief: Fiscal Year* 2010 at 143–147 (2010), http://www.dhs.gov/xlibrary/assets/budget_bib_fy2010.pdf; Michael May, Jay Davis & Raymond Jeanloz, *Preparing for the Worst*, 443 Nature 907, 908 (2006).

references in the popular press, and much of the information about nuclear forensics, especially the more recent developments, remains highly classified as national security information.[333] However, much has recently become evident in public commentary, principally in relation to discussion of the risk of nuclear terrorism.[334] The more recently available information establishes that the techniques of nuclear forensics have evolved dramatically in conjunction with the evolving environment of risk, and have become remarkably variegated, sophisticated, and more accurate for achieving attribution. The science has reached the point that what is public has drawn the attention not only of the scientific community and members of the military establishment, but academics and the popular media such that a typical characterization in the popular discussion of nuclear security is that the nuclear forensics developments are "astounding."[335]

Most significant is the political impact. Nuclear forensics has drawn legislative attention in the United States Congress. The best measure of that impact is ground-breaking legislation, the 2009 Nuclear Forensics and Attribution Act.[336] The legislation provides $30 million per year, additional to forensics capabilities already in place, to establish a National Technical Nuclear Forensics Center under the Department of Homeland Security, to plan, supervise, integrate, develop, and improve federal nuclear forensics capabilities. It also established a National Nuclear Forensics Development Program for academic development of pathways from undergraduate to postdoctorate in the specialties in nuclear and geochemical science to remedy the shortage, widely lamented in the forensics scientific community, of new cadres of scientists capable of implementing nuclear forensics technology.

However, as to international legal and institutional capability, the legislation simply states,

> It is the sense of the Congress that the President should—
>
> (1) pursue bilateral and multilateral agreements to establish... an international framework for determining the source of any confiscated nuclear or radiological material or weapon, as well as the source of any detonated weapon and the nuclear or radiological material used in such a weapon
>
> (2) develop protocols for the data exchange and dissemination of sensitive information relating to nuclear or radiological materials and samples of controlled nuclear or radiological materials... and
>
> (3) develop expedited protocols for the data exchange and dissemination of sensitive information needed to publicly identify the source of a nuclear detonation.

---

333 *See*, e.g, William J. Broad, *Addressing the Unthinkable, US Revives Study of Fallout*, N.Y. TIMES, Mar. 19, 2004, at A1; William J. Broad, *New Team Plans to Identify Nuclear Attackers*, N.Y. TIMES, Feb. 2, 2006, at A17.

334 *See generally* Allison, *supra* note 9.

335 Charles J. Hanley, *Nuclear Terror Strike Could be Difficult to Track, Report Says; Report Raises Concern on Adequacy of U.S. Specialists and Databases*, STAR LEDGER 29 (June 14, 2009).

336 Nuclear Forensics and Attribution Act, H.R. 730, 111th Cong. § 3 (2009).

Virtually nothing is said as to what should be agreed or what the international legal framework for such cooperation might be. The importance of this deficiency cannot be overestimated. The international piece, so far unspecified, is critical. This is because the process of attribution comes down to sampling, and it is the scope of sampling, how international and inclusive, that ultimately determines the quality and efficacy of attribution capability. As attribution is the heart of nuclear forensics, sampling is its lifeblood. It is sampling that enables the empirical and conceptual premise of modern nuclear forensics, and ultimately determines its realization in reducing nuclear risk.

Sampling means establishing pre-catalogued material and data that can be compared to data that the tools of nuclear forensics can obtain from nuclear material that has been collected, either by interdiction, or post-detonation. *Signature* is the term that refers to such distinguishing characteristics of particular material, from which the origin and history of the material may be determined. Signature must be referenced to particular points in the processing of the nuclear material, since the signature is modified as the material is processed. However, there are fixed indicia identifying different points in the processing. Particularly, *fingerprint* is the term generally used to refer to the two elements that appear in isotopes that come in hard-to-alter combinations. These characters can be related to the specific production facilities and operating histories of nuclear plants. If there is access to measure the composition of a country's uranium or plutonium, the isotopic details of its production facility can be recorded to establish the fingerprint for this comparison.

So, as the nature of sampling indicates, nuclear forensics is a science of process. The principal indicia forensics seeks to discover are indicia of process. As to nuclear weapons, nuclear forensics both seeks and depends upon the information that arises from the process of weaponization of nuclear material. And herein lays its extraordinary capacity as a tool for reducing nuclear weapons risk. The data on which nuclear forensics depends for sampling is the inevitable product of weaponization of nuclear material. Signature cannot be avoided because weapons grade nuclear material does not exist as such in nature. The material must be processed to bring it to weapons use. The process of enrichment of uranium is undertaken to increase the amount of fissile U-235 found in uranium ore. The process of plutonium production occurs inside an operating nuclear reactor. These processes establish different ratios of isotopes, which constitute the fingerprint of the material, and also establish the trace elements resulting from the fabrication process involved. Thus it is the process necessary to make weapons-grade material that provides distinctive signatures composed of physical, chemical, elemental, and isotopic properties of the material as well as the facilities in which it was processed, and its fabrication into a bomb. Even after a nuclear explosion, most of the nuclear material remains for potential examination against samples in that only a fraction gets converted into energy and fission products, and the radioactivity of the debris makes it detectable, identifiable, and collectible. Uranium isotopes vary in composition and impurities that can disclose not only how the nuclear material was processed, but even where it was mined. Weapons-grade plutonium also can be identified in relation to its production process and thus location.

This data is what can serve to build the bridge from the domain of science to the domain of political and strategic decision. Even after a detonation, forensics science can disclose the efficiency of the bomb design, which can also help narrow the list of who might have built it. Additionally, debris from a detonation can provide traces of the bomb components that give clues as to the construction process and possible sources. These findings, as well, can be compared against a database of known weapons designs, currently such as is maintained by the United States Nuclear Emergency Search Team.[337]

None of the data is of value for attribution without the archived information to which the signatures of collected material can be compared. This is true as to the basic empirical aspects of nuclear forensics, which depend on analysis of nuclear and other radioactive material, and also as to computer modeling, which utilizes the chemistry and physics of known nuclear processes to predict the signatures that would derive from those processes. One way or the other, any attribution hypothesis must be tested against archived samples and data, for forensics to be able, with any reliable degree of accuracy, to exclude or identify specific facilities or stockpiles as the source or processing of particular nuclear or radioactive material.

Nuclear forensics is most reliable in *ruling out* sources when data from those sources is archived, in contrast to identification of source. However, as archived data increases and becomes more comprehensively representative of existing nuclear facilities, the likelihood of identification of source increases. So the efficacy of a forensics regime for the identification of source depends on the depth and scope of the available database. Its significance is ultimately determined by the available database. The more that databases reference nuclear material stockpiles and processes existing around the world, the more accurate and robust the capacity for identification.

Though nuclear forensics is focused on physical source identification, its maximum value is as part of a larger process of attribution. There is today little doubt that nuclear scientists can take the tiniest amounts of nuclear material and identify not only what the material is, but also when it was formed, what process formed it, and the ambient environment in which it was created.[338] Whether or not that identification can lead back to the state responsible for producing and losing or transferring or using those materials may be determined in a given case, also by what other intelligence resources may contribute. Nuclear forensics is certainly not the sole resource for a maximal attribution capability. Nuclear forensics is most effectively part of a broader application of intelligence resources, such as is currently brought to bear upon an intercept of illicit

337 Jeffrey T. Richelson, *Defusing Nuclear Terror*, VOL. 58 BULL. OF THE ATOMIC SCIENTISTS 38 (Mar./Apr. 2002).

338 *See* Alexander Glaser & Tom Bielefeld, *Nuclear Forensics: Capabilities, Limits and the "CSI Effect,"* (July 24, 2008), *http://www.princeton.edu/~aglaser/talk2008_forensics.pdf* (discussing techniques of isotopic identification); Michael May, APS/AAAS REPORT ON NUCLEAR FORENSICS 5 (Feb. 16, 2008), http://cstsp.aaas.org/files/mayaaas.pdf; *See also* Arnie Heller, *Identifying the Source of Stolen Nuclear Materials*, SCI. & TECH. REV., 13, 15 (Jan./Feb. 2007) (discussing the embedding of ambient particles during nuclear process).

transfer. A similar confluence of intelligence resources, both technical and human, would be brought to bear on a future nuclear event, be it interdiction or detonation. Maximizing attribution capability means exploiting all forensics, inclusive of all intelligence resources, to the ultimate goal of informing political and strategic decision. Not only do non-nuclear forensics capacities, such as human intelligence, cyber-detection, fingerprints, and documentary evidence contribute in themselves to build the evidence for attribution, but all sources relate synergistically, each focusing the other in an ongoing collaborative effort to determine the source and actor(s). However, even by just narrowing the field of potential countries of origin, nuclear forensics can be enormously helpful in preventing mistaken attribution that human intelligence might otherwise indicate.

Perhaps most importantly, unlike human intelligence sources, nuclear forensics does not depend on political predisposition. Moreover, the nuclear criminal does not have the ability to conceal fingerprint, which could confuse other criminal forensics. Though there is some risk of so-called "spoofing," to mislabel the return address of fissile material, the scientific consensus is that any such attempt would require considerable scientific sophistication, and is penetrable. It is likely it would only delay rather than prevent attribution.[339] Even if a terrorist organization or rogue state could secure the necessary sophistication, certain key data points of current forensic science still could not be negated, and would reveal such attempt.[340] Even after an explosion, isotopic history of the material that cannot be altered is present and available for analysis.

Thus, in relation to political and military decision occurring after an interception or detonation, nuclear forensics uniquely enlightens the process of assessment and response. The light shed by nuclear forensics affords greater reliability than other intelligence sources that may be employed by virtue of its objectivity. Nuclear forensics is more likely to provide reliable evidence than other intelligence resources, because it is science. As science, it is beyond the bias of more distinctly human and subjective intelligence resources, which naturally suffer from their human, and therefore, political nature.

The evidence obtained through nuclear forensics, like all evidence, may be used to strategic purpose. Given the seriousness of the threats involved, that strategic purpose is likely to be articulated as self-defense. Self-defense, as a matter of political reality, and under international law, is of course, a prerogative of sovereignty. But the sustainability of the claim of self-defense, for pre-emptive action or otherwise, will depend on its basis in fact, as the invasion of Iraq so dramatically demonstrated. The failures of intelligence that led to the invasion of Iraq on the justification of the presence of WMD

339 May, *supra* note 338.

340 Michael Miller, *Nuclear Attribution as Deterrence,* 14 THE NON PROLIFERATION L.REV. 33, 41 (Mar. 2007). *See also id.* at 52; *See also,* M.J. Kristo, D.K. Smith, S. Niemeyer, G.B. Dudder, UCRL-TR-202675, *Model Action Plan for Nuclear Forensics and Nuclear Attribution* at 8 (Mar. 3, 2004), https://e-reports-ext.llnl.gov/pdf/305453.pdf; *See also* May, *supra* note 338, at 30.

were not failures of science. It is now well documented that, in making the case for the invasion, the George W. Bush Administration "concealed dissent on nearly every element of intelligence and included interpretations unsupported by the evidence."[341] Forensic fact can be repressed, distorted or treated selectively to support strategic purpose. But that does not negate its value for deterrence or its significance for legitimacy of response. Indeed, quite the opposite. The lack of evidence of an ongoing Iraqi nuclear program is what prevented legitimization by Security Council resolution, with the opposition led by France, normally a principal U.S. ally on matters nuclear.

II. EXPANDED DETERRENCE

The potential of nuclear forensics to serve deterrence goes well beyond mutually assured destruction (MAD). Indeed, it is fundamentally distinguishable from MAD. MAD depended wholly on "launch on warning," and massive nuclear retaliatory response against a previously surveilled and identified opponent. But depending on the breach of nuclear security involved in a particular nuclear forensics case, the spectrum of response based on forensics analysis is much more extensive and variable. It could range at one extreme from nuclear retaliation, non-nuclear military force applied preemptively or in response to an attack, to overt or covert suppression through intelligence or diplomatic agency, political and/or economic sanction against a government, criminal prosecution of individuals, or grounds to pressure or sanction a government or a commercial entity to improve nuclear security. In other words, nuclear forensics casts a therapeutic light for risk reduction as far-ranging and variegated as the landscape of contemporary nuclear risk.

Nuclear forensics may shed light on inadequacies in the lockdown or transport of nuclear material, including among allies. In the event of breach of security, it can provide early warning of a planned attack. In revealing the *who* and *where* of breach of nuclear security, it can motivate implementation of security measures to seal the breach. Utilized synergistically with other intelligence resources, it may aid in identifying illicit nongovernmental or governmental for-profit networks, thereby discouraging clandestine or negligent transfer of nuclear materials. It threatens and concerns those responsible for nuclear security with risk of identification, whether governmental officials, those in the nuclear industry charged with security, rogue actors within government, rogue governments, or rogue individuals in the nuclear industry. Ultimately, by way of connection with identifiable individuals or entities, it also threatens terrorist networks striving to obtain nuclear materials and technology.

In affording expanded deterrence, nuclear forensics can also serve to prevent the mistaken attribution, that in a nuclear weapons context, is certain to be of dire consequence. For the fateful scenarios that nuclear weapons risk indicates, the process of nuclear forensics is cautionary, injecting fact and time, to constrain the political pressure that would inevitably follow on a nuclear event. The time required to make key

---

341 *See* Jackson, *supra* note 326.

determinations, such as identification by way of the half-lives of the isotopes involved, can give political leadership a basis for avoiding premature and precipitate response on insufficient evidence. Although the nuclear forensics scientific community continually strives to reduce the time for drawing nuclear forensics conclusions, and a principal concern is the time that may be required,[342] such delay as it exists, is justified as necessary for objective assessment and to achieve credibility.

Given the range of possible connections between non-state actors and the state source of nuclear materials, nuclear forensics may not resolve attribution in a nuclear terrorism scenario. Attribution will typically present a mix of technical and political questions. Such questions will be whether the material was intentionally transferred, whether there is a significant risk that the data provided by any state is a sound basis for its exclusion, whether there are likely to be undisclosed materials and facilities involved, or whether spoofing or some other attempt at gaming attribution may be involved. However, nuclear forensics would nevertheless inject the natural caution of scientific examination into the process of attribution. This could help contain the political firestorm that would follow on a nuclear event of any significant magnitude. It would help to achieve a deliberative time frame, such as was neither practicable nor deemed necessary under the launch-on-warning logic of MAD.

Nuclear forensics also presents perhaps the most profound contrast to MAD in that it addresses the non-state actor nuclear risk not comprehended by the traditional nonproliferation architecture. When non-state actors were first perceived as presenting nuclear risk, deterrence was not seen simply as diminished, but as negated. The 9/11 terrorists were a befuddlement for traditional deterrence theory, both because they were willing to invest their own annihilation, and because of the obscurity of association with government. After 9/11, this was acknowledged in the National Security Strategy of the United States, in its statement the following year that "traditional concepts of deterrence will not work against a terrorist enemy."[343] The corresponding presidential sound-bite went further. President George W. Bush declared:

> Deterrence—the promise of massive retaliation against nations—means nothing against shadowy terrorist networks with no nation or citizens to defend. Containment is not possible when unbalanced dictators with weapons of mass destruction can... secretly provide them to terrorist allies.[344]

However, in the years following this assessment, deterrence was brought into the discussion of nuclear risk presented by non-state actors; and the George W. Bush

---

342 *See* David E. Sanger, *America's Deadly Dynamics with Iran*, N.Y. TIMES, Nov. 6, 2011, (article noting expressions of concern by Obama Administration over time requirements indicated by "table-top" exercises).

343 *National Security Strategy*, *supra* note 2, at 15.

344 *See* George W. Bush, Commencement Address at the United States Military Academy in West Point, New York 38 WEEKLY COMP. PRES. DOC. 944, 946 (June 10, 2002).

Administration changed its view. In response to the October 9, 2006, nuclear test by North Korea, President Bush declared the United States would hold North Korea "fully accountable" if it passed nuclear materials or weapons to terrorists.[345] The 2006 U.S. National Security Strategy, accordingly, was modified to declare "a new deterrence calculus" that "[s]tates that harbor and assist terrorists are as guilty as the terrorist, and they will be held to account."[346]

This deterrence by indirection was not an entirely new approach to nuclear deterrence. It was somewhat reminiscent of the United States response to the Soviet Union's transfer of nuclear weapons to Cuba. President Bush's declaration that "transfer of nuclear weapons or material by North Korea to states or non-state entities would be considered a grave threat to the United States, and we would hold North Korea *fully accountable* of [*sic*] the consequences of such action,"[347] was akin to President Kennedy's threat to hold the Soviet Union responsible, though indirectly, for any launch of missiles from Cuba.[348]

But what was new was that deterrence, in relation to affecting foreign governmental action and decision, was brought into the conversation about how to meet the challenge of nuclear terrorism. It was a new proposition that, by focusing the connection between non-state actors and government, the non-state actor risk could be addressed as a matter of state responsibility, thereby to achieve a new measure of deterrence.

The connection, as made by the Bush administration, was simplistic, and probably unrealistic.[349] The new policy sought to address the nuclear risk presented by rogue states and terrorist networks, as co-conspiracy, envisioned as the handoff from government to terrorist of nuclear material, nuclear technology, or even a portable weapon.[350] Perhaps because it was so simple, this apparition was used to sell invasion and regime

---

345 Tanalee Smith, *Bush Warns North Korea Against Nuclear Proliferation*, ASSOCIATED PRESS WORLDSTREAM, (Nov. 15, 2006). *See also* Graham Allison, *Deterring Kim Jong II*, WASH. POST, Oct. 27, 2006, at A23. "America's challenge is to prevent [North Korean transfer of nuclear weapons] by convincing Kim that he will be held accountable for every nuclear weapon that originates in North Korea. This requires clarity, credibility about our capacity to identify the source of a bomb that explodes in one of our cities (however it is delivered by whomever) and a believable threat to respond."

346 *Strategy for Winning the War on Terror* in *National Strategy for Combating Terrorism* at 15 (2006), http://www.cbsnews.com/htdocs/pdf/NSCT0906.pdf (the National Strategy for Combating Terrorism is also *available at* http://georgewbush-whitehouse.archives.gov/nsc/nsct/2006/).

347 *Id.*

348 Kennedy, *supra* note 325.

349 North Korea had in fact threatened in May 2003 to sell plutonium to the highest bidder. Michael A. Levi, *Deterring Nuclear Terrorism*, [20] ISSUES IN SCI. & TECH., 70 (Apr 1, 2004). Such posturing was, in all likelihood, designed simply to get the attention of the U.S., and against North Korea's other interests.

350 "North Korea is a known weapon proliferator, and there is a danger that the rogue state may sell nuclear technology to non-state entities." Jim Garamone, *Rumsfeld: North Korea Test Threat Must be Taken Seriously*, AM. FORCES PRESS SERV. (Oct. 5, 2006), http://www.defense.gov/news/newsarticle.aspx?id=1476. *See also Institutionalizing Our Strategy for Long-term Success* in *National Strategy for Combating Terrorism* at 20 (2006), http://www.cbsnews.com/htdocs/pdf/NSCT0906.pdf.

change for Iraq.[351] For an American public traumatized by 9/11, the false portrayal of Saddam Hussein in conspiracy with al Qaeda was compelling, with polls indicating about 70 percent of the American people were led to believe Saddam Hussein was personally involved in the attacks of 9/11.[352]

The potential connections between terrorist and government are, in actual fact, of considerably more subtle and wide-ranging possibility, than nuclear conspiracy between government and terrorist. The specter drawn by the Bush Administration, of a rogue state handing over a nuclear weapon to terrorists for their use in attacking the United States or its allies, truth be told, is probably the most unrealistic of the various scenarios by which a terrorist network might obtain nuclear material. No government is likely to make attribution so simple. No government is likely to so unnecessarily risk being on the bulls-eye of a U.S. retaliatory response, by trusting its fate to alien fanatics. This would be an irrational choice against interest under virtually any conceivable circumstance. It is conceivable that extreme elements within a government, or individuals seeking financial gain, might pass off nuclear material. But the prospect of a rogue regime deliberately handing a nuclear weapon to a non-state group of actors that insists on its own radical agenda, over whom the transferor government is not likely to have any effective or continuing control, is probably the least likely lead-up to nuclear attack that one might imagine. If concealment of state participation is sought, whether for an attack on the United States or for profit, there are far more concealable and controllable means than taking chances with fanatics. As noted in congressional hearings on North Korean nuclear risk, "They may be evil. They are not stupid.... Any tramp steamer and a Scud launcher, which they can buy for $100,000, can launch a missile to an apogee of 180 miles. That is perfectly adequate... for an EMP attack which would devastate all of New England."[353]

However unlikely the scenario of a government passing off a nuclear weapon to terrorists, the instinct was sound to address the nuclear risk presented by rogue states and non-state actors by examining their potential connections. Indeed, more realistic consideration of these connections suggests significant and innovative opportunity for an expanded deterrence. The relevant risk scenarios range from situations of

---

351 Two days after the invasion of Iraq (Mar. 21, 2003), Bush wrote a letter to congressional leaders in which he argued: "The use of armed force against Iraq is consistent with the United States and other countries continuing to take the necessary actions against international terrorists and terrorist organizations, including those nations, organizations, or persons who planned authorized, committed, or aided the terrorist attacks that occurred on Sept. 11, 2001." Letter from President George W. Bush to the Speaker of the House and President Pro Tempore of the Senate (Mar. 21, 2003), http://www.cnn.com/2003/ALLPOLITICS/03/21/sprj.irq.letter/index.html.

352 "[The Bush] administration's attempts to tie Saddam to the terrorist attacks of Sept. 11... worked so well that nearly 70 percent of Americans believed Saddam was 'personally involved' in the attacks." *See* Jackson, *supra* note 326.

353 *Addressing a New Generation of Threats from Weapons of Mass Destruction: Department of Energy Nonproliferation Programs and the Department of Defense Cooperative Threat Reduction Program: Hearing Before the H. Comm. On Armed Services*, 111th Cong. 15–16 (2009) (statement of Rep. Roscoe G. Bartlett, Member, H. Comm. on Armed Services).

complete lack of *mens rea* on the part of a government, such as the inadequate securing of nuclear facilities, to engagement in the marketing for profit of nuclear materials and technology, and/or lack of understanding or concern about the dual-use potential of nuclear energy cooperation. In response, then, a contemporary concept of deterrence, that truly reduces nuclear risk, must be sophisticated and inclusive enough to influence the variety of paths whereby states could provide such nuclear access opportunities to non-state actors.

These potential nuclear risk connections between states and non-state actors all evidence a common core. Nuclear weapons opportunities for non-state actors all depend on state action or inaction. Terrorism by means of nuclear material is unlike other terrorism in that a government must be proximately involved. This is simply because nuclear material and the facilities for processing nuclear material are controlled by governments. The science-based consensus is that even well-funded and technically proficient terrorists are not able to produce highly enriched uranium (HEU) or plutonium without state involvement. Producing plutonium requires complex and expensive reactors and reprocessing facilities, and the enrichment of uranium requires substantial physical plant and sophisticated technologies. Both weapons-grade plutonium production and enrichment of uranium also require employment of a sophisticated labor force. Because weapons-grade material is not found in a natural state, there is a necessary connection between the nuclear risk presented by non-state actors, and the states that are the only source of weapons-grade material. Terrorists cannot obtain the wherewithal for weaponization and a nuclear attack without first acquiring fissile materials, plutonium or HEU, and that material must come from a state source. Government must be in the chain of custody, whether by acting in support of terrorism or by failing to effectuate nuclear security.

Because it is states that possess the means for creating the nuclear risk that terrorism can employ, states can be the agents for reducing such risk. Even a "dirty bomb" (radioactive dispersal device or RDD) scenario, whereby radioactive material could be joined to a conventional weapon to produce havoc in an urban setting, depends on state connection, if only by way of state jurisdiction for the security of radiological material. Thus for addressing the nuclear weapons risk represented by non-state actors, states and state responsibility *can* be the focus. Deterrence of non-state actors is achievable by influencing states, though terrorists are spoken of as quintessentially non-state actors. Moreover, because deterrence depends on rational behavior, and there is an imponderable component of the irrational in influencing ideological terrorists, indirect influence by way of potential suppliers becomes even more important.[354]

354 *See, e.g.*, Alexander L. George, *The Need for Influence Theory and Actor-Specific Behavioral Models of Adversaries* in KNOW THY ENEMY: PROFILES OF ADVERSARY LEADERS AND THEIR STRATEGIC CULTURES, 2d ed., (U.S. Government Printing Office 2003); Keith B. Payne, *Deterrence: A New Paradigm*, NATIONAL INSTITUTE FOR PUBLIC POLICY at 3 (Dec. 2–3, 2003) (presentation at the 34th IFPA-Fletcher Conference on National Security Strategy and Policy, Security Planning and Military Transformation After Iraqi Freedom).

The challenge, therefore, is to persuade governments, whether rogue, unfriendly, or ally, to achieve better and better nuclear security, and to repress and punish activity that could result in terrorist use of nuclear materials.

The attribution capability of contemporary nuclear forensics is available to instill this motivation—not conclusively, not certainly, but significantly. Because non-state actors must depend on state control or state failure to control nuclear material, the capacity of nuclear forensics to point the finger of responsibility at government extends deterrence to non-state actors. To the extent nuclear forensics can narrow the list of possible sources of a nuclear event, and at its most efficacious, identify the source, to that extent, government is motivated to reduce and prevent the circumstances under which terrorists could acquire nuclear technology, material, or weapons.[355] This includes motivating states to avoid the variety of ways they might otherwise create risk with non-state actors, ranging from negligent nuclear security to various forms of negligent or intentional transfer of nuclear materials or technology. Though attribution is likely to be imperfect, it thus affords an expanded deterrence.

The expanded deterrence available through nuclear forensics attribution capacity should be understood as expanding to direct influence over a broad population of non-state protagonists of nuclear risk. This population is comprised not just of terrorists and their ideological masters and managers. It also includes nuclear scientists and engineers who, because they possess the relevant technical expertise and skills, might be employed, irrespective of ideological commitment, to build nuclear weapons and the various delivery systems that could be used. Contemporary nuclear risk includes—indeed requires—this human capital. Individuals may be insulated and protected by secretive regimes, such as those of North Korea, Iran, or Syria, and hold positions of governmental authority, such as that of Dr. A. Q. Khan, who supervised Pakistan's nuclear program. Nevertheless, such protagonists of nuclear risk are vulnerable to exposure.[356] The members of the relevant scientific and engineering community, worldwide, like members of other epistemic communities, are known to one another, and accordingly, are known to intelligence services. They are also of small numbers, so that the task of identification is limited. They may be identifiable in relation to the necessary knowledge and skill base for handling nuclear materials, or otherwise through their identification with an identified state source of nuclear material.

---

355 There is evidence that identification of source can be instrumental not only in encouraging states to establish better security for nuclear materials, but that it can be helpful in motivating states away from nuclear weapons development. An extensive *Wall Street Journal* examination of the factors that motivated Libya to surrender its WMD programs and cut ties to terrorist groups concludes that the principal factor was intelligence that identified illicit connections, both as to the source of material and parties involved. The *Wall Street Journal* reported that U.S. officials gave Libya a compact disc containing recorded conversations between the chief of the Libyan nuclear program and representatives of the A. Q. Khan network. The Libyan case is evidence that the identification of source can have remarkable impacts on state policy. Judith Miller, Op-Ed., *How Gadhafi Lost His Groove*, WALL ST. J. 14 (May 16, 2006).

356 This would most importantly include the nuclear engineers and scientists demoted in pay, privilege, or rendered surplus upon the breakup of the Soviet Union.

To the extent source identification may include the identification of who worked on intercepted material or a detonated bomb, these individuals risk identification. To the extent they are facing a credible forensics capacity, they will be aware they could be found, made subject to criminal prosecution, or suffer extreme extrajudicial sanction in the real world of national security enforcement, given the high stakes involved. Thus the deterrence that may be derived from source identification may also serve to deter nuclear scientists and engineers from participating in the various phases of building and delivering a bomb. The same is true, to a lesser degree, of the various intermediaries utilized to provide the funding and transport of illicit nuclear materials and their weaponization. Deterrence, of course, will vary, depending on individual situations and motivations, but to the extent nuclear forensics can put all these people at risk, and they are made aware of that capability, nuclear risk is reduced.

III. THE LEGAL AND INSTITUTIONAL EMPOWERMENT OF NUCLEAR FORENSICS

Nuclear forensics programs today exist within national security establishments of a number of governments. Related work has gone forward at the international level, but is dependent on ad hoc arrangements for cooperation among these governments and their forensics laboratories. Nuclear forensics developments to date reflect the prevailing view that nuclear security, practically and legally, is a state responsibility. States determine, as a matter of sovereignty, within their continuing discretion, the nuclear security activities of their bureaucracies, agencies, or any commercial or academic nuclear resources under their jurisdiction. The only exception to this national discretion model is data collection imposed on a government pursuant to mandate and sanction by the United Nations Security Council, implemented through the International Atomic Energy Agency (IAEA), as occurred for Iraq, and more recently Iran and North Korea.

However much resource and bureaucracy is devoted to nuclear forensics within the United States government, or any government, it falls far short of what is necessary and possible for a truly credible nuclear forensics capacity and deterrent. There are two aspects to this inadequacy, both systemic to the national discretion model. First, the credibility of nuclear forensics is naturally and severely compromised when it is the handmaiden of the national strategic agenda of any state. The false attribution involved in the invasion of Iraq and other situations, such as a case of alleged North Korean transfer to Libya[357] are exemplary and will forever be available to frame any national government's attribution claims as suspect. Second, the collection and processing of forensics data exclusively under national direction is at odds with the inclusiveness on which attribution capability, and therefore deterrence, depends. This is the most critical flaw in the national discretion model—that nuclear forensics capability depends on international inclusiveness, and any nuclear facility which any government keeps

357 Dafna Linzer, *U.S. Misled Allies About Nuclear Export: North Korea Sent Material to Pakistan, Not to Libya*, WASH. POST (Mar. 20, 2005).

out of the database means less attribution capacity and greater uncertainty. It is the very nature of attribution capability that accuracy, and therefore credibility, is compromised within any non-proliferation architecture to the extent confined to national governmental control. And that is precisely the critical shortcoming of the present system and its present course—deficiency of database.

While it is essential to engage whatever human intelligence may be available, the integrity of data is always at risk when generated on a national basis. This is the lesson from the Bush Administration's declaration to its Asian allies as part of its effort to isolate North Korea, that Pyongyang had exported nuclear material to Libya. Legitimacy was lost when it was later revealed, through officials with detailed knowledge of the transaction, that U.S. intelligence had in fact determined that it was Pakistan that sold the material to Libya through the now notorious illicit network of Pakistan's top nuclear scientist, Dr. A. Q. Khan, after obtaining it from North Korea. There was no evidence North Korea was aware of the second transaction. These findings were confirmed by the assessments of the IAEA.[358] The result was also a loss of credibility for the identification of nuclear source. The Bush Administration's similar manipulation of intelligence on WMD in orchestrating the invasion of Iraq, which was later exposed as involving concealed dissent on key elements of claimed intelligence, surely created a cynicism concerning national claims of identification of source, made deep and pervasive by the tremendous expenditure of treasure and blood that followed.

For any nuclear forensics investigation, the international nature of the database, the breadth of its collection and management, remains the critical consideration. Even the nuclear forensics investigations that are undertaken today when material is intercepted, are typically dependent on multiple sources from multiple nations, well beyond the confines of the nuclear weapons club. Credible and effective use of nuclear forensics also requires internationalization because the objective is to expose and address a threat that is typically transnational.[359] Nuclear forensics cases concern material that has moved through different states. Whether upon interdiction or nuclear detonation, nuclear forensics grapples with the transport of the nuclear material, which is sourced in one location and transported to others before reaching the point of interdiction or detonation. That makes the maximal process almost invariably international, and requires widespread participation to achieve even a minimal attribution capability.

As internationalization measures the strength of nuclear forensics capacity, controls by national government are the measure of its weaknesses. Consensus among the

---

358 This misrepresentation, it was reported, was to prevent China and South Korea from leaving the six-party nonproliferation talks with North Korea, a strategy that backfired with North Korea's announcement that it had nuclear weapons and would not rejoin the talks. *Id.* "North Korea predictably reacted with outrageous violations intended to capture U.S. attention. The U.S. negotiator, Charles 'Jack' Pritchard, was constantly subverted by then Undersecretary of State John Bolton… [Writing] in 2003, Pritchard said, 'I asked myself, 'What am I doing in government?''" *See also* Sidney Blumenthal, *Swaggering to Nowhere*, SALON.COM, (July 13, 2006), http://www.salon.com/2006/07/13/bush_foreign_policy/.

359 *See* May, *supra* note 338, at 7, 24.

scientists involved is that the new capacities to collect and analyze data available from a nuclear interception or detonation far exceed the ability to obtain useful information, primarily because of the lack of sufficient database of the world's fissile materials for the necessary comparisons to determine source on a consistent basis of reasonable accuracy.[360] Because the capability of forensics depends on the extent of the database, it cannot be adequately constructed without broadly international coordination and consolidation. Current assessments are all that the databases developed under the current national discretion model, even considered collectively, fall far short of what is necessary, as confirmed by the congressional findings published in 2010 as part of the Nuclear Forensics and Attribution Act.[361] There currently is no single database, but only distributed databases, many of them small, and subject to multiple national decisional authorities. There are no consistent standards for the contribution of data, and there is no collectively comprehensive design for rapid forensics response.[362] Any actual casework is restricted to state-to-state agreement,[363] constrained by the varying and inconsistent national security restrictions and commercial proprietary restrictions imposed erratically by different governments. All of this undermines the functionality of nuclear forensics, especially given the need for rapid collecting, processing, and comparing data upon a nuclear event.[364]

So how do we achieve an internationally inclusive and internationally legitimate attribution capability despite the fact that the data is ultimately controlled by the nation state? This fundamental problem is not ignored in the current deliberations on nuclear forensics capacity. Indeed, it appears front and center in the Congressional legislation, by way of the findings mandating the United States executive branch to enter into agreements with other states for the sharing of nuclear forensics data and protocols for the processing of that data for attribution.[365] But what is generally being proposed perpetuates the traditional design of non-proliferation infrastructure going back to the Nuclear Non-proliferation Treaty (NPT). That design copies the asymmetry of nuclear weapons possession and depends purely on consent, envisioning agreements among the nations with the most advanced and substantial nuclear weapons-related capabilities.[366] Present cooperation is similarly limited. Experts and laboratories from different countries have participated together with the IAEA in limited programs for

---

360 *Id.*

361 *See* Nuclear Forensics and Attribution Act, *supra* note 336.

362 Joint Working Group of the American Physical Society & The American Association for the Advancement of Science, NUCLEAR FORENSICS: ROLE, STATE OF THE ART, AND PROGRAM NEEDS 15 (2008), https://seaborg.llnl.gov/docs/nuclearForensics_role-stateoftheart-programneeds.pdf.

363 *Id.* at 61.

364 Kristo et al., *supra* note 340.

365 *See supra* discussion pages 116–117; Nuclear Forensics and Attribution Act, *supra* note 336.

366 Thus, while calling for broader participation, it has been proposed that forensics capacity could be accomplished through agreement of the major nuclear weapons powers, most importantly agreement between the United States and Russia. William Dunlop & Harold Smith, *Who Did It? Using International Forensics to Detect and Deter Nuclear Terrorism*, ARMS CONTROL ASS'N, at 6, Oct. 2006, http://www.armscontrol.org/act/2006_10/CVRForensics#Sidebar1.

the sharing of unclassified information, and the processing of actual forensics cases. This networking may result in collaboration on a particular forensics case, bringing into play multiple facilities and capabilities. Typically the databases drawn on include the IAEA Illicit Trafficking Database (ITDB), which is composed of commercial nuclear material samples, data obtained through the administration of IAEA safeguards,[367] and data obtained in connection with the seizure of illicit traffic in nuclear materials.[368] Other sources include the Malicious Acts Database and the databases within agencies of the United States government, and other governments and laboratories.

In 1996 a Nuclear Smuggling International Technical Working Group (ITWG) was formed specifically to achieve cooperation among the IAEA and national and non-governmental entities troughout the world in identifying the source and routing of interdicted nuclear materials, and to work on pre-detonation nuclear attribution to support prosecution of illicit material traffickers.[369] The nuclear forensics laboratories participating mutually committed to undertake the characterization of confiscated nuclear or other radioactive materials. There have been international meetings and round-robin analytical trials under the aegis of the ITWG toward developing protocols for the collection of evidence and forensic analysis, including the further development of forensic databanks. Such agreements and activities are, for the most part however, exclusively among the principal established nuclear weapons powers, which of course, is to take advantage of the forensics expertise residing primarily within the scientific and intelligence communities of these states. This natural inclination of exclusivity is counterproductive to drawing in the substantial and critical data of nuclear risk that now extends well beyond the control of the major nuclear weapons powers. A recent report on nuclear forensics by a premier group of American nuclear scientists determined that the nuclear material that could be used by a state or terrorist organization to build a nuclear weapon can be found in at least 40 countries.[370] Agreements on forensics among the major nuclear weapons powers, by perpetuating the asymmetry of the traditional non-proliferation architecture, naturally run counter to encouraging provision of the necessary data for a truly global database.

There have been numerous calls for international data sharing as to known nuclear material, by scientists and governmental officials citing the need for comprehensive

---

367 It is reported that Bush's threat to hold North Korea accountable for any nuclear transfer was premised on the U.S. ability to access the IAEA's data concerning North Korea's facilities and material. David E. Sanger & Thom Shanker, *U.S. Debates Deterrence for Terrorist Nuclear Threat*, N.Y. TIMES A10 (May 8, 2007).

368 Id. The IAEA Illicit Trafficking Database (ITDB) is the IAEA's information system on illicit trafficking and other unauthorized activities involving nuclear and radioactive materials. IAEA, *IAEA Illicit Trafficking Database Fact Sheet*, (last visited Jan. 24, 2010), http://www.iaea.org/NewsCenter/Features/RadSources/PDF/fact_figures2007.pdf.

369 Sidney Niemeyer & David K. Smith, *Following the Clues: The Role of Forensics in Preventing Nuclear Terrorism*, Vol. 37 ARMS CONTROL TODAY 14, 14–15 (July 1, 2007).

370 Joint Working Group of the American Physical Society & The American Association for the Advancement of Science, *supra* note 362.

access to nuclear signatures.[371] And there is no question that the collective judgment of the nuclear forensics community is that the more comprehensive the nuclear data available for sampling, the more promising and more credible the forensics enterprise.[372] But the call for more comprehensive access and collection of data is always based on the assumption that only ad hoc exclusively consensual arrangements between governments or their agencies and laboratories are politically sustainable. And these agreements, such as they are, or are generally contemplated to be, are for data sharing driven and controlled by the principal nuclear weapons powers.[373]

There are databases in numerous states.[374] But they are separated by national jurisdiction, national law—and time. With time for consultation, governmental authority controlling one data bank venue may be able to gain access to data in others. But the more serious a nuclear event, be it interdiction or detonation, the less likely political pressure for response would allow time for access and use. Moreover, among governments that would have to make their data available, there would be political roadblocks to revealing information that could result in retribution against a likely source which the government that controls the data might well choose not to target.[375]

The IAEA has suggested as a solution to such concerns a distributed architecture database that would protect information until the occurrence of an event.[376] But the same factors preventing or limiting sharing of information would still operate in the important scenarios of risk, i.e., the crisis scenarios, to render dysfunctional any pre-planned sharing of data. Moreover, even in time of peace, the nuclear nations that have data on foreign facilities, will not want to share that data, when it might compromise their own intelligence sources, which would normally appear the case.[377]

---

371 *See*, e.g., May et al., *supra* note 332, at 907–908. *See also* Andrew R. Grant, Acting Director, Office of Weapons of Mass Destruction Terrorism, Bureau of Int'l Sec. and Nonproliferation, U.S. Department of State, National Technical Nuclear Forensics Center Before the House Committee on Homeland Security Subcommittee on Emerging Threats, Cyber Security, and Science and Technology, Opening Statement, (Oct. 10, 2007) (documenting need for international cooperation); Matthew Phillips, *Uncertain Justice for Nuclear Terror: Deterrence of Anonymous Attacks Through Attribution*, Vol. 51 ORBIS (Aug. 6, 2007); IAEA, *Technical Guidance Reference Manual: Nuclear Forensics Support*, No. 2 IAEA NUCLEAR SEC. SERIES 1, 31–36 (2006).

372 It is widely agreed that "forensic databases are essential for successfully applying analytical data to existing information on the sources, methods, and origin of nuclear materials throughout the world" and that "this ability to compare signatures with existing knowledge and data is at the heart of case development." Kristo et al., *supra* note 340, at 25.

373 *See*, e.g., May et al., *supra* note 332, at 907–908.

374 The nuclear lab at Karlsrughe has developed an extensive joint database between Russia and the European Union. The Lawrence Livermore National Laboratory has established database sharing with the European Union, and also with laboratories on the Asian subcontinent, such as with Kazakhstan. Kristo et al., *supra* note 340, at 16–17.

375 *See* Levi, *supra* note 349.

376 IAEA, *Reinforcing the Global Nuclear Order for Peace and Prosperity, supra* note 301.

377 "I have discussed this aspect in depth with people at LLNL and I am highly pessimistic if the US (or any other state) will allow their database of weapons knowledge to be divulged. This is a matter not of the type of information, but how the US acquired it. Sources and methods are the most highly protected pieces of the US intelligence infrastructure. Only in the most critical cases where a post-detonation

Ultimately, whether post-detonation, or in relation to interdiction of nuclear weapons related material, the critical problem remains—insufficiency of readily accessible data, and national control over that data that can paralyze the processes for credible attribution and deterrence. The existing databanks are at best tied together in a distributed form, with their usefulness dependent on the willingness of national governments and laboratories to provide data in particular time-bound circumstances. Collation and cooperation to maximize information have taken place on an ad hoc basis between various governmental archives, nuclear laboratories, and the IAEA. Indeed, the European Community (EC) has gone on record as favoring this format. It is reported that in light of the national security sensitivities involved, the nuclear forensic specialists at the European Commission "see more promise in a decentralized system of shielded national databases, to be queried in emergencies."[378] A decentralized system of distributed databases is also clearly the drift of the nuclear forensics legislation recently passed by the United States Congress.[379] It is further recently reported that the United States, the European Community, and the International Atomic Energy Agency are involved in seeking consensus for a proposal to build a system of nuclear "libraries."[380] However, the existing databases, whether utilized separately or together, only include data to the very limited extent willingly made available by the nuclear powers, and states whose facilities have been subject to inspection under Security Council mandated international surveillance regimes such as those that have erratically operated in Iraq, Iran, and North Korea.

Data sharing is likely to be dysfunctional in crisis so long as national governments impose highly discretionary limitations of many sorts arising from considerations of national security and protection of national security intelligence, proprietary interests, or domestic or international political concerns. All efforts to date for data collection have generally failed to engage a priority of counterproliferation among governments, including the principal nuclear weapons powers. Still many hundreds of buildings with separated plutonium and HEU stocks exist within dozens of countries, outside of any database. These facilities also of course manifest gross disparities in security standards, and vulnerability to terrorists.[381]

---

investigation may be used as a prelude to action, would I foresee any illumination of these data... and only then this would come at the highest levels." E-mail from Daniel Chivers, Nuclear Research Scientist at the Lawrence Livermore National Laboratory and Department of Nuclear Engineering, University of California, Berkeley, to author (Oct. 5, 2009) (on file with author). By contrast, the proposal here is not to impair national bases or reveal data such as U.S. intelligence services have gathered about other countries nuclear weapons related resources. The proposed international forensics database would call on governments only to provide information on their own fissile production facilities.

378 Hanley, *supra* note 335.

379 *Id.*

380 Rachel Oswald, *Distrust Mires Effort to Develop International Nuclear Forensics Database*, Global Sec. Newswire (Dec. 24, 2009).

381 *Id. See also* Allison, *supra* note 9, at 61–86.

Going forward under the existing infrastructure of counterproliferation will accordingly also fail to achieve the significantly expanded deterrence that the extraordinary capability of nuclear forensics could provide. The credibility on which deterrence depends is lacking. This is reflected, for example, in the opinion attributed to senior nuclear experts during the Bush Administration, that "when it comes to other countries, many of that library's (nuclear forensics data) shelves are empty… the huge gap is one reason that the Bush administration is so far unable to make a convincing threat to terrorists or their suppliers that they will be found out."[382] The huge gap has not been closed.[383] And the huge gap cannot be closed, so long as the international community remains stuck in a quixotic narrative of national limitation of forensics data. The theme for a new narrative must be one of accommodation of national concerns within a comprehensive international system, that would open the door to achieving legitimacy, credibility, and thereby the greatest deterrence.

Nuclear forensics is a counterproliferation resource with great potential for deterrence, but lack of universality cripples accuracy, undermines credibility, and ultimately defeats deterrence. The evolving and constantly improving capacity for nuclear forensics to significantly enhance international nuclear security through an expanded deterrence will remain unrealized to the extent it is limited by incomplete participation in the collection of data. The need, therefore, is for universality, both in substance and process. Specifically the need is for: (1) an internationally comprehensive, and comprehensively accessible database; (2) internationally comprehensive and consistent standards as to what information should be supplied; (3) internationally comprehensive standards as to how that data should be stored, processed, and analyzed; and (4) internationally agreed standards for indicating to policy makers the accuracy and certainty of forensics conclusions. A Security Council mandate for the establishment of an international nuclear forensics data bank could provide the foundation to free the potential of nuclear forensics, and make all this feasible.

What would be the composition of the international nuclear forensics data bank to achieve the necessarily comprehensive resource? The science of nuclear forensics instructs its content. The database would have to provide data sufficient to identify the method of production and probable source of fissile material.[384] Therefore it would be composed of pre-designated categories of samples and other data drawn from nuclear facilities on the same basis worldwide. The categories would be determined by standards for comparison and identification of the source of interdicted or detonated material, to identify the chemical and physical properties of the plutonium and enriched uranium associated with the production facilities from which the material is drawn. This information would be consolidated into a single reference system—archived and catalogued to constitute an internationally comprehensive data bank.

---

382 Sanger & Shanker, *supra* note 367.

383 The United States and Russia may constitute the biggest part of that gap. Together they are assessed to possess 87 percent of the world's processed plutonium and highly enriched uranium.

384 See Kristo et al., *supra* note 340; See also May, *supra* note 338.

The science of nuclear forensics also instructs how the data would be processed—the protocols for assembling the data, and for its analysis after interdiction, or post-detonation, to extract reliable signature. The data would have to be processed according to a single set of internationally agreed scientific protocols and standards. Altogether, the material so processed would, in effect, define attribution.

The international database would be vast, but certainly not beyond the currently computerized capability for access. Its very size would ensure huge gain in forensics capability. That gain would include not just the volume of data, but also accelerated forensics capability as the result of pre-arranged protocols for collection and analysis of samples, both for building the database, and matching after interdiction or detonation.

What has already been achieved within the limitations of the national discretion model indicates prospects for acceptance of this design. There is solid evidence of willingness of nations to share information about their nuclear production processes and material. Such agreements, though limited, have already been reached between the United States and other nations of the former Soviet Union, such as Russia, Kazakhstan, and Tajikistan.[385] Also, many governments have already demonstrated willingness to share significant signature data, though of course some more than others, and therefore we already know the areas of sensitivity and resistance, such as have appeared in the cooperative efforts involving the United States, the EC, and Russia.[386]

At the practical level, there also has been significant progress, both as to arrangements for data collection and for its processing, though the results remain far short of the necessary data bank. For example, within the U.S. national effort a knowledge base is being designed that could serve as part of and the model for an international database and forensics process.[387] As to processing, significant collaboration to develop appropriate protocols is already being achieved. It is reported by a premier grouping of American nuclear scientists that "an international community of experts has begun developing mutually agreed-upon techniques for performing reliable nuclear forensic analysis, and the analytic techniques are peer reviewed and regularly benchmarked in

---

385 *See Institutionalizing Our Strategy for Long-term Success*, *supra* note 350.

386 *Fact Sheet: The United States-Russia Working Group on Counterterrorism*, EMBASSY OF THE U.S., (June 20, 2008) (*available at* http://merln.ndu.edu/archivepdf/russia/State/factsheet_ctwg.pdf).

387 "We are already establishing a knowledge management system for nuclear signatures, processes, origins and pathways...." It has been disclosed the design is a process that can be accessed by simple employment of computer analysis. "As an example, when key words are entered, the system will find the relevant information..," though "distributed across several government sites...with different levels of controlled access." Lawrence Livermore nuclear engineer Frank Wong, a leader in the knowledge base effort, quoted in *Nuclear Forensics: Identifying the Source of Stolen Nuclear Materials*, LAWRENCE LIVERMORE NATIONAL LABORATORY (Jan./Feb. 2007), https://www.llnl.gov/str/JanFeb07/Smith.html. The Lawrence Livermore Laboratory and seven other Department of Energy (DOE) national laboratories have been mandated by the FBI and Department of Homeland Security to develop the U.S. forensics capability for nuclear and radiological materials.

internationally accepted tests using unfamiliar samples."[388] The technology also continues to advance to even greater efficacy.[389]

The IAEA, as presently operating, offers a natural synergy with forensics data banking in a mandatory system. The IAEA safeguards regime includes taking environmental samples in all facilities and locations where it has safeguards agreements to verify activities. It already maintains a database on sample results of nuclear fuel cycle facilities. Its role could be expanded to achieve both the forensics and accounting objectives, serving both for identification of source in relation to a nuclear event, and providing the intelligence for tracking to prevent a nuclear catastrophe. This could be supplemented with a legal and regulatory framework for the registration, administration, and control of radioactive sources that has been recommended by many experts, drawing on the experience and expertise already available.

The political inclination and practical means are obtainable. The fundamental problem remains structural—a deficiency of legal and institutional basis for achieving a truly international and comprehensive database. The scientists agree that though nuclear signatures as currently archived can narrow the field of potential sources, current banking of nuclear signatures is not anywhere near adequate for a robust identification capability.[390]

Nuclear forensics capability, as other means of counterproliferation, is locked within the constraints of the national discretion model. It is therefore necessary to change the model to achieve a credible and robust nuclear forensics capacity. No doubt the national constraints that currently compromise nuclear forensics attribution cannot be simply dismissed. They reside in reality-based considerations of national security and proprietary interest, for example, the concern not to disclose data that would reveal otherwise secret reactor-fuel production technologies. The feasibility of an international nuclear forensics data bank depends on formulation so as not to be perceived as too prejudicial to such interests, despite the national security benefit of participation in a databank of global capability.

How would the design for an international nuclear forensics databank achieve the necessary accommodations to realize its potential? Legitimacy in nuclear examination comes from capitalizing on expertise drawn together under international aegis. This has been well demonstrated by the operations of the IAEA, which enjoys credibility because it draws together a recognized community of professional and scientific expertise that, even when operating under Security Council mandate and an implicit and/or explicit political agenda, is broadly recognized as committed to maintaining scientific neutrality. What is required for the success of an international nuclear forensics databank, this indicates, is a similar epistemic embodiment of international nuclear forensics for management of the databank.

388 May, *supra* note 338, at 27.

389 This includes sequencing of forensics techniques, such as already developed under the Nuclear Smuggling International Technical Working Group. IAEA, *supra* note 371, at 26; *See also* Niemeyer & Smith, *supra* note 369.

390 *See*, e.g., May et al., *supra* note 332, at 907–908; *But see* Kristo et al., *supra* note 340, at 15.

Most likely, the management capability could be formed within the IAEA,[391] which has endorsed an international archiving role for itself,[392] being already deeply involved in nuclear forensics.[393] But whether within, or in addition to the IAEA, the international institutionalization of expertise to set the standards for sample collection, and the protocols for processing and analysis is necessary. Historical experience already indicates this as the way to maximize the acquisition of information, while minimizing national security and proprietary concerns.

There is a broad range of data for which nondisclosure cannot be justified on the basis of national security or commercial interest. That information, according to forensic science, is adequate to constitute the baseline data required.[394] The expertise that drives the field, according to its own evaluation, is capable of identifying the sampling and process data that could be drawn from any nuclear facility, without significantly impinging on national security and proprietary interests.[395] The consensus is that contemporary nuclear forensics can allow provision of non-sensitive information that can establish nuclear signature for effective attribution.[396]

Intelligence sources can remain secure, because the proposed data bank requires only information on a government's own nuclear resources, not the information it may have gained from spying on others. Moreover, although resistance may appear in the intelligence communities, the scientists—those who actually know what is involved in securing adequate data for attribution—have made a point of stating that data-sharing can be accomplished without prejudice to national security interests.[397]

---

391 Chivers, *supra* note 377.

392 Former Director-General of the IAEA Mohamed ElBaradei stated his support for the IAEA constructing an international database for nuclear material characteristics. IAEA, *supra* note 301.

393 The IAEA has sponsored a working group to study pre-detonation identification of nuclear materials. IAEA, *supra* note 371. It has also established its own limited data archiving, particularly insofar as nuclear material has been identified pursuant to specific Security Council mandated inspection regimes, such as for North Korea, Iran, and Iraq under Saddam Hussein. *See* IAEA, *supra* note 368; *See also* S.C. Res. 1540, *supra* note 124; Allen S. Weiner, Chaim Braun, Michael May & Roger Speed, *Enhancing Implementation of U.N. Sec. Council Resolution 1540: Report of the Ctr. on Int'l Sec. and Cooperation* (CISAC) (Sept. 2007), http://iis-db.stanford.edu/pubs/22070/1540_Final_Report_w_cvr.pdf.

394 This information includes physical, chemical, and isotopic properties identified through such measures as uranium enrichment percentage, isotopic ratios, and time dating. Chivers, *supra* note 377 .

395 "We believe that authenticated and secured access to forensic signatures of such (nuclear weapons source) materials can be ensured with good will, international cooperation and new technologies." Joint Working Group of the American Physical Society & The American Association for the Advancement of Science, *supra* note 362, at 25.

396 Chivers, *supra* note 377.

397 Thus Michael May, retired Director of the Lawrence Livermore National Laboratory, is reported to have explained, concerning nuclear forensics attribution discussions with the Russian counterparts, that the paranoia, at least on the Russian side, comes from its spy agencies and not from its nuclear scientists, "Usually on technical issues they are not distrustful because they know the facts. The Russian Scientists that I've met... they were not paranoid. They were realistic people." Oswald, *supra* note 380.

The proposed international nuclear forensics data bank would seek to capitalize on this practical and political feasibility. Through responsible international management by the professional epistemic nuclear forensics community, the design can be to maximize the role of expertise and science, and minimize the national security paranoia that might otherwise stifle what is an extraordinary opportunity to improve nuclear security.

The science also indicates there is technology available to address national security and proprietary concerns. Division can be made between non-sensitive and sensitive information. Even the latter could be made available to the data bank under special agreements restricting its disclosure, and/or utilizing various encryption techniques, such as "hash" codes to encapsulate analytical information. This would provide confidentiality, and the codes, operating like passwords, would interrogate the database only in the event of nuclear crisis.[398] Also possible is agreement for release of information only under certain pre-defined circumstances.

Security Council action to create and implement an international nuclear forensics data bank could provide the legal basis for realization of this capability. The establishing resolution would impose the obligations on *all states*, to address the global risks inherent in the spread of nuclear weapons related materials and technology by providing the non-sensitive baseline data. This would lay the basis, first and foremost, for the disclosure of pre-designated samples from *all nuclear facilities* capable of production of fissile material at levels for nuclear weapons development. Those samples would be collected and subject to internationally vetted and accepted protocols, designated and managed by the international body of nuclear forensics experts, also established under the authority of the Chapter VII resolution authorizing the international nuclear forensics databank.

The resolution establishing this counterproliferation capability would have to embody the principle of equality of application. This would be an essential aspect of fundamental differentiation from the traditional, and collapsing, non-proliferation architecture. This foundation for equitable and equally binding counterproliferation obligation of all states would not just eliminate the well-worn excuses for non-proliferation noncompliance. It would serve to achieve legitimacy. Through international nuclear forensics management, a baseline of compliance would be established for all, including the principal nuclear weapons powers. These governments, notwithstanding the differentiated status of nuclear weapons and non-nuclear weapons states NNWS under the Nuclear Non-proliferation Treaty, would be providing samples of their own fissile material and processes to achieve the advantages obtainable for all states from a comprehensively international nuclear forensics data bank. Their national security and proprietary concerns would be protected by the same baseline of disclosable information as every other state, as well as by special provisions for assuring secrecy through available encryption techniques, or access on specified conditions. The principle of equality of application

---

398 Joint Working Group of the American Physical Society & The American Association for the Advancement of Science, *supra* note 362, at 26.

would universalize the nuclear security achieved. Especially significant for the major nuclear weapons powers, and motivating those governments to sign on to the system, is that they would obtain previously unobtainable means to trace intercepted fissile material, not only for revealing source or nuclear security lapses worldwide, but to locate weakness in their own nuclear military and commercial nuclear facilities if illicit transfer is intercepted.

The principle of equality of application embodied in the proposed resolution would be compromised by any facilities not publicly acknowledged, such as the facilities known or thought to exist in Israel, Iran, and North Korea. The possibility of hidden facilities would certainly constitute some weakness in the system, though not so significant as to disable it. It is said by experts that "today, most nuclear powers have a fairly thorough accounting system of (their own) nuclear materials, and there are a finite number of sources of weapons grade material, all of which are known,"[399] Secrecy and the few outliers, therefore, should not result in any great gaps in the databank. The likely venues of secret facilities, being known, and few in number, would not create sufficient uncertainty to defeat the credibility of attribution. The venues where secret facilities are thought to exist, however, would mark the points of special interest in the process of elimination by which nuclear forensics achieves accuracy of attribution.

There are other considerations that counter the secrecy concern. Secret facilities, if they exist, may be revealed if challenge inspections are available, or by covert collection means, such as those employed by the intelligence agencies of the United States and other governments. Also, as to the governments most likely to hide facilities, such as North Korea or Iran, the international inspections that have occurred under Security Council mandate, have resulted in significant archiving of samples from their existing disclosed facilities, and may continue to do so.[400]

The strength and greatest significance of the international nuclear forensics data bank, however, would be the motivation it generates for any government to avoid being named on the suspect list, by cooperating at least as to its known facilities.[401] Refusal to provide the designated data would focus suspicion in the event of interdiction or post-detonation. Nondisclosure by some would not preclude the benefits of more general participation, and most governments would seek not to be on the suspect list. The more states that participate, the greater the incentive for all to participate and provide

399 Miller, *supra* note 340, at 50.

400 Dmitri Trenin, *Untangling Iran's Nuclear Web*, MOSCOW TIMES (Oct. 5, 2009).

401 It would be possible to even further minimize this risk, to the extent the system could be supplemented by the right to engage in "special inspections" currently available to the IAEA as to states that have signed on to the additional protocol to the Nuclear Non-proliferation Treaty. *See Model Protocol, supra* note 315; *See also IAEA Safeguards Overview: Comprehensive Safeguard Agreements and Additional Protocols, supra* note 228. It could also be supplemented, on the incentive side, by making participation a condition of various benefits of existing nuclear cooperation, such as a condition for trading for nuclear exports from the Nuclear Suppliers Group, as has been done in connection with the IAEA Additional Protocol. *Id.*; *See also* IAEA, *Safeguards and Verification: Status of Additional Protocols*, (last visited Jan. 30, 2012), http://www.iaea.org/OurWork/SV/Safeguards/protocol.html.

the information that exonerates, to get a seat where most states would be sitting in the relative safety of presumptive innocence.

For counterproliferation, the disclosure and transparency achieved through an international data bank would be a major step forward. Despite elaboration of regulations and systems by the IAEA, the governments with nuclear weapons capacities currently have no strong incentive to provide complete reports on their nuclear facilities and the materials that move through them.[402] There is no particular monitoring regime sufficiently widespread for there to be a compelling downside for being absent. However, with an international nuclear forensics data bank established, any government would have a strong incentive to demonstrate and advertise its compliance. An international data bank would operate without the resistance inherent in the current infrastructure, because all governments would be motivated to participate to insure their own nuclear security, in a variety of critical respects, including the security of nuclear material worldwide, and the means to exclude their being targeted, whether for critique, sanction, or attack, or to avoid false attribution. With intercepts of illicit transfers of nuclear material occurring more and more frequently, and the risks of nuclear detonation becoming more and more likely, that motivation should be great.

Currently, any government cheating on its obligations under the Nuclear Non-proliferation Treaty can reasonably conclude it will not be caught. But the government refusing to cooperate in providing data for the international nuclear forensics data bank would be clearly identified. Whatever the prospects for cheating the IAEA, or avoiding obligations under the Nuclear Non-proliferation Treaty, the misrecreant government's leadership that would resist providing samples of all its facilities and materials would be aware it would face seriously enhanced risk of attribution upon the occurrence of a nuclear event. This self-enforcing dynamic of the international nuclear forensics data bank would also avoid the monitoring conundrum presented by dual-use technology. Whatever the use, whatever the weaponization, virtual or real, the data bank could fully function to achieve an expanded deterrence, because all that it would require of states is that they meet the baseline for data collection.

The integrity of the process of attribution, along with information from intelligence agencies, technical resources, through political evaluation, would determine the international data bank's success in achieving credibility, and therefore legitimacy, before or after a nuclear event. That integrity must include agreed-upon forensics procedures and standards, chain-of-custody requirements, and cross-checking and peer review requirements, articulated and administered by a high-level expert panel.[403] To the

---

402 Orde F. Kittrie, *Averting Catastrophe: Why the Nuclear Nonproliferation Treaty is Losing its Deterrence Capacity and How to Restore It*, 28 MICH. J. INT'L L. 337, 415–416 (2007).

403 "To be a robust scientific method, one must incorporate peer review at some level. This is being done within the Smuggling International Technical Working Group, whose forensics exercises use at least two independent laboratories to reach conclusions with a good amount of peer review on the results. This may be seen as creating an undesirable latency in the process, but this review would be critical to international cohesion for action and thus provides a greater deterrent effect." Chivers, *supra* note 377.

extent such analytical systems are in place and refined, they will facilitate, expedite, and help achieve support for responsible political and strategic decision. They will also serve rational evaluation in a political environment, post-detonation, when the pressure for precipitate and potentially ill-considered response will be great.

To fully realize the expanded deterrence an international nuclear forensics databank could generate, publicity is essential. The challenge is to convince state and non-state actors who would otherwise engage in illicit proliferation activity, or might neglect responsibility for nuclear security, that the international community has the means to identify them in relation to transfer or detonation. Deterrence requires credibility based on capability, but also sufficient clarity of message concerning attribution.

The importance of publicity for securing the deterrence value of nuclear forensics has not been lost on policymakers. It appears as a principal consideration in the recent surge of interest and investment in nuclear forensics. The recent statement of the National Security Strategy of the United States declares, "We will ensure that our capacity to determine the source of any attack is well-known, and that our determination to respond overwhelmingly to any attack is never in doubt."[404] The United States State Department has announced that "Nuclear forensics is a critical component of President Obama's larger nuclear materials security efforts . . . ."[405] The United States Defense Threat Reduction Agency is taking a lead in reporting how successful nuclear attribution techniques have become. There are surely reasons not to fully disclose attribution capabilities, insofar as details might serve efforts to spoof or defeat attribution.[406] Also, certain attribution capabilities may not be disclosed because of their relation to intelligence activities. However, there is no reason for restraint in trumpeting the fact of forensics capability. That capability can be conveyed, today, with information already in the public domain, and by publicity given to nuclear forensics exercises, as has been the technique for establishing credibility in other arenas and programs of counterproliferation, such as the Proliferation Security Initiative (PSI).[407] But there could be no better way to secure the publicity for an expanded deterrence, than a Security Council resolution promulgated under the authority of Chapter VII of the United Nations Charter requiring all states to comply in the establishment of an international nuclear forensics databank.

---

404 Similarly, the National Strategy for Combating Terrorism announced by the Bush Administration in September 2006, states, "Should a WMD terrorist attack occur the rapid identification of the source and perpetrator of an attack will enable our response efforts and may be critical in disrupting follow-on attacks. We *will* develop the capability to assign responsibility for the intended or actual use of WMD via accurate attribution—the rapid fusion of technical forensics data with intelligence and law enforcement information." *Strategy for Winning the War on Terror, supra* note 346, at 15.

405 Ambassador Bonnie D. Jenkins, All-Party Parliamentary Group. on Transatlantic and International Security, U.S. Department of State, Global Threat Reduction (Feb. 4, 2010) (*transcript available at* http://www.state.gov/t/isn/rls/rm/136802.htm), *reported in* Oswald, *supra* note 380.

406 Miller, *supra* note 340, at 43–44.

407 *See infra* pages 195–204.

B. Internationalization of National Counterproliferation Intelligence

I. THE INCONGRUITY OF NATIONAL INTELLIGENCE RESOURCES AND TRANSNATIONAL NUCLEAR RISK

National security today is foremost about intelligence. 9/11 and the killing of Bin Laden gave public clarity to that reality. For counterproliferation, the dependence of international security on intelligence resources is particularly and increasingly compelled by the clandestine nature of nuclear weapons risk represented by nuclear terrorism and secret nuclear weapons programs of governments. In this new world of nuclear risk, intelligence brought to bear internationally can be the difference between security and disaster. An intelligence capability commensurate with the transnational nature of contemporary nuclear risk is therefore what is required.

To the contrary, counterproliferation intelligence resources remain, for the most part, national resources. For the nuclear weapons era that the NPT was designed to address, the national compartmentalization of intelligence resources was suited to the threat. With nuclear weapons confined to the original five nuclear weapons powers of the NPT, openly advertising their arsenals was a natural feature of MAD. Intelligence resources were accordingly structurally settled as instruments of national security. The international organization of resources was confined to the respective spheres of influence of the United States and Soviet Union. Sharing arrangements were limited to be within each of the two spheres of global power, to the most trustworthy national relationships, such as between the CIA of the United States and Britain's MI6.

Intelligence resources today are of a different character. Intelligence sources are prolific and separated in multifarious and fluctuating groupings of governments and their agencies. They include resources unlimited by national borders and resources employing ever-new and varied technologies, such as satellite imagery and cyber-spying. Risk is similarly internationally expanding, and similarly evolving into many of the same new technologies.

Intelligence continues to bear critically on all aspects of contemporary nuclear risk; not just terrorist risk, but also state-to-state risk reminiscent of the cold war. Reliable intelligence remains vital, in particular for assuring compliance with safeguard agreements, and disarmament measures. Transnationally, that includes monitoring transfers of nuclear weapons-related materials and technologies involving governments or non-state actors. However, counterproliferation intelligence, as a national capability, is in important respects at odds with gaining effective intelligence on clandestine nuclear weapons programs and hidden transfers of nuclear material and technologies. State-based agencies have historically relied on the physical boundaries of state borders to intercept security threats. That perspective is surely now inadequate. It should be great cause for concern that the list of belated discovery of concealed nuclear weapons-related transfers and programs is now long and getting longer.[408]

The national character of counterproliferation intelligence resources is least suited to the spread of nuclear weapons and technology that can involve non-state actors. The leaders of terrorist organizations, such as al Qaeda, feed their monstrous schemes on transnational relationships and transnational communications technologies for recruiting, financing, and operations. Between governments, mechanisms such as export-import controls and border controls can flag nuclear risk, such as by identifying discrepancies between what is reported and what is identified as actually being transferred. But transnational weapons-related transfers involving non-state actors are designed to circumvent such controls. Transnational intelligence capacity is accordingly all that much more vital and challenged if the bad actors are unidentified and are working around national borders. This is especially so given the short time span so often characteristic of terrorist operations.

Terrorists are the delinquent foster children of globalization. Terrorism, because of its likely collation of international technological, human, and material resources, naturally depends on transnational networking. Today's networked world is its natural incubator. For nuclear terrorism, such connectedness is the perfect environment, given the transnational resources necessary to sustain it, particularly since its success depends on transporting fissile material from source to target.

Notwithstanding the transnational nature of nuclear risk today, intelligence gathering remains, for the most part, nationally based and nationally circumscribed. There is some distinctly international institutional capacity, for example, by way of a small intelligence office at the IAEA.[409] Additionally, the IAEA and other institutionalizations of counterproliferation, such as the Nuclear Suppliers Group (NSG), may receive intelligence forwarded from national intelligence agencies. However, intelligence

---

408 For a history of Iraq's secret nuclear program, *see* Federation of American Scientists, *Iraqi Nuclear Weapons—Iraq Special Weapons*, (Nov. 3, 1998), http://www.fas.org/nuke/guide/iraq/nuke/program.htm. For a chronology of North Korea's program, *see Chronology of U.S.-North Korean Nuclear and Missile Diplomacy*, ARMS CONTROLS ASSOCIATION, (last visited Feb. 1, 2012), http://www.armscontrol.org/factsheets/dprkchron; *see also*, Volha Charnysh, *North Korea's Nuclear Program*, NUCLEAR AGE PEACE FOUNDATION, (Sept. 3, 2009). For information about the failure to detect the transfer of nuclear technology between North Korea and Syria, *see* Peter Crall, *U.S. Shares Information on NK-Syrian Ties*, Vol. 38 ARMS CONTROL TODAY (May 2008). For information about the secret transfer of nuclear technology from Israel to South Africa that jump-started its program, *see* David Albright, *South Africa and the Affordable Bomb*, Vol. 50, No. 4 BULLETIN OF THE ATOMIC SCIENTISTS 37, 39 (Jul/Aug 1994); *See also* McGreal, *supra* note 263.

409 Presently, the IAEA is said to have only two active small intelligence units, one that analyzes open-source Intelligence and one that assesses imagery. Moreover, it is criticized as lacking staff with a professional intelligence background equal to demands of effective counterproliferation intelligence. See, Elaine M. Grossman, *Boost in IAEA Intelligence Capability Looks Unlikely in Near Term*, GLOBAL SECURITY NEWSWIRE, June 22, 2009, http://www.nti.org/gsn/article/boost-in-iaea-intelligence-capability-looks-unlikely-in-near-term/.

capacity pertinent to counterproliferation is largely confined within limitations variously imposed by different governments, with in-depth state-to-state sharing the exception rather than the rule. When sharing does occur, it occurs on an ad hoc basis, generally in relation to military or counterterrorism operations, such as has occurred between the United States coordinating anti-terrorism operations with Pakistan, Yemen, and the Philippines, and regionally, through coordination within the European Community.[410]

There are a variety of explanations for the limitations imposed on counterproliferation by the almost exclusively national sourcing and implementation of intelligence. There is resistance to sharing because of concerns about free-riding, in that different nations make different contributions to counterproliferation intelligence, sometimes because of different capability, sometimes not. Differences in language are also not insignificant as an inhibition on intelligence sharing. The translation of considerable information to overcome linguistic barriers between national intelligence agencies can be both expensive and problematical.

But the incongruity between the national resource of intelligence and counterproliferation runs much deeper. The dependence of international intelligence sharing on discretionary cooperation of national intelligence agencies is not just limiting in relation to counterproliferation. It is in tension with counterproliferation. National intelligence agencies navigate for their own ends as nationally defined. As sources of information for international intelligence, they are always suspect. As national agencies, the principle focus and priority of each is internal security, which often means telling a different intelligence story at home than abroad. This is reinforced, most importantly, by the need to protect resources and methods from disclosure, and to prevent endangering ongoing operations.

The consequence is that in areas in which intelligence sharing could be most helpful, it may be the most severely restricted. This can be seen, for example, in the distrust that has severely undermined the U.S. relationship with Pakistan's Inter-services Intelligence Agency (ISI), which U.S. officials have repeatedly accused of aiding the Taliban, despite Pakistan's ostensible alliance with the United States in fighting Islamist militants in Pakistan.[411] The killing of Bin Laden, in a protected compound in Pakistan, only heightened, to an unprecedented level, this long-standing distrust.

The tension also arises from concern that intelligence received from another nation's intelligence service is likely to be biased by that government's political perspective, and/or designed to manipulate the recipient government. This dynamic received great attention, of course, after it was discovered that the invasion of Iraq was falsely premised on the presence of WMD.[412] The lead up to the invasion demonstrated, probably

---

410 *See infra* pages 146–147, 153–156.

411 *See*, e.g., Matthew Rosenberg, *Karzai Told to Dump U.S.*, Wall St. J., Apr. 27, 2011, at A10, Col. 4, http://online.wsj.com/article/SB10001424052748704729304576287041094035816.html.

412 See, e.g., House of Commons, Foreign Affairs Committee, *The Decision to go to War in Iraq, Ninth Report of Session 2002–03*, (July 3, 2003), http://www.fas.org/irp/threat/ukiraq0703.pdf.

more than any other recent set of events, the vulnerability of WMD counterproliferation to disinformation through selection of intelligence to influence policy, by withholding, exaggerating, or distorting information.[413]

The difficulty is compounded because the most substantial and technically empowered intelligence capabilities are held and controlled by a small number of major states, including those capable of being the biggest bullies on the block. The relatively great intelligence resources of a government, such as that of the United States or China or Russia, only heightens fear within governments of lesser intelligence capacity, that any counterproliferation intelligence that may be available for them through sharing, will be infected with foreign national bias, to justify otherwise unjustifiable action, particularly the use of force.

The invasion of Iraq bears many lessons, but surely at least one great lesson for counterproliferation is that everything possible must be done to separate intelligence capability to detect WMD, from national strategic policy. At least prior to the invasion of Iraq, it was conventional wisdom among professional intelligence officers that it is of the utmost importance that intelligence gathering be separated from policy-making, to avoid so-called "politicized intelligence."[414] Within highly developed national intelligence organizations, such as the CIA, that separation is normally regarded as a hallmark of professionalism, essential to maximize objectivity.[415] The same principle applies to international sharing of counterproliferation intelligence, but even more importantly, because of the greater potential for manipulation that haunts any sharing between nations of intelligence so critical to national security.

The risk of misinformation is great because of the pervasive and extreme fear that claims of WMD development can generate. Disinformation can not only cripple counterproliferation, but can generate the political preconditions for military action—even massive military action, as for Iraq, sold by politicians to their intimidated constituencies as WMD interdiction. The legacy of the WMD premise used to justify the invasion of Iraq, that the regime of Saddam Hussein was arming itself and terrorists with weapons of mass destruction, will forever epitomize the perversion of counterproliferation intelligence, to which nationally based counterproliferation intelligence is so susceptible.

The selection and distortion of nationally based intelligence, while evident in the extreme in the invasion of Iraq, is to some degree to be expected. Counterproliferation

---

413 See Michael Duffy, James Carney, Massimo Calabresi, Matthew Cooper, Adam Zagorin, John F. Dickerson, J.F.O. Mcallister, & Andrew Purvis, *Iraq: A Question of Trust*, TIME MAGAZINE, at 2, (Jul. 21, 2003), http://www.time.com/time/magazine/article/0,9171,1005234-1,00.html. *See also*, Peter Eisner, *How Bogus Letter Became a Case for War*, THE WASHINGTON POST, Apr. 3, 2007, http://www.washingtonpost.com/wp-dyn/content/article/2007/04/02/AR2007040201777_pf.html/.

414 Concerning "politicized intelligence," See Katarina Zivanovic, *International Cooperation of Intelligence Agencies against Transnational Terrorist Targets*, THE QUARTERLY JOURNAL 119 (Winter 2008), http://www.pfpconsortium.org/file/2789/download.*See also*, Mark M. Lowenthal, INTELLIGENCE: FROM SECRETS TO POLICY (CQ Press1st ed. 2000).

415 *Id.*

intelligence dependent on direction and use by national governments will characteristically be skewed to serve national policy. The consequence is the debasement of international intelligence sharing, diminished credibility, and unwillingness to share, altogether severely constraining the counterproliferation potential of intelligence. Tragic demonstration of this occurred on March 11, 2004, in relation to a terrorist bombing in Madrid. Some of the alleged perpetrators of that bombing, which killed and injured 191 people, had been identified by the French and Spanish police as terrorism suspects as early as 2001, and were living openly in Madrid. Germany and Norway also had information that could have provided additional evidence of the risk.[416] But all the evidence came to naught, for lack of a transnational apparatus for connecting the dots.

International intelligence collation has become more important to achieve as nuclear weapons risk has become more and more characterized by clandestine networking across national boundaries. The mechanisms traditionally used by governments to limit risk, such as border controls and inspections, have become less relevant, and the sharing of intelligence and transnational means of interdiction, is becoming ever more important. Opportunities for the interception of transnational communications and international cooperation in uncovering transnational networking have become crucial to protecting populations from WMD, and most significantly, nuclear risk. Because nuclear risk is naturally transnational, it brings along with it the greatest need for international cooperation, including the capacity to act quickly. But to maximize efficacy and credibility, the separation of national intelligence gathering and counterproliferation policymaking must be maintained. Accomplishing that separation points the way, necessarily, to the international institutionalization of intelligence sharing.

There is broad consensus in studies of intelligence sharing that it is the perception of mutual interest and the resulting trust that is key to both the quality and level of sharing. Different disciplines; political sociology, social psychology, foreign affairs studies, and game theory all identify the same key element that explains one actor's willingness, be it an individual or government, to share and trust information with another. That key is the conviction of the provider that the recipient of the information shares the same goal and desired outcome. Thus the better defined and focused the common interest, the greater the sharing of intelligence that results.[417] That is as true for counterproliferation intelligence as any other intelligence. The academic studies do

416 Peter Finn & Keith B. Richburg, *Madrid Probe turns to Islamic cell in Morocco*, THE WASHINGTON POST, Mar. 20, 2004; *See also*, J. Lichfield, E. Nash, S. Castle & J. Bennetto, *Europe must share terror intelligence*, THE INDEPENDENT, Mar. 17, 2004.

417 This is confirmed by many studies. For political sociology, *see* James S. Coleman, FOUNDATIONS OF SOCIAL THEORY (Belknap Press of Harvard University Press 1990); Russell Hardin, TRUST AND TRUSTWORTHINESS (Russell Sage Foundation 2002); For social psychology, *see* Carl Hovland, J. Irving, & H. Kelley, PERSUASION AND COMMUNICATION (Yale University Press 1953); For social constructivism, *see* Alexander Wendt, SOCIAL THEORY OF INTERNATIONAL POLITICS 359 (Cambridge University Press 1999), and for game theory applied to intelligence sharing, *see* Richard J. Aldrich, *Transatlantic intelligence and security cooperation*, Vol. 80, No. 4 INTERNATIONAL AFFAIRS 731, 731–753 (2004); Jeffrey Richelson, & Desmond Ball, THE TIES THAT BIND: INTELLIGENCE CO-OPERATION BETWEEN THE UK/USA COUNTRIES (Unwin Hyman 1990); Loch Johnson, BOMBS, BUGS, DRUGS AND THUGS:

not claim any counterintuitive or other special insight in arriving at this conclusion. Rather the studies simply confirm the common sense proposition that common purpose generates cooperation. When sophisticated academic studies are so humble as to confirm common sense, we get about as close as possible to the truth of the matter.

II. THE IMPERATIVE FOR INTERNATIONAL INSTITUTIONALIZATION OF INTELLIGENCE

Thus for more effective counterproliferation intelligence, what must be done is to reorient national intelligence resources to the internationally shared perception of nuclear threat. Though counterproliferation intelligence is nationally sourced, by establishing an international process for corroborating, collating, and analyzing intelligence around the counterproliferation objective, intelligence sharing can be substantially improved and increased. Common commitment can be expected to generate greater trust, and greater trust can be expected to generate greater levels of cooperation.

Greater sharing of intelligence would mean establishing a process for collation of intelligence that requires the checking of one source against another. This is among the most effective ways to minimize the bias and manipulation that currently inhibits the sharing of information by intelligence agencies on a bilateral or multilateral basis. In the lead up to the invasion of Iraq, the intelligence attributed by the George W. Bush Administration to U.S. agencies was significantly at odds with other intelligence sources, such as reports of the UN authorized inspectors. However, there was not then, nor is there now, any mechanism to resolve such competing intelligence claims. If there were such mechanism, the U.S. and British governments, when challenged on the claims that the Iraqis were trying to buy yellowcake from Niger, *could not have relied*, as they did, on other intelligence of which the international community was not aware.[418] The question, immediately would be—Why was the information not shared? The threat of political backlash for lack of an answer might well have prevented the deception that in fact occurred. Instead, the IAEA could only protest that what the Americans and British claimed, was at odds with its own limited information.[419]

A mechanism, that through collation and other processing of intelligence, could analyze and evaluate competing claims, by diminishing the risk of bogus intelligence and manipulation, would increase the willingness of governments to share intelligence.

INTELLIGENCE AND AMERICA'S QUEST FOR SECURITY 152–70 (New York University Press 2000); Vincent Crawford & Joel Sobel, *Strategic Information Transmission*, Vol. 50, No. 6 ECONOMETRICA 1431, 1431–51 (1982) and for international political theory, *see* Andrew Kydd, *Trust, Reassurance and Co-operation*, Vol. 54, No. 2 INTERNATIONAL ORGANIZATION 325, 325–57 (2000).

418 *See Iraq Uranium Claim Sows Confusion*, BBC NEWS, July 12, 2003, http://news.bbc.co.uk/2/hi/americas/3061665.stm. *See also*, Lynne Jones, *The Uranium from Africa Claim*, (last visited Mar. 21, 2011), http://www.lynnejones.org.uk/lynne-jones-mp/uranium.htm

419 Mohamed ElBaradei, IAEA, Presentation to the U.N. Security Council (Mar. 7, 2003)(*transcript available at* http://articles.cnn.com/2003-03-07/us/sprj.irq.un.transcript.elbaradeI_1_nuclear-inspections-iaea-iraq-nuclear-capabilities?_s=PM:US).

Presently, there is no means for receiving states to be assured the intelligence proffered has not been manipulated or falsified, or for the sending state to be assured against unauthorized disclosure. The creation of an international intelligence mechanism mandated by the Security Council could provide that means, improving the quantity and quality of information provided, and credibility as received.

An international intelligence capability focused solely on counterproliferation would also establish the political legitimacy essential to the sharing of intelligence. Granted that one government will not allow another government, or indeed any international institution, to control its intelligence operations, governments, even those with the greatest national intelligence resources of their own, will accept coordination and joint analysis directed towards a shared intelligence objective. There are many examples of this, not only if there is a high degree of trust to begin with, such as between the United States and Great Britain, but even if there is substantial distrust. Thus the United States has provided and secured significant intelligence on terrorism through intelligence sharing with a variety of Middle Eastern and Asian governments, despite these governments' strong differences with the United States on fundamental political subjects, such as U.S. policy towards Israel. If there is a focused and significant mutual interest, even intelligence agencies that otherwise may be deeply suspicious of one another, may importantly cooperate. This has been true, for example, as between the CIA and Pakistan's ISI.[420] Pakistan cooperates with the United States in intelligence coordination for some counterterrorism, while using as agents of political influence in Afghanistan individuals and groups that the U.S. counts as enemies.

Credibility of international intelligence comes not from singularity of source, but from multiplicity. Credibility depends on the degree to which conclusions represent a collation and critique of information from diverse sources, the proverbial "confirming source," as any professional reporter knows. Credibility is achieved by a process that highlights, not hides, existing differences. International institutionalization of intelligence can put forth a synthesis of counterproliferation intelligence that is not only better informed than any single national or limited allied effort, but that is legitimated, not undermined, by inviting doubt and critique.

Mutual interest in counterproliferation cannot be expected to eliminate the perceived need of national intelligence agencies to conceal their sources and methods. However, international institutionalization of counterproliferation could create the means to significantly mitigate this concern and thereby encourage intelligence sharing. Being international, that process could cleanse any identification of the national source of intelligence provided, and any clues as to sources and methods of the provider, just as national agencies currently redact raw intelligence they share, to protect

420 Thus the ISI is said to have been "forthcoming with intelligence pertaining to militants it views as threats to the Pakistani regime while refusing to share information pertaining to groups it hopes to use as levers in Afghanistan. . . . " Kathy Gannon & Adam Goldman, *Pakistan's Intelligence ready to slit with the CIA*, THE ASSOCIATED PRESS, Feb. 24, 2011.

sources and methods before sending intelligence on to foreign governments.[421] But the ability of an international institutionalization to cleanse intelligence is a different and much more significant capability than redaction of nation-to-nation intelligence. An international intelligence apparatus can operate not only to redact sources and methods of the provider, but also protect the identity of the provider. This is not characteristic of most bilateral or even multilateral intelligence sharing, as it occurs today, being restricted to governments that are willing to partner closely, who operate therefore within the limits of awareness of one another's identity and intelligence resource. Protection of the identity of intelligence providers through international cleansing would, by contrast, liberate intelligence that otherwise would be shared only among the most trusted allies.

The European Union has accomplished this as a permanent feature of European intelligence,[422] indicating a suitable model for a more multilateral counterproliferation intelligence capability. The European Military Staff "cleans" intelligence that is shared by European Union members. This is done by collating intelligence provided by national authorities and performing additional analysis circulated under the name of the European Military Staff, which impedes any nation from directly discovering the original provider.[423] In intelligence-sharing situations in which protection of the source is critical, when an intelligence officer staffing an international fusion center has information from his nation to share, it can first be sent to personnel at the center. The center personnel are then able to "clean" the intelligence, removing any indicia of origin.

A Security Council mandated internationalization of nuclear counterproliferation intelligence could similarly operate to protect source, and thereby encourage intelligence sharing. It could also, by virtue of its vetting and cleansing capacity, enforce the separation of intelligence gathering and policy that is so critical to maintaining reliable, and therefore actionable, intelligence.

The security reassurance an international intelligence process along these lines would provide would not be absolute. Any organization is susceptible to leakage of classified information, as any sophisticated intelligence officer naturally will assume. Moreover, depending upon the sophistication of the material that is provided, and despite redaction to remove all clues as to sources and methods, it may be possible in particular instances for those made aware of particular intelligence to make an educated guess as to the likely source. Nevertheless, the cleansing of national source identification at the international level, by substantially reducing risk of source identification, would afford an opportunity to gain intelligence presently excluded from bilateral or multilateral

---

421 Zivanovic, *supra* note 414, at 137.

422 *See* Bjorn Muller-Wille, *For Our Eyes Only: Shaping an Intelligence Community Within the EU*, No. 50 EUISS Occasional Papers, (Jan. 2004), www.iss.europa.eu/uploads/media/occ50.pdf. *See also*, Dr. Mai'a K. Davis Cross, *EU Intelligence Sharing & The Joint Situation Centre: A Glass Half-Full*, European Union Studies Association, (Mar. 3–5, 2011), http://euce.org/eusa/2011/papers/3a_cross.pdf.

423 James Igoe Walsh, *Security Policy and Intelligence Cooperation in the European Union*, European Union Studies Association 1, 15 (Apr. 2009), www.unc.edu/euce/eusa2009/papers/walsh_12C.pdf.

state-to-state sharing, because the participant governments would be much better assured that sources and methods could and would be successfully concealed.

An international counterproliferation intelligence facility, also, by stipulating the standards and parameters for supplying intelligence, would help to avoid inordinate caution about sharing. Such standards can include stipulated triggers for intelligence sharing. These triggers would be similar to those already articulated by the Nuclear Suppliers Group for identifying what intelligence, about what sorts of transactions, should be shared. Such triggers would similarly serve to identify suspected illicit transactions in fissile materials and nuclear weapon or dual-use technology, such as the IAEA currently tracks, employing such triggers despite its very limited intelligence resources. The provider also could be assured as to how, and within what limits and under what conditions, the information would be used. The setting of uniform benchmarks and standards would also expand opportunity to establish standardized technical terms, and common security procedures and trainings, to enhance the quality of intelligence, whatever the source.

Uniform standards and benchmarks defining the informational demand would provide further assurance to all participants, even those with the most substantial intelligence assets to protect, such as the United States, that neither security of methods and sources, nor individual or corporate privacy rights will be unduly sacrificed by sharing. Standards and benchmarks can be developed and administered to provide different levels of access to information, for assurance of security for the information, thereby encouraging its provision. Thus, for example, access to databases could be managed and controlled according to specific standards and conditions. The response to the request of a government pleading a need for more detailed access, more revealing of national source or its sources or methods than generally allowed, could be conditioned on the permission of the sender government. Or the sending government, on its own initiative, could be allowed to append detailed conditions for the use to be made of intelligence it provides, and stipulate limits on circulation, to prevent damage to its interests. This would include avoiding disclosure that could compromise other bilateral or multilateral intelligence sharing, a concern often dissuading governments from engaging in broader intelligence sharing.

As reflected by IAEA nuclear safeguards timeliness detection goals, it is essential to get timely warning of a military diversion of fissile fuel production. The intelligence challenge is not only collation and analysis, but speed. For some of the likely scenarios, addressing interception of a fissile material transfer involving terrorists, the time line may be critical. The faster intelligence is shared, the faster agencies can elevate their attentiveness and focus on tracking the location and possible destination of the material.[424] The importance of timing was demonstrated in March 2011, when Malaysian authorities were able to intercept a cargo ship from China that was destined for Iran.

---

424 IAEA, *Combating Illicit Trafficking in Nuclear and Other Radioactive Material*, No. 6 IAEA Nuclear Security Series 92 (2007), http://www-pub.iaea.org/MTCD/publications/PDF/pub1309_web.pdf.

On boarding, weapon components labeled as boiler parts were discovered.[425] This intercept could not have taken place without timely sharing of intelligence. The same would hold true of reporting of lost or stolen nuclear material. To the extent that sharing of intelligence could provide expeditious notification of loss or theft, it enables a government to muster a more timely intercept of the danger coming its way.[426]

As to all such interception, there are contrary dynamics at work. Any state can refuse to share information if it deems the security risk to be too great. There could well be a national security operation by the United States or any other government for which, notwithstanding the advantages of international intelligence sharing, the downside risk of disclosure that could impair that operation would be determined to be too great to tolerate. National security concerns can always trump intelligence sharing. But availability of this self-protection is also why states such as the United States, with the most substantial intelligence resources and the most to lose without the option of self-protection, would be willing to sign on to an international intelligence-sharing mechanism. They can protect against disclosure if that is critical, but still obtain the advantages from sharing if national security is not seriously threatened by the risk of disclosure.

The government that has had material lost or stolen may not be inclined to report for fear of international embarrassment or generating panic. However, an international mandate to disclose would help convince that government to disclose. This would not be absolute assurance against negligent or deliberate failure to report, but the existence of the system would incentivize disclosure, by putting governments at greater risk for nondisclosure. This would be both because of the enhanced risk of political consequence and penalty for violating the international mandate, but also because it is harder for any government to cheat or not comply with intelligence and reporting requirements if others are providing intelligence that indicates material unaccounted for by the government experiencing the diversion of material.

Better organized and shared intelligence will also serve indirectly to reduce nuclear risk in relation to non-cooperative governments. Transparency engenders predictability, and predictability engenders stability. To the extent the activities of proliferating governments, such as the Iranian or North Korean governments, face exposure under uniform internationally implemented standards applied to their customers or suppliers, other governments and entities in their respective regions accordingly would be less inclined to be involved.

Intelligence internationally administered would not eliminate the concerns about intelligence skewed for political purpose. In the 1991–1998 period, U.S. intelligence

---

425 *Ship Detained and Containers with Weapon Components Seized, Police Confirm*, THE STAR ONLINE, Mar. 17, 2011, http://thestar.com.my/news/story.asp?file=/2011/3/17/nation/20110317183449&sec=nation.

426 2009 IAEA reporting indicates that since 1993 there have been 1,562 reported incidents of lost or stolen nuclear materials. It is probably a very conservative number as to actual incidents due to under-reporting. See Mark Heinrich, *IAEA May Need Intelligence Arm Against Atom Terror*, REUTERS, Apr. 1, 2009, http://www.reuters.com/article/2009/04/01/us-nuclear-security-interview-sb-idUSTRE5305I920090401.

officers actually participated in some of the inspections in Iraq. The head of the United Nations Special Committee (UNSCOM), Rolf Ekeus, later observed that some of the Iraqi resistance to inspection may have been attributable to Iraqi suspicions that such participation might be used to help find targets for U.S. bombing.[427] The United Nations Security Council sought to alleviate that concern, when in drafting Resolution 1284, it provided that inspections staff should be international civil servants, who should not take instructions from any government. This experience instructs that a similar policy of administrative neutrality should pervade the formulation of inspection capacity under the international system here proposed, to assure it is maximally robust and legitimate.

There are more subtle gains to be realized through the establishment of an international institutional process. Mainly, these advantages relate to processing the sheer volume of counterproliferation intelligence, which comes from a wide variety of sources, both open and clandestine. Today, most intelligence processed by national intelligence agencies is so-called "open source intelligence," made up of information gleaned from the media, government, academic articles, commercial and governmental satellite imagery, and internet communications, including deep (meaning not accessible through standard search engines) internet sites.[428] Communications technology has turned open source intelligence into the dominant intelligence resource of the 21st century, and the resource best adaptable to meeting contemporary security threats. Even if clandestine nuclear weapons-related production may be involved, open source data, such as export-import data, may provide the best clues.[429] There is also communications and other electronic intelligence which, for example, can reveal a proposed nuclear material deal or transfer. Some of these sources are not quite so open but also generate increasingly voluminous information. There is so-called *measurement and signature intelligence,* obtained from sensing instruments identifying distinctive features of source, emitter, or sender to obtain identification and measurement that can, for example, reveal the construction of an otherwise secret nuclear facility. There is *imagery intelligence*, which consists of satellite images and photos taken from above an intelligence target, whether from a plane, drone or satellite.[430] There is *close-in signals intelligence,* which may penetrate and exploit a nuclear conspiracy, by way of cell phones,

---

427 Michael E. Brown, Owen r. Cote, Jr, Sean M. Lynn-Jones, & Steven E. Miller, GOING NUCLEAR: NUCLEAR PROLIFERATION AND INTERNATIONAL SECURITY IN THE 21ST CENTURY (MIT Press 2010).

428 The more refined classification of intelligence sources is human intelligence (HUMINT), which ranges from conversations to interrogations; signals intelligence (SIGNIT) meaning electronic and communications intelligence; measurement and signature intelligence (MASINT) which is technical intelligence obtained from sensing instruments; and imagery intelligence (IMINT) consisting of satellite and aerial photographic images. NATO, *NATO Glossary of Terms and Definitions* 2010, http://www.dtic.mil/doctrine/doctrine/other/aap6.pdf.

429 Open source information is generally thought to account for the great majority of intelligence processed by Western governments, as much as 90 percent, as distinguished from human and clandestine intelligence. *See* Andrew Rettman, *EU Intelligence Services Opening up to Collaboration*, EUOBSERVOR.COM, Jan. 18, 2011, http://euobserver.com/18/31656.

430 NATO, *supra* note 428.

laptop computers, local area networks, and other information infrastructure. Indeed, this can be the most productive source of information for counterproliferation. It should be recalled that what was officially described as a treasure trove of intelligence seized with the killing of Bin Laden, was the common stuff of cell phones, computers, and flash drives.[431]

Intelligence from all these sources is mushrooming from the faster and thicker globalization of communications, and is spreading in multiple languages. Drawing counterproliferation intelligence out of the morass of potentially relevant data requires a high level of professional skills. It also requires maximal organization of skills that can fully engage the new technologies, such as computer and media-related skills.[432] The characters that could be found in a Le Carre novel may still appear in the occasional real life spy story, as the public image of the spy game.[433] But such stories are today only the off-Broadway dramas of our Internet-connected world. The principal productions are the ones whose characters are intelligence officers staring at computer screens, exercising multiple technical skills, mainly by processing mounds of raw data, looking for the dots that need to be connected.

That the great majority of intelligence data is now open source data, means that trust between governments becomes less important for deriving the benefits of intelligence sharing, and distrust less a constraint on sharing. Obtaining open source data, unlike clandestine data, does not involve violating national laws, and usually does not involve the need for secrecy to protect sources and methods. Moreover, the credibility of open source information, unlike information obtained secretly, can be checked without exposing sources and methods. Thus an international counterproliferation intelligence capacity, as part of the mandatory system here proposed, would not be so necessarily dependent on information that member states *choose* to provide, at least not for most of the data requiring analysis.

But an international institutionalization of counterproliferation would empower counterproliferation intelligence through its gathering and organization of intelligence professionalism into an "epistemic community."[434] That observation, of importance for understanding the informal dynamics of regulatory capability, and now prolific in social science literature, describes the commonality of culture and values and norms shared within any class of professionals. Bringing together professionals who share the same values and objectives creates the group capability to formulate standards of competence and professionalism, and elevates their overall performance, especially transnationally, which is what counterproliferation of nuclear weapons is all about.

Finally, among the most important gains secured by creation of the international institutionalization here proposed, would be new opportunities for compliance and

---

431 Siobhan Gorman & Adam Entous, *Spies Comb bin Laden Intelligence Haul*, WALL ST. J., May 4, 2011.

432 *Id.*

433 *See* Devlin Barrett, *FBI Footage Shows Russian Spies Around NYC*, WALL ST. J., Oct. 31, 2011.

434 *See, e.g.*, Peter Haas, *Introduction: Epistemic Communities and International Policy Coordination*, Vol. 46, No. 1 INTERNATIONAL ORGANIZATION 3 (Winter 1992), http://links.jstor.org/sici?sici=0020-8183%28199224%2946%3A1%3C1%3AIECAIP%3E2.0.CO%3B2-%23.

sanction. History has well demonstrated that counterproliferation sanctions will only be applied by the United Nations Security Council in response to the actions of governments most resistant to counterproliferation measures, as exemplified by the machinations of Saddam's Iraq, and the regimes ruling North Korea and Iran. The members of the Security Council simply bring too many other significant interests to the table, usually economic or strategic, to sanction lesser cases of purposeful or negligent noncompliance with counterproliferation measures. The mandatory structure here proposed, therefore, cannot rely on Security Council sanction or the threat of sanction as the sole, or even the principal, means to assure compliance with standards of counterproliferation. To make the structure effective, we need to enlist any and every intermediate means for achieving leverage to be applied to a noncompliant government. The institutionalization of intelligence sharing could afford such additional means. For non-cooperation and noncompliance, deprivation of intelligence is the obvious sanction a government would and should risk. Reneging on the shared commitment could mean limitation of access to intelligence and databases otherwise available to all member states. Specifically, deprivation of intelligence on nuclear proliferation is likely to be perceived by any government as a significant cost of noncompliance. This would certainly be the cost imposed on any rogue regime, or state designated "of proliferation concern."

There is other, more subtle, possible leverage that the proposed institutionalization can secure, not only for compliance and sanction, but also for deterrence. Among any membership, leverage is achieved through the threat of public identification of noncooperation and noncompliance, that can have political consequence. This will vary, of course, depending on the government involved and the international identity it seeks. Potential identification of China or Pakistan as noncompliant, we know, from the history of proliferation, has a far different impact than complaint about North Korea or Iran. But in general, the political leverage that an international mandatory system could provide, identifying nuclear weapons related activity as delictual, irrespective of the targeted state's consent to the applicable standards, would constitute an important empowerment of counterproliferation.

III. FEASIBILITY

Despite the advantages to be gained from the international institutionalization of counterproliferation intelligence, there is the critical matter of feasibility. Is such institutionalization achievable? Can we secure a robust international counterproliferation intelligence capacity, with sharing of intelligence as its hallmark? Can we also meet the national security and secrecy concerns of the nations that would have to participate, on a broad and deep basis, to make it work?

The key again is common interest. If there is a shared perception of serious threat, and the common goal of meeting that threat is sufficiently well focused, the concerns conventionally thought to limit intelligence sharing become manageable, or are overcome. Common threat and common objective can engender institutional change quickly for the intelligence community. The evidence of this is at hand. It was evident in the aftermath of 9/11, in the warning it brought home to many nations. 9/11 provoked a dramatic reversal of the resistance to intelligence sharing, both within the United States intelligence establishment and among nations. The former director of the CIA's intelligence in the U.S. Counterterrorism Center has observed that immediately after 9/11, not only did the various intelligence agencies within the United States government work much more closely together than ever before, but the United States shared leads and information with dozens of countries, even including Syria, Sudan, and Iran. The normal inhibitions about sharing intelligence were overcome on a broad and deep basis.[435]

The prospect of a nuclear 9/11, being that much more horrendous, should be relatively greater inducement available for improving international intelligence sharing. This is evident in the comment by Secretary of Defense Robert Gates that "... if you ask every senior leader what keeps them awake at night, it's terrorists getting weapons of mass destruction, especially nuclear."[436] Global perception by governments of the extraordinary scale of the threat is no longer in question. What is still lacking is a common international response. The mechanics of intelligence sharing should follow, as they did after 9/11, but even more emphatically as an imperative that no responsible leadership can afford to ignore.

To design an international counterproliferation intelligence capability, the need is to create the mechanism for collation and analysis that can reveal dangerous proliferation, particularly as it may involve transnational terrorism. It requires drawing in the resources for applying all means available on a worldwide basis to spot suspicious transactions and other activities related to acquisition of nuclear weapons, including physical evidence and imagery, communications intercepts, agent access, history, and interpretation of political culture and motivation, to determine whether illicit proliferation is in progress, and how best to respond. It must be sufficient to reveal the networked nature of terrorism, including black-market sales. It must have tracking capability and infrastructure that facilitates connecting the dots, with a premium placed on speed and efficiency to identify nuclear threat as early as possible, and thereby maximize the time for interception and prevention. It should include cross-agency connections, both international and national, assuring, for example, that

---

435 "Conventional rules limiting the sharing of information were suspended in favor of sharing everything with everyone. In all, the CIA passed WMD related leads and analysis to over two dozen countries. In fact, in the process of averting a WMD-enabled al-Qaeda, the United States and its allies were able to thwart attacks in the formative stages in several countries." Rolf Mowatt-Larssen, *Preventing Nuclear Terrorism: A Global Intelligence Imperative*, No. 155 THE WASHINGTON INSTITUTE FOR NEAR EAST POLICY POLICYWATCH (Apr. 30, 2009), http://washingtoninstitute.org/print.php?template=C05&CID=3048. Rolf Mowatt-Larssen is the former director of the Office of Intelligence and Counterintelligence at the U.S. Department of Energy and former head of the Central Intelligence Agency's Weapons of Mass Destruction Department at the Counterterrorism Center.

436 Garamone, *Gesture of Respect*, *supra* note 2.

a significant export that is denied as an unacceptable proliferation risk by one government is also flagged to other governments, and also to the IAEA, to compare with its information resources. The flagging should require the IAEA reciprocally to inform governments, and if need be, the Security Council, of its suspicions. The decisional network must be as efficient as possible with a dominant objective being to avoid burdensome and retrograde bureaucratization.

The people capable of bringing this together within an international agency include the professionals from the national intelligence agencies. The endeavor must be international, but the fact remains that much if not most of the expertise and resources needed are national. The strategy, therefore, must be to join national human resources with the international objective of counterproliferation.

The means are already evident in the various liaison arrangements achieved between some national intelligence agencies and international institutions, such as those established within the European Community and NATO. NATO has an Intelligence Division that integrates intelligence received from NATO nations. But it has no independent intelligence-gathering function, and simply acts as a central coordinating body for the collation, assessment, and dissemination of intelligence within NATO.[437] It is the European Union arrangements that are the most comprehensive and evolved in relation to national sovereignty, and are therefore most instructive as to how a comprehensive international counterproliferation intelligence capacity can be built. The European Union has encouraged intelligence sharing among its members through a number of its institutions. These include the EU Joint Situation Centre (Sitcen), the Intelligence Division of the EU Military Staff, Europol, and the EU Satellite Centre (Satcen). Neither independently nor together do these institutions constitute a comprehensive European Intelligence Agency with a role such as the CIA undertakes in the United States. But the European arrangements do provide a variety of significantly integrated intelligence functions for the sharing of intelligence within the EU system.

To support and encourage intelligence sharing and joint analysis, the national intelligence agencies of the European Union utilize the mechanisms of liaison officers and seconded staff that can be the model for a fully international intelligence-sharing capability. Each member state of the European Union supplies at least one of its professional intelligence officers to work in the intelligence division of the European Union Military Staff, and Europol similarly works with staff members seconded from the national agencies. Sitcen draws together EU intelligence and also is manned by intelligence officers seconded from the EU member states. These officers provide two-way communication; supplying intelligence garnered from their respective national agencies, and communicating intelligence from the European institution to national agencies that appear to need it. There is also communication between the European Union intelligence agencies, and political, diplomatic, and technical facilities, such as imagery

437 *See* NATO, NATO HANDBOOK (2001), http://www.scribd.com/doc/52480427/NATO-Handbook-2001.

from the European Union Satellite Centre in Spain. These resources are all joined so as to maximize the specialized contribution of each to the joint effort. Thus Europol collects, shares, and disseminates intelligence that includes terrorist threats, and the European Union Military Staff analyzes material bearing on military concerns. The European intelligence institutions also provide mechanisms for the selective sharing of intelligence among national authorities on a broad range of particular subjects and threats, including organized crime, terrorism in all its forms, and the military affairs of the European Union. The cooperation and collaboration includes, for example, the development of common intelligence databases and various other joint projects.

The intelligence officers manning an international counterproliferation office, similarly could include, along with some permanent IAEA staff, intelligence professionals who are in liaison with the national intelligence offices from which they are seconded or received their training. This cadre of professionals, working together, could similarly capitalize on their diverse resources and specialties to contribute to the singular focus and objective of counterproliferation.

The benefits of such organization are often more subtle than the benefits of direct intelligence sharing, but nevertheless significant. These include the personal contacts that develop into positive action. For example, we see this manifest by way of the more informal associations that have grown up around the European Union's intelligence work on counterproliferation and terrorism, such as the Berne Group, established in 1971. The Berne Group brought together the security services of the member states of the EU, and then took the concrete step of establishing a Counter Terrorist Group in 2001 that includes the EU's 27 national intelligence services, plus those of Norway and Switzerland. It also participates in international intelligence sharing with the formal and official institutions, Europol and Sitcen.

With human intelligence resources coming from different national intelligence agencies, how can security of sources and methods be secured so as to most encourage intelligence sharing? This is accomplished directly, by providing for that protection. The Intelligence Division of the Military staff of the European Community, for example, while collating and analyzing intelligence that comes from intelligence agencies of different nations, removes any identification of source, performs additional analyses, then circulates the result under its own name to prevent discovery of the name of the original provider.[438]

The arrangements of Europol are further instructive on how files may be shared yet protected. Europol operates by way of stipulated requirements to protect individual privacy and private commercial rights of confidentiality. Also, even though analysis that is general or strategic may be accessed by any member state, if intelligence bears on specific cases concerning specific states and is operationally related, its circulation is restricted. It is made available only to the member state or states that provided the information that resulted in opening the file, and those states that the initiating

438 Walsh, *supra* note 423.

member state authorizes to view the intelligence.[439] Member states may decline to provide intelligence "harming essential national security interests," "jeopardizing the success of a current investigation or the safety of individuals," or "involving information pertaining to organizations or specific intelligence activities in the field of state security."[440] Such discrimination between types of data sharing minimizes secrecy and security concerns. It also facilitates prompt assessment and response to the extent data thereby becomes more manageable.

The same can be accomplished for a comprehensively international counterproliferation intelligence capability mandated by the Security Council under Chapter VII, acceptable even to states with the most substantial intelligence resources to protect. Sitcen, established in 2002, is a relevant model for a viable joint international mechanism, in that it monitors and assesses intelligence involving the same subject matter that would concern the international agency here proposed. Sitcen's focus is WMD proliferation and terrorism. Its work is essentially analytical rather than operational or involving policy formulation. But Sitcen is where all available relevant information and intelligence on terrorism and WMD proliferation is brought together for integration into an all-source intelligence report. This report is the product of overlapping relationships among Europol, the EU Military Staff, and the intelligence agencies of member states. Most of what Sitcen reviews is open source information. But member states provide both closed and open source intelligence to Sitcen, and each member state can stipulate who is allowed to see the information under the so-called originator principle, including the authority to exclude even EU parliamentarians who have high-level security clearance.[441] This *originator principle* can similarly serve the sharing of information for a comprehensively international counterproliferation agency, by encouraging the generation and collation of intelligence through prioritization of security threats. It can facilitate the dissemination of intelligence by allowing its release only if there is a threat justifying the dissemination, and only to the states likely to be impacted, for the formulation and implementation of specific countermeasures.

Considered altogether, there have been some impressive results of intelligence sharing within the European Union. In early 2001, for example, an al Qaeda plot to bomb targets in Europe was foiled through this organized sharing of intelligence, resulting in the apprehension of 18 people and weapons and explosives in a number of European countries.[442]

---

439 Europol Convention Article X.7, July 26, 1995; these rules are more fully stated in Council of the European Union, *Council act of November 3, 1998 adopting rules applicable to Europol analysis files*, 1999/C 26/01 (Nov. 3, 1998), http://eurlex.europa.eu/LexUriServ/LexUriServ.do?uri=OJ:C:1999:026:0017:0018:EN:PDF.

440 *Id.* arts. 4,5.

441 Eveline Hertzberger, *Counter-Terrorism Intelligence Cooperation in the EU*, EUROPEAN FOREIGN AND SECURITY STUDIES POLICY PROGRAM 69. *See also* Andrew Rettman, *Secret Documents Group Was Like "Bad Le Carre Novel," MER Says, EUObserver.com*, Nov. 18, 2010, http://euobserver.com/18/31296.

442 Swedish Security Service, ANNUAL REPORT 2001 31 (2001), http://www.sakerhetspolisen.se/download/18.7671d7bb110e3dcb1fd80009807/annual01.pdf

However, it should be noted that notwithstanding such success, European counterproliferation intelligence sharing, like counterproliferation intelligence sharing worldwide, remains fundamentally a matter of government-to-government consent. It is devoid of the concession of national sovereignty that distinguishes the European Union as a regional government in areas of concern other than intelligence sharing. Despite the comprehensive intelligence-sharing arrangements, each member state decides what information it will or will not share. Moreover there is no institutionalized sanction for failing to share intelligence, or for distorting it, or for failing to keep it secure, other than risk of political repercussion.

So in this crucial regard, European intelligence sharing, while the broadest, deepest, and most institutionalized international intelligence sharing, is foundationally different than the international institutional apparatus here proposed. A mandatory counterproliferation system, under the aegis of a Security Council mandate, would be designed to achieve a legally binding and much more proactive intelligence capacity to deter and expose clandestine nuclear activity and smuggling. Inclusion of discretionary limitation such as the originator principle would enhance rather than detract from this capability, and the capability would be pre-emptive as well as preventive. This could include, for example, seeking out, monitoring, and even infiltrating black-market networks, or particular transactions involving a potentially fatal transfer of material. In other words, the domain of the proposed international intelligence mandate, while limited to information bearing on counterproliferation, would extend as warranted to each and every stage of global counterproliferation, to break the linkage that might otherwise result in a nuclear detonation.

Being proactive, an international intelligence mechanism authorized by Security Council resolution under Chapter VII would enable intelligence for matching information from different sources, which those sources might not otherwise provide. It could also require the raw data on which particular intelligence that has been submitted purports to be based, a critical capacity which might have resulted in a far different picture being painted for the international community and the U.S. domestic constituency before the invasion of Iraq.

An international apparatus could also take advantage of specialization of governments as to regional intelligence and different intelligence assets, whether human or technical. While Western governments are best endowed to provide technical assets, the governments of a particular region, e.g., the Middle East and South Asia, have the most immediate and direct and solid intelligence on their region. Because the intelligence required under the proposed international capability would be narrowly circumscribed to only proliferation relevant intelligence, the diversity of other interests becomes less significant as constraint on cooperation. The mutual interest in counterproliferation as key, would induce cooperation whatever a regional government's other relations. At least any government would be motivated to avoid becoming the target of some form of retaliation because it had intelligence that could have prevented a nuclear weapons plot from succeeding. Once international institutionalization establishing universal norms and obligation is in place, the same dynamic is created for all governments not to be identified as delinquent as for the proposed international forensics data bank, or any other feature of a mandatory counterproliferation regime. No government will want to risk identification as having failed to fulfill the mandated obligation that could have prevented disaster.

The concealment that could cause a failure could indeed be serious to the point of suicidal, and that should seriously dissuade those who would otherwise conceal. The collation of one government's intelligence with that of others, all should understand, is what can reveal a nuclear weapons threat before its culmination in catastrophe. That lesson was well apparent, by analogy, in the determination of the 9/11 report that, had there not been profound informational disjunctions within the government of the United States, the perpetrators might well have been intercepted.[443]

The institutional objective must be an apparatus not apart from national intelligence capabilities, but one that can motivate and maximize intelligence resources, wherever they may exist, to contribute to the multifaceted multilateral task of counterproliferation. In accordance with the regime here proposed, this would draw on the intelligence services of the more than 150 states that agree in some form to current IAEA supervisory jurisdiction. And a mandatory system would be reinforced, not inhibited, by drawing in a maximal diversity and breadth of national intelligence resources.

Such a broadly international mechanism should not have to prevent or discourage other multilateral intelligence sharing. Thus in 2002, intelligence officials from the United States, Canada, and four European countries operated a counterterrorism center in Paris, for pooling intelligence and coordinating antiterrorism operations.[444] This and similar subgroupings focused on counterproliferation need not be foreclosed by the existence of a global infrastructure for intelligence sharing. Nor would there be any necessary sacrifice of relative efficiencies, such as speed of response. Where there are problems of redundancy or overlap, integration with the broadly international infrastructure may need to occur. But the proposed mandatory structure would not require the sacrifice of any present capacity. Short of full integration, liaison arrangements and the borrowing of expertise can nevertheless serve the shared objective of counterproliferation.

Such cooperation has already resulted in substantial securing and building of counterproliferation assets. In the mid-1990s, despite the failure to reach hard-sought unanimous agreement on a Comprehensive Nuclear Test Ban Treaty (CTBT), a provision promoted by the United States and other major governments, including Russia, allowed individual countries to contribute and coordinate their national technical means to monitor nuclear testing. This was agreed, despite resistance from countries

443 *See* David Johnston, *9/11 Congressional Report Faults F.B.I.-C.I.A. Lapses*, N.Y. Times, July 24, 2003, http://www.nytimes.com/2003/07/24/us/9-11-congressional-report-faults-fbi-cia-lapses.html. *See also* National Commission on Terrorist Attacks upon the United States, *supra* note 91.

444 *La France Abrite Une Cellule Antiterroriste Secrete En Plein Paris*, Le Monde, Sept. 13, 2006, http://www.lemonde.fr/societe/article/2006/09/13/la-france-abrite-une-cellule-antiterroriste-secrete-en-plein-paris_812394_3224.html, *and La Collaboration Antiterroriste Confirme*, Radio France, Sept. 8, 2006.

arguing the greater powers would use their superior monitoring capabilities to the disadvantage of other governments. The result was an International Monitoring System (IMS), which includes over more than 300 monitoring stations in over 200 countries, for verifying compliance with the CTBT. These stations already send a flow of information via satellite to an International Data Centre which monitors and analyzes the data, and makes it available to the state participants. Although the CTBT was not ratified by the U.S. Senate and has not entered into force for the United States, the United States cooperates and contributes. The IMS has continued to serve for verifying nuclear testing and data sharing by means of an international data center, global seismological, radionuclide, hydroacoustic, and infrasound networks. For parties to the CTBT, by way of a voting procedure, it also may allow on-site inspections on a challenge basis. The IMS has operated effectively and importantly. Resourced by national systems, it provided the international means to detect and measure the India and Pakistani tests in 1998, and later, the North Korean nuclear testing.

A mandatory international counterproliferation intelligence capability would appear to be best situated within the International Atomic Energy Agency. Given the IAEA's role as the international center for securing nuclear safety, safeguards, and security, the IAEA is the logical candidate. The IAEA already contains a number of different departments dealing with different aspects of nuclear risk, that include a small intelligence unit.[445] Locating a much stronger intelligence capacity with a broad mandate established under Chapter VII within its already comprehensive framework promises the maximum synergies with other aspects of counterproliferation.

The IAEA is uniquely positioned, not only because it is the institution that administers the current safeguards system, but also because it has a track record for integrating the operational and political aspects of counterproliferation. Effective counterproliferation intelligence must include the capability and sensibility to work on both the operational and political fronts. The comprehensive intelligence task is not only to institutionalize corroboration and evaluation of information, but also to determine capabilities and intentions. It is notable that the IAEA, notwithstanding deficiency of its own intelligence capacity, was able to contradict American and British claims of evidence that Saddam Hussein had tried to buy the uranium powder known as yellowcake from the African country of Niger, as based on nothing other than forged documents.[446] The record of the IAEA indicates it can meet the credibility challenge with skill, and achieve success. However, up to the present, it has done so only under

---

445 Under the current organization, IAEA member states provide the agency with limited intelligence reports to assist them in enforcing compliance with the NPT and nuclear safeguards and that is all. *See* Justin Alger & Trevor Findlay, *The Costs of Nuclear Disarmament*, INTERNATIONAL COMMISSION ON NUCLEAR NONPROLIFERATION AND DISARMAMENT, Sept. 2009. The agency's safeguards department does have two small units that are able to offer intelligence functions. The first unit looks into open-source intelligence which is information that is publicly available. The second unit analyzes IMINT. A third unit was given an intelligence function to look into illegal trafficking but has been ineffective due to a lack of technical personnel assigned to the unit. *See* Grossman, *supra* note 409.

446 Jones, *supra* note 418.

ad hoc direction of Security Council resolutions. The lack of a more permanent and refined mandate and the political caution that deficiency engenders, helps explain the delay that has characterized counterproliferation in both the Iranian and North Korean contexts. The need, therefore, is to provide the IAEA the continuing authority under a counterproliferation resolution to do what the IAEA has demonstrated it is capable of doing.

What should be the specifics of the intelligence authorization? Most important would be mandated access to information. This would include data declarations such as for the international forensics data bank,[447] access to and copying of documents, and access to interview nuclear workers, including the scientists and engineers of a given facility, at least if there are grounds to suspect the diversion of material to weapons use. Consistent with the Additional Protocol, such access should be allowed, however, without the burden to establish grounds to suspect a violation, so long as the inspection is limited to assuring that a given facility is sufficiently safeguarded in compliance with IAEA safeguard standards. The specific mandate should include that all states must submit to inspections consistent with the Additional Protocol, including the right to inspect facilities by surprise, take materials samples for forensics analysis, and install monitoring equipment—more or less the access promised to UN inspectors by Iraq in 2002–2003.[448] Fundamentally, this would constitute an advance over the Additional Protocol's current utility by making its provisions mandatory and universally binding, instead of voluntary. The large number of signatories to the Additional Protocol to date, including nuclear weapons powers such as the United States, demonstrates the Additional Protocol is appropriate for universal application and acceptance by the great majority of states, making it a prime candidate for such imposition as part of a mandatory system.

---

447 *See supra* pages 128–145.

448 The IAEA Safeguards Agreement under Article 3 was codified in 1972, with the stated goal of detection of diversion of significant quantities of nuclear material from peaceful to weapons programs. IAEA, *The Structure and Content of Agreements between the Agency and States Required in Connection with the Treaty on the Nonproliferation of Nuclear Weapons*,INFCIRC/153 (CORRECTED) (June 1972), http://www.iaea.org/Publications/Documents/Infcircs/Others/infcirc153.pdf. Signatories must provide ten-year fuel cycle research and development plans, identify the activities and identities of persons or entities carrying out R&D, export-import information, and description of facilities, along with being subject to more intrusive inspections. It was demonstrated to be inadequate by the 1990s with the revelations of long ongoing development of the North Korean and Iraq covert facilities. The Additional Protocol, issued in 1997, had the principal objective of assuring the subject state has no undeclared activities, requiring states to make comprehensive declarations of all their nuclear material and nuclear-related activities, and permits the IAEA to conduct environmental sampling and access to any location to check for undeclared nuclear material or activities Model Protocol, *supra* note 315. The Bush Administration argued for acceptance of Additional Protocol on the basis that it reduces insecurity among neighbors in a regional context. United States Mission to International Organizations, Statement by Deputy Assistant Secretary of State Andrew K. Semmel, Alternate Representative of the United States of America to the Second Session of the Preparatory Committee for the 2005 NPT Review Conference, Geneva, Switzerland, (May 5, 2003).

Defining the parameters of the international intelligence mandate could also benefit from the experience of administration of long-standing export-import controls under the guidelines of the Nuclear Suppliers Group. The triggers for mandatory reporting could be virtually the same guidelines the NSG has established. One is the sale of any materials designed specially for nuclear use, including fissile material and nuclear reactor related equipment, particularly equipment related to reprocessing and enrichment. Another trigger would be intelligence pertaining to dual-use technology and equipment.[449] Also, guidelines for providing information on the movement of any nuclear material or technology could be developed, consistent with current interdiction standards referenced by the IAEA, taking into account the practicable limits of intelligence resources and their coordination. The changing nature of technology would require regular review of the categories to ensure their relevance. The relevant intelligence would include intelligence on both ostensibly legal as well as clandestine transactions, on the well-founded assumption that all transfers of nuclear material and technology, legal or not, can ultimately constitute dangerous proliferation depending on who gets what, for what purpose.

The proposed intelligence authorization for the IAEA would be consistent with the IAEA General Conference resolution in 2002 adopting an integrated approach to protection against international terrorism, and calling for coordination of physical protection of nuclear material and nuclear installations, with material accountancy, detection of, and response to, trafficking in nuclear material, and emergency preparedness measures. The IAEA already employs an integrated approach to identify proliferation threats and vulnerabilities. Making the related intelligence function universal and mandatory, would be to the service of the same objectives.

Physical protection and accountancy as to nuclear materials is a complex and large task—in fact huge, given the extensive spread and variegated use of nuclear material; and all are agreed that verification cannot be perfect. However, modern materials accounting, including the statistical and computer-based recording of quantities, are powerful tools, made ever more so through ever-improving technologies for assessing inventories and material balances to verify or detect a loss. Such accounting is instructive as to what operational and safety measures must be implemented for a given facility.[450] Already there is much experience to draw on. The first Nuclear Materials Management and Safeguards System (NMMSS) implemented in the United States in 1976, has been internationalized through procedures and requirements evolved through the work of the IAEA. There is simply no good reason why the evolved system could not be universally applied. The IAEA already has registry requirements for states

---

449 *See* Nuclear Suppliers Group, *What are the Guidelines?*, (last visited Jan. 28, 2012), http://www.nuclearsuppliersgroup.org/Leng/02-guide.htm; *See also* Brandon King, *The Nuclear Suppliers Group at a Glance*, ARMS CONTROL ASSOCIATION (last visited Jan. 28, 2012), http://www.armscontrol.org/factsheets/NSG.

450 *See* Siegfried S. Hecker, *Towards a Comprehensive Safeguards System: Keeping Fissile Material out of Terrorists' Hands*, Vol. 607, No. 1 ANNALS OF THE AMERICAN ACADEMY OF SOCIAL AND POLITICAL SCIENCE 126–128 (Sept. 2006).

that hold safeguarded materials, though presently this includes only a small fraction of the total fissile materials worldwide.[451] Universal application of this registry and the monitoring it enables, together with universal application of the Additional Protocol allowing greater access to inspectors, would be a world of difference for improving counterproliferation.

The internationalization of intelligence should not constitute the obstacle it currently represents, when seen in the broader perspective of what internationalization of intelligence under Security Council mandate can achieve. Currently IAEA financing allows only a very limited intelligence staff, comprised of one unit reviewing open-source information, another analyzing imagery intelligence, and reportedly, much less than adequate staffing for intelligence on illegal trafficking.[452] This paltry state of IAEA intelligence capability is consistent with its original NPT referenced, and thereby limited, mission of monitoring non-proliferation and safeguards agreements in the relatively settled nuclear age gone by. But current IAEA intelligence capacity is in no measure equal to the current challenge, and development of the proactive intelligence capacity that is here proposed. The cost of an international intelligence capability, in relation to what is at risk seen in the broader perspective of counterproliferation, enabled by Security Council resolution, would be trivial. In the arena of international intelligence, as in the other arenas of counterproliferation, the world can afford counterproliferation, but not its failure. As with counterproliferation more generally, the common sense of threat and mutual interest is now, or shortly must be, at the stage at which the means here explained, for all its advantages, can be realized. If not, the only alternative is to wait for a nuclear detonation to motivate the international community to do what is necessary. The Security Council has declared "its resolve to monitor closely any situations involving the proliferation of nuclear weapons."[453] Unless it establishes the necessary international means to do so, which must include institutionalized international intelligence capability, that declaration will be recognized only in the irony of a mushroom cloud.

C. Export-Import Controls

1. THE CLUB THAT CANNOT COUNTERPROLIFERATE

Closely related to international intelligence as means to enable counterproliferation, is the administration of export and import controls. These controls depend on intelligence both to identify nuclear material and technology transfer, and to discern intention on both the supply side and demand side of a transaction. The need is to identify whether a transaction is suspect, and whether it involves a government or non-state

451 *Id.* at 126.

452 Grossman, *supra* note 409.

453 S.C. Res. 1887, *supra* note 324.

actor or commercial interest of proliferation concern. Export-import controls, accordingly, require both objective and subjective evaluations. Both aspects present a variety of difficulties that could be alleviated or eliminated by a Security Council authorization of mandatory counterproliferation that includes export-import controls.

To see the shortcomings of the current institutionalization of export-import controls, it is necessary to appreciate the differences in nuclear risk as static, and risk that is moving. Nuclear risk, in the form of facilities operating in place for peaceful use and the military triad of ground-based, trackable submarine-based, and air-based nuclear weapons, awaiting launch, was pretty much the whole story during the Cold War. Clandestine movement, such as provoked the Cuban Missile Crisis, was exceptional. For nuclear risk situated in place, the counterproliferation means are clear—best practices for security. Securing nuclear materials in place is still the most readily available and politically practicable means for enhancing nuclear security, though it is likely to remain far from any "gold standard"[454] until we can achieve an authoritative mandate that obligates all states to adhere to such standards. But for in-place and trackable nuclear risk, it *is* known what needs to be done, and what needs to be done is clearly doable.

The more challenging and troubling aspect of contemporary nuclear risk is that it is often moving; moving more, and in more directions than ever before, as the commerce in nuclear materials and technology expands. Today's globalized nuclear markets involve multiple suppliers and buyers, and virtually unlimited possible transshipment connections. Proliferation involves both states and non-state actors working aggressively to circumvent export controls through front companies, transporting nuclear-related materials under a false or incomplete shipment manifest, and laundering of the related financial transactions.

The A. Q. Khan network well demonstrates the challenge. That organization was able to provide extensive support to Libya's nuclear program through reselling used nuclear parts. It also manufactured nuclear plant parts in Malaysia, then shipped them as "used machinery," and imported other necessary tools, furnaces, and other equipment from European countries, via Dubai, through sham companies.[455] The Khan network thus included in its supply chain countries never before deemed relevant to nuclear weapons risk. Such networks dramatically expand nuclear risk, not only by increasing the number of governments that can be nuclear weapons enabled, but by increasing the number of states involved in proliferation, and the associate risks of accident, theft, and the opportunities for terrorism to obtain its ultimate weapon.

The appropriate course for counterproliferation, to address the contemporary mobility and multifariousness of nuclear weapons risk, would be a global system of export controls to monitor and stem the flow. Anything short of a fully comprehensive

---

454 Allison, *supra* note 9, at 143.

455 David Albright & Corey Hinderstein, *The A.Q. Khan Illicit Nuclear Trade Network and Implications for Nonproliferation Efforts*, STRATEGIC INSIGHTS (July 9, 2006), http://www.nps.edu/Academics/centers/ccc/publications/OnlineJournal/2006/Jul/albrightJul06.html.

export-import security system is to that extent susceptible to breach. But the internationalization of export-import controls, such as it is, is not global. It exists only in the form of four self-enclosed groupings of states, the Nuclear Suppliers Group, the Australia Group, the Missile Technology Control Regime, and the Wassenaar Arrangement on Export Controls for Conventional Arms and Dual-Use Goods and Technologies.

The dysfunctional nature of the current complex of control regimes begins with the fact of different state memberships, representing different collections of state interests. Each grouping operates according to its own member-generated demands to achieve consensus. There are no penalties or sanctions even as to members' failure to comply with the group's export guidelines, conditions, or controls. The four groupings have no formal relationship. There is no coordination or orchestration among them. Collectively, they play a discordant mix of disconnected notes.

Of the four groupings, it is the Nuclear Suppliers Group and Missile Technology Control Regime (MTCR) that most directly concern nuclear weapons related materials and technology. The MTCR is designed "to limit the risks of proliferation of weapons of mass destruction."[456] However, for export-import control as counterproliferation means, the most pertinent grouping is that of suppliers of nuclear material and technology, thus named, the Nuclear Suppliers Group. This is an arrangement of about 50 nuclear supplier states to coordinate export controls, particularly the transfer of equipment, materials, and technology that could be used for nuclear weapons programs in states other than those recognized as nuclear-weapons states within the framework of the NPT.[457]

Relatively recent experience of the Nuclear Supplier Group attempting to implement restrictions on the transfer of nuclear technology reveals why even a determined effort to improve international export-import control under the present regime of counterproliferation is fated to fail. In February 2004, the Bush Administration suggested two proposals to the NSG that would have placed restrictions on the transfer of nuclear technology. The first proposal called on NSG member states to prevent the transfer of uranium enrichment or reprocessing technology to states that did not already possess operating facilities for those activities. The second would have tied a state's eligibility for receiving nuclear technology to its adoption of the Additional Protocol with the IAEA.[458] The proposals were shuffled around for a year and half, and other member states offered their own similar proposals. Canada offered an alternative in September 2005 that ultimately became the model for subsequent negotiations.

---

456 Missile Technology Control Regime, *Guidelines for Sensitive Missile-Relevant Transfers*, http://www.mtcr.info/english/guidetext.htm.

457 *Fighting the Nuclear Fight: When Nuclear Sheriffs Quarrel*, *supra* note 247.

458 Wade Boese, *No Consensus on Nuclear Supply Rules*, Vol. 35 ARMS CONTROL TODAY (Sept. 2005) (reporting on the current state of export control negotiations), http://www.armscontrol.org/act/2005_09/NoConsensusNukeSupply and *also* Ian Anthony et al., *Reforming Nuclear Export Controls: The Future of the Nuclear Suppliers Group*, No. 22 SIPRI RESEARCH REPORT 74 (2007), http://books.sipri.org/files/RR/SIPRIRR22.pdf.

That proposal distinguished between objective and subjective criteria for evaluating export of enrichment or reprocessing technologies. Objective criteria, such as a government not being in violation of its IAEA safeguards, would be obligatory to approve a transaction. More subjective criteria, such as whether the importer's program would be economic, would not restrict the exporter.

No agreement was reached at the meeting in 2005 as the U.S. sought to ensure that the final version would preclude Iran from meeting the criteria, and thereby bar Iran from eligibility for the transfer of enrichment and reprocessing technology. Negotiations continued until 2008 when the U.S. abandoned its proposal.[459] As of June 2011, no consensus had been reached by the member states of the NSG to adopt specific export control guidelines.[460] A month later, the NSG reached a consensus and adopted new guidelines for the export of enrichment and reprocessing technology. Under the new rules, a potential recipient state must meet certain conditions in order to be eligible for the technology. These include being a party to and in full compliance with the NPT, not being cited by the IAEA board of governors or secretariat for safeguards deficits, complying with a comprehensive safeguards agreement with the IAEA, reporting on national export controls as called for under United Nations Security Council Resolution 1540, adhering to international nuclear safety norms, and having a bilateral agreement with the uranium enrichment and reprocessing technology (ENR) supplier state covering retransfer and assuring safeguards in perpetuity.[461]

The Carnegie Endowment for International Peace had this to say about the new guidelines:

> These changes will have no effect in substance, because while the specific "subjective" criteria are gone, exporters are instead provided great overall leeway in judging the legitimacy of a recipient state's quest for ENR (Uranium Enrichment and Reprocessing Technology). The final text of the guidelines urges suppliers to take "into account, at their national discretion, any relevant factors as may be applicable." On top of that, the final text also refers back to language in the existing NSG guidelines' Paragraph 4 which states that "suppliers reserve the right to apply additional conditions of supply as a matter of national policy."[462]

---

459 Wade Boese, *U.S. Joins Others Seeking Nuclear Export* Criteria, Vol. 38 ARMS CONTROL TODAY (May 2008) (reporting on the US dropping its proposal), http://www.armscontrol.org/act/2008_05/NuclearExport.

460 Center for Nonproliferation Studies, *Nuclear Suppliers Group*, INVENTORY OF INTERNATIONAL NONPROLIFERATION ORGANIZATIONS AND REGIMES, at 4, (Aug. 8, 2011), http://www.nti.org/e_research/official_docs/inventory/pdfs/nsg.pdf.

461 Mark Hibbs, *New Global Rules for Sensitive Nuclear Trade*, NUCLEAR ENERGY BRIEF (July 28, 2011), http://carnegieendowment.org/2011/07/28/new-global-rules-for-sensitive-nuclear-trade/4atv and *also* IAEA, *Communication Received from the Permanent Mission of the Netherlands regarding Certain Member States' Guidelines for the Export of Nuclear Material, Equipment and Technology*, INFCIRC/254/Rev.10/Part 1a (July 26, 2011), http://www.iaea.org/Publications/Documents/Infcircs/2011/infcirc254r10p1.pdf.

462 Hibbs, *supra* note 461 (parenthesis added).

The U.S. based Arms Control Association also noted the same problems with the new guidelines, adding that the NSG is "not a formal organization, and its guidelines are not legally binding."[463] Whatever progress the specified conditions might appear to accomplish, as noted, is negated by the absence of any obligation, in conformance with the current consent-based architecture of counterproliferation.

The monitoring and regulation of global flow is what export-import control is intended to accomplish. However without any global mechanism or uniform global standards for regulation being imposed, export-import control, as an aspect of current counterproliferation, will remain dramatically unequal to the task. Export controls are supposed to monitor and regulate the sale of nuclear materials and technology of dual-use or direct weapons use. The goals are to limit such transfer and to impose substantial additional risks of exposure and costs of evasion on proliferators, whether governments or commercial interests. The current regime, however, falls far short of these goals. It has not prevented the development of nuclear weapons programs substantially achieved through commercial imports, by all the states of proliferation concern, including particularly North Korea's program for increasing its nuclear weapons arsenal.[464] The international system of export controls surely epitomizes what the former Director-General of the IAEA must have had in mind, in decrying non-proliferation as "in tatters."[465] To the extent there is any international system of export-import controls, to the extent it operates at all, it is weak, erratic and does not even apply for much of the world.

Its deficiency, like other aspects of counterproliferation, comes down to the limitation of its components within the purely consensual framework of counterproliferation that rests on the NPT. Within this framework, export control can be only as robust as developed and administered by a particular government. A supplier state may develop a serious and detailed export-import control regime to limit the transfer of its own nuclear weapons related material and technology abroad. As might be expected, the nuclear material and technology supplier states, with more highly developed legal infrastructure, such as the United States, nationally impose and implement significant controls on their own exports. Current internationalization of export controls relies on drawing together such traditional suppliers among more developed states in best position to impose controls. From a global perspective, however, this is sorely inadequate. Supplier states of more recent technical vintage, such as India, China, and Israel, are not so constrained. And non-nuclear weapons states broadly resist and object to export-import controls, complaining that the Nuclear Supplier Group is a cartel designed to deny technology to less developed states. The UN Institute for

463 Daniel Horner, *NSG Revises Rules on Sensitive Exports*, Vol. 41 ARMS CONTROL TODAY (July/Aug. 2011) (report on adoption of new guidelines), http://www.armscontrol.org/act/2011_%2007-08/Nuclear_Suppliers_Group_NSG_Revises_Rules_Sensitive_Exports.

464 Jim Mann, *N. Korean Missiles Have Russian Roots, Explosive Theory Suggests*, L.A. TIMES, Sept. 6, 2000, http://articles.latimes.com/2000/sep/06/news/mn-16274.

465 *See* Lauria, *supra* note 6.

Disarmament Research issued a 2008 report on the implementation of Security Council Resolution 1540 by regional institutions that identified Association of Southeast Asian Nations (ASEAN) states as being particularly suspicious of export controls, as a barrier to economic development, and representing a deliberate attempt to deprive the region of new technologies and competitive edge.[466]

The four groupings of states that constitute the limited internationalization of export-import controls are wholly dependent on voluntarism and decision by consensus. The groupings, including most importantly for nuclear counterproliferation, the NSG, have great difficulty agreeing on standards, let alone securing any general implementation and compliance. Consensus is required either to establish standards or change control lists or guidelines. Such standards as are promulgated are often ambiguous, with no authoritative interpretation, and no compulsory procedures. Thus NSG guidelines set forth a general *non-proliferation principle* yet call upon members themselves to make risk assessments as to exports.[467] Majority action on standards or their implementation can be held up by one dissenting member. There are no checks or periodic reports for evaluating compliance with guidelines. There is no requirement or coordination of information as to export denial by member governments, not even a requirement to advise businesses as to suspected end-users.[468] Thus denial by one supplier government that could red-flag potential proliferation for other supplier states may never be recognized after that singular denial. This is despite considerable evidence that individuals and corporations are continually seeking to game export controls relating to nuclear materials and technologies, finding alternative avenues for proliferation, if one is closed.[469]

These deficiencies have increased over time as the result of institutional entropy. Within each grouping, cohesion and common purpose, and the potential for action, naturally diminish with expansion of membership. These state groupings of export controls were originated by the United States and its allies in Western Europe and other governments with similar foreign policy orientations, such as Japan, with similar perception as to the threats arising from sales of nuclear material and technology. The memberships have now expanded to include former members of the Warsaw Pact, and new members from the more general expansion of the European Union, which requires new members to take on its export regime. Thus the MTCT, for example, has grown from an original membership of seven to more than thirty. The more governments

466 United Nations Institute for Disarmament Research, *Implementing Resolution 1540: The Role of Regional Organizations*, (2008), http://www.unidir.org/bdd/fiche-ouvrage.php?ref_ouvrage=978-92-9045-190-7-en.

467 M. Beck, *Reforming the Multilateral Export Control Regimes*, THE NONPROLIFERATION REVIEW 17–18 (Summer 2000), http://cns.miis.edu/npr/pdfs/72beck.pdf.

468 See U.S. General Accounting Office, *Report to Congressional Committees: Nonproliferation Strategy Needed to Strengthen Multilateral Export Control Regimes*, GAO-03-43 (Oct. 2002), http://www.gao.gov/new.items/d0343.pdf.

469 Daniel Horner, *NSG Makes Little Headway at Meeting*, ARMS CONTROL TODAY (July/Aug. 2010), http://www.armscontrol.org/act/2010_07/NSGMtg.

involved, the more disparate the perceptions among the members as to their respective security interests. With expanding memberships, the harder it becomes to achieve consensus on which states, commercial entities, and technologies should be targeted for restriction. More members under a consensual regime also means more commercial interests to be accommodated, and greater difficulty in agreeing how and where to compromise those interests in the interest of counterproliferation. Consensus, if achieved, is qualitatively compromised by the multiplied demands. In the earlier days of state groupings of export controls, when the memberships were smaller with a stronger shared community of interest and objective, decision was easier and international export control operations more effective in identifying and reacting to sales evidencing nuclear weapons risk. Consensus process under expanding membership means that each additional state member is another state with power to stymie the entire process, thus altogether driving the process to the lowest common denominator for any decision and action.

Consensus process at the international level leads to a related national regulatory lethargy. A United States Government General Accounting Office study has noted that information such as export denial, to the extent shared, is not shared on a timely basis. Nor are agreed changes implemented through national law efficiently enough to assure the results intended. The Government Accounting Office study highlighted that even the United States, the supplier state supposedly most concerned with implementing export control restrictions, has commonly taken as much as a year to conform U.S. law to changes agreed by the Nuclear Suppliers Group.[470]

Proliferation that export controls must address, whether at the national or international level, mostly concerns what are ostensibly legitimate commercial transactions. The transfer of nuclear weapons related material and technology that occurs through black-market sales appears to be of much smaller dimension in the overall makeup of proliferation. Proliferation disguised as legitimate commerce is cheaper, easier, and less risky and dangerous for buyers and sellers than proliferation through black markets. Smuggling imposes additional costs and risks. Those seeking to proliferate thus naturally prefer regular commercial channels to black-marketeering. Thus, for example, Saddam Hussein's regime set up shell companies, and employed agents organized in difficult to decipher financial and shipment operations for its proliferation procurement.

The Iraqi regime of Saddam Hussein was neither very exceptional nor strenuous in avoiding monitoring or any regulation of this activity. The market simply cooperates with any such trade given the great profits to be obtained. Proliferation transactions have involved even supplier states that are often proactive about export control. Iran's and North Korea's nuclear programs were developed with imports approved by supplier states such as Russia, China, Germany, France, and Pakistan. Canada was a principal supplier for the development of India's nuclear weapons program. Because nuclear

---

470 *See* U.S. General Accounting Office, *supra* note 468.

proliferation is big business, it is not easily declined, even by a counterproliferation inclined government claiming adherence to the NPT regime. And now, particularly of note is that the United States, the prime promoter of export controls, has become a principal nuclear partner of India, securing an exemption from the Nuclear Suppliers Group, despite the fact that India developed its nuclear weapons program in defiance of the NPT.[471]

Difficulties of export control also arise from the technology that must be monitored. National and international export control arrangements are having an increasingly tough time adjusting to the changing technology that counterproliferation must target and list for controls. As a general proposition, legal and regulatory bureaucracy can at best follow, not lead, technology in its evolution. Legal and institutional management of technological change is typically a game of catch-up. And the race to identify, monitor, and control technologically evolving nuclear export risk is accelerating. As dual-use technologies evolve, with increasing rapidity, it is becoming harder to identify and catch transactions and technologies dangerously related to nuclear weapons development. Control is dragging well behind its targets. Add that consensus process is required to identify the subjects and agents of nuclear weapons risk, and export control is in greater danger than ever of losing the game of catch-up. None of the control groupings of states move with anything near the necessary speed. Far from it. They are encumbered not just by consensus process, but by the fact that the implementation of counterproliferation directed export controls must, in a world of sovereign states, depend upon tedious implementation of international prescription through diverse national law. Any international management of export control, to be effective under current arrangements, must negotiate the wide variety of different national legal systems and national political and economic pressures that ultimately determine implementation. Moreover, given that so much of nuclear risk extends across borders, by way of multinational companies and global commercial networks, export control must also overcome cross-border complexes of joint ventures and multinational ownership that were purposefully and specifically designed to work around national export-import controls.

Finally, explaining the deficiency of current counterproliferation export-import controls, is that the national governments, that are the only avenue for the implementation of export controls, are highly susceptible to pressures from down-home economic interests. National export control naturally brings along with it the concerns of domestic producers who perceive export controls as burdensome and costly, both in implementation and effect, particularly in foreclosing marketing opportunity. Worse—export controls are perceived by domestic producers as discriminatory in giving advantage to suppliers located in nations that do not equally implement export controls. Domestic producer complaints about fairness have political force. Domestic producers, understandably, do not remain quiet and compliant while seeing business go

471 *Fighting the Nuclear Fight: When Nuclear Sheriffs Quarrel*, *supra* note 247.

to suppliers from countries outside the ambit of the established export-import groupings of governments. Today, with new technology producers, such as Israel, China, and India, this dynamic is of much greater significance than ever before. Domestic producers can commonly make the convincing case to their governments that a particular export control is a useless and foolish compromise of national competitive position. Their governments, in response, are inclined to lighten up on controls.

II. INSTITUTIONALIZATION OF EXPORT-IMPORT CONTROLS UNDER SECURITY COUNCIL MANDATE

Scholars who have made a holistic study of the current assemblage of export-import controls as they bear on counterproliferation describe it as a "hodgepodge"... for which "almost any change would be an improvement."[472] Even viewed from the national perspective of the United States, the nation ostensibly most committed to export controls, the general observation voiced is that "the existing system of export controls is broken."[473]

Within the structural limitations of the current international export-import groupings of states, a significant fix is unlikely. The Nuclear Suppliers Group, like the other groupings, is disabled from reforming itself, because any change in its regime is constrained by the same consensus principle of operation that presently undermines its efficacy. However, the NSG has provided guidance for states on how to go about the business of export-import control, both operationally and substantively. This warrants saving what is worth saving, and indicates international effectiveness if the decisional deficiency can be addressed and overcome. Export control, just as other means of counterproliferation, must be reframed in a larger way, beyond its current limitations. A counterproliferation regime mandated by the United Nations Security Council is the change that could be transformative enough to fix export-import control where it is most wanting.

First, it is apparent that internationalization of export/import control, in effectuating a mandatory global regime, would eliminate its current identification as the handmaiden of a limited number of developed states. It would relatedly dispel the charge that export control arrangements constitute a cartel of developed nuclear states designed to prevent the rest of the world from obtaining technology. If the institutionalization of export controls for counterproliferation was mandated for a single organization promulgating standards to apply equally to all states and all traders in nuclear material and technology, perception of anti-competitive unfairness would be much less likely. This would be particularly so if the constitution of the single organization is sensitive to the importance of equitable and geographical representation in its membership and

---

472 Michael Beck & Seema Gahlaut, *Creating a New Multilateral Export Control Regime*, ARMS CONTROL TODAY (Apr. 2003), http://www.armscontrol.org/act/2003_04/beckgahlaut_apr03.

473 Sam Nunn Bank of America Forum, *Executive Summary: Globalization: Technology Trade and American Leadership: A New Strategy for the 21st Century* (Mar. 2000).

staffing. The resistance from many governments thus could be assuaged and reduced, if not eliminated. Moreover, broadening through a globalized administrative mechanism is simply necessary for effectiveness. That the Khan network used Malaysia for nuclear weapons-related production, and Dubai as a transshipment hub,[474] demonstrates there is no longer any point in restricting export control to membership of nuclear supplier states. Today, related production and transshipment can occur almost anywhere, including the developing world, in which significant natural deposits of nuclear material are located in countries such as Gabon, Niger, and Namibia. The fact that it was the alleged purchase of yellowcake from Niger by Saddam Hussein's regime that was used to justify the invasion of Iraq, demonstrates the need to extend an international export regime everywhere, along with sound global export-import intelligence administration, for accurate and legitimate counterproliferation.

But would the fix by way of a Security Council resolution ultimately really rest on the broad base of legitimacy necessary to sustain global administration of export controls? The key again is the shared interest and perception of nuclear threat that a Security Council counterproliferation mandate would represent, and its universality, which would draw together export control into one organization applying uniform standards for all states. The first and fundamental step in this direction already has been taken pursuant to the commonality of interest formulated as Security Council Resolution 1540, in 2004, insofar as this resolution requires all states to criminalize proliferation to non-state actors and to establish, review, and maintain appropriate and effective export control regimes.[475] That is, counterproliferation as it relates to export controls, has already been universalized as applying to all states, notwithstanding the limitations of Resolution 1540.[476] What remains is to build the architecture to make its universality the predominant reality.

Reorganizing and building export control capacity pursuant to a mandatory resolution under Chapter VII could be the basis for a procedural and substantive capability that would substantially overcome if not eliminate the current defects. As a truly international mandate and institutionalization of export controls, it would encompass all states as obligated to conform. Its membership, for purposes of decision, would be expansion to all supplier states, and so globalized, would include Israel, India, and Pakistan, the potentially most significant suppliers outside the current NSG membership. It could bring together the best of the present export control formulation, expertise, and experience for the singular mission of efficient yet comprehensive instruction in export control that is currently lacking. The information sharing alone would be a considerable net benefit, potentially encompassing common approaches to licensing and export denials, better and more pervasive understanding of the technologies involved and the risks they represent, and provision of information as to end-user

474 Albright & Hinderstein, *supra* note 455.

475 S.C. Res. 1540, *supra* note 124.

476 *See supra* pages 71–77 (discussing the counter-proliferation deficiencies of Security Council Resolution 1540).

risk, transshipment risk, and best practices. Such universalization would also help to simplify and harmonize documentation and implementation for national governments. The growing number of states capable of being nuclear suppliers undermines implementation of controls. More members means more governments not inclined to restrict profitable nuclear exports, and also more governments without the domestic institutional capacity and legal infrastructure for timely and effective implementation of any decisions agreed at the international level. This is especially true as membership expands to countries with less refined technical and legal resources. A Security Council mandate could respond to such deficiency by including financial support specifically dedicated to assist states without the economic or expert resources or legal infrastructure to insure adequate implementation. The support could be directed to providing a permanent staff of experts to assist governments in developing adequate legal and institutional capacity for implementation where it is lacking. It could also provide the expertise lacking in most nations' bureaucracies for the technical questions that export control of dual-use nuclear material and technology often involves.

Counterproliferation export control, organized and administered through a single international institutionalization, is likely to generate better articulation and uniformity of standards and their implementation. As to feasibility, it is also important to recognize that internationally generated export-import controls capable of uniform application are already at hand, though only as guidelines issued by the NSG. The problem to overcome is the constraint of consensus voting, and this would be accomplished if the standards, by virtue of Security Council authorization under Chapter VII, become obligatory for all nations. The essential work of determining target lists, and states and transactional parties of proliferation concern, of course, would not be without controversy. Such matters never are, particularly in light of the huge sums involved, and the consequent pressure from commercial interests. But with international administration of export controls under Security Council mandate, and a voting structure freed from the drag of consensus voting, much more can be accomplished.[477]

As for further development of appropriate uniform international standards, there is much to build on, given the extensive experience developing and implementing export controls at the national level. This would include rules on the transfer of intangible technologies, transshipment, information sharing on end-users, harmonized export documentation and model laws, and establishing rules on timing and best practices for the implementation of decisions. But more significantly for the internationalization of export control, a mandatory regime would employ standards that are already apparent and available as international standards, but that currently have limited, if any, impact. Most readily, the guidelines agreed by the Nuclear Suppliers Group could be transformed from guidelines that can be ignored, into binding requirements of counterproliferation. This would include the "criteria based standards" encouraged by

477 The international administration could also include a binding dispute resolution mechanism similar to that established for international trade organizations, to give further legitimacy to determination of standards, their application, and determining whether there is violation.

the Bush and Obama Administrations, and adopted in a reformulation by the Nuclear Suppliers Group, but which the Carnegie Endowment for International Peace and the Arms Control Association and others have criticized as currently of little if any utility.[478] Thus borrowing from the useless to make it useful, the standards for export would include that the governments of the buyer and supplier must not be cited by the IAEA board of governors or secretariat for safeguards deficits, that the governments must comply with a comprehensive safeguards agreement with the IAEA, must report on national export controls as called for under United Nations Security Council Resolution 1540, must commit and adhere to international nuclear safety norms, and that the governments of jurisdiction over a transfer must have a bilateral agreement covering retransfer and assuring safeguards in perpetuity of the facilities involved. This could all become great muscle for a robust international counterproliferation regime. Another obvious candidate as condition for export, if not directly mandated by Security Council resolution, would be the requirement that the governments on the supply and demand side of any transaction have signed the Additional Protocol.[479]

Standards inherently equitable as uniform, would work to diminish the political resistance to implementation of export control at the national level. And an important aspect would also be reporting requirements and their evaluation, to assure the highest level of transparency. By thus leveling the playing field of nuclear supply competition through uniform standards, and providing the transparency and mechanism for assurance of uniform compliance, international administration of export/import controls would counter concerns of competitive disadvantage, and in this important respect, as well, enhance legitimacy.

A single administration guided by and dominated by professionalism not subject to veto of its standards or procedures by any nation would facilitate targeting transactions and targeting of individuals, entities or governments "of proliferation concern." It could establish a tiered list of end-users, differentiating, for example, those who should be denied export or import of controlled technologies, a list of end-users and states of proliferation concern for reporting purposes, and a watch list. This could also operate to establish criteria for license determinations, and could achieve transparency by assuring that denials as well as approvals are communicated to all governments. The importance of this should not be underestimated. Such transparency can be precisely what it takes to find and reveal patterns of clandestine proliferation.

There is no question that most governments involved in the supply of nuclear material and technology have demonstrated a willingness to accept internationally promulgated baseline standards as to the preconditions for transfer of nuclear weapons related materials and technology, and therefore that the mandate of international export-import control by the Security Council would have traction. The governments within the memberships of the existing four groupings of states that

478 *See supra* pages 165–166, and notes 462 and 463.

479 *See supra* pages 80–81 *and supra* notes 228, 229 (concerning the substance of the Additional Protocol).

constitute international export control have come to accept at least guidelines and general principles on export control, and the trigger lists demonstrate much agreement as to what materials are considered subject to restriction.[480] This is despite the burden of decision by consensus, and the complaints about unfair competitive disadvantage. So not only would the professionally developed standards be more broadly acceptable under a mandatory universal system that more naturally negates any basis for such complaints; there is no justification for refusing their implementation on a uniform basis as representing the consensus of experts concerning threat levels of various types of shipments. There is simply no justification for national differentiation as to any of this, and the broader the application, the greater the legitimacy to support compliance.

The IAEA would have an important role in the internationalization of export-import control, whatever the particular shape of any formal IAEA connection to international administration of export-import controls. International export control, to be most effective, must be fit within the broader framework of mandatory counterproliferation, requiring implementation and reporting by all states as to nuclear weapons related material and technology, and integration with the IAEA's role for review of suspect transactions and facilities. The IAEA is already focused and working in the arena of export-import control. The IAEA secretariat has recommended that "states should provide extensive information related to exports, procurement inquiries and export denials to allow the Agency greater ability to detect undeclared nuclear activities."[481] The NSG's guideline on condition of supply, that governments should provide assurances for peaceful use and full scope IAEA safeguards, also already indicates a significant export-import role for the IAEA. By allowing the IAEA to verify declarations made by states about their nuclear materials and activities, this guideline effectively requires members to limit their nuclear-related trade to non-nuclear states that are not suspected of having clandestine weapons programs or supporting terrorism, and that have cooperated with the IAEA in instituting safeguards.[482] The A. Q. Khan network demonstrated conclusively the need to have reporting by all nations about their exports and imports of dual-use items for the IAEA to combat and intercept illicit nuclear trafficking. Such reporting relates fundamentally to IAEA assessment of

---

480 See, e.g., Nuclear Suppliers Group, *Development of the NSG and the Philosophy of Nuclear Export Controls*, Oct. 15, 2009, http://www.nuclearsuppliersgroup.org/Leng/PDF/2009-Development_of_the_NSG-Export_Controls-R_Goorevich.pdf; IAEA, *Communication Received from Certain Member States Regarding Guidelines for Transfers of Nuclear-related Dual-use Equipment, Material, Software and Related Technology*, INFCIRC/254/Rev.7/Part 2a (Dec. 7, 2007), http://www.nuclearsuppliersgroup.org/Leng/PDF/infcirc254r8p2.pdf (NSG Guidelines Part 1).

481 Pierre Goldschmidt, *Priority Steps to Strengthen the Nonproliferation Regime*, POLICY OUTLOOK 2 (Feb. 2007), www.carnegieendowment.org/files/goldschmidt_priority_steps_final.pdf.

482 IAEA, *Communication Received from Certain Member States Regarding Guidelines for Transfers of Nuclear-related Dual-use Equipment, Material, Software and Related Technology*, INFCIRC/254/Rev.9?Pat 1a, at 1–6, (Dec. 7, 2007), http://www.nuclearsuppliersgroup.org/Leng/PDF/infcirc254r8p2.pdf.

countries nuclear programs and apparent safeguards inconsistencies.[483] The reporting requirements can also serve to assist countries identify and close gaps in their export regimes before they are exploited. There must be procedures to ensure confidentiality as in other areas of counterproliferation intelligence. But what is required and feasible is a much more cohesive and complete integration of the broad range of IAEA activities and international administration of export-import controls, to maximize effectiveness of the totality of counterproliferation means.

There is good evidence for the viability of a single comprehensive multilateral export control regime. The EU already has managed to accomplish a single control regime whereby its member states all conform to uniform criteria and practices, though export decisions are made and implemented at the national level. This is notwithstanding the considerable economic interests involved, and the political pressures they generate within the national governments involved. By leveling the playing field, with all governments conforming to the same standards, and thereby reducing or eliminating the perception of unfairness or uncertainty through uniform application, a single international control regime can better accommodate these interests. If the authoritative basis for an EU-style control regime is secured by way of a Security Council counterproliferation resolution, the same model should work as well for a global system of counterproliferation export-import control.

D. Internationalization of the Nuclear Fuel Cycle

Counterproliferation can operate closer to the source of nuclear weapons risk than safeguards or export-import controls—by controlling the birthing of fissile material. At the most fundamental level of counterproliferation, there is the simple reality that the reduction of the production of weapons usable fissile material is the reduction of nuclear weapons risk. Accordingly, preventing unlimited national fissile material production is the objective in ongoing negotiations with Iran and North Korea, and is more broadly being considered a basis for counterproliferation.

The general strategy is to reduce the number of nuclear production facilities worldwide through some collective organization of governments, and international control of nuclear fuel supply. This is alternatively referred to as *multi-nationalization*, *internationalization*, or *multi-internationalization* of the nuclear fuel cycle. Although the terms are not always clearly distinguished, *multi* puts the emphasis on joint government control of supply, *internationalization* puts the emphasis on international supervision, and *multi-internationalization* refers to both. Multi-internationalization of the nuclear fuel cycle is sought to reduce all the risks that inhere in nuclear power production, be they the risks of diversion of material to production of

483 Ian Anthony et al., *Reforming Nuclear Export Controls: The Future of the Nuclear Suppliers Group*, No. 22 SIPRI Research Report 63 (2007), http://books.sipri.org/files/RR/SIPRIRR22.pdf. Albright & Hinderstein, *supra* note 455.

nuclear weapons, or access for nuclear terrorism. Also generally envisioned is that internationally controlled fuel-cycle facilities and fuel banks could be used to deal with storage of fissile material and retiring nuclear waste. Multi-internationalization thus is seen as a means for addressing the entire chain of fissile material; not only the risks attendant on fissile material production and use, but also the risks involved in transport and disposal.

There are a number of reasons why multi-internationalization is appealing. It can serve as the means to limit enrichment to the level of peaceful use, and provide incentives against construction of national facilities less subject to international supervision and monitoring. It allows for more comprehensive and effective security for existing facilities, which in turn lessens susceptibility to diversion or theft or attack by a terrorist organization. Distribution from fewer sites also means less risk of accident. Multi-internationalization can also create incentive for controlled production through economies of scale that translate into price. On the tail end of the nuclear production cycle, it can reduce reprocessing and disposal risks, by having disposal managed by an international agency, including take-back provisions returning spent fuel to suppliers, thus removing any need for reprocessing capabilities, and also incentivizing governments to join to minimize the costs and problems of disposal of nuclear waste.

Multi-internationalization also can be a means to obtain greater transparency and accounting for nuclear materials and activities through the ongoing involvement and presence of international staff, and the additional informational resources involved. It can enhance reporting and thereby better flag diversion of material. This is increasingly significant as now complemented by the developing authentication technologies of nuclear forensics. Multi-internationalization would make possible major improvement over current accounting, which allows governments to report only what they are willing to report, with the IAEA having the formidable task of chasing down the truth, as in the cases of Iraq, Iran, and North Korea.

The fewer the facilities, the fewer would be the inspections and other monitoring required, reducing the cost of nuclear security. Moreover, enhanced transparency would be gained on both the supply and demand sides of fissile material production. Multi-internationalization, by putting participants under a greater degree of scrutiny, affords much greater opportunity and efficiency in the investigation of accounting anomalies in the host country, or the state securing supplies from the internationally managed facility. This would be in sharp contrast to the NPT regime. A multi-international enrichment mandate could prevent the breakout scenario whereby a country obtains technology and material as a party to the NPT, then withdraws from the NPT under Article X of the treaty, scraps safeguards, and uses what was obtained for peaceful use for a nuclear weapons program, as North Korea appears to have done.

Beyond achieving greater transparency and security in fissile material production, most important is that international provision and regulation of fissile material production is a means to assure the limitation of enrichment to levels below weapons use.[484] To the extent consolidation of fissile material under international supervision is achieved, that removes national facilities capable of higher levels. Removing present or prospective national facilities also reduces the problem of assuring, on a continuing basis, that different national facilities, declared to be for peaceful use, are not involved in the production of nuclear weapons.

The first nuclear detonations brought quick recognition of the need for international regulation of fissile material production. Proposals for the multi-internationalization of nuclear fuel production appeared as early as the 1946 Baruch Plan, by which the United States proposed that states should transfer ownership and control over civil nuclear activities and materials to an international atomic development agency. Multi-internationalization has been a subject of investigation and discussion ever since, involving a multitude of conferences; international working groups; and numerous proposals ranging from guarantees by existing suppliers, to international fuel bank proposals, international licensing and supervision, international consortia of government suppliers, conversion of existing national facilities to multinational ones, and construction of international facilities, including regional fuel cycle centers.[485] The common feature of all such proposals is some form of collective control and management of fissile material production for peaceful use.

Globalization of the nuclear energy market has resulted in actual, currently functioning, international joint ventures and other consent-based cooperative arrangements. These are both governmental and commercial, addressing the nuclear fuel cycle in whole or in part. They include the AREVA, addressing the whole fuel cycle,[486] British Nuclear Fuels undertaking waste management and reprocessing services, and EURODIF, which enriches uranium in France, and provides enriched uranium to its co-financing international partners, Belgium, Italy, and Spain. URENCO is another multilateral endeavor, with state participants sharing the technology under a single entity. URENCO provides uranium enrichment services from plants located in a few European countries under commercial-industrial management and a governmental joint committee, providing oversight of technology and staffing, along with

484 Arjun Makhijani, Lois Chalmers, & Brice Smith, *Uranium Enrichment: Just Plain Facts to Fuel an Informed Debate on Nuclear Proliferation and Nuclear Power,* Institute for Energy and Environmental Research, at 5–6,(Oct. 14, 2004), http://www.ieer.org/reports/uranium/enrichment.pdf.

485 There are currently about a dozen detailed proposals for nuclear supply to limit proliferation of enrichment and reprocessing capabilities. These proposals have come from governments, intergovernmental organizations, and nongovernmental organizations. *See* e.g., Gareth Evans & Yoriko Kawaguchi, *supra* note 38. IAEA, *Multilateral Approaches to the Nuclear Fuel Cycle: Expert Group Report to the Director General of the IAEA,* INFCIRC/640 (2005), http://www.iaea.org/Publications/Documents/Infcircs/2005/infcirc640.pdf. *See also,* Fiona Simpson, *Reforming the Nuclear Fuel Cycle: Time is Running Out,* Arms Control Today (Sept. 2008), http://www.armscontrol.org/act/2008_09/Simpson.

486 AREVA is a French public multi-national conglomerate which provides facilities at every stage of the nuclear energy process: from mining, to processing, to the dismantling of reactors. Its main shareholder is the CEA, the French equivalent of the US Department of Energy.

substantial safeguards. Such dual layer management shows that multi-nationalization can be made to work successfully, providing sufficient economic incentive for states to join in, while providing international oversight and safeguards.

Other regional schemes include Russia's construction of the International Uranium Enrichment Center at the Angarsk Electronic Chemical Combine, bringing together two existing nuclear fuel service providers, one in Russia and the other in Kazakhstan.[487] This scheme provides for intergovernmental participation in management and profits, with access to the technology, similar to what the EURODIF consortium has done in France since the mid-1970s. Armenia and Ukraine have joined as material suppliers for the site. Under this arrangement, each member state agrees not to pursue nuclear enrichment facilities of its own.

These developments hold promise to improve counterproliferation, by reducing the number of fissile material production facilities, and offering opportunities for more comprehensive safeguards and inspections. However, multi-nationalization of the nuclear fuel cycle has not so far found traction as a major means of counterproliferation. There is resistance based on the sovereign prerogative to develop national capacity for peaceful use of atomic energy, claimed to be enshrined in Article IV of the Nuclear Non-proliferation Treaty. Other reasons for resistance are perceptions of inadequate economic incentives and assurance of supply for the governments that commit on the demand side, and the maintenance of competitive pricing. Without such assurance, it is unlikely multi-internationalization can proceed very much further.

The dramatic increase of proliferation risk in recent years, though, has brought with it greater attention to multi-internationalization as a counterproliferation strategy. A proposal focused almost exclusively on supply has already secured considerable international political support and financing. This is the concept of a guaranteed fuel bank managed by the IAEA for states without existing fuel production facilities. President Obama endorsed the concept in his Prague speech on nuclear risk.[488] Warren Buffett committed $50 million to launch the nuclear fuel bank, provided $100 million could be raised from other sources. This was accomplished by March 2009 with contributions from the United States, the European Union, Norway, the United Arab Emirates, and Kuwait. The fuel bank would consist of existing national facilities under international management to assure supply, or the actual physical production of uranium specifically for an international fuel bank, with the IAEA serving a supervisory role.[489] An alternative formulation is a virtual fuel bank as the fall back safety network should a regional or other multinational facility fail to provide as promised.

As with all aspects of counterproliferation, the goal is to draw into the system as many governments as possible. Because counterproliferation is currently purely

487 Anya Loukianova, *The International Uranium Enrichment Center at Angarsk: A Step Towards Assured Fuel Supply?*, Monterey Institute of International Studies (May 1, 2008), http://www.nti.org/analysis/articles/uranium-enrichment-angarsk/.

488 Obama, Remarks in Prague, *supra* note 7.

489 See, e.g., U.N. Secretary-General, *supra* note 4.

consent-based, the various proposals for internationalization of the nuclear fuel cycle have taken an incentive-based approach that integrates some degree of regulation. The announcement of the new United States nuclear cooperation agreement with the United Arab Emirates, for example, indicates a determined effort to maximize legal and practical counterproliferation constraints and assurances available in the existing system. It is reported, that as conditions for the agreement, the United Arab Emirates has promised that it will not develop its own fuel, but will purchase nuclear fuel for its reactors from outside suppliers, that it will store nuclear waste externally, and will allow monitoring and snap inspections by the IAEA.[490] This incentive-based approach focuses primarily on assurance of supply and competitive pricing. It encourages, but does not assure, nuclear security. It is not a model that will draw in the outliers, such as Israel, India, and Pakistan, to any similar arrangement in their own regions.

There has been a serious effort to bring counterproliferation regulation and multi-internationalization together more definitively in the project to achieve a Fissile Material Cut-off Treaty (FMCT). But the effort only demonstrates the difficulty of accomplishing counterproliferation for internationalization within a purely consensual framework. The proposed treaty is intended as an outright ban of the production of fissile material usable for the production of nuclear weapons. It has been on the UN's agenda since 1957 and on the Conference on Disarmament agenda for more than 15 years, and appears to be in suspension with no apparent prospect of success despite continuing calls for adoption. A few states have blocked negotiations by linking the FMCT to other disarmament issues or by refusing to negotiate until preconditions have been met. More generally, there is no agreement on such fundamental issues as the definition of *fissile material*, whether to include existing stockpiles, and the level of verification.[491] What we see is that, while economic incentives may motivate cooperative fissile material production, limitation is a different matter, not amenable to accomplishment within the consensual architecture of the NPT. For the outliers, such as Israel, India and Pakistan, it is least likely to be achievable.

---

490 Jay Solomon, *U.S. Plans to Sign Nuclear Pact With U.A.E.*, WALL ST. J. A7 (Dec. 12, 2008), *available at* http://online.wsj.com/article/SB122904102094400097.html.

491 The U.S. draft defines fissile material as uranium enriched to more than 20 percent in U-235 or U-233 and plutonium containing less than 80 percent Pu-238. Russia proposed a ban on only weapons plutonium and uranium containing more than about 90 percent of the isotopes Pu-239 and U-235, respectively. The NNWS want to include a ban on Tritium, a hydrogen based material used to boost the power of nuclear weapons, even though it is not a fissile material. The U.S. and other NWS support an exclusion for previously produced fissile materials, while NNWS like Pakistan assert that existing stockpiles will "freeze existing asymmetries," which threaten their security. Although President George Bush was adamantly opposed to verifications as a threat to national security, President Obama has been more forthcoming to a treaty that "verifiably ends the production of fissile materials." However, the NNWS want a comprehensive verification regime that will impose more equal safeguards standards on the nuclear weapons states (NWS). See, e.g., International Panel on Fissile Materials [IPFM], *Global Fissile Material Report 2006: First report of the International Panel on Fissile Materials*, (2006), http://fissilematerials.org/library/gfmr06.pdf

An agreement for multi-internationalization of the nuclear fuel cycle can include a condition precluding independent national enrichment, along the lines of what Russia has stipulated for the Angarsk facility. The arrangements for that facility incentivize participants with a share in profits.[492] But any non-compliance, short of credible evidence of a nuclear weapons program, is likely to go unchecked. Within a purely consensual system, any deal done is, at the end of the day, primarily and predominantly a matter of economic incentives. If those incentives diminish, or are overcome by a government's inclination to develop a weapons program, multi-internationalization as a counterproliferation strategy fails.

Furthermore, it is not only governments resisting counterproliferation that may refuse to cooperate in multi-internationalization. Many of the proposals to internationalize the nuclear fuel cycle require that a state be a signatory to the NPT as a condition of participation.[493] This raises the concern that multi-internationalization reinforces the distinction between the NWS and NNWS. It is another haunting from the false nexus of the NPT, that provides the argument for those governments resisting, that internationalization compromises the commitment to nuclear disarmament and peaceful use embodied in the NPT.[494]

If the multi-internationalization of fuel supply is to be significantly employed for counterproliferation, there must be a basis for leveraging adherence and compliance beyond uncertain and fluctuating economic incentives. A system must be sufficient to achieve adherence and compliance on the part of governments not adequately employing safeguards for their own enrichment facilities, or inclined to enrichment for weapons development. Some schemes for multi-internationalization of the nuclear fuel cycle suggest accomplishing this within the current consensual regime by adding to the agreement for any multi-internationalization, the authority of its management to close or restrict facilities and supplies if there is failure to conform to safeguards. But presented with any such condition as part of a consensual system, governments will not sign on. No government will become party to an arrangement that could allow an outside authority to shut out its lights.

Moreover, multi-internationalization, even if achieved, is not necessarily to the good for counterproliferation. A wholly consent-based system could generate negative impacts even for states that would sign on. Internationalization includes, naturally, significant issues of reprocessing and disposal of spent fuel. Under a purely consensual system, driven principally by economics, the most likely repositories will be poorer countries with lax environmental regulations, and high levels of corruption, where democratic political opposition is least likely, and consent is most easily obtained.

---

492 IAEA, *Communication received from the Resident Representative of the Russian Federation to the IAEA on the Establishment, Structure and Operation of the International Uranium Enrichment Centre*, INFCIRC/708 (June 8, 2007), http://www.iaea.org/Publications/Documents/Infcircs/2007/infcirc708.pdf.

493 *See, e.g.*, *id.* at 133.

494 *Id.*

Allowing such venues to become the world's nuclear trash-cans would not only create immediate health and environmental risks, but the new risk of unsecured material that could become a component of nuclear weapons production..

Thus multi-internationalization within the current consensual framework does not necessarily serve counterproliferation. Indeed, without assurance that a multinational arrangement and its suppliers and customers would conform to international standards, multi-internationalization could actually increase nuclear weapons risk. The establishment of a joint nuclear enrichment facility for Arab states was discussed by the Arab Atomic Energy Agency at the Riyadh Summit, in 2007, which called for "joint Arab action in the field of peaceful uses of nuclear energy leading to a regional or Arab nuclear fuel cycle ...."[495] The notion of a joint Arab enrichment facility, particularly one that might include Iran, is obviously anathema for Israel, and probably anathema for Saudi Arabia and the United States as well. Internationalization within the current consensual framework of counterproliferation could also contribute to nuclear weapons risk insofar as it would enhance the capacity for such combinations of governments to have big power reactors. Given the ease of conversion to weapons development that dual-use technology allows, inadequate regulation or enforcement could create new opportunity for nuclear weapons-related development. With the still evident desire of some governments to have nuclear weapons, such as Arab governments seeking to counter an Iranian nuclear threat, exclusively consent-based multi-internationalization could become the problem instead of the solution. It could become the means to subsidize the expense, and accomplish the complicated and challenging work, of constructing reactors capable of producing the fissile material for nuclear weapons.[496]

Whatever the arrangement for multi-internationalization of the nuclear fuel cycle, the concerns of nuclear safety, security, and safeguards would remain. Standards of safety, security, and safeguards, including those pertaining to assurance of no clandestine facilities, would nevertheless need to be addressed. But the consensual regime based on the NPT is incapable of providing the necessary assurance. An Expert Group reporting to the Director-General of the IAEA on Multilateral Approaches to the Nuclear Fuel Cycle noted that a new binding international norm would be a change in the scope of Article IV of the NPT, which the authors of the report interpret as assuring the right of each party in good standing to choose its national fuel cycle on the basis of its sovereign consideration", and that "waiving this right would thus change the bargain of the NPT."[497] The Expert Group nevertheless concedes, that for the non-nuclear weapons states, "such a new bargain can probably only be realized through universal principles, applying to all states."[498] This latter conclusion *is* surely correct. Implementation

---

495 Mohamed I. Shaker, *The Internationalization of the Nuclear Fuel Cycle: an Arab Perspective*, at 36, (2008), http://www.unidir.ch/pdf/articles/pdf-art2729.pdf.

496 *See* Henry S. Rowen, *This "Nuclear-Free" Plan Would Effect the Opposite*, WALL ST. J. A17 (Jan. 17, 2008), *available at* http://online.wsj.com/article/SB120053467872896313.html.

497 IAEA, *supra* note 485, at 12.

498 *Id.*

of universal principles *is* what is required. But as the Expert Group also recognized, the current counterproliferation architecture, resting exclusively on the NPT, cannot obligate a government to participate in an international arrangement for fuel supply under certain terms, and cannot, in itself, assure compliance with safeguards.

If facilities capable of producing weapons-grade material are to be prevented from doing so, while assuring supply through multi-internationalization for peaceful use, universal norms would have to be applied to all production. This also would require mandatory integration of production and disposal with export-import control, monitoring and verification. As counterproliferation, multi-internationalization of the fuel cycle must operate in tandem with export controls and other counterproliferation means such as IAEA inspection authority to help prevent the construction of clandestine facilities or use of declared facilities for nuclear weapons-related production. So oriented, multi-international nuclear production could operate not only to dissuade clandestine production, but would serve to deflate any government's employment of the excuse, so pronounced in Iran's nuclear development, that its national nuclear facilities are necessary for energy supply, and would assure the right to obtain nuclear fuel for peaceful use granted under Article IV of the NPT. An adequate international arrangement, meaning internationally mandated assurance of supply and waste management, could not only eliminate incentives for national nuclear fuel cycle production of proliferation concern, but would identify and delegitimize the deception used to conceal nuclear weapons related activity.

Assuring such compliance is where all the proposals, confined within the current consensual framework, break down.[499] A framework for compliance could be established, however, in the formulation of a counterproliferation resolution under Chapter VII of the United Nations Charter. The necessary formula, if internationalization of nuclear fuel supply is to be an effective mechanism for counterproliferation, is a design that fits together assurance of supply with robust regulatory authority. This would not be to eliminate but to recognize the limits of market mechanisms. However, a system effective for counterproliferation must add the capacity for authoritative supervision and credible enforcement. The only possible source for the necessary authority, and for the imposition and enforcement of international standards, would be a counterproliferation mandate under the Chapter VII authority of the Security Council. The mandate would be—No nuclear enrichment for the peaceful use of atomic energy, by nuclear weapons or non-nuclear weapons states, other than at fully safeguarded and regularly inspected national facilities, or multi-internationalized facilities. However structured, invested and managed, this requires that the infrastructure assure supply

499 This is so, for example, of the proposal by the National Resource Defense Council of the United States for a licensing authority similar to government regulatory licensing in the United States. A thoughtful and creative proposal, it ultimately loses its way by including the fantasy of a standing international military force to fill the compliance void. Thomas B. Cochran & Christopher E. Paine, *International Management of Uranium Enrichment*, at 5, (2009), http://docs.nrdc.org/nuclear/files/nuc_09052901a.pdf.

without limitation on any ground other than the politically neutral grounds of nuclear security and related environmental security. It would mandate fully safeguarded multi-international facilities, and the obligation of any state to use the supply available from those facilities as the only exception to national facilities declared to be for peaceful use that are fully safeguarded and open to IAEA inspection.

Fitting multi-internationalization of the nuclear fuel cycle within mandatory counterproliferation under Chapter VII of the United Nations Charter requires overcoming the obstacle of NPT Article IV, which guarantees signatory states the right to peaceful use of atomic energy. Probably the NPT would continue to be claimed a barrier to multi-internationalization of the fuel cycle. Unfortunately, this is one more way the NPT may be used to undermine counterproliferation. However, an international arrangement assuring supply at reasonable market prices, and waste disposal, within the contemporary reality of the globalized nuclear energy market, is compatible with the spirit and language,[500] if not the negotiating history, of the Article IV guarantee of rights of peaceful use. The convincing case can be made that multi-internationalization of the nuclear fuel cycle can facilitate and expand national opportunity for use of nuclear energy for peaceful development. In that way multi-internationalization can be said to serve the only legitimate purpose of Article IV. Even without a right of each individual state to itself manufacture fissile material, multi-internationalization can certainly be promoted as enhancement of the right of each NPT party state to peaceful use. This includes that multi-internationalization would enhance the right to peaceful use by providing the means for states without adequate resources of their own, to overcome the technological and other hurdles involved in building their own fissile material production facilities. Multi-internationalization can also be justified as providing greater safety for the individual states obtaining their supply from beyond their own borders.

The Article IV objection to multi-internationalization can be even more clearly overcome because international enrichment need not disallow development of indigenous enrichment facilities, so long as any national fissile material production is fully compliant with criteria set by the IAEA. The alternative of adequately safeguarded and supervised national facilities, either by way of licensing[501] or other supervisory arrangement, as well as multi-international enrichment, also avoids appearance of discrimination between supplier and customer states. This dual arrangement could provide new and significant opportunities for transparency, and security and safety for national facilities that otherwise might escape effective regulation. Allowing the international or national option could also serve to assure nuclear supply on a timely and predictable basis and thereby make multi-internationalization more attractive.[502] But to assure counterproliferation, there must be the obligation to choose between a

500 Nonproliferation Treaty, Article IV, July 1, 1968, 22 U.S.C. § 88.

501 Cochran & Paine, *supra* note 499, at 3–5.

502 There are many complexities that would have to be worked out. These include location, the degree of control of the various participants including international management or ownership, safeguards, the safety and security of both host and customer, and transport between them, fuel fabrication for different reactors requiring customized fuel assemblies, host and customer economic terms, and

fully safeguarded and monitored national facility or international facility, that only a mandatory system can provide.

The bottom line for organization of nuclear fuel supply is that an international mandate is required to preclude a host country or a country collective from jeopardizing the assurance of supply, or engaging in activity that could enable proliferation. Compliance with that mandate must operate at the level of management, and as between the partners to a particular arrangement. Any such multi-internationalization would have to be monitored, advised, and regulated by the IAEA for both supplier and consumer states, backed by the possibility of Security Council action under Chapter VII if there is deliberate and continuing noncompliance.

If multi-internationalization of nuclear fuel supply were to be realized under a counterproliferation mandate of the Security Council, the entire matter of legitimacy would be transfigured. As an international mandate, it could assure supply on a non-discriminatory basis employing professionally generated non-politicized standards. Multi-internationalization of the fuel cycle, as a means for counterproliferation illustrates as much as any area of counterproliferation, the importance of avoidance of classification of states, and the importance of universal application of uniform standards. Incentivizing the system with a mandate of nondiscrimination is what would empower multi-internationalization as means of counterproliferation. It could incentivize potential proliferators to abandon national nuclear enrichment development, and to secure safeguards for all fissile material. Insofar as international guarantee of supply would delegitimize the outliers and/or rogue governments, it would also serve counterproliferation.

All proposals for multi-internationalization exclude states not complying with IAEA safeguards, and that would have to be the condition *sin qua non* also under a mandatory regime. Currently, this is noted to be a principal obstacle for some governments' acceptance of a multi-international system, in that a government such as currently rules in Iran would not agree to comprehensive safeguards.[503] But isn't that just the point justifying a Security Council counterproliferation mandate; that Iran, like all other states, should be required to comply with international safeguards, and upon refusal, would be designated as in breach of an international obligation.

To maximize legitimacy, any international management authority could be, and should be, designed to apply equally to the nuclear enrichment facilities for energy purposes of nuclear weapons states as well as non-nuclear weapons states. If multi-internationalization is feasible as to all peaceful use, it is feasible irrespective of which states possess nuclear weapons. Multi-internationalization thus can become another means to overcome the NPT nexus of counterproliferation and nuclear disarmament,

---

legal relations including controls on proliferation risks. Spent fuel storage is one important area that has received inadequate attention in pending proposals. However, reprocessing is not likely to be denied, since with the exception of Japan, all reprocessing facilities are in nuclear weapons states, and it is clearly not in their interest to leave spent fuel with its plutonium content unprotected. *Id.*

503 Evans & Kawaguchi, *supra* note 38, at 143.

and also to fill the legitimacy deficit inherent in the asymmetry of nuclear weapons possession.

E. Interdiction of Nuclear Weapons Related Transport; The Proliferation Security Initiative

1. COUNTERPROLIFERATION DESIGNED TO BE LEAST LEGAL; AN ACTIVITY, NOT AN ORGANIZATION

The Proliferation Security Initiative, a counterproliferation strategy claimed to be the pre-eminent counterproliferation legacy of the Bush Administration,[504] calls on participating states to block dangerous shipments of WMD material in their ports, territory, air space, or on their vessels. It is based on a set of interdiction principles[505] to which the participating states subscribe. That is the extent of anything akin to a legal and institutional foundation. The PSI in some sense is a challenge to the international institutionalization of counterproliferation, having been promoted as "an activity, not an organization."[506]

PSI truly was a different concept for nuclear counterproliferation, not so much for its content, as for the philosophy it represented. It posits that counterproliferation in the age of WMD proliferation requires above all, speed, efficiency, minimal political constraint, and therefore minimal institutionalization, and nominal concession to legality.[507] Its philosophy is one response to the failing of the NPT. The PSI strategy proposes that instead of seeking to live with, or reconstruct the legal and institutional framework for counterproliferation, it should be made primarily a political and strategic enterprise,

---

504 *See, eg.*, John Bolton, SURRENDER IS NOT AN OPTION: DEFENDING AMERICA AT THE UNITED NATIONS AND ABROAD 122–129 (Threshold Editions 2007).

505 The PSI principles call on all participating states to join in committing to:"[A]) Undertake effective measures, either alone or in concert with other states, for interdicting the transfer or transport of WMD, their delivery systems, and related materials to and from states and non-state actors of proliferation concern. . . .

[B]) Adopt streamlined procedures for rapid exchange of relevant information concerning suspected proliferation activity, protecting the confidential character of classified information provided by other states as part of this initiative, dedicate appropriate resources and efforts to interdiction operations and capabilities, and maximize coordination among participants in interdiction efforts.

[C]) Review and work to strengthen their relevant national legal authorities where necessary to accomplish these objectives, and work to strengthen when necessary relevant international laws and frameworks in appropriate ways to support these commitments." Office of the Press Secretary, The White House, *Proliferation Security Initiative: Statement of Interdiction Principles* (Sept. 4, 2003), http://www.state.gov/t/isn/c27726.htm.

506 John Bolton, *An All-Out War on Proliferation*, FINANCIAL TIMES (Sept. 7, 2004) (*available at* http://merln.ndu.edu/archivepdf/wmd/State/36035.pdf). *See also* John Bolton, U.S. Department of State, Stopping the Spread of Weapons of Mass Destruction in the Asian-Pacific Region: The Role of the Proliferation Security Initiative (Oct. 27, 2004) (*transcript available at* http://merln.ndu.edu/archivepdf/wmd/State/37480.pdf).

507 *See,* e.g., John Bolton, Under Secretary of State, U.S. Department of State, Testimony before the House International Relations Committee (Mar. 30, 2004) (*transcript available at* http://commdocs.house.gov/committees/intlrel/hfa92866.000/hfa92866_0.htm). PSI was touted for its lack of legal

turning on the exigencies of the moment. It is what the U.S. Department of State Director of Policy Planning tellingly called "*a la carte* multilateralism."[508] Thus understood, PSI, perhaps more than any area of counterproliferation, raises the fundamental question of the extent to which counterproliferation should be framed by law.

Though the PSI addresses WMD transport both by air and sea, the focus is mainly maritime shipping rather than air transport, for obvious practical and political reasons.[509] And though the PSI applies broadly to any WMD proliferation, it specially designates "states of proliferation concern," today most notably, of course, North Korea and Iran, for heightened surveillance and presumably a greater likelihood of interdiction when shipments involve these states.[510] The PSI has evolved through a series of meetings and agreements to include 18 "core-participants" and the "support" of over 60 additional states. Interdiction exercises and actual interdictions have been conducted by the core members. By 2008, the number of actual interdictions was said to be more than 35, and today would be substantially larger.[511]

Even with the number of interdictions claimed, it is impossible to make any judgment about overall success of the PSI, because so little has been made public about

---

structure and procedure as its strength for counter-proliferation. "(D)on't mistake PSI for a multilateral institution in the conventional sense. There's no headquarters, no secretary-general, no talkfests—and, perhaps most important of all, no French or Russian veto." *The New Multilateralism*, Editorial, WALL ST. J. A22 (Jan. 8, 2004). *See also*, Susan F. Burk, U.S. Dept. of State, The Proliferation Security Initiative, Remarks at the Global Transshipment Control Enforcement Workshop, (May 2004) (*available at* http://2001-2009.state.gov/t/isn/rls/rm/32899.htm

508 *See* Richard N. Haas, THE RELUCTANT SHERIFF: THE UNITED STATES AFTER THE COLD WAR 88 (5th ed. 2002) *and* Richard N. Haas, Remarks to the Chicago Council on Foreign Relations, Chicago (June 26, 2002) (*transcript available at* http://www.cfr.org/world/richard-n-haass-director-policy-planning-staff/p4758). It can also be seen as representative of the George W. Bush administration's claim of multilateral justification by way of "coalitions of the willing"; meaning ad hoc coalition building at the behest and under the leadership of the United States. *See*, e.g., Bolton, *supra* note 507.

509 It has been suggested that countries could deny over-flight rights to aircraft which are suspected of transporting WMD material, or that suspected aircraft could be "escorted down" for searching if necessary. Australia, for one, has been reluctant to embrace this part of the PSI. Certainly any use of force involving an aircraft mid-flight would be of the gravest consequence. *See* Nicholas Kralev, *U.S. Seeks Asian Aid for Ship Searched*, WASH. TIMES (June 17, 2003).

510 The State Department does not publicly disclose incidences of interdiction, so it would be hard to prove empirically that these countries are targeted for interdiction at a disproportionate rate. However, the State Department has openly said that North Korea and Iran were of "particular concern." *See* John R. Bolton, Under Secretary for Arms Control and International Security, Testimony to the Committee on International Relations, U.S. House of Representatives (June 4, 2003) (*transcript available at* http://foreignaffairs.house.gov/112/bol062311.pdf). *See also* Interview with John Bolton, Undersecretary of State for Arms Control and International Security, ARMS CONTROL TODAY (Nov. 4, 2003), *available at* http://www.armscontrol.org/aca/midmonth/2003/November/Bolton.

511 After the second year of PSI, Secretary of State Condoleezza Rice claimed there had been 11 interdictions in the previous nine months. By July 2006, it was claimed PSI had interdicted more than 30 shipments, including exports to Iran's nuclear and missile programs. Robert Joseph, U.S. Under Secretary for Arms Control and International Security, *Remarks to the Capital Hill Club* (July 18, 2006) (*transcript available at* http://www.mtholyoke.edu/acad/intrel/bush/joseph.htm). *See also* Wade Boese, *Interdiction Initiative Successes Assessed*, ARMS CONTROL ASSOCIATION, Aug. 2008, http://www.armscontrol.org/act/2008_07-08/Interdiction.

its operations.[512] However, the little that is known gives cause for skepticism about the claims of success. For example, one episode of the few reported in any detail, was a claimed success for PSI of a 2003 interdiction of a shipment of uranium centrifuge enrichment parts from Malaysia to Libya on board a German-owned ship, the *BBC China*. Credible sources, however, contend that BBC China was an intelligence operation separate from the PSI.[513] There also are known incidents of PSI search of vessels on the basis of intelligence reports that turned out to be false.[514]

The authors of the PSI characterized it as an international partnership of countries,[515] and implementation of the statement by the president of the UN Security Council in January 1992, which called for UN member states to take greater steps to prevent proliferation.[516] PSI was announced by the Bush Administration with vague claim to legality by way of declaration that the PSI is "consistent with national legal authorities and relevant international law and frameworks, including the UN Security Council."[517] The joint subscription to interdiction principles has since been supplemented by bi-lateral agreements, particularly with the "flag of convenience" states under which a large portion of international shipping operates.[518]

There is, surely, something to be said for the Bush Administration's stated objectives of avoiding the burdens of bureaucracy and the political disabilities of institutionalization, risking a veto, or other impairment of interdiction. Moreover, there is reason

---

512 One public statement that shed some light on PSI operations was at the 2009 Operational Experts Group meeting where it was noted that PSI has "helped to block export licenses to block coolers to Iran's heavy water program, coordinated with (PSI) partners to off-load, inspect and return to country of origin ammonium perchlorate and chromium nickel steel plats (dual use components) bound for Iran, tracked off-loaded and inspected, and conducted laboratory analysis of components use in missile fuel, and prevented a ballistic missile-related North Korean cargo flight to Syria." Tony Foley, U.S. Acting Deputy Assistant Secretary of State, Opening Remarks at PSI Regional Operational Experts Group Meeting (June 22, 2009) (*transcript available at* http://dtirp.dtra.mil/pdfs/psI_remarks.pdf).

513 U.S. Assistant Secretary of State John Wolf disclosed to the publication *Arms Control Today* that the BBC China was a "separate" operation from PSI, that was part of the action against the A.Q. Khan network, designed to influence Libyan disarmament. *See* Wade Boese, *Key U.S. Interdiction Initiative Claim Misrepresented*, ARMS CONTROL ASSOCIATION (Aug. 2005), http://www.armscontrol.org/act/2005_07–08/Interdiction_Misrepresented. *See* Ron Suskind, THE ONE PERCENT DOCTRINE 268–69 (Simon & Schuster 2006).

514 *See* Wade Boese, *False Claims of PSI Success,* WASH. TIMES A16 (Aug. 17, 2005) (The BBC China, touted as an interdiction success, finding centrifuge components destined for Libya, reportedly has been falsely attributed to PSI.)

515 Office of the Press Secretary, The White House, *supra* note 505.

516 Statement of the President of the Security Council, 3046th mtg., UN Doc. S/23500 (1992) (*transcript available at* http://www.undemocracy.com/S-23500.pdf).

517 The U.S. has said that the PSI "is consistent with and a step in the implementation of the UN Security Council Presidential Statement of January 1992, which states that the proliferation of all WMD constitutes a threat to international peace and security, and underlines the need for member states of the UN to prevent proliferation." Office of the Press Secretary, The White House, *supra* note 505.

518 "More than 50 percent of commercial shipping fleet dead weight tonnage is now subject to rapid action consent procedures for boarding, search, and seizure by the United States." Office of the Spokesman, U.S. Department of State, The United States, and the Republic of the Marshall Islands Proliferation Security Initiative Shipboarding Agreement, (Aug. 14, 2004), http://www.state.gov/t/isn/trty/35237.htm.

for building support for international interdiction by starting with those states most willing, then expanding membership as effectiveness and credibility are developed; a not unusual form of international capacity building.

But is PSI, and the approach to counterproliferation it epitomizes, effective? That is impossible to fully determine without access to confidential information on its operations. With so little disclosed publicly, presumably to protect revealing the scope and design of PSI to proliferators, and because of the political implications of actual interdiction, outside operational evaluation is difficult. It has been disclosed that PSI operates by means of an Operational Experts Group, consisting of military, law enforcement, intelligence, legal, and diplomatic personnel from more than 20 PSI member governments, that works to discuss, plan, and test interdiction. However, there is no PSI process publicly known. The substance of all PSI activities is kept secret. The resultant lack of transparency and accountability has not gone unnoticed, and has been criticized as unreasonably opaque, even from within the U.S. government.[519]

Though it impossible to assess PSI operationally from public sources, there is something significant to be learned about effectiveness of interdiction from the episode that is said to have inspired the PSI, which did receive considerable publicity. This was the boarding of a North Korean vessel on the high seas by forces of the United States and Spain. The episode illustrates the challenge in the hard cases involving a "state of proliferation concern." Indeed, this particular encounter involved not just a state of proliferation concern, but nuclear-armed North Korea, which has threatened that interdiction of one of it ships would constitute an "act of war."[520]

In December 2003, Spanish Special Forces rappelled from a helicopter onto the moving deck of an unflagged cargo ship in the Indian Ocean, while Spanish snipers stood by. The United States Navy had been tracking the ship for a month, having surveilled the loading on board of what appeared to be WMD related cargo. Neither the United States nor Spanish forces acted until a legal justification was found for seizure of the ship. The ship was apparently freshly painted with the name *So San*, but no ship named *So San* was registered, and the captain repeatedly raised and lowered the flag, apparently in an effort to avoid detection. This made available a legal basis for interdiction—that the ship was "without nationality," and therefore could be stopped and searched without violating any state's jurisdiction. American forces arrived a day after the interception by Spain. They found, hidden below thousands of bags of cement in the ship's hold, crates containing fifteen scud missiles, fifteen conventional warheads, and many barrels of chemicals, which it was determined, were on their way to Yemen.

---

519 *See* U.S. General Accountability Office, GAO-08-21, U.S. Efforts to Combat Nuclear Networks Need Better Data on Proliferation Risks and Program Results (Oct. 2007), http://www.gao.gov/new.items/d0821.pdf. The U.S. Congress responded to the critique, by including in the Implementing Recommendations of the 9/11 Commission Act of 2007, that the Executive establish clear policies, procedures, structures, funding, and performance indicators to measure the results of PSI activities. Implementing Recommendation of the 9/11 Commission Act of 2007, Pub. L. No. 110-53, § 1821 (2007) (codified at 50 U.S.C. § 2911 *et seq*).

520 David E. Sanger, *US Weighs Intercepting North Korean Shipments*, N.Y. Times A1 (June 7, 2009).

The following political denouement was reported by *The Wall Street Journal*:

> Yemen told the U.S. it had a right to the missiles, which it claimed to have ordered nearly a decade earlier during its civil war. After a series of tense phone calls among Yemen's President Ali Abdallah Salih, Vice President Cheney and Secretary of State Colin Powell, the U.S. agreed to let the ship sail on to Yemen and deliver its cargo. The Spaniards were embarrassed. Deputy Defense Secretary Paul Wolfowitz apologized to Spain's defense minister for "what could seem an absurd situation."[521]

In other words, in terms of securing either effective weapons interdiction or international legitimacy, the episode was a fiasco. So it might have been a cautionary tale about the need for greater organization and legally defined process. The lesson drawn by the Bush Administration was, however, different. It *was* for greater preplanning.[522] However, the principal official identified with the PSI, declared the lesson to be, "With Spain, it all worked out well. But with another country, we could have been lost in discussions for days about the legality and other issues."[523] So on the rationale of the need for pre-planning was born the scheme of the PSI, outside any established international organization or legal process, as the way to maximize the ability of the United States and its counterproliferation allies to act expeditiously for interdiction.[524]

What was the appropriate lesson? For interdiction, what is the optimal relationship of process and political and strategic consequence? Would a reformulation of PSI in an institutional framework of prescribed legal process more effectively address the interdiction component of counterproliferation? PSI remains, for the most part, articulated as simply a set of principles which member states are said to be "committed to."[525] The principles are declared as comporting with established law of the sea, particularly concerning the jurisdiction of coastal states and flag state jurisdiction.[526] However, there has been much contention among academic commentators, and governmental and military officials over whether PSI interdiction, in its various potential scenarios, is consistent with customary international law and the Convention on the Law of the Sea (UNCLOS).[527] The question is revealing, because the answer is that the claim of consistency of PSI with the law of the sea is false in its most significant aspects, and

---

521 Carla Anne Robbins, *Why U.S. Gave U.N. No Role in Plan To Halt Arms Ships*, WALL ST. J., Oct. 21, 2003, at A1.

522 *See* Nigel Chamberlain, *Interdiction Under the Proliferation Security Initiative: Counter-Proliferation or Counter-Productive?*, BRITISH AMERICAN SECURITY INFORMATION COUNCIL (2004), *available at http://www.basicint.org/sites/default/files/PUB051003.pdf*

523 Robbins, *supra* note 521.

524 *Id.*

525 Office of the Press Secretary, The White House, *supra* note 505.

526 *Id.*

527 *See* Yann-Huei Song, *The U.S.-Led Proliferation Initiative and UNCLOS: Legality, Implementation and an Assessment*, Vol. 38 OCEAN DEV. & INT'L L., 101–145 (2007) for a collection of contending views on the different jurisdictional scenarios.

that the PSI, as currently formulated, thereby sacrifices, unnecessarily, legitimacy and effectiveness.

II. INTERFACE OF THE PROLIFERATION SECURITY INITIATIVE AND INTERNATIONAL LAW

a. Coastal State Jurisdiction

The PSI secures little if any legitimacy for interdiction. This is true even as to the territorial jurisdiction of state parties to PSI over their own coastal waters. Though the territorial jurisdiction of states extends 12 miles, the right of innocent passage has long been part of customary international law, and is now also enshrined in the jurisdictional rules of UNCLOS. That right is an aspect of the convention, which the United States has recognized as constituting binding international law, despite U.S. rejection of other parts of the convention and U.S. refusal to date to ratify. The right of innocent passage protects a shipment of WMD material that does not constitute a threat to the coastal state, which of course would describe the typical situation of illicit nuclear weapons-related transport, in that WMD typically would be targeted for the point of destination, not somewhere along the route of transit.

UNCLOS was formalized before the advent of WMD interdiction as a major security concern, and therefore was not designed to address counterproliferation. And none of the exceptions to the right of innocent passage can be construed to prohibit the transportation of WMD material nonthreatening to the coastal state. Articles 17 and 21 of UNCLOS list the type of passage that would not qualify as innocent, and none of the listed categories could be deemed applicable to stoppage of a WMD shipment without significant distortion of meaning. Article 19 provides exception only for "any threat or use of force against the sovereignty, territorial integrity or political independence of the coastal State," the use of weapons against the costal state, "any act aimed at collecting information to the prejudice of the defense or security of the coastal State," or "any act of willful and serious pollution contrary to this Convention."[528] Of particular relevance under Article 23 of UNCLOS is that ships carrying nuclear weapons are explicitly given the right of innocent passage,[529] a provision surely supported in its origination by the nuclear weapons states.

The apparent inconsistency between the right of innocent passage under UNCLOS and PSI has been a subject of particular protest by governments outside PSI.[530] Interdiction in relation to the right of innocent passage is especially of concern to the littoral states of Indonesia and Malaysia, both of which have refused to sign on

528 U.N. Convention on the Law of the Sea, Article 19, *opened for signature* Dec. 10, 1982, 1833 U.N.T.S. 397 (entered into force Nov. 16, 1994) (UNCLOS).

529 *Id.*, at art. 23.

530 *See* e.g., Ivy Susanti, *Indonesia Questions US Proposals on Proliferation Initiative*, JAKARTA POST, Mar. 16, 2006, http://www.redorbit.com/news/international/430553/indonesia_questions_us_proposals_on_proliferation_security_initiative.

to PSI. The counterproliferation mandate of Security Council Resolution 1540 arguably now pre-empts the right of innocent passage to the extent inconsistent with transit of weapons of mass destruction; but under what circumstances and to what degree remains entirely unclear. The same apparent inconsistency pertains to passage through narrow straits. Even if the straits in question are within the jurisdiction of a PSI participant, UNCLOS, under Articles 37 and 38, provides a right of transit passage that would restrict PSI interdiction no less than the right of innocent passage through territorial waters.

b. High Seas Jurisdiction

The legitimacy challenge posed by WMD interdiction will be greatest, of course, when interdiction requires the use of force. The likely locus for any use of force is not coastal state jurisdiction, but the high seas. This is not only because of the geographical extent of high seas jurisdiction compared with coastal state jurisdiction, but also because of the general recognition in customary international law, now embodied in UNCLOS Articles 86–94, that high seas jurisdiction is exclusively the jurisdiction of the flag state. It is consequently on the high seas that "states of proliferation concern," such as North Korea or Iran, have the greatest claim to freedom from interdiction. High seas interdiction without the permission of the flag state is also, surely, crucially provocative, and the fact that North Korea has declared that it would regard the interdiction of one of its ships on the high seas as an "act of war" confirms this. That North Korea can take this position, secure in its legitimacy, is evidenced by the restraint shown by the U.S. Navy in following the vessel named *So San* for a month without any confrontation, and requesting the Spanish to implement interdiction only after the "stateless vessel" rationale became available. More generally in the case of North Korea, and similarly demonstrating the limits on interdiction, the call to inspect vessels suspected of violating sanctions has been restricted to action requiring consent of the flag state, and not authorization of the use of force.[531]

Flag state jurisdiction cannot be ignored, because it is embodiment of the general principle of freedom of the seas. It is of critical importance to securing the interests of the global economy and the world's major navies, and is a principle of international law firm and universal in its political basis. For both air space and the seas beyond 12 nautical miles (the territorial sea), a ship is subject solely to flag state jurisdiction, and interdiction is not legitimized under international law unless the flag of transport is not identified or the vessel or aircraft is engaged in piracy, trafficking in illicit narcotics, unauthorized broadcasting, or activity analogous to the now ancient exception for slave trade. Even for the United States, notwithstanding its initiation and leadership of PSI, there is ever-present the important countervailing interest in maintaining the legal foundation for freedom of navigation, for U.S. naval and air forces, and for commercial shipping.

531 UNSC Res 1874 UNDoc S/RES/1874 (June 12, 2009).

Consequently, the PSI has evolved with particular attention to reconciling interdiction on the high seas with the principle of flag state jurisdiction. The approach has been two-pronged; securing the agreement of PSI participant states to cooperate in interdiction on the high seas of their own flag vessels, and bilateral agreements with so-called "flag of convenience" states, such as Liberia, Panama, and the Marshall Islands. The United States asserts these bilateral agreements and commitments from PSI partners now render over 50 percent of the world's commercial shipping "subject to rapid action consent procedures for boarding, search, and seizure by the United States,"[532] and therefore constitute a major expansion of international legitimacy for counterproliferation.

The flag of convenience bilaterals, technically a response to flag-state jurisdiction on the high seas, are artifice, however, in relation to the relevant political considerations. A flag of convenience is just that, a device that shipowners use to avoid regulation; to obtain low registration fees, avoid taxes, and employ cheap labor. There is no genuine link between the real owner of a vessel or its cargo and the flag the vessel flies. In many cases, the flag of convenience registry is not even run from the country concerned. All of the paperwork for the Liberian registry, for example, is done by a private company in the United States.

So what is the significance of agreements with flag of convenience states for WMD interdiction? A bilateral boarding agreement between the United States and a government it can easily leverage, such as that of Panama or Liberia, is hardly basis for international legitimacy. More to the point of any particular interdiction, because the flag of convenience has no bearing on the actual ownership of ships or cargo, flag of convenience jurisdiction is largely irrelevant to the political interests that can be ignited by an interdiction.

The irrelevance of flag-state jurisdiction to the actual political consequences of interdiction is exemplified by the fact that Panama and Liberia have the highest volume of flag of convenience global trade.[533] The flag of convenience agreements provide no legal standard of process or substance to test a decision by the United States government or any government to undertake an interdiction. If there is significant political consequence to the interdiction of a vessel of Panamanian or Liberian registry, Panama or Liberia will be irrelevant to the source of difficulty. When a more dangerous nation's cargo or other commercial interest is affected, the consequences could be quite significant, as significant as North Korea's claim that the interception of any of its ships would be treated as an "act of war."

532 Office of the Spokesman, U.S. Department of State, *supra* note 518. Through November of 2011, the U.S. entered into ship boarding agreements with the following governments; Antigua and Barbuda, Bahamas, Belize, Croatia, Cyprus, Liberia, Malta, Marshall Islands, Mongolia, Panama, and St. Vincent and the Grenadines. *See* U.S. State Department, Proliferation Security Initiative, *Ship Boarding Agreements*, (last visited Jan. 17, 2012), http://www.state.gov/t/isn/c27733.htm

533 UNCTAD Secretariat, *Review of Maritime Transport* 2009, UNCTAD/RMT/2009, at 54, http://www.unctad.org/en/docs/rmt2009_en.pdf.

None of this is remedied by Security Council Resolution 1540. The legislative history of Resolution 1540 makes clear that it was not intended to effect flag-state jurisdiction, just as it was not intended to alter coastal-state jurisdiction and the right of innocent passage. The Bush Administration, in the negotiations and debates leading to Security Council Resolution 1540, sought and failed to obtain support for inclusion of a maritime interdiction provision. Russia and China threatened to veto any resolution that endorsed the PSI, and Resolution 1540 was agreed only after the United States accepted China's demand to drop a provision authorizing the interdiction of a vessel suspected of carrying WMD.[534] A similar effort through the International Maritime Organization during revision of the 1988 Convention for the Suppression of Unlawful Acts Against Navigation resulted in similar rejection of nonconsensual boarding on the high seas. The 2005 protocol to the convention reaffirms that boarding seaward of any state's territorial sea is not permitted without the express authorization of the flag state, or its failure to communicate timely response to a reasonable request, any reasonable suspicion of the presence of WMD notwithstanding.[535]

c. Self-Defense

To close the gap in the available legal justification for interdiction on the high seas, the Bush Administration asserted that a ship can be stopped under the general right of self-defense.[536] However, while Article 51 of the United Nations Charter provides for the right of self-defense, the long prevailing understanding in international law has been that the self-defense justification is limited to situations of armed attack or imminent armed attack. As was commonly pointed out in the debate over the Bush pre-emption doctrine,[537] in the principal precedent indicating U.S. practice, the *Caroline* case, the self-defense justification for the use of force was declared as applying only when the necessity is instant, overwhelming, and leaves no choice of means, or time for deliberation.[538] Critics note, without contradiction, that without the limits of imminence

534 Wang Guagya, China's ambassador to the United Nations stated that such provision had been "kicked out" of the resolution. *See* Michael Richardson, *Between a Rogue and a Hyperpower*, S. CHINA MORNING POST 17 (Dec. 12, 2003). *See also* William Hawkins, *Chinese Realpolitik and the Proliferation Security Initiative*, Feb. 18, 2005, http://asianresearch.org/articles/2505.html. *See* Valencia, *supra* note 275, at 48. *See* Mary Beth Nikitin, Cong. Research Serv., RL 34327, CRS REPORT FOR CONGRESS-PROLIFERATION SECURITY INITIATIVE 6 (Jan. 18, 2011).

535 *See Protocol of 2005 to the Convention for the Suppression of Unlawful Acts Against the Safety of Maritime Navigation*, IMO Doc. LEG/CONF.15/21 (Nov. 1, 2005) The protocol provides that consent may be given in advance for a WMD-related offense and that authorization to board will be deemed granted if response to a request is not made within four hours from the flag state's acknowledgment of receipt of a request to confirm the vessel's nationality. *Id.* art. 8 bis, para5(d). Similar changes were made to the 1988 Fixed Platforms Protocol. *See id.* art. 8 bis, para. 5(d).

536 *See generally* Michael Byers, *Policing the High Seas: The Proliferation Security Initiative* 98 AM. J. INT'L .L 536, 541 (2004).

537 *Id.*

538 *See* Letter from Daniel Webster to Lord Ashburton (Aug. 6, 1842), quoted in 2 John Bassett Moore, A DIGEST OF INTERNATIONAL LAW 412 (1906).

and necessity, the doctrine of self-defense could be used to justify virtually any use of force, in the most volatile international contexts, e.g., India-Pakistan, China-Taiwan. It is not surprising that in reaction to the torrent of criticism of its raw pre-emption doctrine, the Bush Administration, in contexts other than the PSI, returned to a more traditional inclusion of some notion of imminence and necessity.[539]

The doctrine of self-defense as a basis for unilateral action, embodying the pre-emption doctrine in its most extreme form, is still available for the PSI to cover a broad range of possible circumstances. This reliance on pre-emptive self-defense as justification, however, renders minimal, at best, any legal or political legitimacy. This is not a new lesson in the use of law and legal process to mitigate international crisis. A self-defense justification under Article 51 of the United Nations Charter and Articles 6 and 8 of the Rio Treaty was specifically considered and rejected by those who fashioned United States policy in the Cuban Missile Crisis.[540] As explained in the memoir and study of the crisis, by then Legal Advisor to the State Department, Abram Chayes,

> In retrospect, however, I think the central difficulty with the Article 51 argument was that it seemed to trivialize the whole effort at legal justification. No doubt the phrase 'armed attack' must be construed broadly enough to permit some anticipatory response. But it is a very different matter to expand it to include threatening deployments or demonstrations that do not have imminent attack as their purpose or probable outcome. To accept that reading is to make the occasion for forceful response essentially a question for unilateral national decision that would not only be formally unreviewable, but not subject to intelligent criticism either. There is simply no standard against which this decision could be judged. Whenever a nation believed that interests, which in the heat and pressure of a crisis it is prepared to characterize as vital, were threatened, its use of force in response would become permissible.[541]

The same reasoning applies to avoiding, or at least limiting as much as possible, the use of the self-defense justification in implementation of the PSI.

---

539 The Department of State's Legal Adviser articulated a somewhat narrower view of the doctrine in a memorandum on pre-emption, which returned to the criteria of imminence and necessity associated with anticipatory self-defense. The Legal Adviser wrote that "[t]he President's National Security Strategy relies upon the same legal framework applied to the British in Caroline and to Israel in 1981.... After the exhaustion of peaceful remedies and a careful, deliberate consideration of the consequences, in the face of overwhelming evidence of an imminent threat, a nation may take preemptive action to defend its nationals from unimaginable harm.'" Miriam Sapiro, *Iraq: The Shifting Sands of Preemptive Self-Defense*, 97 AM. J. INT'L L. 599, 602 (2003), quoting William H. Taft IV, Legal Adviser, Department of State, *The Legal Basis for Preemption*, Nov. 18, 2002, http://www.cfr.org/publication.php?id=5250.

540 *See generally* Abram Chayes, THE CUBAN MISSILE CRISIS: INTERNATIONAL CRISES AND THE ROLE OF LAW (Oxford 1974).

541 *Id.* at 65.

Another rationale for forcible interdiction on the high seas was suggested by the Bush Administration, which though not self-defense in any present formulation, is related. This is the concept of a customary norm of interdiction developing by way of a group of states, presumably an expanded "coalition of the willing," acting under the PSI in their mutual security interest. The concept draws on analogy to the ban on transporting slaves, which developed after Britain began halting slave ships in the early 1800s. The proposition it fosters is that at some point the participation of multiple states in the activities of the PSI would establish the necessary normative basis as a matter of state practice.[542] Some academic support has been obtained for this view.[543] Nevertheless, at present it is incontrovertible that the forcible interdiction on the high seas that the PSI envisions is at odds with state practice, customary principles of freedom of the seas and UNCLOS.

III. INSTITUTIONALIZATION OF PSI UNDER SECURITY COUNCIL MANDATE; LEGITIMACY AND EFFECTIVENESS

The formula of the PSI, interdiction based informally on strategic relationships of maritime powers (the core states of the PSI) and leverage over politically insignificant flag states ("flag of convenience states"), is a prescription for minimizing international legitimacy. It is not a foundation for confronting the hard and critical confrontations, such as involving North Korea or Iran. The fundamental deficiency of PSI is the same as all treaty or consent-based approaches to counterproliferation. The "states of proliferation concern" that PSI purports to target are naturally the states not willing to grant interdiction authority to the international community. And the legitimacy that would help reach these cases is not obtained by stretching or distorting established norms of the law of the sea. Though search for WMD may occur when in foreign ports or airports, where there would be domestic criminal jurisdiction available, it is not difficult for proliferators to avoid such jurisdiction, given the global alternatives of modern transport. As in other arenas of counterproliferation, what is lacking is a mechanism, and the procedural and substantive grounding, for obligation of all states to intercept, in all places, illicit transit of nuclear materials and technology.

PSI is definitely an advance in the direction of evolving prerogatives for international interdiction. According to its terms, and the sketchy reports of its operations, it facilitates information sharing, the building of relationships between responsible national officials at the political and operational levels, and enables joint planning

---

542 *See* Paul Wolfowitz, Deputy Secretary of Defense, *Remarks to Proliferation Security Initiative Conference*, (Dec. 17, 2003) (*transcript available at* http://www.defense.gov/transcripts/transcript.aspx?transcriptid=2817). *See also* Ruth Wedgewood, *Interdicting North Korea*, WALL ST. J. A12 (Apr. 28, 2003). *See also* Wenwei Guan, Student Disarmament Research Associate, Simons Centre, The Proliferation Security Initiative and Implications for International Law (2004); *and* The Proliferation Security Initiative: an Interview with John Bolton, Arms Control Today (Dec. 2003), http://www.armscontrol.org/act/2003_12/PSI.

543 Wedgewood, *supra* note 542.

and sharing of best practices for conducting interdictions.[544] It is possible, that as the number of states participating in PSI increases, and the activities of PSI increase, a customary norm may develop to accord legitimacy to interdiction on the high seas without flag-state consent.[545] However, there would still be the need for articulation of substantive and procedural standards within an organizational format. This is because the lack of standards seriously increases the risks of conflict resulting from interdiction, by leaving unnecessary uncertainty as to critical questions and expectations. How are the "states of proliferation concern," whose ships are subject to interdiction, to be determined? Does this extend to commercial ventures trading with such states, within such states, or only those flying the flag of such states? How and on what basis is it to be determined which vessels flying under flags of states not "of concern" but with shipments from states (or entities from states) "of concern" may be interdicted? How is the risk-laden decision to interdict to be made? Upon what burden of proof? What cargoes would qualify for interdiction? Does dual-use technology, for example, which is the subject of normal commercial sale, subject a vessel or aircraft to interdiction if somehow involving a "state of proliferation concern"? Under what command and control is the actual interdiction to be accomplished? Is there any redress for states or commercial interests when losses occur from interdiction, when it is justified or when it is not justified? The PSI is said to include a standard of good cause for interdiction.[546] What does this mean for the reality of interdiction? Good cause is probably in large measure a political determination. Nevertheless, legitimacy will depend on the process by which the determination is made.[547] Even the little publicly known about actual interdiction, such as the *So San* affair, indicates serious mistakes of fact and judgment have already been made as to precisely such questions.[548] Some of the questions may have been addressed in the practice exercises taking place among the participants in the PSI.[549] But without formal and legal articulation, unnecessary and inflammatory problems of consistency and notice will remain, not the least of which is notice to the state that is the subject of confrontation, particularly in a potentially nuclearized context, such as interdiction of a North

544 Office of the Press Secretary, The White House, *supra* note 505. *See* http://www.state.gov/t/isn/c10390.htm for latest information on PSI.

545 *See* Wolfowitz, *supra* note 542; *and* Wedgewood, *supra* note 542; *and* Interview with John Bolton, Undersecretary of State for Arms Control and International Security, *supra* note 510.

546 *See* Office of the Press Secretary, The White House, *supra* note 505. *See* Bureau of Nonproliferation, U.S. Department of State, Chairman's Statements, 2003–2004, http://www.nuclearfiles.org/menu/key-issues/nuclear-weapons/issues/proliferation/psi/2004-06-01_krakow-chairmans-statement_fco_gov_uk.pdf.

547 In relation to the Cuban Missile Crisis, Chayes writes "The Rio Treaty did not set up a *standard* permitting an objective conclusion on that issue by the method of reason. It established a process for deciding the question by the method of politics." Chayes, *supra* note 540.

548 *See* William Safire, *Bush's Stumble: The So San Affair*, N.Y. TIMES A1 (Dec. 19, 2002).

549 As of 2012, PSI participant states have conducted nearly thirty interdiction exercises. *See* Peter Crail, *The Proliferation Security Initiative (PSI) at a Glance*, ARMS CONTROL ASSOCIATION (last visited Jan. 27, 2012), http://www.armscontrol.org/factsheets/PSI.

Korean or Iranian vessel. The unresolved questions and unexplained procedures have become the principal basis for the lack of international legitimacy and adherence, particularly and most significantly as China has charged as the reasoning for its own nonsubscription to PSI.[550]

If all of these determinations are effectively in control of the United States through "a collection of interdiction partnerships,"[551] which is said to be the current strategy, legality and legitimacy are inevitably trivialized. It is the same problem of unilateralism the Kennedy Administration recognized in rejecting the Article 51 self-defense justification during the Cuban Missile Crisis. Moreover, as recognized in the stewardship of that crisis, international action of such magnitude and risk, by a superpower, without multilateral endorsement, establishes precedent enhancing the risks of unilateral action by other governments at other potential flashpoints of major conflict, the list which today most obviously would include India-Pakistan, the Middle East, Taiwan-China, and the zone of North Korea's paranoia.

The need for detailed articulation of standards of substance and process, both to minimize risk of international conflict and to obtain international legitimacy, argues for the PSI to become an organization, not just an activity. And is there truly any good reason to avoid an institutional formulation of substantive and procedural standards? A preeminent rationalization for non-institutionalization of PSI interdiction is that proliferation risk involves non-state actors such as al Qaeda,[552] and that responding to the new non-state actor threats may require acting outside of traditional frameworks and norms. But this is a non sequitor that deflects the relevant question. Whoever is doing the proliferating, a government or non-state actor, the question is: What does effective interdiction require? For interdiction, every operational aspect of the PSI is based on state-initiated or state-directed action. Interdiction at sea is by its nature a state-focused activity, in which legitimacy inevitably involves what is a firm general consensus on jurisdictional standards. This was probably the principal accomplishment of UNCLOS. Thus its designation of jurisdictional limits remains strongly supported by the United States, despite continuing U.S. resistance to adoption of the convention.[553] Even though non-state actors and rogue states may utilize maritime transport, the political and military risk is state-to-state, as illustrated by the *So San* episode.[554] And despite the bilateral dynamics of the PSI, there has been no claim, by

---

550 Thus Ye Ru'an, Vice President of the China Arms Control and Disarmament Association, has written, "How can the PSI participants ensure that interdiction operations are conducted based on accurate, unbiased and non-politicized intelligence? Who should be held accountable for interdictions in which no WMD-related cargo is found or, worse still, for interdictions that touch off an armed conflict." Ye Ru'an & Zhao Qinghai, *The PSI: Chinese Thinking and Concern*, THE MONITOR: INTERNATIONAL PERSPECTIVES ON NONPROLIFERATION, Vol. 10 No. 1, 2004, 22–24.

551 Office of the Press Secretary, The White House, *supra* note 505.

552 *See* Wolfowitz, *supra* note 542.

553 See Keith Johnson & Laura Meckler, *To Parry China: US Looks to Sea Treaty it Hasn't Signed*, WALL ST. J. A12 (Nov. 18, 2011).

554 *See* Bolton, *supra* note 507.

any of its proponents, to deal with terrorism as such by ignoring applicable legal standards. Indeed, a basic principle of the PSI, from its inception, has been to call for the cooperation of states and adherence to international law to achieve interdiction of non-state proliferators.[555]

Legitimacy cannot be achieved by an informal arrangement, completely opaque as to standards and procedures. The PSI has achieved substantial political enlargement through the growing list of participants, and through endorsements such as that of the EU.[556] United Nations Security Council Resolution 1540 laid the groundwork for possible integration of PSI with the architecture of the United Nations by providing support for at least the basic tenets of the PSI.[557] But the refusal to integrate the PSI into a broader architecture is myopic. One way or another the PSI will have to be reconciled to the United Nations Charter, and various regional security arrangements. Given, for example, that North Korea has declared that PSI interdiction of its ships would constitute an act of war, in any confrontation with North Korea, the question of the relationship of PSI interdiction to Security Council action or inaction will be provoked. This is true, also, of all other crisis scenarios. The PSI, as currently formulated, purports to allow any participant state, to present a good-cause request to another. Suppose for example, India, which has so far refused to join PSI, did join and requested of a flag state with which it has good relations, to interdict a shipment of WMD material between Pakistan and China, Pakistan having proven to be a major proliferator. Should such situations, rife with potential for military escalation, be resolved solely on a bilateral basis between India and the state to whom the request is directed? This is apparently the present prescription of the PSI in its confinement to flag-state jurisdiction as currently configured. Does not interdiction result in precisely the situation in which diplomats and public international lawyers should be able to turn to an institutional format that can facilitate and legitimate action in the mutual interest of the international community, to prevent a disastrous escalation?

Because the use of force may be involved, institutionalization by means of the Security Council's authority under Chapter VII of the UN Charter would be the appropriate modality. The institutionalized and internationalized council of governments enhances legitimacy, as James Madison noted long ago in reference to a much simpler

555 The principles of interdiction state that "PSI participants are committed to the following interdiction principles… consistent with national legal authorities and relevant international law and frameworks, including the UN Security Council,"and that partner countries should "[r]eview and work to strengthen their relevant national legal authorities where necessary to accomplish these objectives, and work to strengthen when necessary relevant international law and frameworks in appropriate ways to support these commitments." Office of the Press Secretary, The White House, *supra* note 505.

556 Council of the European Union, 10052/04, Non-Proliferation: Support of the Proliferation Security Initiative (PSI), June 1, 2004, http://www.consilium.europa.eu/uedocs/cmsUpload/st10052.en04.pdf.

557 *See* S.C. Res. 1540, *supra* note 124; U.N. SCOR, 4956th mtg., U.N. Doc. S/Res/1540 (2004).

international order.[558] In echo of Madison's observation, China and other members of the Security Council, resisting early drafts of what became Security Council Resolution 1540, made clear they would oppose any formulation that could suggest a priori unlimited authorization of interdiction. But they were not objecting to WMD interdiction as such; only to control by the United States and its closest allies. Not only could such objection be overcome by Security Council authorization, but by allowing potentially objecting states the opportunity for critique and a role in fashioning the action involved, endorsement may be secured that otherwise would not be available. China is the only remaining one of the five permanent members of the Security Council still not brought within PSI's core group of states. Bringing China in by means of the internationalization of the PSI, and securing an international mandate, would be mutually reinforcing accomplishments.

This need not make counterproliferation interdiction subject to veto. Failing endorsement under the Security Council authorized process, the United States and any of its partners in PSI could act in alliance, or independently, if the interdiction situation was thought to be sufficiently dire, notwithstanding lack of broader organizational support. What *would* be accomplished is a priority of available justifications and means for interdiction. First would be to act pursuant to the new Security Council mandate. If that were not politically feasible, the alternative would be to act on the basis of what has been accomplished under PSI, the boarding agreements and experience of coordinated action between governments. That would remain a fall-back position for cases in which there is no better international alternative, which is effectively the currently claimed prerogative of the PSI.[559] Finally, the United States or any other state could rely on anticipatory self-defense as justification, though then at the lowest level of legitimacy.[560] If the United States and allied governments determine that

---

558 It is the salutary principle enunciated by James Madison in the Federalist Papers that "when the national councils may be warped by some strong passion, or momentary interest, the presumed or known opinion of the impartial world, may be the best guide that can be followed." James Madison, *The Federalist no. 63: The Senate (Continued)*, March 1, 1788.

559 It was declared on behalf of the George W. Bush Administration that "where there are gaps or ambiguities in our authorities, we may consider seeking additional sources for such authority, as circumstances dictate. What we do not believe, however, is that only the Security Council can grant the authority we need, and that may be the real source of the criticism we face." John R. Bolton, Under Secretary for Arms Control and International Security, *Legitimacy in International Affairs: The American Perspective in Theory and Operation*, Remarks to the Federalist Society, Washington, D.C., (Nov. 13, 2003) (*transcript available at* http://www.fed-soc.org/doclib/20070324_bolton.pdf).

560 The customary right of pre-emptive self-defense was constrained by the criteria of a "necessity of self-defense, instant, overwhelming, leaving no choice of means, and no moment of deliberation." R.Y. Jennings, *The Caroline and McLeod Cases*, 32 AM. J. INT'L L. 82, 89, 91–91 (1938). *See also* Ian Brownlie, INTERNATIONAL LAW AND THE USE OF FORCE BY STATES, 257–64 (Oxford 1963); William W. Bishop Jr., INTERNATIONAL LAW: CASES AND MATERIALS 916–917 (3d ed. 1971). The George W. Bush Administration famously advanced the proposition that the threat of weapons of mass destruction justified pre-emptive action without such imminence. *National Security Strategy*, *supra* note 2, at 15. Former UN Secretary-General Kofi Annan responded that that this modern version of the doctrine of anticipatory self-defense "represents a fundamental challenge to the principles on which, however

a ship is transporting a nuclear threat, they would probably attempt interdiction, no matter what justification may be available. U.S. officials have said as much.[561] But the best strategy would maximize the opportunity for international law and legitimacy in anticipation of confrontation, by making it possible for action to come by way of the maximal international endorsement and sanction under a Security Council counter-proliferation mandate.

The institutionalization of interdiction would also serve to generate legitimacy for gathering the intelligence to justify interdiction. From the initiation of the PSI, it has been recognized that one of the important advantages to be gained from international cooperation on interdiction is the sharing of information. One of the initial principles of interdiction calls on participants to "adopt streamlined procedures for rapid exchange of relevant information concerning suspected proliferation activity."[562] However, United States representatives have declared that under PSI, in responding to an interdiction request, "each state will need to decide for itself whether good cause has been shown; i.e., each state will need to decide for itself whether the information provided by the requesting state warrants acceding to the request."[563] No process has been indicated for joint intelligence evaluation, and as these statements indicate, any international process is absent. Part of the challenge of institutionalization, therefore, would be to design a mechanism efficient enough and sufficiently uncompromising of intelligence sources, to prove effective. There is no perceivable downside to such development, and much to be gained for legitimacy and effectiveness, which could help to bring in maritime states such as China, India, Indonesia, and Malaysia.

In the characterization of the PSI as "an activity and not an organization," a recurring theme is that effective interdiction requires avoiding the time constraints imposed by the deliberative processes of international organization.[564] Some of the flag-state boarding agreements accordingly allow as little as two hours for response to a boarding request, with lack of such response defaulting to de facto authorization. But this does not accurately reflect the time-span realities of interdiction. As indicated by the *So San* episode, and the tracking by the U.S. Navy for more than a month, interdiction of WMD material at sea does not, by its nature, have to be accomplished in a matter of

imperfectly, world peace and stability have rested for the last 58 years... If it were to be adopted, it could set precedents that resulted in a proliferation of the unilateral and lawless use of force, with or without justification." *What They Said in New York*, IRAQ TIMES 17 (Sept. 24, 2003).

561 For example, during a PSI meeting in Brisbane in July 2003, John Bolton, the Bush Administration's point man on PSI stated that the United States had "a general right of self-defense" if there was a serious belief that North Korean vessels were carrying material for use in WMDs. Greg Sheridan, *US "Free" to Board N Korea Shipping*, AUSTRALIAN 1 (July 9, 2003).

562 *See* Office of the Press Secretary, The White House, *supra* note 505.

563 U.S. Dept. of State, Bureau of International Security and Nonproliferation, *Proliferation Security Initiative Frequently Asked Questions (FAQ)*, at 5, (Jan. 11, 2005) (*available at* http://merln.ndu.edu/archivepdf/wmd/State/32725.pdf).

564 This theme was introduced in the very origin of the PSI. *See* Judith Miller, *Panama Joins Accord to Stem Ships' Transport of Illicit Arms*, N.Y. TIMES (May 11, 2004).

hours. Interdiction of WMD material typically does not involve any risk of immediate launch such as characterized the Cuban Missile Crisis. And even in that historic context of unparalleled nuclear weapons risk, the time span for resolution was the now iconic "thirteen days."[565] The Cuban Missile Crisis surely demonstrated that the time allowances for interdiction of transport, if carefully managed, can facilitate rather than limit efficacy of response to WMD-related crisis. It provides a compelling case study to support the conclusion that the allowance of time for consultation, organizational endorsement, and negotiation can be critical for crisis control.[566]

It is highly unlikely that in crisis the "collection of interdiction partnerships," that is said to constitute the PSI, would be more effective than a well-designed process for securing a broadly international endorsement. The greater the number of interdiction partnerships, the more awkward and time-consuming it becomes to achieve political and/or military action by working through bilateral relations. But the more numerous the state participants, the greater the case for publicly defined substantive and procedural norms, including a multilateral process designed to minimize obstructionism.

The counterproliferation effectiveness of interdiction of transport thus can be enhanced by a reformulation of PSI under a Security Council mandate. And there is already legal basis for this advancement. A Security Council counterproliferation resolution comprehending interdiction of transport would be a fundamental evolution, but not a sharp break with prior legal development. Security Council authorization under Chapter VII of the United Nations Charter has been generally accepted as authorizing interdiction of vessels in contexts ranging from the embargo against Rhodesia in the 1960s, to the First Gulf War and the sanctions that followed NATO acting in the former Yugoslavia. Furthermore, besides the various Security Council resolutions that have mandated transit interdiction, Security Council Resolution 1373 highlighted the connection between the international terrorism threat and the "illegal movement of nuclear... and other potentially deadly materials," and declared this nexus to be, in the triggering words of Chapter VII, a "threat to international security." Resolution 1540 reinforced this by requiring every state to criminalize proliferation. The U.S. Deputy Assistant Secretary of State for Nuclear Non-proliferation has gone so far as to state that "PSI and 1540 are complementary."[567] Altogether, then, there is basis for the necessary movement forward.

As for the actual prospects of a Security Council resolution inclusive of PSI, it is important to note that the rejection of interdiction endorsement during the passage

565 As memorialized in the book and movie of that name. *See generally* Robert Kennedy, THIRTEEN DAYS: A MEMOIR OF THE CUBAN MISSILE CRISIS (3d ed. 1999). *See also* THIRTEEN DAYS (New Line Cinema 2000).

566 *See generally* Chayes, *supra* note 540.

567 Andrew K. Semmel, Principal Deputy Assistant Secretary of State or Nuclear Nonproliferation, Remarks to Asia-Pacific Nuclear Safeguards and Security Conference (Nov. 8, 2004) (*transcript available at* http://merln.ndu.edu/archivepdf/wmd/State/38256.pdf).

of Resolution 1540 was in view of a PSI initiated, led, and dominated, by the United States, not negotiated within the broader framework of the United Nations.[568] China's opposition to any such authority can be appreciated, China having the world's third largest merchant fleet composed of over 2,000 ships.[569] A more comprehensive design, however, orchestrated through the Security Council, that provided assurance of more broadly initiated counterproliferation interdiction, would surely afford a greater likelihood of Security Council authorization by states with a priority shipping perspective. Political viability in general would be greatly enhanced by providing China, India, and Indonesia with some say in the process, even if only by way of participation in the Operational Experts Group as it functions within the current PSI.

There is in fact movement in this direction. The International Commission on Nuclear Non-proliferation and Disarmament has recommended reconstituting PSI "within the UN system as a neutral organization to assess intelligence, coordinate and fund activities, and make both generic and specific recommendations or decisions concerning... interdiction."[570] This recommendation fits full-square within the regime here proposed. It has received endorsement by President Obama, who in his Prague speech on nuclear risk, called for transmuting PSI into an international institution.[571] Additionally, the U.S. State Department has already taken the position that PSI is one means for states to comply with their obligations under UN Security Council Resolutions 1718, 1737, 1747, 1803, and most notably, 1540. This is notwithstanding that Resolution 1540, while mandating WMD interdiction, was a rejection of endorsement of the PSI.[572]

The deficiencies of Resolution 1540 in addressing interdiction of nuclear proliferation, as well as the legitimacy deficit of PSI, indicate what is needed. Specifically, the need is for an explicit authorization for interdiction on the world's oceans. This would include that flag states have an affirmative duty to participate, establishing flag-state duties and interdiction rights. It would also include mandate to assure accountability as to the intelligence foundation for specific interdiction, and standards as to cargo subject to seizure and the methodology of interdiction.

The Security Council resolution authorizing all this probably would be confined to general guidelines and establishing a procedural mechanism for implementation, more or less in the manner of Resolution 1540's statement of principle as consistent with international law. The mandate should be such as to maximize coherence with UNCLOS, and its designation of jurisdictional zones, and designed to minimize interference with

---

568 These expressions of opposition came principally from Cuba, China, and Indonesia. *See* Anthony Bergin, *The Proliferation Security Initiative—Implications for the Indian Ocean*, 20 INT'L L. J. OF MARINE & COASTAL L. 85, 92 (2005).

569 *Id.*

570 Evans & Kawaguchi, *supra* note 38, at 253.

571 Obama, Remarks in Prague, *supra* note 7.

572 The word "interdict" was removed and changed to "take cooperative action to prevent illicit trafficking" in WMD, apparently in relation principally to China's objection. For a history of Resolution 1540's development, *see* Merav Datan, *Security Council Resolution 1540: WMD and Non-State Trafficking*, DISARMAMENT DIPLOMACY, Apr./May 2005, http://www.acronym.org.uk/dd/dd79/79md.htm.

freedom of navigation and commercial shipping. UNCLOS, in providing limited rights of boarding on the high seas without the consent of the flag state for piracy or narcotics trafficking or unauthorized broadcasting, demonstrates the rationale that there is a shared international interest in proscribing the subject activity. Illicit transport of nuclear weapons-related technology and material would certainly suit the same rationale. Indeed, today, WMD interdiction would be the best candidate one could conceive for inclusion on the list of boarding justified as exceptional to flag-state jurisdiction. Pending the difficulty of amending UNCLOS, it is necessary to trump the limited and antiquated interdiction allowance list of the treaty. If there were intelligence vetted through institutional process establishing that a state-flagged vessel was illicitly transporting WMD, flag-state jurisdiction should be permeable; and this is what could be legitimated only by Security Council resolution.

Placing a more international interdiction facility within Chapter VII would be most significant for the most significant threat. PSI is not only constrained by the strong international commitment and interests reflected by flag-state jurisdiction, but provides interdiction authority only as to commercial shipping, not as to military or other government vessels, or aircraft. Proliferation by such other means has been reported.[573] This is a gap that legally can be closed only by Security Council action under Chapter VII, at least to make clear that governmental vessels are also subject to interdiction in appropriate circumstances, as determined by the Security Council.

Direct amendment of UNCLOS to make the necessary accommodation of either flag-state or coastal-state jurisdiction, given the consensual basis of UNCLOS, presents no near-term prospect. Any effort at amendment would be complicated by substantive and procedural concerns, delaying or defeating what the Security Council could accomplish expeditiously through a counterproliferation resolution. Notably, this was acknowledged even by the Bush Administration despite its promotion of PSI. Only a few months after George W. Bush announced the PSI in 2003, the official most identified with PSI, John Bolton, stated that "the 11 PSI countries also talked about circumstances where one could envision a Security Council resolution that might give authority in certain circumstances." But as reason for not seeking a resolution to articulate the terms for high seas interdiction, he went on to say that "the history of the Security Council in granting enforcement authority, has usually been in the context of a specific problem and a specific country that people were concerned about, and we thought probably it would be best to leave the evolution of that to circumstances as they develop."[574]

---

573 For example, missile shipments were reportedly loaded in North Korea on a Pakistani C-130 in the summer of 2002. *See* David Sanger, *Threats and Responses: Alliances; In North Korea and Pakistan, Deep Roots of Nuclear Barter*, N.Y. TIMES (Nov. 24, 2002). Government owned noncommercial ships obtain immunity under customary international law, codified in Articles 32, 95, 96, & 110 of UNCLOS, except as qualified by other states' rights of self-defense or other violations of international law. As to the immunity of military vessels, *see* UNCLOS, *supra* note 528, at arts. 110, 95, 96.

574 Interview with John Bolton, Undersecretary of State for Arms Control and International Security, *supra* note 510.

So there was, almost from the outset of PSI, recognition that even with the promotion of PSI as "an activity, not an organization," it is the Security Council that can fill the critical gap in PSI counterproliferation. However, it must be noted that Bolton's remarks about the historic situational nature of Security Council action under Chapter VII were made *prior to* the important evolution of Security Council action broadly directed to WMD proliferation that is constituted by Security Council Resolution 1540. Now that Security Council action on nuclear proliferation has evolved in the legislative form of Resolution 1540, there is precedent for interdiction authorization beyond "a specific problem and specific country." Indeed, the very same arguments that were used to justify PSI's informal and noninstitutional character—timeliness, efficiency, and protection of intelligence resources—now argue for dealing with the procedural and legal issues, before, not after, high seas interdiction. As the Bush Administration declared in promoting PSI as "an activity, not an organization," we cannot wait around for a legal debate if identified nuclear risk is on the move.[575] So the point would be to have the legal debate now, to resolve the means for legality and therefore legitimacy before action, rather than through attempts at justification after action and the political turmoil that unilateralism engenders, which, unfortunately, is where we are now for any interdiction on the high seas that clashes with flag-state jurisdiction.

A Security Council counterproliferation resolution that helps fill the high seas gap can only help enhance counterproliferation capacity. High seas interdiction would be well served by legal preparation, creating at least the mechanism and general standards to take account of the relevant interests. That mechanism, put in place before the fact of high seas interdiction, could and should be designed to facilitate the most advantageous balance between freedom of navigation and counterproliferation. It would deflate diplomatic and legal risk, through enhanced legitimacy. China's objection to PSI was stated, "(t)he PSI with its interdiction principles lacks a solid basis in international law."[576] To the extent that basis is provided, grounds for objection are diminished. Moreover legality achieved through an authorized mechanism would importantly invigorate deterrence. Potential proliferators will know that the costs and risks of proliferation have been substantially increased, becoming accordingly less worth the gamble.

575 *Id.*

576 Ru'an & Qinghai, *supra* note 550.

5

COMPLIANCE

A TREATY REGIME cannot be long sustained by sanctions. The common interest that the treaty represents is what assures routine compliance. Compliance is about the benefits of shared objectives. This is certainly true in reference to the Nuclear Non-proliferation Treaty (NPT). Sanctions have been applied only in the rare cases of governments with well-demonstrated records of proliferation. For most governments, their relationship with the NPT and its administration through the International Atomic Energy Agency (IAEA) is directed to improving nuclear security, safety, and safeguards. And the most significant elements for counterproliferation, such as safeguards agreements and the inspection protocols, are adopted and supported by most nations of the world.

Unlike the general run of treaties, however, effective counterproliferation is mostly about finding and countering the miscreant. So sanctions, though applied only against governments of extreme and continuing proliferation risk, are relatively more significant in relation to the NPT than for most treaty regimes. The containment of nuclear risk goes beyond the limits of the cooperative enterprise. The challenge for counterproliferation is most importantly to identify the bad actor to prevent the consummation of weapons-related proliferation. In this regard, counterproliferation is more in the nature of criminal process, than the relatively cooperative regulatory modalities of most international treaty regimes. The priority goal is to defeat the violator, with the threat of sanctions backing the counterproliferation enterprise.

International sanctions in any context are difficult to orchestrate, politically and economically, and are difficult to maintain. The various international sanctions programs have demonstrated this over and over, whether in service of human rights, as in the contexts of Southern Rhodesia and South Africa, or for counterproliferation. For the sanctions hard cases, Saddam Hussein's Iraqi regime, Iran, and the enduring delinquency of the hermit kingdom of North Korea, the application of sanctions has faced three devils of a challenge: first, to establish the evidence required for sanctions; second, to achieve the political consensus for the adoption of sanctions; and third, to maintain sanctions over time, often despite withering consensus, and the countering strategies of the targeted government. The relevant history warrants considerable cynicism, epitomized by the financial tryst that developed between the regime of Saddam Hussein and the son of United Nations (UN) Secretary-General Kofi Annan in the UN Oil-for-Food Program.

The actual imposition of sanctions often has been characterized as counterproductive, even from the most prominent and holistic perspectives for evaluating sanctions as they relate to counterproliferation. The former Director-General of the IAEA, Mohammad ElBaradei, went so far as to declare, "Sanctions don't work as a penalty. They tend to put hard-liners in the driver's seat."[577] That opinion has been echoed by the leaders of governments with important voices, including permanent members of the Security Council, Russia and China, on whose concurrence any Security Council sanctions depend.[578] It is the deep and wide perception that sanctions are not a reliable tool for counterproliferation. And the historical record certainly supports this. The various attempts to employ United Nations sanctions for counterproliferation have come to constitute a classic paradigm of frustrated diplomacy. That paradigm has been shaped by events of threat and counter-threat, promises made and promises broken. This has been the pattern in all the critical cases—Iraq, Iran, and North Korea. And the related weapons inspections under the aegis of the IAEA have reflected the same pattern. Thus, for example, the board of the IAEA found Iran to be out of compliance with its safeguards obligations and encouraged the UN Security Council to hold Iran accountable—a process that began with Resolutions 1737 (2006), and 1747 (2007), 1803 in 2008, and continued with a fourth round of sanctions with Resolution 1929 in 2010, and new U.S. and European sanctions in 2011 and 2012.[579] In response to North Korea's claimed nuclear test on October 9, 2006, the Security Council passed Resolution

---

577 The remark was made in connection with the continuing debate over sanctions on Iran. Quoted in Nuclear Proliferation, CQ GLOBAL RESEARCHER 21, Jan. 2007, *available at* www.globalresearcher.com.

578 *See* Russian Foreign Minister Sergey V. Lavrov on the use of sanctions against Iran, "At the current stage, all forces should be thrown at supporting the negotiating process. Threats, sanctions and threats of pressure in the current situation, we are convinced, would be counterproductive." Mark Landler & Clifford J. Levy, *Russia Resists U.S. Position on Sanctions for Iran*, N.Y. TIMES, Oct. 13, 2009, http://www.nytimes.com/2009/10/14/world/europe/14diplo.html. *See* Bridget Johnson, *China Not on Board With Sanctions to Tackle Iran Nuclear Issue*, THE HILL, Mar. 7, 2010, http://thehill.com/blogs/blog-briefing-room/news/85361-china-not-on-board-with-sanctions-to-tackle-iran-nuke-issue. "As everyone knows, pressure and sanctions are not the fundamental way forward to resolving the Iran nuclear issue, and cannot fundamentally solve this issue," Yang (China's Foreign Minister) said." (parenthesis added). Diplomats from two major European allies said that China had refused even to "engage substantively" on the issue of sanctions, preferring to continue diplomatic efforts with Tehran. *See* e.g., Mark Landler, *Despite Pressure, China Still Resists Iran Sanctions*, N.Y. TIMES, Feb. 26, 2010, http://www.nytimes.com/2010/02/26/world/asia/26diplo.html. *See also* Matthew Lee, *Brazil Rebuffs US, says it will go its own way on Iran,* ASSOCIATED PRESS, Mar. 3, 2010, http://www.bostonsun.com/news/story/y/95002_brazil-rebuffs-us-says-it-will-go-own-way-on-iran.htm; "It is not prudent to push Iran against a wall... The prudent thing is to establish negotiations." (Brazilian President Luiz Inacio Lula da Silva responding to U.S. pressure to impose new sanctions on Iran.)

579 S. C. Res. 1737, U.N. Doc. S/RES/1737 (Dec. 27, 2006); S.C. Res. 1747, U.N. Doc. S/RES/1747 (March 24, 2007); S.C. Res. 1803, U.N. Doc. S/Res/1803 (Mar. 3, 2008); S.C. Res. 1929, U.N. Doc. S/Res/1929 (June 9, 2010).

1718 imposing sanctions.[580] Further sanctions were imposed on North Korea by the Security Council, in 2009, after a second North Korean nuclear weapons test, with the goal of forcing North Korea to return to the six-party talks and halt its nuclear weapons program.[581] Both for Iran and North Korea, "smart" or "targeted sanctions," such as financial controls, were added. In neither case however, Iran or North Korea, is the proliferation risk so far resolved—for the same reason. The member states of the Security Council have other interests invested in relation to the targeted regime that they see as of higher priority than counterproliferation. Such interests compromising sanctions range, for example, from trade, as in the Iran-Russia relationship, or border- and maritime-related issues (including buffering against U.S. regional presence) with respect to the Chinese-North Korea relationship. These are powerful interests that either prevent sanctions entirely, or undermine their escalation. Even if agreements are apparently achieved with the targeted regime, and then betrayed, violated, and denounced, these powerful interests leave no greater sanctions option than reengagement of the same game, gaming that in its worst manifestations, as with North Korea, involves nuclear blackmail, which Iran is reported to have taken as a model to follow.[582]

Whether in response to the carrot of trade or energy supply, or the stick of sanctions, the results have been uniformly the failure to stop nuclear weapons-related activity. Ironically, it was the one case in which a nuclear weapons program apparently was put in abeyance after a sanctions and surveillance regime was imposed—Iraq—that force was applied on the justification of presence of weapons of mass destruction (WMD). The Alice-in-Wonderland nature of that result might seem ludicrous, if not for its deadly seriousness. It was certainly an abdication of any legitimate and credible process of proliferation attribution.

A wholly ad hoc sanctions regime to reinforce a consensual regime is also inadequate because it depends upon negotiated and often delayed access, which allows opportunities for concealment. Thus the IAEA inspected and gave clearance to Iranian facilities for many years before stories of Iran's secret Natanz centrifuge facility appeared in the media, after which further efforts by the IAEA disclosed enriched uranium at Natanz. Then the Iranians cleaned up their Kalaye Electric facility, though it still yielded the investigators traces of enriched uranium inconsistent with Iranian inventory declarations.[583] Moreover, though the Director-General of the IAEA made clear that

580 S.C. Res. 1718, U.N. Doc. S/Res/1718 (Oct. 14, 2006).

581 S.C. Res 1874, U.N. Doc. S/Res/1874 (June 12, 2009).

582 "The hard-liners, perhaps impressed by North Korea's achievement, are now inclined to be more resilient and uncompromising. They say if North Korea could do it, why shouldn't We? Why should we let the United States dictate to us, rather than negotiate with us." *See* Murphy, *supra* note 55 (quoting Professor Sadegh Zibakalam, a professor of politics at Tehran University, "This scenario has been at the back of the minds of some Iranian leaders; that if we reach a stage that we would be respected as an equal partner, then we could do real negotiations and reach a deal over our nuclear program.")

583 IAEA, Doc. Gov/2004 Implementation of the NPT Safeguards Agreement in the Islamic Republic of Iran, Report by the Director General 6 IAEA (Feb. 24, 2004), http://www.iaea.org/Publications/Documents/Board/2004/gov2004-11.pdf (discussing enriched uranium contamination findings at Natanz and Kalaye).

more information would have to be provided, Iran refused to sign the Additional Protocol developed to help IAEA inspectors find undeclared nuclear work. Iran first pledged to follow the Protocol procedures; then renounced it,[584] denying the IAEA additional access or information. Similar patterns of concealment and outright refusal played out in Iraq and North Korea, where the regimes in power proved adept at foiling inspections and conning the inspectors.[585]

There is reason to be more sanguine about so-called *targeted sanctions*, which zero in on particular individuals and financial interests. They have been effective in causing costs, both economic and political, for the targeted regime, principally as wielded by the United States Department of Treasury.[586] It is difficult, even for terrorist networks to avoid using the global financial system, triggering disclosure and record-keeping mechanisms of the system. Given the financial leverage of the United States, this strategy has demonstrated dramatic impact. But thus far it has not achieved counter-proliferation compliance.[587] When individuals are targeted for counter-terrorism, this strategy also raises serious issues of due process and human rights that have provoked significant legal challenge in national courts and the courts of the European Union, potentially undermining sanctions strategy.[588] Moreover, the impact is not indicative of effectiveness of United Nations sanctions as such. Though targeted sanctions have been included in Security Council sanctions, most of their strength and the initiative to use them has come from outside the Security Council, as leverage by the United States acting through its bilateral international relationships.

---

584 *See* Paul Kerr, *Iran, EU Struggle to Start Nuclear Talks*, ARMS CONTROL ASSOCIATION (Oct. 2006), http://www.armscontrol.org/act/2006_10/IranEU.

585 *See* Robert McMahon, *UN Sanctions: A Mixed Record*, COUNCIL ON FOREIGN RELATIONS, Nov. 17, 2007, http://www.cfr.org/un/un-sanctions-mixed-record/p12045.

586 *See* e.g., *The Threat of Terrorist Financing, Subcommittee on Terrorism, Technology and Homeland Security, United States Senate Committee on the Judiciary*, 108th Cong., June. 26, 2003, http://www.treasury.gov/press-center/press-releases/Documents/js5071.pdf (written Testimony of David D. Aufhauser, General Counsel, US Department of the Treasury). *See also* Gerald P. O'Driscoll, Jr., et al., *Stopping Terrorism: Following the Money*, THE HERITAGE FOUNDATION, Sept. 25, 2001, http://www.heritage.org/research/reports/2001/09/stopping-terrorism-follow-the-money. It is reported that for Iran, financial sanctions have even generated internal protests chanting, "we don't want nuclear energy." *See* Farnaz Fassihi, *Iran Currency Woes Spark Rare Strike*, WALL ST. J. Oct. 4, 2012, at A12

587 As to the devastating impact on the Iranian economy of the threat of financial and other economic sanctions, *see* Sill Spindle, Benoit Facucon, & Farnaz Fassihi, *Iran Cracks Down on Dollar Trades*, WALL ST. J. A7 (Jan. 17, 2012). Just how powerful and effective targeted sanctions can be is illustrated by the Banco Delta case, involving sanctions against North Korea. The mere issue by the U.S. Treasury Department of a comment asking why the Banco Delta of Macau was allowing a $25 million deposit from North Korea, accusing the bank of inadequate money-laundering control, and inviting comment as to why it should not be sanctioned, resulted in banks around the world refusing to do business with Banco Delta, and the Macau authorities freezing its accounts, until a deal was struck concerning North Korea's further participation in the six party nuclear talks. David D. Aufhauser, *Terrorist Financing: The Privatization of Economic Sanctions*, 56 FED. LAW 25–26 (Sept. 2009). For a more complete discussion of U.S. Treasury Sanctions, see Orde F. Kittrie, *New Sanctions for a New Century: Treasury's Innovative Use of Financial Sanctions*, 30 U. PA. J. INT'L L. 789 (2009).

588 See, Nada v. Switzerland, App. No. 10593/08 (Eur. Ct. H. R. Sept. 12, 2012), available at http://hudoc.echr.coe.int/sites/fra-press/pages/search.aspx?i=001-11318; A. Tzanakopoulos, *Domestic Court Reactions to UN Security Council Sanctions* in A. Reinisch (ed), CHALLENGING ACTS OF INTERNATIONAL ORGANIZATIONS BEFORE NATIONAL COURTS (Oxford) 2010.

The history of application of United Nations counterproliferation sanctions, disappointing as it may be, does not, however, fully reveal the value of Security Council sanctions for mandatory counterproliferation under Chapter VII. The fact that sanctions may not generally be employed and are highly problematical, does not measure their value for compliance. For it is not just the malefactors that sanctions impact, though that is their immediate and express purpose. Sanctions can operate as a significant dynamic for compliance of the membership at large. The risk of sanctions is a dynamic to counteract incentives such as the tempting profits of proliferation,[589] and can serve importantly to propel general adherence.

"If you want to know the law . . . ," runs the pragmatist declaration of Oliver Wendell Holmes, "you must look at it as a bad man, who cares only for the material consequences such knowledge enables him to predict . . . . "[590] What Holmes said for individual compliance can be said for governments. Being identified as in violation of international standards, is not where most governments want to be. There is much to be lost, both apparent and unknown. The risk of being exposed as violator may negatively impact interstate relations, even though there is little risk of direct sanction for the violation. The real law for governments, as Holmes had it for individuals, is defined, in large measure, by the consequences the violator may pay. The sanctions orchestrated for Iraq, Iran, and North Korea achieved compliance value notwithstanding the failure to achieve more direct counterproliferation objectives, by imposing considerable costs on the targeted governments. Sanctions in the hard cases are persuasive evidence for other governments that compliance with the nuclear weapons non-proliferation regime is the preferred option. Thus as to Iran, even China has moved erratically in this direction, substantially cutting back on oil imports from Iran for a time in recognition of the costs of resisting U.S. and European sanctions on Iran.[591] More recently, China agreed along with the other permanent members of the Security Council, to increase pressure on Iran to allow the IAEA unfettered access to Iran's nuclear sites.[592]

So most governments adhere as members of a treaty regime, not only because they share the mutual interest that inspired that regime, but to avoid the status of recreant. That is especially true today because every government is bound, to varying degree, in the global web of interconnected international interests wherein reputation for compliance creates value. Within governments there is also generally appreciation, that if

---

589 This more subtle dynamic of sanctions is not exclusive to counterproliferation. For example, the dispute resolution processes of the international trade regime of NAFTA includes sanctions as ultimate penalty, though there is little if any likelihood of actual imposition of sanctions, as the NAFTA cases have demonstrated. The sanctions provision for fines and loss of trade benefits within the framework of NAFTA or the WTO is designed to propel international trade dispute resolution, though an actual sanction may be rarely if ever employed. *See generally* Jack I. Garvey, *Trade Law and Quality of Life—Dispute Resolution under the NAFTA Side Accords on Labor and the Environment*, 89 AM. J. INTL' L. 439 (1995).

590 Oliver Wendell Holmes, *The Path of the Law*, 10 HARV. L. REV. 457, 458 (1897).

591 Ilan Berman, *Beijing and Tehran's Coming Divorce*, WALL ST. J. A11 (Jan. 11, 2012).

592 David Crawford, *China, Russia Agree to Pressure Iran*, WALL ST. J. A10 (Sept. 13, 2012).

there is delinquency and disaffection in one international arrangement or endeavor, it may well be paid for by loss of benefits in another.

It remains the global situation, however, that compliance under the NPT is far from secure and barely moving towards nuclear security. Noncompliance by any state when the issue is nuclear security, demonstrates not just weakness in the regime, but the potential for catastrophic failure. And non-proliferation has operated during the last couple decades on either side of the edge of failure. It was only after the first Gulf War in 1991 that it was discovered Iraq had developed an undeclared uranium enrichment program and had conducted other activities for producing nuclear weapons, in sites that had been previously visited by IAEA inspectors. In 2002, following disclosures by an Iranian dissident group, it was determined that Iran had been conducting undeclared nuclear activities for eighteen years. The IAEA reported, as recently as late 2011, that these activities cannot be interpreted other than to be intended for the development of nuclear weapons capabilities.[593] Libya's program, which had also continued for more than three decades, was discovered through intelligence activities, not IAEA inspections. And it was Israel, not the IAEA, that in 2008 discovered and demolished a nuclear facility being constructed in Syria, with the IAEA only later confirming that it was a clandestine nuclear facility.

Such failures of the existing counterproliferation infrastructure are not readily attributable to a lack of operational capability of the IAEA to discover what is hidden. On the face of it, the IAEA operates as intended. The safeguards system represents the best know-how for detection, and for prevention of diversion of fissile material to weapons use, as do the IAEA inspection protocols. Moreover, the IAEA has been endowed with significant inspection authority measured against the monitoring and inspection mechanisms of other arms control legal regimes.[594] The IAEA can, on its own authority, impose penalties such as suspending assistance, and the board of the IAEA is required to report noncompliance to the Security Council, as basis for Security Council action under Chapter VII. Challenge inspections on short notice and related provisional measures may be orchestrated under Chapter VII, and if not successful, the Security Council may move on to the so-called "sliding slope" of Chapter VII providing for mandatory measures, beginning with non-use of force measures including economic sanctions and embargoes, and severance of diplomatic relations; and it can move further, to the use of force.

Ultimately, however, though it may look counterproliferation capable, the existing legal and institutional process always slips on its flawed foundation. Achieving compliance, until the Security Council acts, is not supported by any mandatory disclosure or other legal obligation other than what is agreed by the subject state. Even if a

593 IAEA, Doc. Gov/2011/65, Implementation of the NPT Safeguards Agreement and Relevant Provisions of the Security Council Resolutions in the Islamic Republic of Iran, Report by the Director General 7 (Nov. 8, 2011), http://www.iaea.org/Publications/Documents/Board/2011/gov2011-65.pdf.

594 *See* Sloss, *supra* note 317, at 856.

government agrees to inspection of undeclared sites, it can agree conditionally. If the work of the IAEA is regarded as too intrusive, that government can withdraw completely from any legal obligation, as North Korea has done, cashing in on any advantages it gained while a party to the NPT.

A new grounding for counterproliferation going beyond the global legislation of Security Council Resolution 1373 addressing terrorism and Resolution 1540 addressing WMD would be the basis for overcoming this counterproliferation dysfunction. To be most effective, counterproliferation authority and capability should be and can be established before, not after, discovery of clandestine nuclear weapons development. This is what Security Council Chapter VII action can enable through a permanent and continuing Chapter VII mandate.

Security Council Chapter VII Resolutions 1373 and 1540 opened the door to this opportunity. But the Security Council has not gone further. Resolution 1540, on weapons of mass destruction, did not reach far enough to achieve a comprehensive counterproliferation mandate. The Security Council fell back on the national law model of Resolution 1373 on international terrorism, thereby effectively leaving counterproliferation to the discretion of each government, without stating any standard to assess compliance. The result is that counterproliferation compliance is not in any way compelled. The principal and critical deficiency remains. No matter how many states report, and no matter how many of their laws they report, there is simply no common measure or assurance of efficacy.

Though Resolution 1540 provides that all governments are required to report the measures taken under national law, the designated process of bottom-up implementation through national law and its reporting is fated for failure. Given the profound diversity of national laws and legal systems, diverse reporting capacity among nations and, ultimately, dependence on the agreement of each state, robust counterproliferation cannot be achieved within the current counterproliferation architecture. The global legislation we have on counterproliferation is simply too weak to contend with the gaming of the system that a proliferating government can so easily accomplish, even if a signatory to the NPT, by wielding the power of its legally justifiable veto.

A counterproliferation resolution of real merit must evolve counterproliferation global legislation beyond its current national law and national consent limitations. This is the transformational step that would be the basis for building a global counterproliferation culture of much greater breadth and depth. The difference would not be more likely application of sanctions. Under the proposed counterproliferation regime, it could be expected that the Security Council would act to institute sanctions, as it does presently, only in the most egregious cases of continuing serious noncompliance and evasion. It would also operate cabined by the same disparate interests and political discretion that currently constrain sanctions as a means to ensure compliance. However, sanctions as a tool for counterproliferation would be empowered by their declared legitimacy for any case of noncompliance. A mandatory regime particularly could serve to add vigor, depth, and breadth to the operation of financial controls, to trace and interrupt financing of related international terrorism, including black-market sales and money laundering for illicit transfers of nuclear material and technology. Subsuming financial controls and other targeted sanctions within a mandatory counterproliferation regime would afford much greater impetus and legitimacy to the effort to secure fullest cooperation internationally in identifying illicit transactions, and closing sources down. This has been confirmed recently by India, for example, which has taken the position that it would not allow or support interruption of its purchase of oil from Iran on the basis of sanctions by the United States and Europe, but would comply with such sanctions if imposed by the United Nations.[595]

Greater international institutionalization and international rule-generation does not necessarily improve compliance. To the extent an institutionalized process reaches beyond its legitimacy, to the extent rules are ambiguous or impractical, compliance is reduced or negated. A strong institution promulgating ambiguous rules without adequate mechanisms for implementation will fail. However, with the counterproliferation mandate sufficiently clarified and defined under Chapter VII, a different world of nuclear containment can evolve. Any government considering its nuclear weapons-related option to profit or build its own nuclear weapons capacity would be more inclined to desist. The difference would flow from uniform and nondiscriminatory standards made obligatory for all states. Because nondiscriminatory standards afford legitimacy, and because legitimacy affects compliance, compliance would be enhanced.[596] No longer would the IAEA be in the position of supplicant to each government to choose how far it will go in reporting and granting rights of inspection. Every government would be bound under the Security Council authorization, to cooperate in the implementation of international standards. The standards would be the same standards that most states have already adopted. Thus though the regime would be mandatory, it could rely on the support of the broader membership of the United Nations. The difference would be establishment of a priori obligation for each government, not subject to its discretion to accept or reject. For compliance, it would not impair Security Council discretion, but would predetermine the process, and put the burden of justification on the state charged with proliferation.

As now, sanctions would vary case-to-case. But legitimacy and effectiveness would be enhanced to the extent evaluation and response would be based on uniform criteria of universal application. This means including not only non-nuclear weapons states (NNWS), but nuclear weapons states (NWS) as well, at least as to all peaceful use.[597]

---

595 Benoit Faucon, Rakesh Sharma & Se Young Lee, *Iran Confronts Saudis on Oil Offer*, WALL ST. J. A8 (Jan. 18, 2012).

596 *See* T. Franck, THE POWER OF LEGITIMACY AMONG NATIONS (1990).

597 Currently the nuclear weapons states do adhere to much of the existing infrastructure of counter-proliferation, but limit that participation by what is essentially a national security exemption, wielded at the discretion of each nuclear weapons state. *See* Peter Crail, *IAEA Approves India Additional Protocol*, ARMS CONTROL ASSOCIATION (Apr. 2009), http://www.armscontrol.org/print/3597. (The United States and many other nuclear—weapon states have incorporated provisions of the Model Additional Protocol but with access conditioned on the basis of national security exclusions.) *See* Agreement Between The United States of America and The International Atomic Energy Agency for the Application of Safeguards in the United States (and Protocol Thereto), Part 1, art. 1-2, Nov. 18 1977.

It would include addressing the "three-state problem"—bringing to bear counterproliferation norms and obligations on Israel, India, and Pakistan, the three nuclear armed states that remain outside the NPT. Presently there is no constituency or motivation for these three outliers to join the NPT as nuclear weapons states, and they will not join as NNWS. By way of a Security Council resolution mandating the same counterproliferation obligations for all states, they can nevertheless be required to uphold non-proliferation norms, and to employ best practices as to safeguards, export controls, and engage in intelligence sharing, as well as all other counterproliferation mechanisms.

Security Council authorization is not a counterproliferation cure-all. There are the limits to the Security Council's own legitimacy. Its more progressive posture on counterproliferation would encounter the usual well-grounded complaint that the Security Council is an anachronism representing the interests of a now arbitrary grouping of relatively powerful states, not even all the most significant states as measured by economy, population or strategic power. Security Council reform remains a work in progress, with no readily apparent prospect of success. But Security Council authorization of a mandatory counterproliferation regime is nevertheless the available means for achieving standards that, if uniform and uniformly applied, would maximize counterproliferation compliance.

Counterproliferation is distinctly amenable to uniform application of uniform standards as a global objective. The contrast with terrorism, the principal subject of 1373, is instructive. Security Council Resolution 1373, in mandating the criminalization of terrorism, impacted national criminal jurisdiction, an area of domestic law of most heightened sovereign sensitivity. Yet all states quickly complied with national legislative initiatives.[598] The European Union, the African Union, the Association of South-East Asian Nations, the Organization of American States, and just about every major regional organization also quickly signed on with action plans to implement the Resolution 1373 mandate.[599] This was all despite the fact, and perhaps because of the fact, that terrorism is one of the most ill-defined terms in contemporary international security discourse.[600] Leaving terrorism to national definition was probably inevitable given the inevitably political content of the term as applied.

---

598 Johnstone, *supra* note 126, at 286. Counter-Terrorism Comm., *Survey of the Implementation of Security Council Resolution 1373 (2001) by Member States*, U.N. Doc. S/2009/620 (Dec. 3, 2009), *available at* http://www.un.org/sc/ctc/pdf/GIS2009.pdf.

599 *See* e.g., European Council, *Conclusions and Plan for Action of the Extraordinary European Council Meeting on September 21, 2001*; Association of Southeast Asian Nations, *ASEAN's Stance on Terrorism*, (Nov. 5, 2001), http://www.aseansec.org/12636.htm; Inter-American Committee against Terrorism, *Organization of American States*, http://www.cicte.oas.org/Rev/En; Organization for Security and Co-Operation in Europe, BUCHAREST MINISTERIAL DECLARATION: DECISION ON COMBATING TERRORISM AND THE BUCHAREST PLAN OF ACTION FOR COMBATING TERRORISM 3–4 Dec. 4, 2001, http://www.osce.org/mc/40515; African Union,*The Peace and Security Agenda: Preventing and Combating Terrorism in Africa*, http://www.africa-union.org/root/au/AUC/Departments/PSC/Counter_Terrorism

600 *See generally* George Fletcher, *The Indefinable Concept of Terrorism*, 4 J. INT'L CRIM. JUST. 894 (2006). This was evidenced, for instance, by the inability to arrive a fixed definition for the Rome Treaty establishing the International Criminal Court. *See* e.g., Richard J. Goldstone & Janine Simpson, *Evaluating*

However the legal standards of counterproliferation, such as for safeguards and inspection authority, are very different; not only different, but different in kind. These are not political terms to be easily manipulated through national law as is *terrorism*, but are empirically generated standards that are detailed, precise, and by their nature, uniform. This both explains why they are more appropriate to international mandate, and why there is more resistance. Standards of nuclear security are well articulated and for the most part undisputed as to their substantive content, and are already being implemented on a broad scale. Developed as internationally applicable they are not easily subject to political manipulation. Counterproliferation thus presents a most appropriate goal for implementation through universal norms. For counterterrorism, obeisance to the variability of national criminal law and legal systems comes with the territory—as necessary concession to national sovereignty. Nuclear counterproliferation, by contrast, can and does rely on objective standards that can be applied universally in service of global security.

That so many of the standards for counterproliferation are so widely voluntarily adopted[601] substantiates their viability as mandated standards. Their general acceptance is what can provide legitimacy for a mandatory system. It should be noted that the nuclear weapons states, including most prominently the United States, have also negotiated safeguards for their civil nuclear facilities mainly to encourage transparency by other governments and to alleviate concern that safeguards would put the NNWS at commercial disadvantage.[602] Even the nonsignatories to the NPT, India, Pakistan, and Israel, have submitted to safeguards as to declared facilities. This is strong evidence

---

the Role of the International Criminal Court as a Legal Response to Terrorism, 16 HARV. HUM. RTS. J. 13, 14 (2003). Unlike the standards for counterproliferation, governments can legislate against *terrorism* fully according to their own ends, which often means the use of term to define political opposition, as in efforts to repress the Arab Spring. *See* e.g., Michael Slackman, *Egyptian Emergency Law is Extended for Two Years*, N.Y. TIMES (May 11, 2010).

601 The Final Document of the 2010 Review Conference noted that as of 2010, there were safeguards agreements in force bringing 166 States into compliance with Article II, Paragraph 4, of the NPT, that the IAEA board of governors had approved additional protocols (INFCIRC/540) (Corrected) to comprehensive agreements for 133 states, and that Additional Protocols were being implemented in 102 states. *See* United Nations, *supra* note 59, at 4.

602 All nuclear weapons states (NWS) members have put in force safeguard agreements and the Additional Protocol demonstrating transparency in their civilian nuclear programs. On December 2, 1967, President Johnson stated that the United States was not asking any country to accept safeguards that the United States was unwilling to accept and that... "when such safeguards are applied under the Treaty, the United States will permit the International Atomic Energy Agency to apply its safeguards to all nuclear activities in the United States—excluding only those with direct national security significance." The U.S. has kept this promise and exceeded it. As a measure of good faith, in 1993, the U.S. relaxed its application of the national security exclusion by placing "material deemed excess to its defense needs" under IAEA inspection. Moreover, the other NWS have made similar commitments, though some less broadly than the United States. Russia and China omit Articles 4 through 9 of the Model Additional Protocol, the sections discussing complementary access and wide-area environmental sampling. (Complementary access refers to an increase in access rights of the IAEA to inspect anywhere.) The United Kingdom (UK) and France both allow for complementary access but only the UK allows wide-area environmental sampling. These variations are of limited significance as concerns the

that there is a broad range of safeguards that all states can accept, at least as to declared civil nuclear facilities, and that uniform standards on critical aspects of nuclear security could be uniformly implemented on a mandatory global basis.

Given that the IAEA has built substantial expertise both as to standard setting and effective operational implementation, such mandate would be complemented by the IAEA's track record, and counterproliferation legitimacy thereby would be enhanced. Implementation of uniform standards is practicable through existing mechanisms. The IAEA has demonstrated ongoing capability to articulate and employ uniform standards non-offensive to national sovereignty at large. Indeed, that has been its central task and accomplishment. There is no reason to think the IAEA would not continue to fulfill that task under a Chapter VII mandate which would provide the leverage it currently lacks. The IAEA, with its broad experience and expertise, can administer uniform standards for all states. What is required is the authority and the resources to do so.

At no time in history have nuclear regulators been so well armed with the substantive and procedural means to rebuild every level of counterproliferation architecture. Indeed, much of the task is already accomplished. There is a comprehensive collection of standards and procedures, widely adopted as objective and legitimate, that have been spelled out in considerable detail, and tested through widespread implementation. Standards for security of nuclear material throughout the fuel cycle are well developed, as well as standards for transport, storage, and disposal of nuclear material. There are standards for reliable accounting for nuclear materials to detect diversion of those materials, and for detection and monitoring of trafficking in nuclear materials. There are the IAEA inspection protocols that have been tested through much experience over considerable time. There are defined technical requirements known to nuclear forensics experts for designating nuclear forensics data. The informational and communications requirements for enhanced intelligence sharing and interdiction capacity are already apparent, as employed most elaborately within the European Union. The standards and models for profound improvements are thus available for implementation in virtually all principal arenas of relevant knowledge and technological resources for counterproliferation.

Looking forward, there are also already available sophisticated articulations of what additionally is needed.[603] Nuclear forensics experts know what data nuclear forensics requires to trace the source of interdicted nuclear material, so that the source can be secured or shut down. There are indicators and limits for enrichment that could be imposed to prevent weapons use of fissile material. The pace and degree of additional

---

nuclear weapons states since they are allowed to have nuclear activities and are not required to declare them to the IAEA. The purpose of adherence to IAEA safeguards by NWS is said to be to demonstrate a commitment to act in solidarity with the NNWS members, promote the safeguard system for other countries and share the economic burden of the safeguards system. *See* Uribe, et al., *supra* note 246.

603 *See* e.g., Matthew Bunn, *Appropriate Effective Nuclear Security and Accounting-What Is It?* (Presentation at the Appropriate Effective Material Accounting and Physical protection-Joint Global Initiative/ UNSCR 1540 Workshop, Nashville, Tenn., July 18, 2008), *available at* http://belfercenter.ksg.harvard.edu/files/bunn-1540-appropriate-effective50.pdf.

articulation of standards will necessarily vary according to subject matter. This is also true of the Security Council's role. For each subject area of counterproliferation, there is the question of how much to detail in the counterproliferation resolution, and what to leave for administration by the IAEA or other subsidiary mechanism. The new global legislation, embodied by Security Council Resolutions 1373 and 1540 articulates only general guidelines, and that probably indicates the appropriate level of detail for a broader resolution focused exclusively on counterproliferation. However, a comprehensive Security Council counterproliferation resolution would be newly specific in marking out and making binding the existing protocols of internationally uniform standards of safety, safeguards and security. The "appropriate effective" standards that Resolution 1540 mandated would no longer be open to national governments to define, but would be internationally fixed and obligatory for all states. There is no justification for any government to refuse the standards and procedures of safeguards and inspection protocols that are accepted by most states now as a matter of course. The current lack of any nonconsensual legal obligation to adopt those standards unjustifiably leaves the counterproliferation regime bereft of legitimacy and empowerment that is available.

The details of development will vary necessarily according to subject matter, and some international uniform standards will be much easier to adopt than others. Though implementation of international standards would not depend on consent of each government, the status of standards as international norms will depend on consensus—indeed, must depend for their credibility on general acceptance, though not subject to individual state consent. Thus safeguards and the Additional Protocol, already widely accepted, will be much easier to move fully into place within a mandatory system, than interdiction on the high seas. High seas jurisdiction will remain contentious, given the current incongruity between the Proliferation Security Initiative (PSI) and the Convention on the Law of the Sea (UNCLOS). It will be a considerable challenge to accommodate, if not overcome, the interests that went into securing exclusive flag state jurisdiction on the high seas as a cardinal principle of (UNCLOS). Development of an interdiction process that international commercial shipping interests can find tolerable will not come easily, and states such as China, with huge shipping interests, are likely to resist. But a truly international mechanism is within the realm of the practicable, if done under the legitimacy of securing a Security Council mandate. No doubt this would require transforming maritime interdiction from a U.S. owned mechanism, namely the PSI, to a more broadly endorsed capability, including participation by principal high seas stake-holders such as China, Indonesia, and Malaysia. But as in other areas of counterproliferation, this does not require trashing what has been accomplished through the PSI or any other interdiction means. Nor does it preclude the ultimate option of counterproliferation action by the United States or any other state to claim pre-emptive self-defense. It does mean creating new capacity, that could coalesce with the PSI, and in time fill the legitimacy gap of high seas interdiction. It can create counterproliferation value in the most vulnerable area of the seas, where PSI cannot legally enforce an interdiction mandate, and where action based on a claim of self-defense brings with it high risk of provoking armed conflict.

The empowerment of counterproliferation, whether through the IAEA or any new international institutionalization, presents a potential for overreaching or overly cumbersome bureaucracy, as all institutionalizations do. But any international management of the mandatory regime is unlikely to go beyond standards that are deemed generally acceptable to governments, commercial nuclear interests, and the epistemic community of nuclear experts and regulators. The historical record, and common sense, instruct that the board of the IAEA or any other international counterproliferation management authority would not proceed in the face of substantial opposition from these communities. IAEA governance, being politically sophisticated, and working continually with the relevant political and commercial nuclear interests and elites, can be expected to respect the caution of such counsel in generalizing new standards. If it should go too far, it can be expected it would be reined in by its political constituencies and funders, either informally, or in the unlikely event of a serious arrogation of authority, by the Security Council itself.

Better securitizing of the world's nuclear weapons and materials under a Chapter VII regime will involve substantial cost, though cost, as is generally true of counterproliferation, is sure to be minor in relation to the cost of a targeted nuclear detonation. For many countries, though, it is not only the financial capability, but the necessary expertise that may be lacking. This is well recognized, even under current counterproliferation infrastructure. However, there is also solid indication that where the national counterproliferation burden is genuinely unsupportable from a particular nation's own resources, the international community is willing to respond. The IAEA currently provides assistance, accomplished on the basis of existing funding arrangements with contributions from wealthier governments, to encourage and aid governments to implement nuclear standards of safety, security, and safeguards. The outstanding single example of direct assistance by government would be the Nunn-Lugar Cooperative Threat Reduction Program, under which the United States alone contributed over $7.3 billion to remove fissile material and help decommission nuclear weapons in the former Soviet Union. More generally, in its mandate concerning weapons of mass destruction, Resolution 1540 already laid the basis for financial provision by establishing a voluntary fund to help provide the technical support and expertise to support implementation of the Resolution, to which the U.S. and other relatively wealthy countries have substantially contributed. A counterproliferation resolution could mandate similar ongoing and increased funding as required. Whatever the formula agreed, this could provide the best possible assurance of the necessary financial coordination and sufficiency for robust counterproliferation on a global basis. As success of a mandatory system grows in global breadth and depth, there would be concomitant increase in the funding necessary for the governments with nuclear activities that lack the necessary means. But the motivating mantra has been, and must be, "it's worth it," given the risk and cost of nuclear catastrophe.

6

POLITICAL WILL

THE UNITED NATIONS (UN) Security Council operates generally within its own limits of legitimacy. It is a representative body only as far as the politics of its composition. Its origins in the World War II alliance against Fascism render it today sometimes incongruent with realities of power and interstate influence. Nevertheless, for invigorating and building counterproliferation, the Security Council remains the best available institutional resource to accomplish what must be accomplished. Indeed, it is the *only* resource. There is nowhere to secure fundamental multilateral counterproliferation improvement outside the United Nations Security Council. There was demonstration of this during the 2010 Nuclear Non-proliferation Treaty (NPT) Review Conference, where it proved impossible to achieve even endorsement of universalization of the Additional Protocol, or provisions on noncompliance, or restriction of the right of withdrawal from the NPT.[604] The nuclear weapons states (NWS) and Western non-nuclear weapons states (NNWS) pressed for making the Additional Protocol the verification standard under the NPT, and a condition of supply of nuclear material and technology. The Non-Aligned Movement (NAM), composed of about 115 states, opposed any such provision and insisted on the NPT catechism that any counterproliferation progress depends on progress on nuclear weapons disarmament. That insistence, it can be presumed, meant progress on disarmament however the NAM might define progress, notwithstanding such important progress as U.S.-Russian nuclear arms reductions.[605]

Their position can be justified as legal argument. Sovereign equality *was* the implication of the Grand Bargain. It was inherent in the core commitment to negotiate nuclear disarmament to bring all states to equality at zero. But sovereign equality has always bowed before the political imperative of greater powers, and the asymmetry of nuclear weapons possession. There is nothing in sight that would alter this reality. In the history of non-proliferation, the only significance of sovereign equality remains

604 Potter et al., *supra* note 71, at 1–2.
605 *Id.* at 14.

rhetorical, grounding the complaint that the Non-proliferation Treaty regime has not lived up to its promise, and providing resisting nations, such as Iran and North Korea, a basis for denouncing efforts to monitor and limit their nuclear activities.

An architecture mandated by the Security Council under Chapter VII would, no doubt, run up against the same tired rhetoric of sovereign equality. But sovereign equality has never been a principle of successful counterproliferation, and the legitimacy to support counterproliferation can only be found, unbound from the equitable pretensions of the NPT. It can be achieved by focusing counterproliferation as a goal in itself, as already accomplished to limited extent in the counterproliferation Resolutions 1373, 1540, and the affirming and expanding resolutions that followed.[606] These resolutions can be the harbingers for a newly principled counterproliferation architecture, capable of meeting the challenge of contemporary nuclear weapons risk and inviting broad acceptance by a world of governments increasingly sensitized to the global implications of nuclear risk.

The most significant principle to secure support for a mandatory regime appeared, however, decades before any Security Council counterproliferation resolution. This was the principle that determined the strategy that prevailed in the greatest nuclear weapons near-catastrophe of all time, the Cuban Missile Crisis. In seeking legal and political justification for the quarantine of Cuba, in a time when massive nuclear arsenals of the two singularly great powers were set to the logic of mutually assured destruction (MAD), it was nevertheless possible to persuade multiple governments, both inside and outside the Security Council, of that principle. The principle is that the clandestine development of nuclear weapons, in itself, is illegitimate, because it is too destabilizing of international peace and security, and that reasonable action in response trumps any claim of national sovereignty. This was the basis for unanimous adoption by the Organization of American States (OAS) of a resolution authorizing the "quarantine" of Cuba. The member states of the OAS, some of whom had strongly opposed U.S. policy on Cuba, sided with the United States on the basis of this principle, passing a resolution specifically condemning the threat of clandestine increase in nuclear weapons risk.[607] According to the accounts of the actual participants, this crucially influenced the Soviet decision that made it possible to end the crisis.[608] In the speech that immediately followed the OAS resolution, and that set the terms of the confrontation, President Kennedy stated the same principle as becoming international precedent for the nuclear era. He declared that clandestine increase in nuclear

---

606 *See* S.C. Res 1673, U.N. Doc. S/Res/1673 (April 27, 2006). (Reiterated objectives of Resolution 1540 and expressed the Security Council's interest in promoting full implementation.) S.C. Res 1810, U.N. Doc. S/Res/1810 (Apr. 25, 2008). (Extended the mandate of 1540 for a period of three years with the continued assistance of experts). S.C. Res 1887, *supra* note 324. The Security Council emphasized that the body had a responsibility to address nuclear threats, and that all situations of noncompliance should be brought to its attention.

607 *See Resolution on the Adoption of Necessary Measures to Prevent Cuba from Threatening the Peace and Security on the Continent*, OAS Council, Annex A, OEA/Ser.G/V/C-d-1024 Rev. 2 (Oct. 23, 1962).

608 Kennedy, *supra* note 565.

weapons risk, constituted by the Soviet placement of missiles in Cuba, was a threat to peace and security of the Americas as "a clear and present danger," borrowing that standard from U.S. jurisprudence, and melding it to the vernacular of global nuclear risk.[609]

Today we confront a new kind of clandestine risk that threatens to dramatically disrupt the nuclear weapons status quo—proliferation of nuclear weapons-related material and technology; in its most dangerous aspect, illicit transfer and its relationship to nuclear terrorism. There is clear perception of clear and present nuclear danger, at least among most governments, if not their domestic constituencies. That perception is clear and common despite contention about global access to nuclear energy for peaceful use, or the goal of nuclear disarmament; the crumbling pillars of the NPT. But counterproliferation can move forward on its singular merit. This has been made evident by the passage of Resolution 1540, and the various public and private counterproliferation initiatives specifically and exclusively directed to address any increase in clandestine nuclear weapons risk, such as the announcement, in July 2006, by then U.S. President George W. Bush and Russian President Vladimir Putin, of the creation of a Global Initiative to Combat Nuclear Terrorism.[610] Counterproliferation is already to such extent legitimized in singularity. Proliferation, conversely, is delegitimized by the same principle introduced and made successful in the quarantine of Cuba—that any clandestine increase in nuclear risk is simply too destabilizing a threat to international peace and security, and must be condemned and countered.

There is reason of course to be skeptical that a broad counterproliferation mandate under Chapter VII can be secured. Any debate on a counterproliferation resolution is likely to include, not only assertions of sovereignty, but questions of rationalization with the Nuclear Non-proliferation Treaty, questions of costs and administration, rights in technology and its transfer, intrusiveness of inspections; and also many other questions in relation to the existing NPT regime, and then some. No doubt any draft counterproliferation resolution advancing beyond Resolution 1540 would reflect such concerns, and would have to be adjusted as necessary to achieve adoption of a broad counterproliferation mandate under Chapter VII. This was the case, for example, for the passage of Resolution 1540 itself, in ruling out any right of interdiction that could be used to support ship-boarding by PSI beyond the limits of flag state jurisdiction.[611] As the expressions of resistance to "global legislation" voiced during the debate on 1540 indicate, there is challenging diplomacy to be worked through to move forward from 1540 to a robust, comprehensive counterproliferation resolution mandating universal

609 *See* Kennedy, *supra* note 325. *See Schenck v. U.S.* 249 U.S. 47, 52 (1919) (First articulation of "clear and present danger" language as a limit to First Amendment freedom of speech protection.) For the best known popularization in book and movie, *see generally* Tom Clancy, CLEAR AND PRESENT DANGER (Putnam 1st ed. 1989).

610 *See* Embassy of the U.S., *Joint Statement Announcing the Global Initiative to Combat Nuclear Terrorism*.

611 Principal modifications being, for example, deletion of the reference to "interdiction" to contain the Proliferation Security Initiative (PSI), *See supra* at 201–201, and *supra* n. 572. Also, the sovereign rights of nonparties to the nonproliferation treaties were affirmed. The latter, of course, would have to be eliminated from the proposed counterproliferation resolution as antithetical to its universal application.

measures. Moreover, the different aspects of nuclear security present different challenges for the authority of Chapter VII. The scope and depth of a mandatory regime will necessarily be uneven and its architecture would develop in its different aspects at diverse pace. But within the context of a universal counterproliferation mandate, all the arenas of counterproliferation would find new room for significant progress. The challenges are for the most part manageable. The refinement of that framework can provide the foundation for an international nuclear forensics data bank, for greatly improved intelligence sharing, security of fissile material, enhanced interdiction capability, and for export controls restructured to address globalized supply and spread of nuclear weapons related material and technology. The institutionalization of that agenda under Chapter VII of the United Nations Charter could most certainly achieve a much more effective scheme of nuclear security than we have been able to achieve within the confines of a framework that was designed for a different world.

There is today solid basis for Security Council authority, capacity, and willingness to undertake the necessary development. Under Article 29 of the UN Charter, the Security Council "may establish such subsidiary organs as it deems necessary for the performance of its functions." Beginning in the 1990s, the Security Council became increasingly proactive under Chapter VII of the UN Charter on a variety of the fronts that bear on counterproliferation. Before 1990, sanctions were imposed only in human rights context against Southern Rhodesia in 1968 and South Africa in 1977. Since 1990, sanctions have been imposed and sanctions committees set up more than a dozen times for a variety of global objectives related to weapons and their use. And besides authorization of sanctions, the Security Council has repeatedly acted under Chapter VII to set up legal and institutional mechanisms in response to a variety of use of force threats to international peace and security. For example, after the 1991 Gulf War, the Council established not only the UN Special Commission, but later, the UN Monitoring, Verification and Inspection Commission, with disarmament and verification mandates, and also the Compensation and Boundary Demarcation Commissions. As previously noted, Security Council activism under Chapter VII has also ventured well into domains previously reserved to national law, such as criminal jurisdiction assumed in 1993 and 1994 when the Council used its Chapter VII authority to establish the International Criminal Tribunals for the former Yugoslavia and for Rwanda. And then, most relevantly, Resolutions 1373 and 1540 directly mandated the development of national criminal law to address the threat of international terrorism and weapons of mass destruction (WMD).

Security Council Resolution 1540, and those that have followed in addressing nuclear risk as a threat to international peace and security,[612] can be seen as progressive movement toward a mandatory counterproliferation architecture. The Security Council has reaffirmed and supported expansion of the work of the 1540 Committee, adding resources including a "group of experts" in Resolutions 1673 (2006), 1810 (2008),

612 S.C. Res. 1540, *supra* note 124.

and 1977 (2011). Most recently, in Resolution 1887, the Security Council reiterated its mandatory authority to act against proliferation under Chapter VII, declaring that it "emphasizes that a situation of non-compliance with non-proliferation obligations shall be brought to the attention of the Security Council, which will determine if that situation constitutes a threat to international peace and security."[613]

The aftermath of 9/11 demonstrated that governments and their publics can be aroused for counterproliferation. Fear is always the great motivator. Certainly that was evident in the ease with which the George W. Bush Administration, by promoting fatuous claims of Iraqi WMD development, was able to manipulate the American press and public for the invasion of Iraq and the enormous costs in blood and treasure that followed.[614] A robust response should therefore be available, with adequate leadership, to instead support the honest and truly critical enterprise of global counterproliferation of nuclear weapons risk.

Will the governments of the United States, Russia, China, Great Britain, and France perceive sufficient mutual interest to prevent a nuclear detonation in a large population center on one of their territories?[615] All the permanent members of the Security Council do, today, face that question, whether acknowledged or not. They may see it differently, in the different cast of light of their different filters of national interest. But in the end, there is the same threat to all that nuclear weapons present on an unparalleled scale, and the ineluctable truth that the Security Council is the only institution capable of the international mandatory global authority that is necessary to contain the threat.

In light of resistance of China and Russia to impose sanctions on North Korea and Iran, the perception might be that the counterproliferation mandate here proposed is somewhere on the same fog-shrouded mountain where Senator Sam Nunn said nuclear disarmament resides. But that view is no longer compatible with reality, as well evidenced by the fact that the so-called P5 plus 1, the permanent members of the Security Council plus Germany, now collectively and continually, are pressuring Iran

---

613 S.C. Res. 1887, *supra* note 324.

614 The reliance of the Bush Administration on false assertions of Iraqi WMD programs to justify military action has been well documented. *See* Associated Press, *Study: Bush Led U.S. to War on "False Pretenses,"* Jan. 23, 2008, http://www.msnbc.msn.com/id/22794451/ns/world_news-mideast_n_africa/t/study-bush-led-us-war-false-pretenses/#.TvERaxzmpMo (The article cites a study by the Center for Public Integrity that found that, on 532 occasions, President Bush and administration officials falsely stated that Iraq had WMD capabilities or was trying to obtain them.) The use of false WMD intelligence to justify the invasion of Iraq has also inspired Hollywood. *See* FAIR GAME (Summit Entertainment 2010) (About CIA agent Valerie Plame whose identity was revealed by Bush Administration officials after her husband made public comments challenging the validity of pre-Iraqi invasion intelligence).

615 President Ronald Reagan, in his persona as the great communicator, put the question in more widely empathetic terms when asked to identify the most critical matter of foreign relations, asking us to imagine if "all of us discovered that we were threatened from outer space—from another planet... wouldn't we come together to fight that particular threat?" Quoted by Former Senator Sam Nunn, *The Mountaintop: A World Free of Nuclear Weapons*, COUNCIL ON FOREIGN RELATIONS (June 14, 2007) (*transcript available at* http://www.nti.org/analysis/speeches/nunn-mountaintop-free-weapons/).

for counterproliferation with the threat and actuality of mandatory globally enforced sanctions as indicated by agreement declaring it "essential and urgent that Iran give unrestricted access to the IAEA."[616] The global need is to generalize what is now being undertaken as to Iran, and make it an institutionalized matter of globally applicable standards and process.

It would be mistaken, however, to judge the political will of the members of the Security Council for a broad counterproliferation mandate solely on the experience in targeting a particular state for sanctions. Although China and Russia each have their interests to protect in the context of targeting a particular government, they have shown a willingness to proceed on a broader front of counterproliferation, and their willingness can be expected to be greater, the greater the commitment to equal application of counterproliferation to all states, not just governments viewed negatively by Western powers. The permanent member governments of the Security Council have proven sufficiently sensitized to the gravity of the risk, to make the dramatic evolutionary transition to global legislation on terrorism and WMD. Overcoming Resolution 1540's limitations by authorization of uniform standards under Chapter VII should not be seen as so far beyond the point to which the Security Council has already gone for counterproliferation progress; certainly not out of sight. There is no fog about it, and it is coming ever more clearly into view. The common will is well demonstrated by initiatives such as the G-8 Global Partnership against the Spread of Weapons and Materials of Mass Destruction, launched in June 2002 "to cooperate on non-proliferation, disarmament, counter-terrorism and nuclear safety issues," for which the U.S. pledged a contribution of $10 billion over ten years.[617] It is evident in the Global Initiative to Combat Nuclear Terrorism and the International Convention on the Suppression of Acts of Nuclear Terrorism, which articulate and criminalize acts of nuclear terrorism. Though all such initiatives have remained within the realm of voluntary consent-based cooperation of states, they demonstrate the shared sense of urgency to move forward on counterproliferation. Even China, which historically has been the most recalcitrant of partners on counterproliferation, has shown increasing initiative in the direction of enhanced counterproliferation. China has officially declared counterproliferation to be a priority national policy, and is generally on board for most counterproliferation activities. After some earlier ambiguity by way of resistance to PSI and other counterproliferation initiatives, China, through its accession to a number of international agreements and official declarations, has clearly committed to counterproliferation as a continuing project despite any critique of means. On December 3, 2003, for example, China issued a counterproliferation white paper stating that "(a) developing China needs both an international and a peripheral environment of long-term peace and stability. The proliferation of (weapons of) mass destruction and their means of

616 David Crawford, *China, China, Russia Agree to Pressure Iran*, WALL ST. J., A10, Sept. 13, 2012.

617 *See Statement by G8 Leaders: The G8 Global Partnership against the Spread of Weapons and Materials of Mass Destruction*, June 27, 2002, http://www.partnershipforglobalsecurity.org/Official%20Documents/G-8%20Global%20Partnership/index.asp.

delivery benefits neither world peace and stability nor China's own security."[618] In spite of expressing concern that PSI might attempt "military interception, which is beyond the limits of international law,"[619] China has assisted in interdictions and export control.[620] It has been observed that Chinese leadership now sees nuclear proliferation risk in fuller perspective, including threats arising from the Middle East,[621] and the potential for nuclear terrorism arising in relation to the protests that increasingly appear to plague its dominions, such the separatist activity among the Turkic-speaking Islamic Uighurs in Xinjiang, that the Chinese leadership has characterized as terrorism.[622]

Such movement towards what is here proposed evidences also the compelling realization that use of force is probably the only alternative for negating nuclear weapons proliferation in the critical places where the present architecture is most dysfunctional. That alternative is most apparent today in Israel's nuclear confrontation with Iran and the prediction of an Israeli attack on Iranian nuclear sites if significant progress is not soon achieved in counterproliferation negotiations with Iran.[623] But surely the bombing of increasingly hardened nuclear sites cannot be a universal and ongoing prescription for counterproliferation. The scenario of an attack on Iran's nuclear sites or other similar crisis scenarios such as might concern North Korea's nuclear capability or a radical Islamist takeover in Pakistan are pictures to persuade most governments to achieve new empowerment of counterproliferation that can serve to avoid use of force.

The permanent members of the Security Council are all attuned to the risk of nuclear terror, and all, except perhaps China, have experienced international terrorism to the degree that a nuclear detonation in any one of their cities is their shared nightmare. But a detonation in New York, London, Moscow, or Paris would be a catastrophe for China as well. With U.S. and European and global economic interdependence with China having become bedrock of the global economy, and given China's stake in international trade and investment, China simply cannot afford to ignore proliferation risk.

---

618 *See* Richardson, *supra* note 534. More recently, China has demonstrated a remarkable willingness to step out front as a leading proponent for declaration of international legal obligation on matters of international concern, such as China's surprising recent call, at United Nations climate talks, for legally binding emissions cuts. *See* Patrick McGroarty, *Chinese Overture Jolts Climate Talks*, WALL ST. J. A10 (Dec. 6, 2011).

619 Shirley A. Kan, RL31555, CHINA AND THE PROLIFERATION OF WEAPONS OF MASS DESTRUCTION AND MISSILES: POLICY ISSUES 59 (updated Feb. 22, 2005), http://www.missilethreat.com/repository/doclib/20050222-CRS-chinawmd.pdf.

620 *See id.*

621 "Acquisition of nuclear devices and WMD by domestic terrorist groups is one of the top security concerns for the Chinese government... Concurrently Beijing has shown its readiness to move away from its traditional support for state sovereignty as well as its willingness to display a more assertive diplomacy." Ramon Pacheco Pardo, *Changing Policy Towards the Middle East?*, THE MAJALLA, May 25, 2009, http://www.majalla.com/eng/2009/05/article554255.

622 *See* Chien-peng Chung, *China's War on Terror: September 11 and Uighur Separatism*, COUNCIL ON FOREIGN RELATIONS (Aug. 2002), http://www.cfr.org/china/chinas-war-terror-september-11-uighur-separatism/p4765.

623 Ronen Bergman, *Israel vs. Iran*, N.Y. TIMES MAGAZINE 22 (Jan. 29, 2012).

This is so whatever its particular interests vis à vis Iran or North Korea, or any other relationship with any state.

The different elements of nuclear risk engage different degrees of political will. The response to 9/11 was unprecedented, because the event and the trauma it produced were in so many respects unprecedented and unexpected. For the arduous work of prevention of a nuclear 9/11, there are serious challenges on every front. Multi-internationalization of the nuclear fuel cycle runs up against economic considerations, such as competitive advantage, and national concerns of sovereignty and self-sufficiency. Export-import controls must keep pace with technological developments and rationalized with protection of intellectual property and the potentialities of dual use. Intelligence sharing must be designed to overcome concerns about the disclosure of sources and methods of national intelligence. The 2010 NPT Review conference reflected such concerns in refusing to endorse any of the general proposals pushed by the IAEA. So the challenges are considerable, and various. However, the Security Council, acting under Chapter VII can set the new agenda, by mandating the same objective for each aspect of counterproliferation—to maximize the implementation of uniform criteria, whether for security of nuclear material, intelligence sharing, provision of forensics data, export control, interdiction, or internationalization of the fuel cycle. The differences in political support for the various elements of the counterproliferation regime legitimated by Security Council resolution would have to be resolved in meeting the challenges of implementation. All must be accomplished by developing global uniform standards while resisting the temptation to classify states for extraneous political purposes that run counter to counterproliferation. Altogether, though, if accomplished, there would be fundamental improvement of global nuclear security.

7

CONCLUSION

PROLIFERATION OF THE material and technology of nuclear weapons has come to a most troubled time. The non-proliferation infrastructure that has been forged on many fronts, for many decades, is no longer suited to police the landscape of nuclear risk. That landscape has been fundamentally altered by systemic threats such as nuclear terrorism and nuclear black markets and the accelerating availability of nuclear weapons related material and technology. Counterproliferation must today, if it is to succeed, become a systemic project to meet the nature of the present threat that nuclear weapons present.

What the existing agreements and mechanisms all demonstrate, to the contrary, is a fractionated character. Export-import control is mainly characterized by the small club of traditional supplier states, resented as an international cartel. The separation of sources of counterproliferation intelligence, with no institutional means to overcome overzealous guarding of sources and methods by national intelligence agencies, is the very antithesis of the ability to connect the dots. Nuclear forensics is more accurately characterized by the lack of sharing than the minimal communication between the different databases that do exist. For the substantive standards of counterproliferation, implementation on condition of state consent, exclusively through state-originated legislation, the formula of Resolution 1373 on terrorism and Resolution 1540 on weapons of mass destruction, is a formula that inevitably deprives counterproliferation of the legitimacy and coherence necessary to achieve significantly higher levels of compliance.

Before departing his position as Director-General of the IAEA, Mohamed ElBaradei complained publicly at a meeting of the United Nations (UN) Security Council, that in over 90 states, the IAEA has no verification authority or insufficient authority to ensure non-engagement in clandestine nuclear weapons-related activities.[624] Such

624 Mohamed ElBaradei, U.N. Doc. S/PV.6191, Remarks during the 6191st Meeting of the Security Council 17 (Sept. 24, 2009).

incapacity of the IAEA is simply indicative of the more extensive and pervasive weakness of current counterproliferation. Correction cannot be accomplished through a purely consent-based regime burdened with the counterproductive connection of counterproliferation and nuclear disarmament. What Senator Sam Nunn characterized as the fog-shrouded mountain of nuclear disarmament sits together with the twin peak of rhetoric that has built up around the Grand Bargain of the NPT. Any satisfactory NPT amendment or any other broadly multilateral consensual means for accomplishing significantly greater counterproliferation is simply not to be had. The political barriers are too great under a consensual regime, as most evident in the nuclear hot spots. India and Pakistan remain in nuclear face-off. North Korea and Iran continue on their wayward ways. No Arab government will ever agree to Israel's exclusive possession of nuclear weapons in the Middle East and its privileged status as a nuclear weapons state (NWS) outside the NPT.

The authority, standards, and institutional makings for robust counterproliferation could be made available, however, under a Security Council counterproliferation resolution. The elements are identified. They can be drawn from the past experience in export-import control, interdiction of transport of nuclear weapons related material and technology, coordination of intelligence, multi-internationalization of the nuclear fuel cycle, the banking of nuclear forensics data, and other counterproliferation means. The challenge is to design the more effective operation of each of these means within the authority and empowerment of Chapter VII of the UN Charter.

No international management of uniform standards in service of counterproliferation, even as authorized by the Security Council under Chapter VII, can be a complete solution to the problems and difficulties to be addressed. Making standards of counterproliferation a matter of international legal obligation, not dependent on consent of individual governments, surely would not assure their universal implementation or universal compliance. But this mandate would raise the overall level of both implementation and compliance to a much higher plane of global nuclear security than is currently possible. Analysis of each arena of counterproliferation demonstrates substantial potential for improvement through reframing under Security Council mandate. Intelligence sharing would continue to be constrained by concerns about the disclosure of sources and methods, even operating under an internationally authorized counterproliferation facility that could cleanse intelligence. Intelligence presently lost to counterproliferation, however, would be shared if an international apparatus was in place to cleanse intelligence and thereby offer governments that greater measure of protection of sources and methods. An international nuclear forensics data bank would be compromised to the extent any state failed to provide the necessary data to fingerprint and identify every nuclear facility worldwide. But a Security Council mandate securing baseline forensics data from most states, would dramatically improve the chances of identifying source, and thereby provide a new and powerful dynamic for deterrence of illicit transfer, and for discouraging proliferation.

To the extent the overall architecture of counterproliferation can be transformed for greater transparency and effectiveness, deterrence will be enhanced. The more effective the regime for achieving transparency, the greater the costs and risk for potential proliferators. This is true as to most critical aspects of counterproliferation, whether security of fissile materials, interdiction, sharing of intelligence, or the ability to identify the source of nuclear material. Counterproliferation, as deterrence, is about creating a protection system that proliferators perceive as presenting too much risk of exposure and failure, to warrant undertaking the business of proliferation. A Security Council mandate is the means to generate that perception globally. All governments also would be assured that if they play by the common rules, they will not suffer costs of non-compliance and will obtain as a new "Grand Bargain" the collective achievement of moving towards the common goal of much greater global nuclear security.

Rebuilding counterproliferation architecture under Security Council authority can occur without sacrificing what has been accomplished under the regime of the NPT. It is certainly no small accomplishment that over 180 countries are now party to that treaty, and that they cooperate in the important work of the IAEA, though in extreme variance of degree. Moreover, to the extent counterproliferation sanctions can be justified as based on noncompliance with treaty obligations assumed under the NPT, as has been so of counterproliferation efforts on Iran, Saddam's Iraq, and North Korea, counterproliferation value has been obtained from the NPT despite its flawed foundation. Reduction of nuclear risk through consensual means could and should continue concurrently with a mandatory regime. Indeed, it is likely to be improved as impelled by the common will demonstrated through Security Council mandate for implementation on a global scale. Consensual accomplishment could continue to include, for example, important work for agreed reductions of actual nuclear weapons deployments such as START, removal of hair trigger alerts, and agreements for nuclear crisis communication. The demonstration of common will embodied in a Security Council resolution mandating global application of uniform standards could also be a positive force for entry into force of international agreements such as the 1998 Comprehensive Test Ban Treaty (CTBT), and ratification of the Fissile Material Cut-off Treaty (FMCT).

In light of all this potential, it can be seen that we are at one of those intersections in the evolution of international law and institutions where the road not taken can condemn the journey to avoidable chaos and despair. The Nuclear Non-proliferation Treaty no longer indicates the right road; if it ever did. It should not be too much to expect, without waiting for a nuclear version of 9/11 to occur, for the Security Council to fundamentally reform the framework for counterproliferation by building on a new foundation. Probably a single detonation in New York, Moscow, Paris, London, or Beijing, which the experts predict will occur in chillingly short time frames,[625] would do it. The day after such an event, all the interests that today confound counterproliferation would appear a fool's diversion from

---

625 *See* Dan Farber, *Nuclear Attack a Ticking Time Bomb, Experts Warn*, CBS NEWS, May 3, 2010, http://www.cbsnews.com/8301-503543_162-20003954-503543.html (Reports that various experts believe the likelihood of nuclear detonation in the next ten years to be between 10% and 30%). *See also* Lugar, *supra* note 97. (This report examines a survey of 85 national security experts on the likelihood of a WMD attack).

the critical security challenge, and the world would respond, too late, to the unparalleled danger.

Though the necessary motivation should be available within the permanent membership of the Security Council, it will be facilitated to the degree supported by all governments. Whether the progress here proposed is realized will depend on whether most governments and their constituencies in general can be educated to understand that the global community is today seized of nuclear vulnerability much more pervasive and insidious than in the Cold War era. For many of the world's communities, there may be little sense of the immediate threat. Perception of nuclear risk is still largely dominated by images from the Cold War. Nuclear weapons risk is commonly seen as risk only for the populations of the states engaged in nuclear weapons confrontation. This may be the most important constraint on effective counterproliferation—the gap between global community consciousness, and the reality of the global threat.

Moreover, the perpetuation of counterproliferation as a wholly consent-based enterprise is a concession to national sovereignty that is, in a sense, natural. Sovereignty is the inevitable condition of collaborative international action in a world where power is differentiated by the delineation of states. But nuclear weapons risk opens a dimension beyond sovereignty. There is no other global risk so compelling in the consequences that action by one state can have for all others. Where a government acts to violate international norms in arenas other than nuclear risk, we have now well-established exceptions to the priority of national sovereignty. For interdiction on the high seas, there has long been the exception to flag-state jurisdiction for trade in human slavery and piracy. The Trail Smelter Principle, that activity in one state must not be allowed to cause damage to another, is well established in international environmental law. And yet, for the greatest threat to the moral and physical safety of modern civilization, nuclear weapons risk, international law, and global political culture, remains fixed in a formulation that places national sovereignty above global security.

It is just too dangerous to dwell any longer in the delusional framework of the NPT. This would be true even if there were not available recourse to a new foundation. Albert Einstein's admonition that "since the advent of the Nuclear Age, everything has changed save our modes of thinking and we thus drift toward unparalleled catastrophe,"[626] remains terribly true. No doubt a nuclear detonation obliterating some part of our globalized community, would change the mode of thinking for all those who remain.

The international community can build a new foundation to change direction and prevent that catastrophe or continue to rely exclusively on an architecture that, despite any historic utility, is today critically deficient and dying by all accounts. The troubled history of the Nuclear Non-proliferation Treaty; of refusals of states to join, withdrawals, deceit by signatories, and open defiance as by North Korea, Saddam's Iraq, and an aggressive Iran contemptuous of counterproliferation by the IAEA or any

---

626 Albert Einstein, BULL. ATOMIC SCIENTISTS (May 1946).

other present mechanism, demonstrates well enough that what we have is not strong enough, and is not in itself amenable to the necessary correction.

That there has not been a nuclear detonation targeted on a human population since the reduction of Hiroshima and Nagasaki to rubble in 1945 encourages the inertia that good luck breeds. Anesthetized in that balm of luck, the international community may ignore the compelling evidence that the global good luck will run out sooner rather than later. But the gap between our greatest danger and global consciousness *will be* closed, either by unprecedented trauma, or by a human triumph of understanding and political will. We can respond effectively with a new vision and architecture for nuclear weapons security. Or are we to be, as in the poet's unwitting vision of the nuclear age, "The Hollow Men," "paralyzed force, gesture without motion"?[627] Our need is to affirm that civilization was not built, and is not preserved, by hollow men. Preservation presumes a trust, requiring commitment to acknowledge what is wrong, and make it right, for the human community today, and for future generations.

---

627 T.S. Eliot, *The Hollow Men*, Poetry X Archive, http://poetry.poetryx.com/poems/784/ (last visited Dec. 6, 2012).

Index